Alberta and the Economics of Constitutional Change

Publication No. 3 in the series

Western Studies in Economic Policy

of the Western Centre for Economic Research at

the University of Alberta

Paul Boothe
Editor

This edition published by
Western Centre for Economic Research
University of Alberta
Edmonton, Alberta

Copyright © The Western Centre for Economic Research 1992

Canadian Cataloguing in Publication Data

Alberta and the economics of constitutional change

(Western studies in economic policy: no. 3)
Proceedings of a conference held Sept. 28, 1991
at the University of Alberta.
Includes bibliographical references.

ISBN   0-88864-804-9

1. Alberta–Economic policy–Congresses.
2. Alberta–Economic conditions–1945-
Congresses.*   3. Canada–Economic policy–1991-
– Congresses.*   4. Canada–Economic conditions–
1991-   – Congresses.*   5. Federal-provincial
fiscal relations–Canada–Congresses.* 6.
Federal-provincial tax relations–Canada–
Congresses.*   7. Canada–Constitutional law–
Amendments–Congresses.   I. Boothe, Paul Michael,
1954–   II. University of Alberta. Western
Centre for Economic Research.   III. Series.
HC117.A4A42 1992   338.97123   C92-091236-2

C ontents

iii

Acknowledgements

I would like to acknowledge the contributions of the people and organizations that made the volume possible. On behalf of the Western Centre for Economic Research, I would like to express our appreciation for the support of the Government of Alberta which allowed the Centre to undertake this project. I am grateful to all the authors and discussants who gave generously and freely of their time. I am also grateful to Barbara Johnston and KarrinPowys-Lybbe for research assistance. Finally, I would like to acknowledge the hard work and superior organizational skills of Charlene Hill, without whom this conference and volume would not be possible.

This research was supported by a grant from the Western Centre for Economic Research.

Contributors

Authors (A) and Discussants (D)

Paul Boothe (A) is an Associate Professor of Economics at the University of Alberta and, currently, Visiting Scholar (1991-92) at the School of Policy Studies at Queen's University. After receiving his Ph.D. (UBC) in 1981, he worked for three years at the Bank of Canada and lectured part time at Carleton University. He has taught at the Univ. of Alberta since 1984 and was appointed Visiting Economist at Alberta Treasury for the year 1989-90. Professor Boothe is a member of the executive of the Canadian Economics Association, and an Associate Editor of Canadian Public Policy. He has published extensively in the area of macroeconomics, and is best known for his work for the MacDonald Royal Commission, and his study of government revenue and expenditure in Alberta.

Edward J. (Ted) Chambers (A) is Professor of Marketing and Economic Analysis in the Faculty of Business, and Director of The Western Centre for Economic Research at the University of Alberta. Born in Vancouver, he received his undergraduate and master's degrees at the UBC and his Ph.D. in Economics at the Univ. of Alberta. He has previously held appointments at Whitman College, Rutgers Univ. and the Univ. of Montana. During the 1960s he was Professor of Business in the Graduate School of Business Administration at the Univ. of Washington. He came to the Univ. of Alberta in 1969 to serve as Dean of the Faculty of Business and in 1976 he returned to teaching and research. Since early in 1989 he has served as Director of the Western Centre. He is presently the President-elect of the North American Economics and Finance Association. Dr. Chambers has published extensively in the fields of regional economics and business fluctuations. His present research interests are primarily in western Canada's economic position in the international economy, and in the effects of structural adjustment on resource requirements and allocations in the region. He has consulted for numerous governments and private organizations. He has served as a Ford Foundation Fellow in business, a Humanities and Social Science Research Fellow, A Gulbenkian Foundation Fellow, and a McCalla Research Professor at the Univ. of Alberta

Thomas J. Courchene (D) was educated at the Univ. of Saskatchewan and Princeton University from which he obtained a Ph.D. in 1967. From 1965 to 1988 he was Professor of Economics at the Univ. of Western Ontario. Dr. Courchene spent the fall term of 1986 as a visiting Professor at Ecole nationale d'administration publique (Montreal). In 1987/88 he occupied the John P. Robarts Chair in Canadian Studies at York Univ. Currently, Dr. Courchene is the Director of the School of Policy Studies at Queen's Univ. where he is the Jarislowsky-Deutsch Professor of Economics and Financial Policy and is a member of the Dept. of Economics, the School of Public Administration and the Faculty of Law. Courchene is the author of well over a hundred books and articles on Canadian policy issues, including a four volume series on Canadian monetary policy for the C.D. Howe Institute. His on-going research interests also include financial deregulation and the political economy of Canada's regions. Dr. Courchene was Chairman of the Ontario Economic Council from 1982 to 1985, has been a Senior Fellow of the C.D. Howe Institute since 1980, is a former member of the Economic Council of Canada and is a Fellow of the Royal Society of Canada. He is currently the President of the Canadian Economics Association.

Bev Dahlby (A) is Associate Professor in the Department of Economics at the University of Alberta. He received his B.A. (Hon.) from the Univ. of Saskatchewan, his M.A. from Queen's Univ., and his Ph.D. from the London School of Economics. He joined the Univ. of Alberta in 1978. In 1981-82 he was on leave from the University and worked for Alberta Treasury as Manager of Economic Analysis in the Fiscal Policy and Economic Analysis Branch. His research interests include the economics of insurance, public finance, and applied welfare economics. He has recently completed a paper entitled "Taxation and Social Insurance" which will be included in a book, Tax Policy to the Year 2000 and Beyond, edited by Richard Bird and Jack Mintz and published by the Canadian Tax Foundation.

Wendy Dobson (D) (Ph.D. Economics, Princeton University) is adjunct professor at the Faculty of Management at the Univ. of Toronto and Visiting Fellow at the Institute for International Economics in Washington. Dr. Dobson has served as Associate Deputy Minister of Finance in Ottawa and as President and Executive Director of the C.D. Howe Institute, Canada's leading economic policy research institute. She is a director of several Canadian companies and of a number of voluntary organizations. She is author and editor of numerous books and articles on Canadian and international economic issues, the most recent being *Economic Policy Coordination: Requiem or Prologue?* published by the Institute for International Economics in Washington, D.C.

Richard G. Harris (D) is a Professor of Economics at Simon Fraser University. He received his Ph.D. from the Univ. of British Columbia and taught at Queen's Univ. from 1975 to 1980. He is the former director of the John Deutsch Institute for the study of Economic Policy and has been involved as a consultant to a number of government and international agencies. His area of expertise is international economics, and in particular the economics of international integration. He is the author of a number of books and studies on Canada-U.S. trade, and is currently studying the economics of a North American Free Trade Area, and the economics of constitutional change in Canada.

Paul A.R. Hobson (D) was born in Ireland. He earned his B.A.(Hons) from York University and his M.A. and Ph.D. in Economics from Queen's University. Professor Hobson is currently Associate Professor of Economics at Acadia Univ. He has held visiting Assistant Professor positions with the Departments of Economics at both the University of Western Ontario and Queen's University. His research interests include local public finance, regional economics, and fiscal federalism.

Derek P.J. Hum (D) is originally from the Maritimes and was educated at Mount Allison, Oxford and Toronto. He is presently Professor of Economics at the University of Manitoba and a Fellow of St. John's College. He was formerly Research Director of Mincome, an experimental test of the guaranteed income concept funded by the Canadian and Manitoban governments. His research interests include social policy and intergovernmental relations.

Kathleen E. Macmillan (D) is from Ottawa. She did her B.A. in Economics at Queen's University and her M.A. at the Univ. of Alberta. As an economist and policy analyst she has published widely. She has worked for the Economic Council of Canada, the Canada West Foundation, and, most recently, the C.D. Howe Institute. Ms. Macmillan was appointed Member of the Canadian International Trade Tribunal on March 1, 1989, and on January 18, 1990 was appointed Vice-Chairman.

Robert L. Mansell (A) is a Professor of Economics at the University of Calgary. He received his Ph.D. in Economics from the University of Alberta in 1975, with specialization in regional and resource economics and in econometrics. Dr. Mansell has written many monographs and articles dealing with regional economics, the Alberta economy, resource economics and regulatory issues. He has also given numerous invited papers and talks and has appeared as an expert witness in many hearings before regulatory tribunals, commissions and inquiries. Dr. Mansell has recently written extensively on issues related to the regional economics of Confederation.

Melville L. McMillan (D) is Professor of Economics at the University of Alberta. He received his BA (1964) and M.Sc. (1967) from the Univ. of Alberta and his Ph.D. (1973) from Cornell University. He left the Dept. of Agricultural Economics at the Univ. of Wisconsin, Madison in 1975 to join the Dept. of Economics at the Univ. of Alberta. In 1981, he was promoted to Professor and since then he has served as Associate Chairman, Acting Chairman, Associate Dean of Arts (Social Sciences) and has been Chairman of the Department of Economics since 1987. Professor McMillan focuses his research on the economics of the public sector and, in particular, fiscal federalism and public good provision. His interests include local government, urban and regional economics and natural resource economics. He has published widely in these areas and recently edited a two volume book, *Provincial Public Finances*, that was published by the Canadian Tax Foundation in 1991.

Kenneth Norrie (D) earned his undergraduate degree from the University of Saskatchewan and his Ph.D. in Economics from Yale University. Dr. Norrie is currently Professor of Economics at the University of Alberta. He has an interest in Canadian economic development and public policy formulation. Dr. Norrie has served as: Research co-ordinator for *The Royal Commission on Federal-Provincial Economic Relations* (the MacDonald Commission), Editor, *Canadian Public Policy/Analyse de Politiques*, and the Clifford Clark Visiting Economist with the Department of Finance, Government of Canada.

Michael Percy (A) Professor of Economics (July 1988), is a graduate of the University of Victoria (BA 1972), and Queen's University (MA 1974, PhD 1977). He joined the Dept. of Economics at the Univ. of Alberta in 1979 and teaches in the areas of Canadian economic development and regional economics. He has published three books, and numerous articles in the areas of resource management, regional economics and economic development. His most recent research is in the area of economic modelling and its applications to trade and development issues. He is currently involved in a major project assessing the economic implications for Alberta of alternate constitutional scenarios. In addition to having served as Chair of the Department he was formerly Research Director of the Western Centre for Economic Research. Currently he is Adjunct Professor in Rural Economy at the U of A, Associate Director of the Forest Economics and Policy Analysis Unit at UBC, and Associate Dean (Planning), Faculty of Arts at the University of Alberta.

Bradford Reid (A) is an Associate Professor in the Department of Economics at the University of Alberta. He received his Ph.D. in Economics from the University of Toronto. Professor Reid's research interests lie in the areas of macroeconomics and public finance with particular interest in the issues revolving around government budget constraints. He has published several journal articles examining the impact of deficit financing on economic activity and the choice of debt instruments used to finance public sector deficits.

Ron Schlenker (A) is currently an economic consultant. As well as a B.Sc. degree in Engineering, Mr. Schlenker received his master's degree in economics from the University of Calgary in 1989. His areas of interest and consulting include energy, regional and regulatory economics.

Roger S. Smith (D) received his Ph.D. (Economics) from the Univ. of California (Berkeley) and joined the Univ. of Alberta in 1969. From 1972 to 1974 he was with the International Monetary Fund as an Economist. From 1978 to 1988 he was Dean of the Faculty of Business, Univ. of Alberta; he served as Chairman of the Canadian association of business school deans from 1986 to 1988. He has been a Visiting Scholar at Harvard Law School's International Tax Program, and at the International Monetary Fund, and a Visiting Professor at Erasmus Univ. in Rotterdam. His three books and numerous journal articles have been in the areas of local and provincial public finances, taxation of the transport sector, reform of income taxation, and macroeconomic issues related to saving and the underground economy. He has been involved in research and consulting work in Asia, Africa, the Caribbean, Europe, the Middle East, and Central America, as well as in Canada. Professor Smith holds a joint appointment in the Dept. of Marketing and Economic Analysis of the Faculty of Business and the Dept. of Economics of the Faculty of Arts.

Tracy Snoddon (A) is a Ph.D. Candidate at the University of Alberta's Department of Economics. Prior to entering the Ph.D. program, Ms. Snoddon earned a Masters of Arts degree in economics from Queen's University in 1986 and an Honours Bachelor of Arts degree from the Univ. of Western Ontario in 1985. She has specialized in the Public Finance and Industrial Organization fields and is currently working on her dissertation in the area of intergovernmental transfers in federal government systems.

Wayne Thirsk (D) is currently Professor of Economics and Director of the International Trade specialization in the Applied Studies program at the University of Waterloo. He has taught previously at the Univ. of British Columbia, Rice University in Houston, Texas and the Univ. of Manitoba. He has also been employed as a senior economist at the World Bank and a senior manager at KMPG Peat Marwick in Washington, D.C.

Stanley L. Winer (D) is Professor of Economics in the School of Public Administration at Carleton University. Professor Winer has taught at the Univ. of Western Ontario, at Carnegie-Mellon University and The People's Univ. of China (Beijing), and has held a research fellowship at Haifa University. His research has been concerned with why governments do what they do, especially in the context of taxation. He has a long-standing interest in the political economy of federalism. Other current research topics include the incorporation of public policy into computable general equilibrium models, and empirical investigation of the effects of economic growth on political regression. Professor Winer has been a member of the editorial board of the Canadian Journal of Economics and is a member of the Board of Management of the International Institute of Public Finance. He is the supervisor of the new Ph.D. in Public Policy soon to commence at the School of Public Administration. Professor Winer has published widely in international journals.

Introduction
and
Overview

by Paul Boothe

Introduction

Canadians are struggling with choices regarding their constitutional future. Many interrelated factors—political, social, and economic—must be weighed and the complexity of any choice is matched only by its importance. We must choose soon, and all possible alternatives have profound implications for the way we, our children, and their children will live their everyday lives.

Unfortunately, despite its importance for all Canadians, most of the debate in political circles and the media has focused on the implications for Québec, and, to a lesser extent, on a newly-formed abstraction called the Rest of Canada (ROC). For Alberta, a province that has traditionally had different interests and aspirations than Ontario and Atlantic Canada, this is singularly unhelpful. Albertans need to know specifically how they will be affected by constitutional change.

To aid in the process of informing Albertans about the economic implications of the choices they face, the Western Centre for Economic Research (WCER) at the University of Alberta commissioned a series of five studies by Alberta economists. These studies focus specifically on the economic implications for Alberta of three alternative constitutional scenarios. The studies cover the following broad areas: division of spending responsibilities, redistribution of income, taxation, trade and migration, and the distribution of net federal fiscal balances. The alternative constitutional scenarios were chosen, not because they represent likely or preferred outcomes, but rather because they cover a broad range of possibilities which encompass the scenarios currently under consideration. The alternatives include:

1.   A more centralized Canada without Québec,[1]

2.   A more decentralized Canada which includes Québec, and

3.   An independent Alberta.

An important variant of this last alternative is an independent Western Canada and was considered in some of the studies.

The results of the studies were first presented at a WCER conference in Edmonton in late September 1991. Members of the public, political leaders, public servants, and the media attended the conference. At the conference, WCER brought the authors together with leading economists from across Canada as discussants. The discussants contributed valuable criticism and reaction both as professional experts and, in many cases, as residents of other regions of Canada. Added together with discussion from the audience, the result was an extremely lively and informative exchange of views.

The purpose of this volume is to make the proceedings of the September 1991 conference accessible to a wider audience in Alberta and in other parts of Canada. For those interested in a compact overview of the studies, the remainder of the introduction gives a brief summary of the studies and the discussants' comments. In addition, Roger Smith closes the volume with one Alberta economist's interpretation of the conference as a whole. The volume offers no conclusions—we leave those to the reader. While we recognize that the economic implications are only one aspect of constitutional change that must be considered, it is our hope that the volume will contribute to more informed choices as we approach the critical decisions that lie ahead.

Alternative Constitutional Scenarios

The three common constitutional alternatives examined in each study are:

1.   Canada without Québec—where the federal government takes on a number of the responsibilities currently assigned to the provinces and municipalities,

2.   Canada with Québec—where there is a move toward substantial decentralization of responsibilities along the lines suggested by the Allaire report (1991), and

---

1.   In some of the studies, the absence of Québec has an important effect on the results. In others, the key issue is the degree of centralization.

3.   an independent Alberta—where all responsibilities are moved to provincial
     and municipal orders of government. As part of this third alternative, some
     of the studies also examine the implications of an independent Western
     Canada.

The first alternative is Canada without Québec. In this case we assume
that Québec and the ROC are unable to reach some accommodation to
preserve the federation and Québec chooses political independence. ROC is
assumed to move to a more centralized form of government. On the
economic front, we assume there is free trade and migration between ROC
and Québec, at least for a reasonably long transition period. However, there
is no significant sharing of economic institutions such as stabilization,
unemployment insurance, pensions, defense, and no redistribution of
income to Québec from the ROC through equalization or regional
development programs.[2]

Within the ROC, the relations between the three orders of government
are assumed to change significantly, with a shift of responsibilities from
provincial and municipal to the federal government. The rationale for this
shift could be increased demand for "national standards" in social programs
in the absence of Québec. Thus, even if actual program delivery remained in
the hands of provincial and municipal governments, program design would
be increasingly controlled by the federal government, perhaps through the
use of the federal spending power. Alternatively, the federal government
could continue the current trend of moving to more direct delivery of social
programs. A recent study that recommends changes along these lines
(without predicting the separation of Québec) is Norrie et al. (1991) which
argues the necessity of this type of shift to complete the "social charter"
implied by the Constitution Act of 1982.

To make the more centralized scenario concrete, we assume that primary
responsibility for "people" programs is transferred to the federal
government. For example, in Alberta the federal government is already
dominant in housing, labour, and social security programs. We assume that
primary responsibility is transferred from municipal governments in the area
of culture and from the provincial government in the areas of education and
health. Accompanying this shift in program responsibilities is a concurrent
elimination of transfer programs such as Established Program Financing
(EPF) and Canada Assistance Plan (CAP). Other federal redistribution

---

2.   Of course, full Québec independence is not necessary for this alternative to be relevant.
     Sovereignty-association with a more centralized ROC would have the same implications for
     Alberta. In either case, the political and economic relations between Québec and the ROC
     would have to be worked out, and there could be a long and acrimonious transition to a
     stable relationship—if one were possible. These issues are outside the scope of these studies.

programs that are delivered directly to persons, such as Unemployment
Insurance (UI), Canada Pension Plan (CPP), Family Allowance, and Old Age
Security (OAS) remain, although in cases where Albertans' benefits currently
vary from national norms, benefits are now provided at average rates across
the country. Of course, the federal government would require additional
revenues to discharge its increased responsibilities; alternative methods of
raising this revenue are discussed in the study by Dahlby.

The second alternative is Canada with Québec. In this alternative we
assume that an accommodation between the ROC and Québec is reached in
which Québec remains a full partner in the Canadian federation.
Recognizing Québec's demands as articulated by the Belanger-Campeau
Commission (1991) or Allaire Commission reports (1991), a substantial
degree of decentralization would be required for this alternative to be
feasible. We further assume that the degree of decentralization demanded by
Québec would also be offered to the other provinces, and, at least in the case
of Alberta, that the transfer of responsibilities would be accepted.

Reasonably specific proposals regarding the transfer of responsibilities
are provided by the Allaire report, and are summarized in the table
reproduced at the end of this introduction.

It is difficult to match directly the Allaire report's division of powers
with the division of program areas discussed in this volume. However, a
rough translation that preserves the spirit of the Allaire report is possible.
Following Allaire, we assume that the federal government is left with
primary responsibility for defense (i.e., protection), tariffs and customs (i.e.,
the foreign part of trade and industry), and regulation in a number of areas
(e.g., transportation, weights and measures, fisheries, justice, and so forth)
where national coordination is desirable. However, substantial
responsibilities would be transferred to provinces and municipalities in the
areas of culture, health, housing, labour, and social security. EPF and CAP
transfers are eliminated and federal redistribution programs that are
delivered directly to persons (CPP, UI, OAS, and Family Allowance) are
transferred to the provinces. However, the federal government retains
responsibility for interprovincial equalization.[3] Clearly, a significant
realignment of taxing powers would be needed to support this transfer of
responsibilities, and alternative configurations of taxing powers are explored
in the Dahlby paper.

The third alternative is an independent Alberta. As in the
Canada-without-Québec case, we assume that free trade and migration

---

3. Although this last point is taken from the Allaire report, it could well be in keeping with the
    spirit of decentralization to make provinces jointly responsible for equalization. See Dahlby
    and Wilson (1991) for such a scheme.

between Alberta and its former partners continues, at least for a lengthy transition period. Further, we assume that Alberta will continue along the path toward free trade with the United States—in other words, we assume no significant changes in trading relationships. Of course, this alternative implies a wholesale shift in responsibilities from the federal government to what were previously provincial and municipal governments. The shift would include some areas, like defense, where the provinces have no previous experience. In addition to the responsibilities shifted from the federal government in the more decentralized scenario, interprovincial equalization is also eliminated.

An important variant of this alternative is to consider an independent Western Canada that would include the four western provinces, the Yukon and the western half of the Northwest Territories. This might result in a Western Canadian "federation" in which the current federal government would be replaced by a Western unitary state in which case only two orders of government (Western "national" and municipal) would operate. The same assumptions about trade and migration apply.

A final issue that must be addressed for both the first and third alternatives is how federal assets and liabilities would be divided. To limit the scope of the study, we have purposely ignored questions of transition to any of these alternative futures, but it is necessary to make an assumption about the final division of federal assets and debt (regardless of how it is determined) under each alternative. As discussed in an earlier WCER conference[4] this is an extremely difficult and complex issue. However, in the interests of simplicity, we assume here that fixed assets are left in place, and moveable assets and debt are divided on a simple per capita basis.

Conference Overview

Divisions of Powers Study—Boothe
The goal of the Boothe study is to compare the division of spending responsibilities that can be derived from economic principles to the division implied by each of the three alternative constitutional scenarios. The three principles to which Boothe appeals in assigning spending responsibilities are

1. responsiveness,

2. efficiency, and

3, accountability.

4. See Boothe and Harris (1991).

Responsiveness has to do with governments' ability to provide the level and mix of government goods and services (GGS) that are demanded by the public. A key assumption in the analysis is that preferences over GGS become less similar as the geographic distance between individuals increases, and thus lower orders of government are better able to respond to the demands of the citizens in their jurisdiction because those demands are more similar.

Efficiency has to do with governments' ability to deliver particular GGS at the lowest cost. Boothe argues that most GGS have more-or-less constant costs as supply increases, thus the efficiency principle gives little practical guidance in the assignment of spending responsibilities. An exception to this general rule is in cases of "externalities" or spillovers—where events in a given jurisdiction have effects in other jurisdictions. These spillover effects may be positive or negative. In cases where the spillovers are between neighbouring jurisdictions, it may be most efficient to eliminate negative effects through coordination between governments. In cases where spillovers affect many provinces, it may be more efficient to centralize that particular spending responsibility under a higher, encompassing order of government.

The final principle, accountability, has to do with governments' ability to match the benefits from a particular program with its costs so that recipients of benefits demand the socially-efficient level and mix of GGS. Boothe argues that this principle also generally leads one to decentralization since it is lower-order jurisdictions that are best able to effect the cost and benefit alignment.

An examination of spending by the various order of government reveals that Albertans receive about 13% less than the Canadian average from the federal government, but about 20% and 10% more than the national average from their provincial and municipal governments, respectively. Albertans receive 37% of their GGS from the federal government, 45% from the provincial government, and 18% from their municipal governments. Of the fourteen program areas examined, the federal and provincial governments are each dominant in six, with Alberta municipal governments dominant in the remaining two.

Using the three principles to compare the assignment of responsibilities under the alternative scenarios and the status quo, Boothe establishes the following ranking: more decentralized Canada, independent Western Canada, status quo, independent Alberta and more centralized Canada. He argues that the first two options improve over the status quo in both responsiveness and accountability, while providing for jurisdictions that are large enough to capture economies of scale and internalize spillovers where necessary. The loss of potential economies of scale and increased coordination costs to deal with spillovers contribute to the low ranking of the independent Alberta scenario. Finally, low ranking of the more centralized Canada option is a result of its significant loss of both responsiveness and accountability.

In his wide-ranging comments, discussant Thomas Courchene of Queen's University agrees with the ranking of constitutional alternatives suggested by Boothe. However, his reasons for supporting the ranking are substantially different. Specifically, he argues that the effect of globalization and the Free Trade Agreement (FTA) with the United States has been to change the economic axis of Canada from east-west to north-south. Thus, today Canadians are less tied together by an economic policy "railway" than by a social policy railway. Focusing on one of Boothe's key assumptions, Courchene argues that, rather than having differing social interests (and thus different preferences for government social programs), Canadians in different regions (and particularly in Alberta) have substantially different economic interests. In Courchene's view, it is this difference in economic interests that supports the decentralization advocated by Boothe.

Stanley Winer of Carleton University also highlights the importance of Boothe's assumption regarding the differences in preferences between regions in Canada. He argues that there are good reasons to think that Canadians view themselves primarily as members of groups that cut across provincial boundaries. For example, members of minority groups who reside in several provinces may feel that their rights would be better protected by a federal government that can represent the interests of all the members of their group. Winer conjectures that reliance on the Bill of Rights in the United States has led over time to the gradual erosion of states' rights in favour of the federal government. He predicts that the 1982 entrenchment of the Canadian Charter of Rights and Freedoms will ultimately lead to the same trend in Canada.

Redistribution Study—Reid and Snoddon

The goal of the Reid and Snoddon study is to examine the implications of the constitutional scenarios for government redistribution programs. Because virtually all government activities have some element of redistribution, Reid and Snoddon confine their attention to federal programs which "are explicitly designed or are generally perceived to transfer resources from higher-income to lower-income agents." This definition captures seven federal programs: Equalization, Established Program Financing, the Canada Assistance Plan, Family Allowance and Old Age Security programs, the Canada Pension Plan, and Unemployment Insurance. The study assesses the ability of different orders of government to finance existing programs, and makes no comment on their desirability.

By necessity, this is a partial-equilibrium study—that is, no account is taken of the second-round effects these changes may have on individual behaviour or the economy as a whole. Thus, they assume that the goal and structure of the programs remain the same regardless of the constitutional scenario examined. Further, the distribution of population and economic activity across Canada is unaffected. Program costs (with the exception of UI and CPP where costs can be allocated directly) are allocated to regions based on their contribution to total federal revenue. Finally, program costs allocated to regions are "grossed-up" to include the portion of expenditure that is financed by federal borrowing. This adjustment ensures that the "hidden" costs of expenditures—those currently financed by borrowing—are also considered.

In their examination of the status quo for 1988, Reid and Snoddon show net transfers from Alberta for redistribution were in the order of $314 per person. Canadians in Atlantic Canada received over $2000 per person, and Québecers received almost $600 per person. The largest net contributor to redistribution was Ontario at almost $1100 per person.

These figures have important implications for the alternative constitutional scenarios. Based on the 1988 data, a more centralized Canada without Québec would gain in the order of $4 billion in redistribution no longer paid to that province. The federal government would have these extra funds at its disposal, but would require substantially more revenue to take over the redistribution programs currently shared with the provinces. As Reid and Snoddon point out, provincial natural resource revenue is an obvious place for an increased federal presence. In addition, some Alberta redistribution programs would be reduced if they were funded at the national average by the federal government.

A more decentralized Canada in which Equalization is the only major federal redistribution program, would benefit Alberta and especially Ontario, but would hurt Québec and Atlantic Canada. Clearly, a transfer of tax room from the federal to provincial governments would be necessary. To make this option viable for Atlantic Canada, there would have to be a significant enrichment of Equalization. Provincial pension and unemployment insurance programs, even in the Ontario and Alberta, would be less diversified and thus somewhat more costly.

Finally, an independent Alberta would gain the full amount of federal redistribution. However, programs such as UI would be more costly to operate given the lack of diversification of the program and the substantial volatility of the Alberta economy. The most substantial gains would accrue to Ontario, and the costs to Atlantic Canada, Manitoba, and Saskatchewan might well be unsustainable. Interestingly, the costs of maintaining all current redistributive programs in an independent Western Canada would result in a savings of about $100 per person in Alberta.

Discussant Derek Hum from St. John's College, University of Manitoba, finds himself in agreement with much of the Reid and Snoddon study. He makes a careful distinction between transfers that are driven mostly by demographic factors (for example, Family Allowance and OAS) that are essentially unaffected by constitutional change, and programs (for example UI and equalization) which could be dramatically different under alternative constitutional scenarios. He points to the importance of using common sense in interpreting the Reid and Snoddon results. Assumptions that put practical bounds on the kind of hypothetical changes considered—such as assuming that all transfers to persons continue to be funded at their current levels—are unlikely to remain intact in the face of profound constitutional change.

Ken Norrie of the University of Alberta argues that Confederation is really about sharing wealth between individuals and regions. While some of this sharing, such as progressive income tax and redistribution is explicit, much of it is done implicitly through the programs examined by Reid and Snoddon. Norrie asks whether a federal withdrawal from social programs implied by decentralization will lead to reduced spending in some provinces or will be compensated for by higher levels of equalization. Norrie doubts the latter will occur, because he believes that a federal government whose main tasks are to service debt and explicitly redistribute income will lack legitimacy.

Norrie points out that a reconsideration of redistribution would be necessary even if we were not faced with choosing between constitutional options. This re-examination is dictated by the federal government's fiscal situation and its progressive withdrawal from the funding of social programs. Finally, he reinforces Tom Courchene's point that in the future Ontario may be less willing to support redistribution to other regions as more of the second-round benefits accrue to the United States rather than returning to Ontario.

Taxation Study—Dahlby

The goal of this study is to examine the implications of the alternative constitutional scenarios for taxation in Alberta and ROC. After reviewing the current state of taxation in Canada, Dahlby turns to a discussion of principles for the assignment of taxation powers in a federal state. He appeals to two principles: efficiency and equity. Efficiency concerns arise in federations when the burden of the tax is borne by individuals outside the jurisdiction imposing the tax, "when taxes distort the location decision of economic activity, or when two governments tax the same base."

Dahlby next outlines the "accepted" theory of taxation in federations where personal and corporate income tax (PIT and CIT) are assigned to the central government for efficiency reasons, PIT and resource revenues (RR) are assigned to central governments for equity reasons, and sales taxes and property taxes are assigned to provincial and municipal governments, respectively. Dahlby argues that there are a number of problems with applying the "accepted" theory to the Canadian federation. First, the theory ignores the need (discussed in the Boothe study) to align the benefits and costs of GGS in order to control the size of the government sector. Second, as Dahlby puts it, "history matters." When the Canadian federation was founded, provinces retained primary responsibility for their citizens' social welfare and ownership of their natural resources. Finally, concentrating taxing powers with the central government reduces the ability of provincial governments to use tax policies to deal with varying economic conditions.

Evaluating the alternative constitutional scenarios, Dahlby suggests that a more centralized Canada without Québec might be able to provide more generous transfers to remaining provinces—thus leading to lower provincial tax rates. However, he warns that Québec's departure would likely result in "a greater tendency for Ottawa to impose uniform standards in areas of provincial jurisdiction and more pressure for the federal government to obtain a larger share of resource rents." Finally, with Ontario representing nearly 50% of the population of ROC, its interests would largely determine federal tax policy.

In the more decentralized scenario, Dahlby compares the suggested tax assignment of Mintz and Wilson (1991) with his own. Mintz and Wilson suggest that the federal government withdraw from the sales tax field and increase the provinces' share of PIT to 50%. He contrasts this with his preferred assignment where, given their primary responsibility for income security, provinces control direct taxes (PIT and CIT) and the federal government has exclusive control of indirect (sales) taxes. Dahlby cautions that both these proposals increase the scope for inefficient tax exportation and competition. The harmonization of PIT across jurisdictions, for example, would require interprovincial cooperation.

Without the current net fiscal transfers from Alberta to other parts of Canada, tax rates would be lower in an independent Alberta. In this environment, Dahlby argues that there would be substantial gains to Alberta to harmonize its tax system with those of its neighbours, especially the

United States. The volatility of the Alberta economy could lead to greater use of tax incentives to diversify the economy. In addition, the province would do well to look for more stable revenue sources (for example, a sales tax) to offset the volatility of resource revenue. Finally, the importance of saving a portion of the revenue from depleting natural resources would become even more important in an independent Alberta.

In his discussion of Dahlby's paper, Mel McMillan of the University of Alberta makes a number of observations. He suggests that Canadians may feel they get more "value" for their tax dollars because transfers between orders of government obscure the relationship between costs and benefits of government services. Because they are recipients of intergovernmental grants (and, in Alberta's case, substantial resource revenues), provincial and municipal governments seem to provide more services at lower cost. Arguing that provincial taxation of resource rents leads to distortion of resource allocation and attendant inefficiencies, McMillan calls for reconsideration of provincial ownership of resource revenue. He also points out that calculations of tax burdens under alternative constitutional scenarios depend crucially on assumptions regarding responsibility for the federal debt. It is unlikely that the federal government will be willing to transfer revenue sources to the provinces without being relieved of some of the burden of the national debt. Finally, McMillan suggests that, in the event of Québec choosing independence, limiting the federal government to the sales tax field (Dahlby's assignment) may be one way of counteracting the centralizing tendencies of a Canada where Ontario is 50% of the population.

Wayne Thirsk of the University of Waterloo proposes to look at taxation in a different framework: distinguishing between residence-based (sales and property taxes) and source-based taxes (income taxes). Residence-based taxes are less likely to be exported and are less susceptible to tax competition, and thus seem appropriate for provincial and municipal governments. When pure public goods (goods for which benefits accrue to all regardless of who pays) are being financed, source-based taxes should be used to minimize inefficient migration in search of greater net fiscal benefits. However, Thirsk argues that most of the services provided (for example, health care and education) by provinces and municipalities are not pure public goods and therefore residence-based taxes provide appropriate financing. Finally, Thirsk disagrees with the conjecture that Québec independence will lead to centralizing pressures in the ROC. Rather, he argues, political realities are such that provinces such as Alberta will insist on substantial decentralization as a precondition to remaining in a federation increasingly dominated by Ontario.

Trade and Migration Study—Chambers and Percy

The goal of this study is to assess the implications of the alternative
constitutional scenarios for Alberta's trade and migration flows. It departs
somewhat from the other studies which assume that trade and migration
patterns are unchanged. In this paper, Chambers and Percy look at how
alternative constitutional arrangements might alter these flows as changes in
the structure of the Alberta economy take place.

Chambers and Percy begin with a review of the four potential gains from
Confederation first enumerated by Maxwell and Pestieau (1980). The four
sources of economic surplus are:

1.   sharing of overheads,

2.   gains from trade (specialization),

3.   increased market power in international trade, and,

4.   insurance and stabilization.

They argue that the first two sources of surplus are relatively
unimportant for Alberta. With many GGS provided at roughly constant unit
cost there is little gain for Alberta in this area. Gains from specialization will
accrue as long as trade with other provinces and the United States remained
possible. Indeed, it may be that some of these potential gains were not
realized in the past because of the distortions that arose from the
tariff-induced east-west alignment of economic activity.

Chambers and Percy argue that potentially large gains for Alberta are
found in the increased market power and insurance and stabilization aspects
of Confederation. They point to Canada's market power with the United
States as an important factor in the successful resolution of the softwood
lumber dispute, and they argue that it is unlikely that British Columbia, by
itself, would have been able to avoid a United States tariff on its softwood
exports. Of course, market power is a two-edged sword. The ability to make
trade-offs in this kind of international bargaining means that sometimes the
interests of one region are sacrificed for the benefit of another. It may well be
that, given its small size, Western Canadian interests are traded off to protect
industry in Québec or Ontario.

Given the high volatility of the Alberta economy, the potential gains
from insurance and stabilization are also important. Unfortunately, as
Mansell and Percy (1990) show, past federal action has increased, rather than
reduced the volatility of the Alberta economy. However, a key private
insurance mechanism, the ability to migrate to and from other regions in
response to economic conditions, has been widely used.

How important are these potential gains for the Alberta economy, and how might the structure of the economy change in a different constitutional environment? Chambers and Percy present an exhaustive set of statistics describing the current structure of the Alberta economy. In addition to documenting the high volatility of the Alberta economy, they collect important information about the current patterns of trade and migration. On the trade side, they show that while the bulk of Alberta exports are sent abroad and to other western provinces, Ontario remains an important destination for Alberta exports of primary and processed commodities. On the migration, side a similar pattern emerges. While the majority of migrants to Alberta are from abroad and other western provinces, Ontario is an important source and destination of Alberta migrants.

Chambers and Percy argue that when trade and migration are considered, an independent Alberta is the least attractive of the constitutional scenarios. Alberta would be a small, volatile economy with little market power and reduced migration opportunities. They question Alberta's ability to maintain its relatively large agricultural subsidies as an independent state. While an independent Western Canada would have enhanced migration opportunities and market power, these opportunities would be further improved by including Ontario. Their study gives little guidance in choosing between the more centralized and more decentralized alternatives, although they suggest that Québec independence might lead to a reduction in agricultural protection in the ROC. Finally, they argue strongly that any revitalized Confederation must address the inequity and inefficiency of the current mechanism for redistributing the economic surplus from Confederation.

In her comments on the Chambers and Percy paper, Wendy Dobson of the University of Toronto draws attention to five characteristics of the international environment:

1. the world will be characterized by low inflation,

2. there will be global production in key industries with increasing reliance on information technologies,

3. there will be increased interdependence—the policies of one government will affect others, and thus policy coordination will grow in importance,

4. the world economy will grow more slowly with increased movement toward "managed trade" by powerful states, and

5. we will move toward continental economic integration, and, especially important for western provinces, we will become increasingly integrated with newly-industrialized countries (NICs) of the Pacific Rim.

With these characteristics in mind, Dobson divides the constitutional scenarios being considered into two groups—scenarios that imply integration (a more decentralized Canada) and disintegration (a Canada without Québec and an independent Alberta). She argues that is unhelpful to assume that the FTA with the United States will remain intact in the disintegration scenarios—since the agreement is unlikely to survive in its present form and the likely changes will have significant consequences for Canadians in all regions. In Dobson's view, the only option that ensures rising living standards for all Canadians is one that maintains the economic union. Finally, commenting on all the conference papers, she is disturbed by the lack of discussion of what she believes will be the crippling transition costs of any disintegration scenario.

Richard Harris of Simon Fraser University comments on two elements of the Chambers and Percy study. He draws an important distinction in reacting to the volatility of the Alberta economy. The key issue is whether a decline in resource prices should be viewed as a cyclical phenomenon that will be reversed in the future or as a secular decline. Obviously, these alternative interpretations give rise to very different policy prescriptions. Harris places considerable importance on what he calls the "option" value of labour mobility. He cites as evidence the current black-market price of $10,000 to $30,000 for United States green cards (which permit holders to work in the United States). The option value of mobility is what parents would be willing to pay to insure that they and their children could work in all regions of Canada. Harris argues that Canadians value this option very highly.

Finally, Harris takes issue with Chambers and Percy over the independent Western Canada scenario. If Québec chooses independence, he believes that this option should be examined carefully. Rapid growth in the NICs may put upward pressure on resource prices—in which case, Western Canada could find itself in a long-term secular upswing.

Fiscal Balances Study—Mansell and Schlenker

The goal of the study by Mansell and Schlenker is to "estimate the regional distribution of fiscal balances under existing and selected alternative constitutional arrangements." This exercise is useful in determining "the extent to which regional grievances concerning equity, stability, adjustment, and distribution might be alleviated or amplified under various types of changes in the allocation of powers." Mansell and Schlenker caution that their analysis is essentially an accounting exercise, and that the "second-round" economic effects of fiscal transfers are not considered. They cite Whalley and Trela (1986) who show, for the year they examined, that the "second-round" effects significantly amplify the impact of fiscal transfers.

To perform their analysis, Mansell and Schlenker make a number of modifications to Statistics Canada's Provincial Economic Accounts for the years 1961 to 1989. These modifications are dominated by accounting for the effects of national energy pricing policies. For example, in the early part of the period analyzed, Alberta received an implicit subsidy from energy-consuming regions as prices were set above world levels. Later in the period, it was the energy-consuming regions that were subsidized though energy prices that were set below world levels.

Mansell and Schlenker use two alterative conceptual approaches to allocate the costs of "national overhead." In the "cash-flow" approach, benefits of federal expenditures are allocated to the region in which the expenditures are made. This is consistent with the view that most of the benefits of say, the federal bureaucracy, accrue to the regions in which public servants spend their salaries. In the "benefits" approach, the benefits of federal expenditures are allocated to all regions on the basis of their contribution to total federal revenue. This allocation is consistent with the view that expenditures on say, the National Capital Region, confer equal benefits on residents of Edmonton and Ottawa-Hull.

In assessing the status quo, Mansell and Schlenker argue that the substantial net fiscal transfers they find have resulted in Courchene's (1978) cycle of transfer dependency in Atlantic Canada. In Alberta, where net fiscal outflows over the three decades have exceeded $125 billion dollars, the result has been to exacerbate economic instability, to worsen Alberta's prolonged recession of the 1980s and to neutralize provincial government efforts to stabilize the economy.

Based on their analysis, Mansell and Schlenker establish the following ranking (from best to worst for Alberta) for the constitutional alternatives considered: more decentralized Canada, independent Alberta, status quo, and more centralized Canada. Focusing first on the worst alternative, Mansell and Schlenker argue that, while the province would find net fiscal transfers reduced in a more centralized Canada without Québec, Alberta would lose a strategic ally in the protection of provincial rights in the economic sphere. Countering a current argument, they find little in the Free Trade Agreement with the United States that would protect Alberta from another National Energy Program-type federal attack on provincial resource revenue, and thus they are worried about Alberta's position in a more centralized ROC.

An independent Alberta would realize large gains by eliminating the net fiscal transfers to other regions. While, in theory, the Alberta economy would be more volatile, Mansell and Schlenker remind us that past federal policies have increased, rather than reduced the volatility of the provincial economy. Volatility could be reduced by an aggressive program of public-sector savings along the lines of the Alberta Heritage Savings Trust Fund (AHSTF) which was developed in the 1970s. However, they also argue, that many of these gains could be realized with relatively modest reforms in institutions within the existing Canadian federation.

Mansell and Schlenker believe these reforms would be best accomplished within the framework of a more decentralized Canada. Under this option, Alberta would be protected from discriminatory federal policies such as the NEP, and would gain from the removal of inefficient federal regional development schemes and unemployment insurance. They argue that the removal of these policies would actually reduce the volatility of the Alberta economy, while leaving the province free to gain the benefits of economic integration discussed by Chambers and Percy.

Kathleen Macmillan of the Canadian International Trade Tribunal views the Mansell and Schlenker study as an important contribution to the current constitutional debate. However, she urges caution in interpreting the results. In particular, she draws attention to the lack of second-round effects in the analysis. Macmillan argues that the study can provide little evidence regarding what the Alberta economy would be like in the absence of the large fiscal transfers that Mansell and Schlenker document. Finally, she calls attention to the fact that fiscal balances are only one part, albeit an important one, of the equation in looking at the economic implications of alternative constitutional scenarios.

Paul Hobson of Acadia University claims that the size of the federal transfers out of Alberta may well be consistent with the equity goals of the Canadian federation. Indeed, taking a broad definition of equity, he suggests that all Canadians should be provided with the same level of public services regardless of their region. He argues that the fact that the federal government continued to transfer large amounts out of Alberta during a period in which Alberta experienced a deep and prolonged recession may simply show the small size of federal transfers for stabilization purposes relative to the transfers for regional and personal redistribution. In his view, resource rents should be explicitly equalized to the extent that they allow provinces to provide public goods and services at a lower tax costs to their citizens.

References

Allaire, J. (1991). *Un Québec libre de ses choix: Rapport du Comite constitutionnel du Parti liberal du Québec*. Québec: Parti liberal du Québec.

Belanger, G. & Campeau, J. (1991). *Rapport du Commission sur l'avenir politique et constitutionnel du Québec*. Québec: Assemblee nationale du Québec.

Boothe, P. & Harris, R. (forthcoming). Alternative divisions of federal assets and liabilities. *Canadian Public Policy*.

Courchene, T. (1978). Avenues of adjustment: The transfer system and regional disparities. In M. Walker (Ed.), *Canadian Confederation at the Crossroads* (pp. 143-186). Vancouver: Fraser Institute.

Dahlby, B. & Wilson, S. (1991). *Fiscal capacity, tax effort and optimal equalization grants*. University of Alberta discussion paper.

Mansell, R. & Percy, M. (1990). *Strength in adversity: A study of the Alberta economy*. Edmonton:, University of Alberta Press.

Maxwell J. & Pestieau, C. (1980). Economic realities of contemporary confederation. Toronto: C.D. Howe Institute.

Mintz, J. & Wilson, T. (1991). The allocation of tax authority in the Canadian federation. In R. Boadway, T. Courchene & D. Purvis (Eds.), *Economic dimensions of constitutional change*, Vol. I (pp. 169-188). Kingston: John Deutsch Institute.

Norrie, K., Osberg, L. & Boadway, R. (1991). The constitution and the social contract. In R. Boadway, T. Courchene & D. Purvis (Eds.), *Economic Dimensions of Constitutional Change*, Vol. I (pp. 225-254). Kingston: John Deutsch Institute.

Whalley, J. & Trela, I. (1968). *Regional aspects of confederation, Vol. 68. Collected Research Studies of the Royal Commission on the Economic Union and Development Prospects for Canada*. Toronto: University of Toronto Press.

Exclusive Québec Authority		
Social affairs	Energy	Research and
Municipal affairs	Environment	development
Agriculture	Housing	Natural resources
Unemployment insurance	Industry and commerce	Health
Communications	Language	Public security
Culture	Recreation and sports	Income security
Regional development	Manpower and formation	Tourism
Education	Family policy	

Shared Authority (or distributed according to authority)		
Native affairs	Justice	Post office and
Taxation and revenue	Fisheries	telecommunications
Immigration	Foreign policy	Transport
Financial institutions		

Exclusive Canadian Authority		
Defence and the	Currency and common	
territorial security	debt	
Customs and tariffs	Equalization	

Source: Allaire (1991).

Constitutional Change and the Provision of Government Goods and Services

2

by Paul Boothe

Introduction

As Canada begins a critical round of constitutional negotiations, Albertans and Canadians in other regions are being called upon to consider carefully what it is they "want" of the Canadian federation. Many factors must be considered. For Québec, some of these factors relate to preserving their distinct language and culture and their identity as a francophone nation in North America. In Alberta, questions of political representation, participation in national institutions, and the economic well-being of Western Canada are paramount. The purpose of this paper is to contribute to Albertans' discussion of what they "want" from confederation by looking at one of the economic implications of constitutional change for Alberta: the assignment of spending responsibilities among federal, provincial, and municipal governments.

The constitutional alternatives examined in this paper are common to all the studies presented at this conference:

1. a more centralized Canada without Québec,

2. a more decentralized Canada with Québec, and

3. an independent Alberta or an independent Western Canada.

All the alternatives will be compared to each other and to the status quo. The alternatives were chosen, not because they represent predictions regarding our constitutional future, but rather to give a range of possibilities which provide some information about the choices Albertans face.

Obviously, economic implications are only one part of a larger picture that Albertans need to consider as we develop our constitutional position, and the assignment of spending responsibilities is only one of those economic implications. Other important economic implications of constitutional change are addressed in companion papers presented at this conference. However, in one sense, the assignment of spending responsibilities is one of the key issues in constitutional design precisely because it derives directly from what we "want" of the federation. Put another way, we can ask how can we design our government to give us what we want in some optimal way?

The plan for the paper is as follows: the remainder of the introduction will be devoted to a brief discussion of our current situation and some of the external forces which will affect our future direction. In Section 2, we lay out some principles which can be used to evaluate and compare the assignment of spending responsibilities which correspond to our constitutional alternatives. Some facts about the current situation are presented in Section 3, and the alternatives are described in detail and compared in Section 4. Given the restricted focus of the paper, conclusions must likewise be restricted, and the paper concludes with a brief summary and some observations regarding our future choices.

The current situation

Canada is one of the most decentralized of the industrial federations. Compared with citizens of many other nations, Canadians have an enviable standard of living and level of social security. However, strong forces are currently working to change the Canadian constitution. While in Québec these forces may spring from the will of Québecois to preserve their distinct language and culture in North America, in Western Canada, the key issues relate to the sharing of decision-making and institutions and the distribution of wealth across regions.

Fiscal federalism in Canada is currently under tremendous strain. Over the past three decades, the federal government has moved significantly into areas of provincial responsibility through its expanded use of direct transfers to individuals and the use of its spending power to affect the design and delivery of provincial programs. The provinces have likewise moved into federally-dominated areas such as immigration and international trade. Both orders of government jointly occupy a number of program areas. In sum, the current system of program delivery is characterized by overlap, confusion and conflict between the programs of the two orders of government.

More recently, as part of its deficit-reduction efforts, the federal government has unilaterally reduced the growth of federal transfers relating to social programs, leaving provinces to fund an increasing share of these growing programs. Reductions in transfers in the Canada Assistance Plan, for example, have affected different provinces differently, pitting so-called "have" and "have-not" provinces against one another.

Both orders of government have put in place policies which interfere with the marketplace or impede the free flow of goods and people within the federation and thus weaken the Canadian economic union. On the federal side, Courchene (1986) lists the National Energy Program, unemployment insurance, regional development (DREE, DRIE, Western Diversification Office, Atlantic Canada Opportunities Agency, etc.), federally-sanctioned agricultural marketing boards and grain transportation subsidies, and federal procurement policy (for example, the CF-18 decision) as examples. Although they are probably less significant, provincial barriers fragment the economic union through the use of employment standards, procurement policy, interprovincial trade barriers (beer is an oft-cited example), and differential tax treatment for corporations.

Finally, there is substantial evidence of large, persistent net transfers out of some provinces as a result of federal expenditure and taxation. The massive cost of Confederation to Alberta is documented in Whalley and Trela (1986) as well as in Mansell and Schlenker (1990) and Horry and Walker (1991). According to Horry and Walker, for the year 1988 the net cost of confederation to every Albertan was in the range of $1700. This is indicative of the serious fiscal imbalance which currently exists.

External factors

In addition to the internal strains discussed above, a number of external factors are working to change the federation. Drawing on Courchene (1991), we look at three factors: the effects of globalization, the federal debt and deficit, and the Free Trade Agreement (FTA) with the United States. Courchene argues that globalization is having the effect of transferring the federal government's power to act effectively in two directions. Some of its functions, such as regulation of trade and industry, are being transferred "up" to transnational bodies that seek to regulate those transnational corporations which use components from many countries to produce "global" products. He cites the adoption by an number of countries of the bank capital standards of the Bank for International Settlements as an example of a transnational regulatory body at work. At the same time, power is being transferred "down" to "global" consumers, so that international market forces, not national governments, set standards and discipline industry.

The size of the federal deficit, debt, and corresponding interest payments are such that the federal government is now engaged in an exercise of "expenditure shifting" (called "deficit offloading" by the provinces) to its provincial partners. This is having the effect of progressively eroding the federal government's power to affect the design and delivery of programs or to enforce "national standards." The federal government's recent threat to use "other methods" to punish provinces that do not abide by the *Canada Health Act* is a signal that it is very aware of this problem.

Finally, the FTA is working to change the traditional flow of goods and services in Canada from east-west to north-south. Thus, the economic links that bind the federation are weakening as Canadians find other markets in which to buy and sell their products. In addition, the second-round effects of interprovincial transfers are now less likely to return to central Canada through the purchase of manufactured goods or services. Rather, transfers to have-not provinces are now just as likely to be spent buying goods and services from the United States. Thus, the effective cost to Ontario (and Québec) of making these transfers is increasing.

Accountability and the federal deficit

A final issue to be addressed before examining constitutional alternatives has to do with the relation between our constitutional structure and the federal deficit and debt. The 1980s saw the buildup of a mountain of federal debt and corresponding interest payments so that now almost one-third of all tax revenue goes to pay interest on the federal debt. While a number of reasons for this massive debt buildup have been advanced, little attention has been paid to how the structure of our federation has contributed to the problem.

A basic law of economics is that people demand more of a good as its price declines. One way the price faced by consumers may fall is when someone else pays a portion of the cost. An important trend in the Canadian federation has been an increasing loss of accountability—giving citizens a clear idea of which government provides a given service, what it costs, and who pays. More and more with national programs, only the benefits are clear. As governments (especially the federal government) increasingly blur the lines between providing a program (allocation) and redistributing income (distribution), the close alignment between who benefits from programs and who pays for them is lost. Consequently, citizens demand more from government because they believe someone else (in another region, or income class, or industry) will pay. The result is increasing demands for government services, and, lacking government determination to impose corresponding tax increases, government deficits.

Basic Principles

Modern governments perform a bewildering array of functions—probably too many to even count. In a federal system with three orders of government, the problem of comprehending all the things that governments do is all the greater. For this reason, modern constitution writers must confine their efforts to assigning constitutional responsibilities under broad general headings rather than attempting to delineate explicitly and exactly what each order of government should do.

In order to evaluate and compare alternative assignments of responsibilities in the face of this complexity, an organizing framework is needed. The purpose of this section is to develop such a framework based on a set of simple economic principles. Later in the paper, we will use the framework to compare the assignment of responsibilities for providing government goods and services (GGS) under the various constitutional alternatives.

We can begin by thinking about the goals of government. Of course, political philosophers have devoted many lifetimes to this question and we could not begin to survey the accumulated body of knowledge here. Concentrating on economic goals, we will follow Bird and Hartle (1972) in assuming "that it is desired to maximize the welfare, broadly conceived, of individuals within a given geographic area." Further, we assume "that the welfare of individuals is determined in part by the extent to which their wants for collective goods and services are satisfied." (p. 47)

Two related complications immediately arise. The first is the economist's well-known problem of having no general theoretical basis for comparing (or trading off) the well-being of one individual for another. This is important because the actions of governments typically make some people better off and others worse off. Sometimes this is dealt with by assuming that all individuals are alike—but this method removes much of what is interesting about federalism. Another method is to confine oneself to making only certain kinds of comparisons—ones where one individual is left with the same level of well being and the other is made better or worse off. This is very restrictive, but it can sometimes be extended to situations where one individual is better off and the other could be compensated so that they are no worse off. Of course, to the person being made worse off with no guarantee of compensation, this is not very satisfying. Because economic theory provides no satisfactory general answer to this problem we must turn to politics to understand how the inevitable conflicts between different groups in society are resolved. In a sense, one way to think about a constitution is to view it as a set of rules that outlines how conflicts should be resolved.

The second complication comes from the fact that we live in a federal state with three orders of government. Thus, an individual can simultaneously be a Calgarian, an Albertan, and a Canadian. Each level of government can (and frequently does) claim to respond best to the desires of the same individual. Which one is right? Here again, the answer is very contentious and there is no definite evidence to settle the question. However, economic theory does give some help in this area. We will assume that individuals are more alike in their preferences regarding GGS the closer they live to one another. In other words, with respect to preferences for GGS, a Calgarian is more like another Calgarian than an Edmontonian, more like another Albertan than a Nova Scotian, and more like another Canadian than an American.

Of course, political scientists and sociologists try to measure preferences directly by looking at public opinion evidence, and there is evidence to support both the view that there is very little variation in preferences across provinces (except Québec) and the view that there is a lot. Economic theory suggests that if people do have different preferences regarding the things that governments provide, and if the costs of moving are small, then "those that like the same things will tend to congregate together, for most collective services have an important spatial dimension." (Bird and Hartle, 1972, p. 50). Even when moving costs are relatively large, people who live together tend to have the same preferences because "they learn their values from the same source, or through observing each other, or through the operation of social controls which instill value systems. From this sharing of common values emerges a sense of identity with the community as well as some degree of common tastes." (p. 50)

The reason that this is important is because higher orders of governments must frequently make decisions which make some groups better off at the expense of others. The Alberta government must sometimes take actions which benefit Edmonton at the expense of Calgary. The Canadian government must sometimes take actions which benefit Ontario at the expense of Alberta. Given our assumption that peoples' preferences diverge as the distance between them grows, one would expect this necessity of trading off among groups to become more frequent as one moves from local to provincial to federal governments.

Of course, an assumption of this nature is, by necessity, controversial. In its defense we offer two arguments. The first is that, while for some GGS (which for our purposes, does not include redistribution) people with common interests are not grouped geographically (for example with Native or women's issues), most GGS have a spatial component which cannot be ignored. The second argument is simply that it is difficult to see how another kind of assumption can work within our present, geographically-based constitutional structure and electoral system.[5]

What do governments do to maximize the well-being of citizens? Economists generally group the functions of governments under three headings: allocation, distribution, and stabilization. As we stated in the introduction, this paper will focus on the allocative role of governments—the provision of GGS—although some overlap with the studies of redistribution and taxation is unavoidable. However, we will define GGS quite broadly. Using Stevenson's (1985) framework, we include government spending and delivery of GGS as well as government regulation and stabilization. Our distinction between spending and delivery recognizes that the federal government often spends on things like social assistance without actually delivering the service. Even though the federal government does not deliver the program, they can affect it by putting conditions on how the money is spent. Regulation is an important function of every order of government (sometimes of the same activity), as is stabilization, and so we include them as "public services" through which governments attempt to maximize citizens' well being.

With these preliminaries complete, we now turn to the central issue of this section: What does economics tell us about the "best" assignment of responsibilities for providing GGS among the three orders of government? To determine this, we must consider both the supply and demand for GGS. On the supply side, we want to assign responsibilities so that GGS are provided as efficiently as possible, i.e. at the least possible cost. To do this,

---

5. Both of the discussants recognize the importance of this assumption to my argument. Professor Winer asks if provinces can be better trusted to protect the rights of minorities than the federal government. In response, I would make two points. First, the protection of minorities is a very small part of what governments do—especially in the range of activities under consideration in this paper. I agree with Professor Winer that this may be a responsibility better entrusted to the courts. Second, I think that most would agree that neither order of government in Canada has an exemplary record of dealing with minorities, and thus history gives us little guidance in deciding where this responsibility should reside.

Professor Courchene argues that preferences regarding GGS are probably very similar across Canada. Rather, he believes that it is economic interests that differ substantially. While this takes me beyond the scope of my paper, I recognize that this provides an alternative way of supporting my argument. For a more formal discussion of this notion, see Mintz and Simeon (1982).

we need to know something about the costs of providing various GGS and whether there are economies of scale in their production. For example, there are clearly economies of scale in the provision of national defense and the infrastructure for international relations, and thus these things are more efficiently provided by the federal government than the provinces or municipalities. When there are no economies of scale, the cost of providing a given good or service is the same regardless of which order of government supplies it. Finally, in some cases there may be diseconomies of scale so that the unit cost of supplying a given service rises as the amount rises. Health economists sometimes argue that unit costs rise after health care systems grow beyond a certain size. So, in general, which order of government can supply services most efficiently depends on the shape of the cost function for particular services.

Unfortunately, according to Bird and Hartle (1972), we know little about the shapes of the relevant cost curves for producing GGS. While some obvious examples of economies of scale were cited above, things such as defense and the maintenance of foreign embassies typically make up a very small proportion of total government spending. Beyond some minimum size, it is difficult to see that there are significant economies in supplying some of the large, labour-intensive spending items as health care or education or social assistance at the national rather than the local or provincial level. Bird and Hartle (1972) argue that for many GGS "there appears to be little evidence of either economies or diseconomies over a broad range of population served." (p. 49)

Turning to the demand side, we want to choose an assignment of responsibilities for providing GGS so that the "right" bundle, i.e., the ones that people want, is provided. If everyone had exactly the same preferences, then it would not matter which order of government provided which services—cost considerations would dominate. However, if individuals in different jurisdictions have different preferences, then lower orders of government are better placed to provide the services that people want since they will not have to respond to the desires of different groups. This leads to what Oates (1972) has called the "decentralization theorem," which states that, except in the case of significant cost saving from exploiting economies of scale or internalizing spillovers (discussed below), it will always be better for GGS to be supplied by lower rather than higher orders of government. Thus, to be as responsive to the wishes of the people as possible, GGS should be provided at as low an order of government as possible.

Another argument for decentralization, accountability, also comes from the demand side. An important element of any demand decision is cost. Ideally, individuals would pay fully for the GGS they received and would demand GGS just up to the point the extra cost was equal to the extra benefit they received. When the cost of GGS which have local benefits is shared by a large number of people in other jurisdictions, recipients of these services are likely to demand more than they would if they paid the full cost themselves. The smaller the jurisdiction, the more likely the recipients of GGS will have to pay for them, and thus the "right" amount of these services will be demanded. Of course, this argument not only supports assigning some GGS at the provincial rather than the federal level, but also at the municipal rather than the provincial level.

Finally, if different jurisdictions provide different bundles of GGS or different ways of delivering them, there may be two kinds of benefits. First, people will have a choice about the GGS they receive and can move if those provided in one jurisdiction seem more attractive than the ones provided where they currently live. In addition, innovation and experimentation by different jurisdictions may lead to the development of better ways to produce and supply GGS. Thus, this is an additional potential benefit from decentralization.

A potential problem with the decentralized provision of GGS comes from the spillover effects or "externalities" that GGS may have. This is potentially very important in regulation. Externalities can be good or bad for neighbouring jurisdictions. For example, if a neighbouring jurisdiction pollutes the air, you may be an unwilling recipient of some of it. On the other hand, if a neighbouring jurisdiction invests in sports broadcasting, you may be a happy recipient. One way of dealing with externalities is to "internalize" them. For example, in our educational broadcasting case, if the federal rather than provincial governments supplied educational broadcasting, all recipients could be made to share the cost. However, presumably it would not be desirable to tailor the programming to a particular jurisdiction's tastes if all jurisdictions shared the cost.

Another way to deal with externalities is through coordination. It may be possible for jurisdictions to cooperate to "internalize" externalities without assigning them to a higher order of government. This may be more useful if the externalities are local, i.e., just between neighbouring provinces rather than between all provinces. It may also be possible if there are a number of different externalities—some which are good and some which are bad—so that there are potential benefits to both parties to negotiate.[6]

---

6. As Professor Winer points out, there is an extensive literature on constitutions built around the notion of "organization" costs—Breton and Scott (1978) being the best-known example. My point here is simply that the organization costs of provinces' bilateral dealings may well be much smaller than those incurred when the federal government imposes rules on all provinces to deal with a dispute between two neighbours.

To summarize the arguments so far, on the supply side, we have little evidence on the cost of providing GGS that would indicate which order of government can most efficiently fulfil a given responsibility. GGS with significant economies of scale (such as defense) should be centralized at the national level. However, few of the large, labour-intensive spending areas are likely to be characterized by significant scale economies, and, thus, cost efficiency provides little guidance in the assignment of responsibilities for providing GGS. On the demand side, decentralizing the provision of GGS to the local or provincial order of government allows the choice of GGS provided to be more responsive to the public's preferences. In addition, accountability and innovation in providing GGS is also enhanced. A potentially important caveat is the case where there are significant externalities in the provision of GGS, especially in regulation. In this case, the provision of relevant GGS may be centralized or be coordinated between lower order jurisdictions.

Facts on GGS

In this section, we look at some aggregate data on the provision of GGS. As we noted earlier, there is an important distinction to be made between spending and actually delivering GGS. Here, we try to highlight where this distinction is necessary. We begin by a brief analysis of current data at a fairly aggregate level for the three orders of government: federal, provincial and municipal. We then turn to a discussion of some specific areas to give illustrations of the division of responsibilities and discuss how other aspects of GGS such as regulation fit into the picture.

Aggregate data on GGS by order of government

An excellent source of recent data on the provision of GGS by program area is Horry and Walker (1991). Using data from Statistics Canada's Financial Management System (FMS) data base and the *Provincial Economic Accounts*, they provide series for a number of years by all three orders of government under fifteen spending headings.[7] Here, the distinction between spending and design and delivery of GGS becomes important. Horry and Walker define "funding"[8] by a given order of government to be the total

---

7. The fifteen headings are Culture and Recreation, Education, General Services, Health, Housing, Interest, Labour, Natural Resources, Oil and Gas, Other, Protection, Research Establishments, Social Security, Trade and Industry, and Transportation and Communications. See Appendix 1 for a list of programs included under each heading.

8. Horry and Walker use "funding" in the same way as we use "design and delivery." An order of government funds or delivers a program if they are unconstrained in designing it.

amount spent, less any grants provided by another order of government specifically for that purpose. That is, any specific grants are treated as funded by the order of government that provides them, since they can only be used for the purpose specified by the grantor. General grants are treated as funding by the receiving order of government, since the recipient has discretion over how the money should be used.[9]

A second point worth noting has to do with the treatment of interest payments. Interest payments are allocated according to the information provided in the *Provincial Economic Accounts* and simply reflect the geographic distribution of government bond holders. In a sense, they are a benefit to particular provinces that has little to do with governments per se (except their propensity to borrow) and much to do with the savings behaviour of the different provinces' residents. Thus, to measure the direct benefits of government spending in Alberta, total spending less interest payments is also presented.

The basic data for 1988 is presented in Tables 2.1 and 2.2 and Figures 2.1 and 2.2. Table 2.1 shows per capita funding by each order of government for Alberta and for Canada as a whole. Looking first at federal funding, we see that neglecting interest payments, the federal government spent $3406.50 per person in Alberta in 1988. This compares with average expenditures across Canada $3910.70. Thus, as we see from Table 2.2, Albertans received about 13% less than the average amount received by all Canadians from the federal government.

Turning to provincial funding, we see that, neglecting interest payments, the provincial government spent $5396.80 per person in 1988, compared with $3657.20 spent, on average, by all provinces. One possible distortion here is the inclusion of expenditures related to natural resources and oil and gas which were $836.20 and $486.00, compared with national averages of $218.70 and $50.80. Alberta spends a good deal on development and support of its resource industry and, in turn, receives substantial revenues from that source. In fact, net revenues in this area are significantly higher in Alberta than in any other province. Removing the effect of these expenditures reduces the Alberta total to $4074.60, which is 20% above the comparable national average.

Turning to municipal funding, we see that Albertans received a total of $1780.60 per person from their municipal governments compared with the Canadian average of $1127.10. Thus overall, while Albertans receive a

---

9.   Of course, this framework for allocating spending is arbitrary. For example, the federal government would treat all EPF grants as federal spending on education and health divided according to some formula. Provincial governments would treat all EPF money as unconditional, and therefore claim all health and education spending as their own.

TABLE 2.1:
Per Capita Spending by Order of Government,
Alberta and Canadian Average 1988

	Federal		Provincial		Municipal	
	Alberta	Nat'l Avg.	Alberta	Nat'l Avg.	Alberta	Nat'l Avg.
Culture	27.5	41.0	94.4	54.2	140.6	111.0
Education	160.0	207.2	971.4	741.1	282.8	259.6
General Ser.	162.2	260.0	279.7	239.3	128.3	103.0
Health	292.8	307.0	1147.5	1021.1	339.2	82.8
Housing	83.5	68.5	67.5	28.2	35.2	17.2
Interest	624.5	1207.2	419.7	570.9	0.0	0.0
Labour	78.9	98.8	64.7	46.5	0.0	0.0
Nat. Res.	60.2	86.3	836.2	218.7	169.3	120.3
Oil & Gas	10.3	17.0	486.0	50.8	0.0	0.0
Other	37.6	92.6	180.6	170.3	219.2	94.8
Protection	406.0	541.6	160.6	136.7	146.6	157.0
Research	33.7	40.5	22.2	11.4	0.0	0.0
Soc. Sec.	1549.1	1749.8	491.1	575.8	15.6	24.6
Trade & In.	379.6	240.8	275.2	149.5	9.9	2.5
Trans. & Comm.	125.1	159.6	319.7	213.6	294.1	154.4
Total	4031.0	5117.9	5816.5	4228.1	1780.6	1127.1
Total less interest	3406.5	3910.7	5396.8	3657.2	1780.6	1127.1
Total less interest and resources	3336.0	3807.4	4074.6	3387.7	1611.4	1006.8

Source: Tables 3.4, 4.4 and 4.13, Horry and Walker (1991).

lower-than-average value of GGS from the federal government, they receive
higher-than-average GGS from both provincial and municipal governments.
Neglecting interest payments and spending on resources, Albertans receive
total GGS which are about 10% higher than the national average. If we
measure the degree of decentralization by the proportion of GGS provided
by each order of government (see Table 2.2), GGS delivered to Albertans are

TABLE 2.2:
Index of 1988 Spending in Alberta by Order of Government
(National average = 100)

	Federal	Provincial	Municipal
Culture	67.1	174.2	126.7
Education	77.2	131.1	108.9
General Ser.	62.4	116.9	124.5
Health	95.4	112.4	409.5
Housing	121.9	239.4	205.2
Interest	51.7	73.5	100.0
Labour	79.9	139.1	100.0
Nat. Res.	69.8	382.4	140.7
Oil & Gas	60.6	956.7	100.0
Other	40.6	106.0	231.3
Protection	75.0	117.5	93.4
Research	83.2	194.7	100.0
Soc. Sec.	88.5	85.3	63.3
Trade & In.	157.6	184.1	391.3
Trans. & Comm.	78.4	149.7	190.5
Total	78.8	137.6	158.0
Total less interest	87.1	147.6	158.0
Total less interest and resources	87.6	120.3	160.0

Source: Tables 3.4, 4.4 and 4.13, Horry and Walker (1991).

more decentralized than the those delivered to the average Canadian. Neglecting interest and provincial resource expenditures, Albertans receive 37% of their GGS from the federal government, 45% from the provincial government, and 18% from their municipal governments. The average Canadian receives 46% from the federal government, 41% from their provincial government, and 12% from their municipal government.

To see which order of government dominates any particular program area, we turn to Table 2.3 and Figure 2.3. In Table 2.3, we present the share of total funding attributable to each order of government for each program

FIGURE 2.1: Per Capita Spending by Order of Government,
Alberta 1988 (dollars)

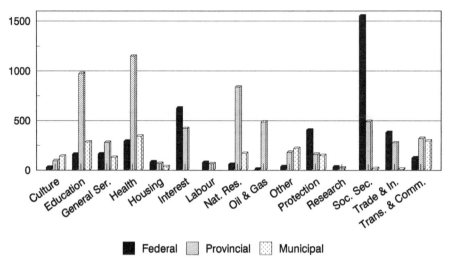

Source: Tables 3.4, 4.4, 4.13, Horry and Walker (1991).

FIGURE 2.2: Index of Spending by Order of Government,
Alberta 19881 (National Average = 100)

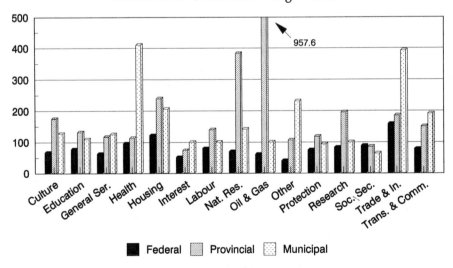

Source: Tables 3.4, 4.4, 4.13, Horry and Walker (1991).

TABLE 2.3:
Share of Per Capita Total Spending by Order of Government, Alberta 1988

	Federal	Provincial	Municipal	Total (dollars)
Culture	10.5	36.0	53.6	262.5
Education	11.3	68.7	20.0	1414.2
General Ser.	28.4	49.1	22.5	570.2
Health	16.5	64.5	19.1	1779.5
Housing	44.8	36.2	18.9	186.2
Interest	59.8	40.2	0.0	1044.2
Labour	54.9	45.1	0.0	143.6
Nat. Res.	5.6	78.5	15.9	1065.7
Oil & Gas	2.1	97.9	0.0	496.3
Other	8.6	41.3	50.1	437.4
Protection	56.9	22.5	20.6	713.2
Research	60.3	39.7	0.0	55.9
Soc. Sec.	75.4	23.9	0.8	2055.8
Trade & In.	57.1	41.4	1.5	664.7
Trans. & Comm.	16.9	43.3	39.8	738.9
Total	34.7	50.0	15.3	11628.1
Total less interest	32.2	51.0	16.8	10583.9
Total less interest and resources	37.0	45.2	17.9	9022.0

Source: Tables 3.4, 4.4 and 4.13, Horry and Walker (1991).

area. Of the 14 program areas (neglecting interest) we see that the federal government is dominant in six: housing, labour, protection, research, social security, and trade and industry. The provincial government is dominant in six fields (education, general services, health, natural resources, oil and gas, other, and transportation and communications), and municipal governments are dominant in only in culture and other, although they have a substantial share of transportation and communications.

Of course, the fields are of very different sizes. For example, some fields like culture, housing, labour, and research are relatively small, while others, like education, health and social security are relatively large. Indeed,

FIGURE 2.3: Share of Total Spending by Order of Government,
Alberta 1988 (percent)

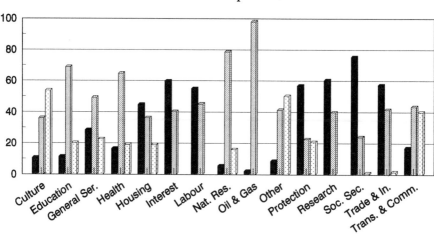

Source: Tables 3.4, 4.4, 4.14, Horry and Walker (1991).

neglecting interest payments and provincial resource expenditures, the latter
three areas make up 57% of total spending on GGS. Thus, while federal and
provincial governments dominate the same number of fields (in this
arbitrary grouping of expenditure items), the province is clearly dominant
overall.

Some specific program areas

Although there is much useful information in the aggregate data
presented above, it is also revealing to look more closely at some of the
specific program areas. Because of their importance in overall
spending—comprising over half of all government spending on GGS—we
focus on education, health, and social security. As we shall see, these
expenditure areas are interesting not only because of their substantial
contribution to overall spending, but also because they include an important
regulatory element and because they illustrate the use of the federal
spending power in influencing the design of programs.

Looking first at education, returning to Tables 2.1-2.3, we see that all
three orders of government are active in this important expenditure area,
with clear dominance by the provincial government. Both federal and
provincial orders of governments give substantial grants to the next lower
order of government for the purposes of education. However, grants to

municipal governments (school boards) from provinces are specific grants and thus are treated as provincial government funding, while federal grants (for post-secondary education) are without condition and, thus, are treated as provincial rather than federal funding.

Returning to our principles outlined in the previous section, we would argue that tastes for elementary and secondary education may differ substantially across provinces. Further, the cost of providing education services is constant or even increasing after reaching some (reasonably small) minimum efficient size. In addition, a substantial portion of the funding for elementary and secondary education comes from school taxes levied at the local level which are directly linked to the services provided. This provides a fairly tight link between the benefits and costs of elementary and secondary education. Thus, our economic principles suggest that these services should be provided by municipal and provincial governments rather than the federal government. It may be argued that some benefits could be reaped at the postsecondary level by specialization and the elimination of duplication at the national level. However, even postsecondary education services seem to differ substantially across provinces—indicating different tastes or needs. Further, given the inevitable forces of regional politics, rather than rationalizing the Canadian postsecondary education system, federal politicians would likely face significant pressure to ensure that all regions have all types of postsecondary institutions for reasons of regional employment and prestige.

Transfers from federal to provincial governments for postsecondary education are unconditional and come as part of Established Programs Financing (EPF). These grants, which have both a tax transfer and cash component, have been unilaterally restricted recently as part of the federal government's deficit-reduction efforts. Provinces, which have the responsibility to deliver the services, have been forced either to reduce services or increase their share of spending on these programs. They have complained about unilateral federal withdrawal from these large and important programs. The most recent federal budget hinted at new federal initiatives in the area of elementary and secondary education—which has traditionally been a provincial responsibility.

The pattern for funding of health care parallels the education pattern closely. Once again the provincial government is dominant, although it receives significant funding from the federal government as part of its EPF grant. Significant grants to municipal governments (in this case, hospital boards) are specific grants and thus are treated as provincial funding. Unlike the case of education, in the area of health, the federal government makes substantial use of its spending power through the *Canada Health Act* (CHA) which outlines five conditions that provincial programs must meet in order to be eligible for full funding.[10] The best-known uses of the spending power in this area by the federal government were the penalties imposed on provinces that allowed physicians to bill patients for amounts above the insured-fee specified by the provincial plan. Although it was argued that this had an important influence on demand and controlling abuse of the system, because of the penalties, all provinces were eventually forced to eliminate so-called "extra billing."

The federal government is also involved in health on the regulatory side through a number of other expenditure areas. A recent example has been federal efforts to enforce regulations banning certain forms of television advertising. Although the courts have brought the federal government's actions into question in this case, it serves to illustrate the intermingling of many of our arbitrarily-divided government expenditure categories.

Recalling our economic principles once again, as in education, we argue that health care is an area where there are few economies of scale to be gained after reaching a minimum efficient size. Indeed, some health economists have argued that diseconomies may occur as the health system grows. In specialized areas where scale economies may exist, we have seen evidence of sharing of specialized services between provinces without any federal involvement—perhaps an indication of relatively small organization costs. With the elimination of extra billing and, in some provinces, of health-care premiums, there is already little to link the benefits of the health care system to its costs. In fact, in Alberta, the Premier's Commission on Health Care recommended a significant decentralization of health care management to the local rather than the provincial level.

Much is made of the fact that the CHA promotes so-called "national standards" in health care which are a basic right of citizenship of all Canadians. However, there is already wide variation in total health spending across provinces,[11] and differences in program design seem to indicate regional differences in preferences for this service. From the standpoint of enhancing the economic union, it is the "portability" rather than the standards or billing methods for health benefits which encourages labour mobility across the federation.

As with education, health has been affected by the recent restraint in EPF payments by the federal government, and provincial governments have been especially vocal in complaining about the unilateral reduction in federal support at the same time as the *Canada Health Act* puts significant constraints

---

10. These conditions relate to: 1) public administration, 2) comprehensiveness, 3) universality, 4) portability, and 5) accessibility.

11. The largest per capita variation, between Alberta and Prince Edward Island, is 77%.

on their ability to respond to rising costs. Some have argued that as its involvement is reduced, the federal government will find it increasingly difficult to enforce "national standards." In the most recent budget, the federal government responded to this concern by hinting that the provinces would be penalized in other ways if they did not comply with the conditions laid out in the CHA.

Finally, in the area of social security, the federal, rather than the provincial governments, is dominant. The federal government currently provides about three quarters of total social security services. This is because the federal government delivers a number of these programs (such as pensions, family allowance, unemployment insurance) directly to citizens. In addition, although the federal government provides funding to the provinces, through the Canada Assistance Plan (CAP), given the numerous conditions imposed, this is treated as federal funding in our framework.

In addition to direct funding, the federal government and the provinces both use the tax system extensively to augment their social security programs. Indeed, together with direct transfers, this leads to substantial overlap, confusion, and even policy conflict between the three orders of government, as individuals face a bewildering web of interrelated income-security programs. Although we are aware of no detailed studies, it has been suggested that this is an area where substantial duplication of programs exist.

Returning to our economic principles, there seems to be little basis for federal involvement in this area because of scale economies, and some reason to believe that programs should be tailored to local needs. However, because many of these programs are mainly redistributive, it may be argued that the reason for federal involvement is the fact that redistribution should be conducted on an individual basis over the entire federation. However, this seems inconsistent with the `redistribution-by-region' which takes place through equalization. In fact, some of the programs in this expenditure area, such as unemployment insurance, which provide different levels of service in different regions, have the unfortunate side effect of hindering labour mobility in the federation, and thus fragmenting the economic union.

In its 1990 budget, the federal government announced that it would restrict the growth of CAP payments to the "have" provinces as part of its deficit reduction efforts. This restriction, recently confirmed by the Supreme Court, has had important effects on the budgets of British Columbia and, especially, recession-battered Ontario. Equally important, the decision has transformed what was essentially an allocative function of the federal government into a specific grant for interregional redistribution performing the same function as, say, equalization.

Comparison of Alternative Constitutional Arrangements

With a set of principles in place to evaluate alternative assignments of
responsibilities and an understanding of the current situation, we are now
ready to consider the implications for Alberta of each of the three
constitutional alternatives proposed. As outlined in the introduction, the
three constitutional alternatives we examine are:

1. Canada without Québec—where the federal government takes on a number
    of the responsibilities currently assigned to the provinces and municipalities,

2. Canada with Québec—where there is a move toward substantial
    decentralization of responsibilities along the lines suggest by the Allaire
    report, and finally

3. an independent Alberta—where all responsibilities are moved to provincial
    and municipal orders of government.

In conjunction with this third alternative, we will also examine some of
the implications of an independent Western Canada. First, we lay out in
more detail specifically how responsibilities will be allocated under each
alternative. We then turn to an evaluation of each of the alternatives based
on the principles outlined in Section 2.

Defining the constitutional alternatives

For a full discussion of the alternatives considered, the reader is referred to
the introduction of this volume. In this section, we focus on the implications
of the alternative scenarios for the problem of providing GGS. The first
alternative is Canada without Québec. We assume that Québec chooses
independence and the rest of Canada (ROC) chooses to remain together
under a more centralized form of government. Further, we assume there is
free trade and migration between ROC and Québec but no significant
sharing of economic institutions such as stabilization or unemployment
insurance or pensions or defense, and no redistribution of income to Québec
from the ROC through equalization or regional development programs.[12]
    Within the ROC, the move to a more centralized form of government
causes a shift of responsibilities from provincial and municipal to the federal
government. This shift could be accomplished through the use of the federal

---

12. Of course, it is not necessary for Québec to separate for this alternative to be relevant. Some
    kind of sovereignty-association with a more centralized ROC would have the same
    implications for Alberta. In either case, the political and economic relations between Québec
    and the ROC would have to be worked out, and there could be a long, possibly acrimonious
    transition to a stable relationship—if one were indeed possible. Given our perspective here,
    most of these issues are outside the scope of this study.

spending power or through a continuation of the current trend of moving to more direct federal delivery of social programs. A recent study which recommends changes along these lines (without predicting the separation of Québec) is Norrie et al. (1991) which argues the necessity of this type of shift to complete a "social charter" implied by the *Constitution Act* of 1982.

To make this alternative concrete for the provision of GGS, we assume that primary responsibility for so-called "people" programs is transferred to the federal government. As discussed above, in Alberta the federal government is already dominant in housing, labour, and social security programs. Primary responsibility is transferred from municipal governments in the area of culture, and from the provincial government in the areas of education and health.

The second alternative is Canada with Québec. In this alternative Québec chooses to remain a full partner in the Canadian federation. Recognizing Québec's demands as articulated by the Bélanger-Campeau Commission or Allaire Commission reports, a substantial degree of decentralization would be required for this alternative to be feasible. We further assume that the degree of decentralization demanded by Québec would also be offered to the other provinces, and, at least in the case of Alberta, that the transfer of responsibilities would be accepted.

Although reasonably-specific proposals regarding the transfer of responsibilities are provided by the Allaire report, it is difficult to match directly their division of powers with the division of program areas discussed in this paper. However, a rough translation which preserves the spirit of the Allaire report is possible. Following Allaire, we assume that the federal government is left with primary responsibility for defense (i.e. protection), tariffs and customs (i.e., the foreign part of trade and industry) and regulation in a number of areas (e.g., transportation, weights and measures, fisheries, justice, etc.) where national coordination is desirable. However, substantial responsibilities would be transferred to provinces and municipalities in the areas of culture, health, housing, labour, and social security. Clearly, a significant realignment of taxing powers would be needed to support this transfer of responsibilities. Finally, the federal government would retain responsibility for interprovincial equalization.[13]

The third alternative is an independent Alberta. As with the first alternative, we assume that free trade and migration continues between Alberta and its former partners, and that free trade continues with the

---

13. Although this last point is taken from the Allaire Report, it could well be in keeping with spirit of decentralization to make provinces jointly responsible for equalization. See Dahlby and Wilson (1991) for such a scheme.

United States. This alternative implies a wholesale shift in responsibilities from federal to what were previously provincial and municipal governments, including some areas, such as defense, where the provinces have no previous experience.

An important variation of this alternative is to consider an independent Western Canada which would include the four western provinces, the Yukon, and the western half of the Northwest Territories. We assume the western Canadian provinces and territories would be replaced by a unitary state with only two orders of government (Western "national" and municipal) would operate. The same assumptions about trade and migration apply.

A final issue that must be addressed for either the first or third scenarios is how federal assets and liabilities would be divided. To limit the scope of the study, we have purposefully ignored questions of transition to any of these alternative futures, but it is necessary to make an assumption about the final division of federal assets and debt (regardless of how it is determined) under each alternative. As we have discussed elsewhere[14] this is an extremely difficult and complex issue. However, in the interests of simplicity, we assume here that fixed assets are left in place and that moveable assets and debt are divided on a simple per capita basis.

Evaluating the alternatives

Before evaluating the constitutional alternatives, it is useful to review the economic principles developed in Section 2. The first is that the level and type of GGS provided should be responsive to the wishes of the citizens. Oates' principle of decentralization indicates that, other things equal, this is best achieved by providing GGS at as local a level of government as possible. The second is efficiency. Whenever possible, economies of scale should be taken into account in determining which order of government should provide a given program. Other things equal, programs which are characterized by economies of scale should be provided by higher orders of government. Programs characterized by diseconomies of scale should be provided by lower orders of government.

Another aspect of efficiency relates to spillovers. Whenever possible, the effects of spillovers between jurisdictions should be accounted for, either by coordination or by assigning the responsibility to a higher, encompassing order of government. The final principle is accountability. Other things equal, citizens will demand the socially-efficient level of GGS when the costs

14. See Boothe and Harris (1991a,b) and Boothe et al. (1991).

are fully paid by those who benefit. Thus, spending and taxing powers should be arranged so that it is clear that the order of government which provides the program also levies the taxes (on those who benefit) to pay for it. To avoid confusion among citizens, the allocation function of government should be kept as separate as possible from the government's function as redistributor of income. For ranking the principles in cases of conflict, we adopt the European Community's rule which assigns all responsibilities to the lower order of government (in the interests of responsiveness and accountability) except in cases where significant cost savings through economies of scale exist or when significant detrimental spillovers cannot be corrected through ad hoc coordination.

Looking first at the more centralized alternative—Canada without Québec—we would argue that this option would result in a substantial decline in the responsiveness of government programs to the desires of citizens in different regions. To the extent that Albertans have different preferences than Ontarians regarding government programs, Albertans would receive the "wrong" mix of GGS, as their wishes would have to be balanced against those of much larger (50% of the population of ROC) Ontario. On the regulatory side, the National Energy Program provides a good case in point. Looking at social programs, if total Alberta spending in the three major areas (education, health, and social security) were moved to the national average, per capita spending on education and health would decline, while per capita spending on social security would rise. In addition, an important source of innovation in government programming— experimentation by provinces with alternative programs and delivery mechanisms—would be lost or greatly reduced.

A further drawback of this alternative from the Alberta perspective is on the macro stabilization front. Westerners have long complained that federal stabilization policy in Canada is generally tailored to economic conditions in central Canada. To the extent that national economic aggregates such as output, unemployment, and inflation are to be stabilized, this is dictated by the sheer size of central Canada relative to the other regions. If economic conditions differ across regions, small regions such as western Canada generally get the "wrong" macro policy. There is little reason to expect that national monetary and fiscal policy will be more responsive to economic conditions in Alberta in a more centralized ROC.[15]

15. The recent federal constitutional proposals make suggestions for changing the conduct of both monetary and fiscal policy in Canada. On the monetary side, despite the fact that the appointment of the Governor of the Bank of Canada would be ratified by the Senate, and Bank directors would be advised by regional "committees," the Bank's new sole focus on price stability ensures that monetary policy would be conditioned primarily by conditions in central Canada. On the fiscal side, the proposed "harmonization" seems likely to reduce the ability of provinces to respond to shocks peculiar to their own economies.

To the extent that there were economics of scale in providing GGS, a move to more centralized government could result in cost saving. Here we have little evidence, although Bird and Hartle (1972) have argued that most GGS are characterized by constant returns to scale, and thus there is little efficiency to be gained through consolidation. In any case, some savings might occur through the elimination of program duplication and conflict between the three orders of government. However, given the forces of regional politics, it is unlikely that there would be any rationalization of the system across regions. Every region would want to receive its "fair share" regardless of potential benefits of specialization. Some spillovers between provinces could be internalized, especially on the regulatory front, but this would have to be balanced with the loss of flexibility which would come from trying to design regulations to fit nine provinces to correct what might be a spillover between two neighbouring jurisdictions.

Perhaps the greatest cost to Albertans of a more centralized Canada would be a further loss in accountability. As we argued in the introduction, we believe the ongoing blurring of lines between allocative and distributive functions of government was one of the main causes of the rise in persistent deficits in the 1980s. Only the inevitable arithmetic of debt and deficits has forced governments to embrace restraint. Given the disparate sizes and economic circumstances of the remaining provinces, it is likely that the already-significant lack of accountability at the federal level would be exacerbated. There is no reason to expect that poorly-designed, inefficient redistributive programs such as unemployment insurance, regional economic development initiatives, and government procurement decisions, for example, the CF-18 contract—all of which serve to weaken the economic union—would not continue to flourish in a more centralized ROC. Given the higher-than-average income of Alberta, Albertans would be called upon to pay a disproportionate share of these inefficient programs.[16]

Turning to the second alternative—a decentralized Canada with Québec—moving more GGS to provincial and municipal governments could enhance responsiveness. To the extent that preferences differ significantly across provinces, this is likely to be an important benefit. On the stabilization side, we can conceive of a division of responsibilities along the lines suggested by Courchene (1990) where given different economic conditions across regions, provinces rather than the federal government, use fiscal policy to achieve stabilization goals. Good examples of provincial stabilization through fiscal policy are found in Alberta's Economic

16. The federal proposals to strengthen the economic union would exempt most of these programs under the heading of "regional development," or, failing that, "national interest."

Resurgence Plan of 1982, and the recent rise in Ontario's deficit to combat the severe recession in central Canada.

A move to a more decentralized Canada might result in the loss of some economies of scale in the provision of GGS. We note, however, that functions with clear economies of scale, such as defense and customs and excise, would be retained at the federal level. In addition, there is no reason that ad hoc coordination or even formal, binding agreements could not be arranged to provide some specialized services—for example, heart transplant facilities.

An important issue in a more decentralized Canada would be the effect of spillovers between provinces. To the extent that the federal government currently acts as coordinator and arbitrator—especially on the regulatory front—some efficiency in the provision of GGS may be lost. A special concern is the potential for provinces, through regulation, to erect barriers to the free flow of goods and people, thereby weakening the economic union. It should be remembered that although provinces are not blameless in this area, many of the important economic barriers in Canada are of federal origin. Some examples of federal programs which fragment the economic union are the regionally-differentiated unemployment insurance plan; regional development programs such as DREE, DRIE, Western Diversification, and Atlantic Opportunities; federally-sanctioned agricultural marketing boards, and so forth. While recent initiatives in the Maritime provinces to enhance the economic union are encouraging, it may be desirable in a more decentralized Canada to enshrine the economic union in the constitution under the protection of the courts.[17]

Our final criterion for evaluating this alternative is accountability. It seems likely that accountability will be improved as the provision of many GGS is moved closer to the citizens who pay for them and benefit from them. Of course, in many instances, the same logic that argues for moving GGS from federal to provincial orders of government, also points to moving some GGS from provincial to municipal governments.

The final alternative to be evaluated is an independent Alberta or independent Western Canada. To make the latter case concrete, we assume that Western Canada breaks down provincial and territorial boundaries and reconstitutes itself as a unitary state. In terms of responsiveness, an independent Alberta would likely be the most responsive of the three alternatives to the preferences of Albertans for GGS. To the extent that preferences for GGS differed substantially across the western provinces and territories, government responsiveness to individual jurisdictions' preferences will be reduced relative to the independent Alberta scenario.

---

17. See footnote 16.

While it is likely that a Western Canadian government would be more responsive to the demands of Albertans than a more centralized federal government, it may be less responsive than a more decentralized Canada. On the stabilization front, clearly an independent Alberta would be most responsive to economic conditions within the province. In the case of independent Western Canada, the four western provinces do have, from time to time, significant differences in macroeconomic conditions. However, these differences are generally less pronounced than the differences between Western Canada and Ontario or Québec. In addition, a larger jurisdiction such as a Western Canadian state might have more resources to deal with severe macroeconomic stabilization problems.

Turning to economies of scale and spillovers, an independent Alberta would probably lose significant economies of scale since programs such as manpower and labour policy (unemployment insurance, training, etc.) would probably be below a minimum efficient size. This would clearly be the case for functions such as defense, customs and tariffs and foreign relations. Here, a Western Canadian state would be preferable to an independent Alberta, although not necessarily preferable to a more decentralized Canada. A similar argument could be made regarding spillovers. An independent Alberta would find it necessary to invest substantial resources in negotiating and monitoring agreements on issues of joint concern with its neighbours, British Columbia, Saskatchewan, and the United States. Agreements would be required in areas in which spillovers are likely—transportation, tax harmonization, justice, the environment and a host of others. Again, these costs would likely be substantially reduced in a Western Canadian state, and perhaps costs would be somewhat higher than those in a more decentralized Canada.

The final issue relates to accountability in an independent Alberta or Western Canada. Maximum accountability would likely accompany an independent Alberta. In this relatively small jurisdiction, the alignment of benefits and costs would, of necessity, be much closer than currently is the case. Some loss of accountability is inherent in a Western Canadian state, especially if it had a unitary structure. This alternative would clearly be much more accountable than a more centralized Canada, but perhaps less so than the more decentralized alternative.

In summary, it is useful to compare all the alternatives using each criterion in turn. A set of numerical rankings is presented in Table 2.4. In terms of responsiveness, an independent Alberta would be most responsive to the demands of Albertans for GGS. This would be followed closely by a more decentralized Canada (with provincial responsibility for macroeconomic stabilization), and then by an independent Western Canada,

TABLE 2.4:
Ranking Alberta's Constitutional Alternatives

Principle	Alternative				
	Central-ized	Status Quo	Decentral-ized	Western Canada	Independent Alberta
Responsiveness	5	4	2	3	1
Efficiency					
Scale	4	3	1	2	5
Spillovers	2	3	4	1	5
Accountability	5	4	2	3	1

1 = best, 5 = worst

the current situation, and finally a more centralized Canada. Economies of scale (which can be increasing or decreasing) and spillovers would be dealt with most efficiently by a more decentralized Canada and a Western Canadian state respectively. The more centralized Canada might also be efficient in dealing with spillovers, although probably not always in the best interests of Albertans. The efficiency principle argues strongly against the alternative of an independent Alberta. Finally, an independent Alberta would be most accountable to Albertans. A more decentralized Canada and Western Canadian state would be more accountable than the current arrangement, and a more centralized Canada would be significantly less accountable.

Conclusions

Given the restricted focus of this paper, our conclusions can be brief. The Canadian federation is currently under a great strain from both internal and external factors. Canadians in all provinces have been called upon to consider what kind of federation they want for the future. Our goal has been to inform Albertans' discussion on the economic implications of various constitutional change in one specific area: the assignment of responsibilities for providing GGS. To this end, we adopted three guiding principles—responsiveness, efficiency and accountability.

We used the three principles to evaluate the assignment of responsibilities implied by three constitutional alternatives: a more centralized Canada without Québec, a more decentralized Canada, and an independent Alberta or independent Western Canada. In our view, the worst possible outcome of constitutional negotiations would be a move toward a more centralized Canada—with or without Québec. Albertans would likely experience a significant further decline in both responsiveness and accountability for the GGS they receive. Although it ranked best in responsiveness and accountability, in our view, an independent Alberta would be the next-worst alternative. An independent province would face a significant loss of efficiency in providing GGS due to its small size and spillovers with its close neighbours. Both of these alternatives are dominated by the status quo.

Our preferred alternative is a more decentralized Canada. We believe this alternative offers the potential to gain many of the efficiencies of being part of a larger country, while at the same time significantly improving on the current level of government responsiveness and accountability. Less desirable, but still preferred to the status quo, would be an independent Western Canada. This alternative (at least the unitary state variation we considered) would improve on the status quo in all respects, but only dominate a more decentralized Canada in minimizing coordination costs of spillovers.

Of course, a new assignment of program responsibilities is just one aspect of the economic implications of constitutional change, and indeed, economic implications are just one factor that must be considered as Albertans determine their constitutional position. Depending on the relative importance they assign to the three principles, others may reach different conclusions. However, we hope that this paper, together with the other papers presented in this conference will help to inform debate on these critical issues as Albertans look forward to their shared constitutional future.

The views expressed in this paper are my own and should not be attributed to any other individual or institution. I am grateful to my discussants Thomas Courchene and Stanley Winer, and to Robert Young for helpful comments. Barbara Johnston and Karrin Powys-Lybbe provided dedicated research assistance. This research was supported by a grant from the Western Centre for Economic Research.

References

Québec Liberal Party. *Constitutional Committee. (1991). A Québec free to choose: Report of the Constitutional Committee of the Québec Liberal Party* ("The Allaire Report"). Quebec City: Allaire, J. et al.

Bélanger, J. et al. (1991). *Report of the Commission on the Political and Constitutional of Québec.* Québec City: Québec National Assembly.

Bird, R. & Hartle, D. (1972). The design of governments. In R. Bird and J. Head (Eds.), *Modern Fiscal Issues: Essays in Honour of Carl S. Shoup.* Toronto: University of Toronto Press.

Boothe, P. & Harris, R. (forthcoming). The economics of constitutional change: Dividing the federal debt. *Canadian Public Policy.*

Boothe, P. & Harris, R. (1991). Alternative divisions of federal assets and liabilities. In R. Boadway, T. Courchene & D. Purvis (Eds.), *Economic Dimensions of Constitutional Change,* Vol. II (pp. 553-574). Kingston, ON: John Deutsch Institute.

Boothe, P., Johnston, B. & Powys-Lybbe, K. (forthcoming). Dismantling confederation: The divisive question of the national debt. In J. McCallum (Ed.), *The Canada Round Series.* Toronto: C.D. Howe Institute.

Breton, A. & Scott, A. (1978). *The economic constitutions of federal states.* Toronto: University of Toronto Press.

Canada. (1991). *Shaping Canada's future together: Proposals.* Ottawa: Minister of Supply and Services.

Courchene, T. (1986). Economic management and the division of powers. *Collected Research Studies of the Royal Commission on the Economic Union and Development Prospects for Canada*: Vol. 67. Toronto: University of Toronto Press.

Courchene, T. (1990). Rethinking the macro mix: The case for provincial stabilization policy. In R. York (Ed.), *Taking Aim: The Debate on Zero Inflation.* Toronto: C.D. Howe Institute.

Courchene, T. (1991). *The community of Canadas.* Paper presented to the Commission on the Political and Constitutional Future of Québec.

Dahlby, B. & Wilson, S. (1991). *Fiscal capacity, tax effort, and optimal equalization grants.* University of Alberta discussion paper.

Horry, I. & Walker, M. (1991). *Government spending facts.* Vancouver, BC: The Fraser Institute.

Mansell, R. & Schlenker, R. (1990). *An analysis of the regional distribution of federal fiscal balances: Updated data.* [University of Calgary discussion paper.]

Mintz, J. & Simeon, R. (1982). Conflict of taste and conflict of claim in federal countries. *Queen's University Institute of Intergovernmental Relations Discussion Paper No. 13*. Kingston, ON: Queen's University, Institute of Intergovernmental Relations.

Norrie, K., Osberg, L. & Boadway, R. (1991). The constitution and the social contract. In R. Boadway, T. Courchene & D. Purvis (Eds.), *Economic dimensions of constitutional change* (Vol. I; pp. 225-254). Kingston, ON: John Deutsch Institute.

Oates, W. (1972). *Fiscal federalism*. New York: Harcourt Brace Jovanovich.

Stevenson, G. (1986). The Division of Powers. In R. Simeon (Ed.), Division of powers and public policy. *Collected Research Studies of the Royal Commission on the Economic Union and Development Prospects for Canada* (Vol. 61). Toronto, ON: University of Toronto Press.

Whalley, J. & Trela, I. (1968). *Regional aspects of Confederation. Collected Research Studies of the Royal Commission on the Economic Union and Development Prospects for Canada* (Vol. 68). Toronto, ON: University of Toronto Press.

APPENDIX 2.1

Culture and Recreation
- recreation
- culture
- other

Education
- elementary and secondary education
- postsecondary education
- other

General Government Services
- executive & legislative
- administrative
- pension plans
- other

Health
- hospital care
- medical care
- preventive care
- other

Housing
- general assistance
- home buyer assistance

Labour
- labour and employment
- immigration
- other
- special retaining services

Natural resources
- fish and games
- forests
- mines
- water
- other natural resources
- environment

Oil and Gas

Commentaries

Thomas J. Courchene, Queen's University

Because Paul Boothe and I are colleagues at Queen's this year and because I had the opportunity to comment on earlier drafts of his paper, I shall use this occasion to elaborate more generally on the interaction between economics, the Constitution, and the options for Alberta.

In this context, the first point is that there is frequently not much correlation between the typical list of economic principles underlying the appropriate division of powers and what actually happens in federations. For example, most public finance economists would assign direct taxes to the national level and indirect taxes to the state/provincial level. Yet the Swiss do exactly the opposite and in addition have created what is generally termed a "tax jungle." And the last time I looked, the Swiss were doing exceedingly well on the economic front. This does not mean that an economic perspective is inappropriate. Far from it. Rather, it means that there are alternative arrangements that can be put in place to compensate for the supposed defects.

Second, I think that there would be general support for Boothe's point that the "lack of accountability" at the federal level can be a contributing factor to the runaway federal deficits. This is what I call "Maxim's maxim." If the financing of a meal at Maxim's were based not on what each person consumed but on an equal-per-capita basis, then I would make sure that my palate became at least as sophisticated as the average at the restaurant. In other words, under these sort of incentives, my ordering preferences would no longer coincide with my initial preference orderings. Despite this, we observe that federations, such as Germany and Australia, that are even more centralized than Canada and also have a generous social contract, do not run such deficits. What gives them accountability? (I know that it would be "politically correct" at this point and in this province to say a Triple-E Senate and for all I know it's part of the answer.) It is important to recognize that Maxim's maxim argues for overspending (large governments) not necessarily deficit financing. But even with respect to large government, the evidence is not clear. In particular, what appears to come out of the political science literature on Canada is that the federal structure has put a brake on social spending in comparison to the European welfare states.

Perhaps we should look a bit deeper in terms of what is driving deficits. By our very history (relative to the United States) we looked to government to play a far more important role. In addition, our rich resource endowment and, until recently, the protective cover of our National Policy provided an "inefficiency corridor" that allowed us to believe and act as if we were "beyond economics" as it were. With the collapse of resource prices on the one hand and the erosion of the protection of the National Policy (via global restructuring in the wake of the 1981-83 recession and more directly with the FTA) on the other, Canadians suddenly found themselves with a continuing appetite for Scandinavian-type social policies but increasingly constrained to adopt North American (United States) tax rates. And now Ontario's Premier Bob Rae is lobbying strenuously for a "social charter," presumably because the underlying economics have become so far out of sync that he fears that we are heading toward American social policy at Scandinavian tax rates. However, the bridge between the desire for European social policy attitudes on the one hand and the necessity of United States tax rates for personal and corporate income on the other is, of course, the GST. This is a tax that allows for greater internal taxation without affecting international competitiveness (except cross-border shopping, because it is not collected). If it is large deficits one is worried about, fear no more because the GST is a veritable money machine. However, if it is large government that worries you, then fear!

Another principle raised by Boothe, and one that is almost universally adhered to by economists, is that the spending jurisdiction ought to also be the one responsible for raising the revenue. While this may be good in theory, it is progressively more difficult to implement in practice. Specifically, with globalization some tax bases are becoming increasingly more mobile. Phrased differently, under increasing globalization, the optimal taxing jurisdiction is becoming larger whereas this is not the case (or at least less the case) with respect to the optimal spending jurisdiction. Thus, one can speak meaningfully about the potential for an EC-wide corporate tax or an Ecotax. What this implies is that the transfers back to the states or provinces must be made as consistent as possible with the tax/spending coincidence principle. In other words, the real problem here is not so much that the federal government collects more in terms of revenues than its expenditure responsibilities would warrant. Rather, the villain is the nature of the incentives embodied in the federal-provincial transfer mechanism (e.g. 50 cent dollars).

But even here one can find that evidence is confounding. I remember way back writing about the vicious circle of transfer dependency for Québec: Québec had the highest minimum wage on the continent, which then resulted in high unemployment rates, increased UI, and equalization, and then the province argued (successfully) for protection for its labour-intensive sectors like textiles. Québec was not bearing the full economic cost of its policies; the rest of us were. Yet, without a change in the underlying nature of these incentives, much (though not all) of this has been shifted around completely in the decade of the 1980s and Québec's entrepreneurial revolution.

Finally, and relatedly, the operations of the interregional transfer system inevitably and intentionally distort the tax price for government goods of services in the equalization receiving provinces. But so does Section 125 of the Constitution (which essentially states that the Crown cannot tax the Crown) under which energy royalties accruing to Alberta cannot be subject to federal tax nor are they included in the incomes of Albertans for tax purposes (as they ought to be if one desired symmetry of treatment between the private and public sector). To be sure, this is not just an Alberta issue—it applies to the provincial hydros and, in reverse, to the Bank of Canada; i.e. without Section 125, the provinces should have their tax share of Bank of Canada seigniorage. (As an aside, who ought to get the seigniorage in the EC, if and when they opt for a EuroFed, will become a very controversial issue). Phrased differently, Section 125 is an incentive for government ownership rather than private ownership. Putting property rights in the Charter may well result in an intriguing court challenge here. In any event, part of equalization (but not as much as recent empirical information suggests) can be viewed as efficiency enhancing to the extent that it mutes any migration triggered by the operation of Section 125. However, both are now entrenched in the constitution.

Somewhat relevant in this context are Boothe's tables adopted from Horry and Walker (1991). He uses the data to make a case for varying degrees of centralization or decentralization. I do not think these data say anything about centralization or decentralization—they are driven largely by the operations of the federal-provincial transfer system. They *do* say something about *dependence*. But as far as I can see, Nova Scotia (whose residents receive more total government spending dollars than Albertans—Horry and Walker, Table 2.b) has the same powers with respect to medicare or postsecondary education or welfare as Albertans. A propos to this, my oldest grandson has a book of riddles, one of which is the following: why do white sheep eat more than black sheep? To spare you the embarrassment that I went through, the answer is "because there are *more* white sheep"! Likewise, Alberta's figures in Horry and Walker suggest greater "decentralization" in Alberta only because there are more rich people, proportionally, in Alberta than in Nova Scotia. What this means is that an independent Alberta is more viable than an independent Nova Scotia, but it seems to me that *within* Canada it suggests little about centralization or decentralization.

To end this first section, then, my point is that economists' hallowed principles may not get one too far in pursuing which constitutional arrangement is, in practice, preferable. The remainder of the paper focuses on alternative constitutional options for Alberta from a quite different perspective.

In his oral presentation Boothe has already alluded to the fact (quoting Daniel Bell) that under globalization the nation state is finding itself too small for the big problems in life and too large for the small problems in life. In my own research, I have argued globalization is transferring some of the traditional functions upward to supranational bodies. At the other end of the spectrum, globalization has some decentralizing elements. Power is being transferred downward to citizens and to international cities. (See Courchene 1991.) The latter is intriguing because as our international cities grow in importance and influence the fact remains that not only are they constitutionless but (to be provocative) your international city is not even in your province. This influence of globalization is the first point.

The second point is that the optimal currency area (in the transactions/trade sense) is increasingly north-south rather than east or west. What this means is that what binds us east-west is less and less an economic railway and more and more a social policy and values railway.

These two observations lead me to make the following assertion. In terms of social policy principles, Albertans' values and preferences *do not differ* in major ways from those of other Canadians. However, *on the economic front, Alberta is distinct*. In other words, instead of Boothe's geographical approach to preferences, namely that Edmontonians are more like each other than they are like Calgarians, and that Edmontonians are more like Calgarians than like Winnipegers, and so forth, I cut through those preferences from a different perspective. Specifically, in terms of adhering to underlying values or principles such as sharing, medicare, social security, Albertans really do not differ from other Canadians including Québecers. (Note that the "distinct society" issue is, at base, an economic issue—namely the ability of Québecers to earn a North American living standard operating in French—even though most of the rest of Canada is a distinct society in largely cultural terms). I should emphasize that I am talking about underlying principles here not, for example, how UI is implemented. When one adds to this conception of the social contract the fact that revealed mobility preferences incorporate substantial west-center interchange (Ontario-born Boothe is now in Alberta while I left Saskatchewan for Ontario), it seems to me that in terms of the options, an independent Western Canada, let alone an independent Alberta, is simply too undiversified to be optimal in terms of ensuring that the scope of mobility for human capital provides adequate access to the sorts of occupational opportunities needed in a global environment. One could argue that an independent Western Canada would eventually develop a greater range of activities, but I think that Rick Harris' reference to the likely value of "green cards" (see Harris' comments later in the volume) carries the day here. In this context, whether the optimal economic unit encompasses Québec as well as Ontario will depend on whether or not the sociocultural preferences of Albertans can be maintained in a Canada without Québec. I suspect that they cannot, because we would likely fragment and, as a result, likely be forced to adopt the American social contract.

However, in terms of the specificity of the Alberta economy, it seems to me that the optimal economic or currency area is increasingly north-south. Since one cannot alter exchange rates on an east-west basis, the two leading options here are a Canada-US currency union or a fixed exchange rate with the United States. Moreover, Alberta's unique economic situation also requires it to have substantial control over its own economic levers. In this sense a decentralized federation on the economic front should be the first best option. (Note that while I argued that social policy preferences were quite uniform across Canada, Alberta will need some flexibility in terms of the manner in which social policy is integrated with economic policy.) The other principal alternative, here, namely a more-centralized Canada, where Alberta has more powers in the decision making at the center, does not appear as inviting. Hence, I have never thought much of a Triple-E Senate as a strategy to improve the economic influence of Alberta at the centre. (This does not mean that a Triple-E Senate cannot be argued on other grounds.) However, if this is the way we are going, at least Alberta should insist that its senators are elected at the time of provincial elections, not federal ones, so that they are more obviously linked to desires and needs of the provinces (rather than to the desires and needs of some "federal" party).

Thus, the challenge is how to design a set of powers and institutions that will allow Alberta (and more generally all of Canada) to integrate east-west in terms of values and north-south in terms of economics (or for Alberta and British Columbia, perhaps a Pacific Rim orientation economically).

How do the new proposals square with this? Alternatively, how might Alberta position itself with respect to the proposals? This constitutes the final part of my comments.

Let me begin with the proposals relating to the Bank of Canada. These are of two sorts—structure and mandate. In terms of the latter, the proposal is to alter the *Bank of Canada Act* to make price stability the sole mandate of the Bank. Apart from the fact that changing the Bank of Canada Act has nothing to do with the Constitution, price stability as the sole mandate is inappropriate. Canada must have the flexibility to do what the 12 European countries are in the process of doing, namely abandoning any notion of an independent national monetary policy and tying their currencies to the European Currency Unit (ECU). Transferred to Canada, this means pegging to the United States dollar. Hopefully, the United States would opt for price stability. The essential point is that in a world of super currencies, a price stability mandate for Canada irrespective of what the Federal Reserve is doing is a recipe for disaster.

In terms of structure, the proposals include

a) ratification of the Governor by the Senate,

b) a more powerful and regionally-based Board of Directors and

c) some regional economic intelligence ability to better inform the regional governors.

This would appear to imply that this will break the existing Parliamentary relationship between the Bank and the Government along, for example, United States Federal Reserve lines. However, that this is what Ottawa has in mind is far from clear from the document. Alberta *should* argue for breaking this link, and should argue for including some powerful regional governors as part of the Board of Directors. However, if the point is to depoliticize the Bank, then the provinces should not have direct input to the directors' appointments. Like the Governor, they should be ratified by the Senate, perhaps with the requirement of a double majority—overall and regional. The advantage of this greater independence is that the Bank will now have a much freer hand in discussing *in public* the fiscal positions of both federal and provincial governments, and vice versa. Presumably, the method of removing a Governor should also be the responsibility of the Senate. This would make a strong and relatively independent central bank. However, the decision to form a currency union with the United States and Mexico as part of an extended NAFTA, just to take an example, should rest with the government, not the Bank. Similarly for any decision to fix the exchange rate to the American dollar. As noted, however, the structure as outlined above is probably not what Ottawa has in mind.

Turning now to the economic union proposals, it is important to distinguish between what has come to be called "negative integration" (i.e. what you cannot do) and "positive integration" (what should be done to enhance the internal market). Section 121(1) and (2) relate to the former.[18] It seems to me that all Canadians should support this. The only problem that I have with 121(1) is that it should be broadened to go beyond "barriers" and "restrictions" and encompass any incentives in policies that distort mobility on a regional basis.

---

18.   Section 121 of the new proposals reads:

121   (1)   Canada is an economic union within which persons, goods, services and capital may move freely without barriers or restrictions based on provincial or territorial boundaries.

(2)   Neither the Parliament or Government of Canada nor the legislatures or governments of the provinces shall by law or practice contravene the principle expressed in subsection (1).

(3)   Subsection (2) does not render invalid

(a)   a law of the Parliament of Canada enacted to further the principles of equalization or regional development;

(b)   a law of a provincial legislature enacted in relation to the reduction of economic disparities between regions wholly within a province that does not create barriers or restrictions that are more onerous in relation to persons, goods, services or capital from outside the province than it does in relation to persons, goods, services or capital from a region within the province; or

(c)   a law of the Parliament of Canada or of the legislature of a province that has been declared by Parliament to be in the national interest.

(4)   A declaration referred to in paragraph (3)(c) shall have no effect unless it is approved by the governments of at least two-thirds of the provinces that have, in the aggregate, according to the then latest general census, at least 50 percent of the population of all the provinces.

(5)   This section shall come into force on July 1, 1995.

Section 91A reads:

91A.

(1)   Without altering any other authority of the Parliament of Canada to make laws, the Parliament of Canada may exclusively make laws in relation to any matter that it declares to be for the efficient functioning of the economic union.

(2)   An Act of the Parliament of Canada made under this section shall have no effect unless it is approved by the governments of at least two thirds of the provinces that have, in the aggregate, according to the then latest general census, at least 50 percent of the population of all the provinces.

(3)   The legislative assembly of any province that is not among the provinces that have approved an Act of the Parliament of Canada under the subsection (2) may expressly declare by resolution supported by 60 percent of its member that the Act of Parliament does not apply in the province.

(4)   A declaration made under subsection (3) shall cease to have effect three years after it is made or on such earlier date as may be specified in the declaration.

Section 121(3) unwinds much of the bite of the first two sections since it exempts regional development initiatives. Available evidence on the economic costs of barriers to the economic union tends to suggest

a) that the federal barriers are probably the more costly and

b) that most of what Ottawa does to distort prices on a geographical basis can come under the rubric of regional policy.

Section 121(3)(c), even though it must be run through the 7/50 requirement in 121(4) allows Ottawa to declare its barriers to be in the "national interest."

Section 91(A) is really about "positive integration"—initiatives that would enhance the economic union. Again, however, it is couched in terms of a federal "declaratory" power, this time the "efficient functioning of the economic union." At the symbolic level, this is clearly a federal power grab. And it is not difficult to imagine circumstances where seven provinces with 50% of the population could be brought into line. Moreover, declaratory powers are in the nature of "trumps"—they can take out a provincial ace, as it were. This is not the European solution, it should be noted, because the "center" in Europe has no "veto," nor does it spend much more than 1% of GNP, again unlike Ottawa.

Nonetheless, I believe that there ought to be some mechanism for moving on the positive integration side of the economic union, e.g. to enhance pension portability, to make transfer of professional and technical certificates more "mobile" across provinces. Alberta should support positive integration, but be extremely wary of the process recommended in the federal proposals. To my mind, it smacks of the 1980-82 mentality with respect to the economic union, namely most things that provinces do fragment the economic union but, almost by definition, Ottawa acts in the national interest. One would wish that this latter point were true!

More generally, I defy anyone to write down a set of economic union principles that would be agreed upon in terms of applying to both the manufacturing and resource sectors alike. More to the point, some of Alberta's corporate tax incentives with respect to the resource sector will almost certainly run afoul of the principles of an economic union. But what if the norms in other energy producing areas (e.g., in the United States) are similar to what Alberta is doing? In my view, what constitutes an appropriate internal economic union within Canada *should not be independent of the fact that the optimal currency area is increasingly north-south and less and less east-west.* Thus, my recommendation for Alberta is that it attempts to pursue alternative approaches (to those in the federal proposals) to enhancing the positive integration aspects of the economic union—ones that enhance the mobility needs of Albertans but at the same time recognize the needs of Alberta on the economic front. At a minimum, this should imply that Ottawa cannot exempt itself from economic union dictates nor should the federal government be the only one to be able to advance economic union proposals. This is not in any way an argument against enhancing the economic union via both negative and positive integration, only that there are better ways to implement this and ways that will contribute more to ensuring that we will in fact end up with an effective economic union.

Despite having departed so substantially from Paul Boothe's paper (and my assigned task), it is nonetheless the case that I do support his ranking of constitutional options for Alberta.

References
Courchene, Thomas J. (forthcoming). Global competitiveness and the Canadian federation. In Marcel Côté (Ed.), *Rearrangements: The Courchene papers*. Toronto: Mosaic Press.

Horry, Isabel & Walker, Michael A. (1991). *Government spending facts*. Vancouver: The Fraser Institute.

Stanley L. Winer, Carleton University

Introduction
In this paper Paul Boothe tackles the difficult problem of evaluating the economic consequences of alternative constitutional arrangements ranging from a fully sovereign Alberta to a highly centralized state without Québec. Professor Boothe ranks these alternatives by applying several criteria which, in his view, allow him to evaluate the pattern of public expenditure that could be expected to emerge in each.

This is an important and challenging project, one that has defied consensus despite decades of constitutional theorizing in Canada. Its importance stems, quite simply, from the tremendous welfare we derive from publicly provided goods and services when the public sector functions well. It is challenging because of profound disagreements about what normative principles ought to be relied upon and about how these principles ought to be applied.

I am not going to question the scenarios chosen for comparison. Even consideration of an independent Alberta makes good sense since the object of the paper is to outline boldly the issues at stake. Nor will I object to the reliance on economic efficiency as the primary basis for normative judgement. I will question the context within which the analysis is conducted, and in the end I will suggest that before we could accept the rankings of alternatives he proposes, Professor Boothe needs to deal at length with two critical issues, one that he acknowledges but neatly assumes away, and one that he has not considered.

The Normative Criteria and the Critical Role of Transactions Costs

Let me quickly review the three criteria that are used to evaluate the pattern of public services in each of the constitutional scenarios chosen for consideration. This will reveal why much greater decentralization is the inevitable outcome of the application of these principles. Then I will go on to explain why we must withhold judgement about the conclusion that radical decentralization is desirable.

The first principle relied upon is referred to in the paper as *responsiveness* and is based on what is known as the *decentralization theorem*. This theorem simply points out that when preferences for public services vary across regions, provinces, or municipalities, the provision by any government of a uniform level or mix of services will almost certainly be less desirable than a situation in which the level or mix of services is matched carefully to the distinct character of demands in each locality.

The second criteria is labelled *efficiency*. Of course the decentralization theorem is also about the relative efficiency of discriminating versus uniform provision of public services. A better term for what is actually referred to is *scale and spillovers*. This principle says that when the cost of public goods falls with the quantity produced, then they ought to be provided in large quantities, presumably by a higher level of government, in order to keep the per unit cost as low as possible. Centralization to deal with interjurisdictional externalities is also desirable for the usual reason.

The third principle is accountability. While this treacherous word has many meanings, it is used here to refer to the idea that the level of government supplying a service ought to be the authority responsible for raising the necessary taxes. This criteria can also be seen as stemming from a concern for efficiency in the allocation of resources. Unless those taxpayers benefitting from a government service are those who also pay for it, there will be a tendency to try and shift the cost to other jurisdictions. And if this does happen, the tax-price of the service would be reduced below the true cost and too much would then be demanded relative to the quantity that maximizes the well-being of citizens in the country as a whole.

In the original conference paper there is also a forth criterion, subsidiarity, which plays a less important role in the analysis than the other three principles. Subsidiarity is borrowed from the European Community and states that when the application of the three primary criteria does not lead to an unambiguous decision, the public service in question should be assigned to the lower level of government. Subsidiarity doesn't add much to the argument in the paper and I am happy to see that it does not appear in the revised version of the paper. If our concern is exclusively with efficiency, subsidiarity adds nothing more than the decentralization theorem and is therefore redundant in the discussion. And if the maintenance of political sovereignty or some other objective is behind this criterion, that objective should be stated directly so we may discuss it properly. One may note here that an analysis of political sovereignty in a federal system would have an entirely different character than that of the present paper; for example, a consideration of breaking Ontario into several smaller provinces would not be out of place in such a discussion.

Now since Professor Boothe concludes that there are not many public services that are subject to strong economies of scale, an assessment I share, it is clear that application of the principles of responsiveness and accountability indicates decentralization of the public sector is a most desirable course of action.[19] This is so even without recourse to the principle of subsidiarity. However, and here I want to introduce one of the two issues that I think have to be given much greater attention, in the absence of any consideration of the nature of the real costs involved in organizing the public sector (as distinct from the costs of producing public services), the result of applying the criterion of efficiency in its various forms is in fact indeterminate.

The first person to see this clearly was the late Jack Weldon (1966), although an earlier paper by Vincent Ostrom, Charles Tiebout, and Robert Warren (1961) came close. Most recently Albert Breton and Anthony Scott (1978) have extensively explored the problem. Breton and Scott argue correctly that, under the extreme assumption of zero organizational costs, there can be a different political jurisdiction for each public service in each locality, several jurisdictions with costless coordination to deal with interjurisdictional spillovers, one central jurisdiction that provides a limitless menu of services finely calibrated to local tastes, or even no government at all (since the cost of enforcing good behaviour by a dictator is zero). Only after the nature of organizational costs have been specified can a meaningful solution to the assignment problem be well defined.

While it is not easy to see what the outcome of such an analysis would be because it is so very hard to measure organization or transactions costs, it is

---

19. There is no reason to stop at independence for Alberta. Why not establish city-states?

in my view unlikely to be one in which responsibilities are neatly divided up between different levels of government as is suggested in the paper. Paul Boothe like many others is motivated by a desire to reduce "overlap, confusion, and conflict" (in his words) between the programs of different levels of government that now characterize the Canadian fiscal system. It must be pointed out, however, that in the real world in which enforcing proper behaviour by government is costly, this state of affairs—more appropriately referred to as *competitive federalism* rather than overlap and confusion—is a valuable institution for ensuring that citizens get what they want. Parliamentary democracy and the Charter of Rights also help in this respect. But Parliament is not a perfect institution either in Ottawa or Edmonton, and recourse to the Charter is a prohibitively expensive course of action in most circumstances. On the other hand, managing competitive federalism requires us to define carefully concurrency of expenditure responsibilities and mechanisms for resolving conflicts between governments. We have been at this task for many decades though, with good success judging by the generally high quality of our public services. I see no reason to throw away our accumulated efforts in this respect by granting tidy monopolies to the various orders of government.[20]

The Assignment of Responsibilities and the Fundamental Problem of Collective Choice

The second issue that must be given much more attention has in fact been acknowledged in the paper. This is the problem of how we decide what should be supplied by government when there are substantial differences among people concerning what they want. This is a fundamental issue in the design of constitutions that simply cannot be avoided. Professor Boothe acknowledges this nasty problem and then does away with it in a clever way.

A key assumption underlying the analysis, to put it more crudely than in Boothe's paper, is that people within a province are essentially alike. Substantial differences in tastes are assumed to exist only between people in different provinces.[21] If this were true, it would surely be the case that provision of services by the federal government on the basis of a political

---

20. Besides the costs of enforcing the behaviour of elected officials, other questions such as the nature of scale economies in the organization of government bureaucracy, the costs of coordinating activities of different levels will also have to be considered. All of this will have implications for the optimal assignment of responsibilities.

21. The actual assumption is more general than this: "We will assume that individuals are more alike in their preferences regarding GGS the closer they live to one another." But this less elegant statement will suffice here.

process that trades off the interests of citizens in different regions would fully please few, and would in many cases be inferior to decentralized provision. But the fact is that there are big differences in tastes within provinces, too. Abortion, minority rights, and protection of the environment are just some of the areas in which opinion is substantially divided regardless of political jurisdiction.

If you were handicapped, would you want to assign exclusive responsibility for all public services to a lower level jurisdiction, or to the federal level where people such as you from all over the country could join in cooperative action? If you were a member of a visible minority, would you want to leave your access to government services to the local majority, or to the political jurisdiction where minorities of all types from all provinces have a mutual interest in insuring equality of treatment? This is an old question, concern for which goes back to the *Federalist Papers* and beyond (1787-88).[22] Consideration of this problem will clearly have implications for the assignment of responsibilities that have not yet been dealt with in the paper. We need people with Professor Boothe's skills to grapple with this issue.

It might be argued that the clash of opinion I have highlighted can be addressed through the Charter of Rights and other aspects of the Constitution, leaving the optimal division of powers to be decided on the basis of efficiency considerations. To conclude my remarks, I want to indicate why such a solution to the problem of reconciling important differences of opinion within a province may have longer term implications for the division of powers that run counter to the radical decentralization suggested in the paper.

The more the Constitution is relied upon to settle conflicts between competing demands or interests, the more it prevents governments from delivering services well tuned to the precise pattern of interests in the province. This will be so to a greater extent at the provincial level than for the federal government. In the first place, discrimination (by which I mean the ability to provide public policies that cater to specific, narrowly defined interests) over the whole country is harder to detect or prove. In the second place, the courts may feel that discrimination over the entire country is more acceptable than overt discrimination within one province. The most recent proposals of the federal government to use the Constitution to reduce interprovincial trade barriers (which benefit small groups in a province at general expense of the citizens in that province as well as elsewhere) may be a good example of what I have in mind here. My guess is that, while the power of all governments to fragment the Canadian customs union will be

---

22. See especially number 10 (Madison) of the problem of "faction."

restricted if the proposals are adopted, the federal government will still be able to conduct what might be called "regional development policy," and will extended the domain of this policy to all provinces by suitable definition of when a region is in "special economic circumstances."

If the Constitution does tilt the distribution of spending powers towards the federal government, satisfaction with the available provincial menu of policies is likely to decline gradually over time relative to the degree of satisfaction with the menu provided by the federal government. To escape the greater constraint at the provincial level on the ability to deliver precisely what they want, people will increase their demands on the federal sector, and responsibility for the corresponding services or policies will shift towards the higher level of government. [23]

In other words, I am suggesting that the Charter of Rights and other constitutional restrictions on government will slowly but inexorably lead to greater centralization of expenditure responsibilities in Ottawa. In the same way I think the Bill of Rights in the United States was one of the important causes of the watering down of federalism there, even though residual rights were always vested in the states.

I would like to see how Professor Boothe ranks alternative constitutional arrangements in a context that includes the additional and broader issues I have raised.

References

Breton, Albert & Scott, Anthony. (1978). *The Economic constitution of federal states*. Toronto: University of Toronto Press.

The Federalist Papers [1871-88]. (1961). New York: New American Library, Mentor Books.

Ostrom, Vincent, Tiebout, Charles & Warren, Robert. (1961, December). The organization of government in metropolitan areas. *American Political Science Review, LV*.

Weldon, Jack. (1966, May). Public goods and federalism. *Canadian Journal of Economics and Political Science, XXXII*, 2.

Winer, Stanley L. (1991). *Taxation and federalism in a changing world*. A paper prepared for the Canadian Tax Foundation conference Taxation to 2000 and Beyond. Toronto.

---

23. The same argument applies in the context of the distribution of the power to tax. See Winer (1991).

3 Redistribution Under Alternative Constitutional Arrangements for Canada

by Bradford Reid and Tracy Snoddon

Introduction

In this study we examine the implications of alternative constitutional scenarios for the conduct of redistributive policy currently undertaken by the federal government in Canada. Since virtually every government spending, revenue-generating, and regulatory activity leads to a redistribution of resources among economic agents, we have found it necessary to limit the focus of our study. We exclude programs for which redistribution is a relatively minor component as well as programs providing direct and indirect transfers to businesses and agriculture. We concentrate instead on the major federal government programs involving direct transfers to individuals and provincial governments that are either explicitly designed or are generally perceived to transfer resources from higher income to lower income agents. Seven major federal programs meet these criteria: equalization, the Established Program Financing grants (EPF), the Canada Assistance Plan (CAP), the Family Allowances and Old Age Security (OAS) programs, the Canada Pension Plan (CPP), and Unemployment Insurance (UI). The first three programs involve federal transfers to provincial governments while the latter four provide transfers directly to individuals.

We focus our analysis on assessing the ability of different orders of government to undertake and finance these major redistributive programs in their current form under different constitutional arrangements. We do not attempt to address the issue of desirability of such programs nor do we address the question of "optimal" redistributive policy. We simply use the current system of federal transfers to provinces and individuals in Canada (i.e., the status quo) as a benchmark for comparisons among the alternative scenarios.

Methodology

Each constitutional scenario is defined by the associated division of taxing powers and expenditure responsibilities between provincial governments and the federal government. Particular attention is given to the reassignment of redistribution expenditure responsibilities that would or may occur under different constitutional arrangements. Some intrusion into the area of taxation is required, however, to estimate the redistribution of resources attributable to these major transfer programs.

Several critical assumptions are common to all three constitutional scenarios considered as well as to our discussion of the status quo. We adopt a "partial equilibrium" analysis to examine each program individually. Using this approach, we make two fundamental assumptions. First, all programs are assumed to remain the same in principle and structure provided they are not eliminated under a particular constitutional arrangement. Second, we assume that the distribution of population and economic activity among the provinces and regions of Canada remains the same across the alternative constitutional scenarios.

We also make an important assumption relating to the allocation of program costs across provinces. While data on federal program expenditures by provinces are readily available, it is more difficult to determine a province's contribution to the financing of these federal programs since most are funded out of federal general or consolidated revenues, a pool of all revenues from provinces and tax sources. To circumvent this problem, we assume that program costs are distributed across provinces in accordance with the distribution of federal revenues across provinces. Two exceptions to this should, however, be noted. Unemployment insurance has, until recently, been funded from both private contributions and federal revenues. To reflect this, costing of the program includes both components. When UI contributions exceed total direct contributions, the necessary provincial cost shares of the excess are determined according to the provincial distribution of federal revenues. Since CPP contributions are not considered part of general revenues and are maintained as a separate account, costing of this program includes only these direct contributions and the investment income from the CPP Investment Account. The distribution of costs across provinces in this case is simply the provincial distribution of CPP revenues. The distribution of federal revenues used in the costing of all other programs includes all federal revenues except CPP and UI contributions.

Finally, our analysis imposes the restriction that total program costs are assumed to equal total program expenditures. This assumption essentially imposes a "balanced budget" restriction on the federal government so that revenues are large enough to finance expenditures in a given time period without borrowing. To assume otherwise ignores the substantial amount of deficit financing that has been and is being undertaken by the federal government and the implications of this for future taxes. We assume the distribution of federal revenues across provinces is unchanged by this "grossing up" of total revenues to their balanced budget level. Accordingly, a province's contribution to the cost of a federal transfer program is calculated as the proportion of actual federal revenues generated from that province multiplied by total program expenditures. This cost share is then compared to the program benefits received by a province, as measured by program expenditures in that province, to determine if the province is a net recipient of resources under a given program. These measures of redistribution are estimated by region for each of the seven programs considered for the years 1986 and 1988.

Using data from these two years, we retrospectively examine the implications of the alternative constitutional arrangements for redistribution had these arrangements been in place in 1986 and 1988.[24] While this approach neglects many other factors that would impact on redistribution in each case, it does avoid the hazards of estimating revenues, expenditures, prices, migration and so on for the future and of having to determine how far into the future to look.

Alternative #1: A more centralized Canada without Québec

The first constitutional arrangement assumes a more centralized Canada without Québec. Greater centralization is defined here as increased federal powers in taxation, redistribution and spending as well as uniformity in the provision of federally provided goods and services. The federal government maintains its current powers and responsibilities and assumes the additional

---

24 It is important to recognize the implications of our assumption of balanced budget funding on our conclusions regarding redistribution programs under different constitutional scenarios. One issue to be examined is the question of whether these programs, as operated in 1986 or 1988, would have been more or less costly to conduct had one of the alternative constitutional arrangements been in place at that time. However, any conclusion about costs/taxes rising or falling is a prediction relative to what taxes should have been in 1986 or 1988 to balance the federal budget, not relative to what taxes actually were in 1986 or 1988.

responsibilities of health, welfare, and postsecondary education. In such a world, programs such as EPF and CAP are no longer necessary as the federal government has the authority and responsibility to enter these fields directly. Equalization transfers to provinces could be continued with some restructuring of the program rules to accommodate the removal of Québec from the formula and adjustment of payment schedules to reflect reduced provincial expenditure requirements.

In this scenario, UI, CPP and OAS, in principle, would remain as they are in the status quo. The Family Allowances program is assumed to continue unchanged with the exception that all provinces now face the same benefit schedule. In the status quo, Alberta and Québec have requested rates different from the flat rate payment available in other provinces. In a more centralized Canada, uniform provision of public goods and services eliminates this option of differential rates.

Alternative #2: A more decentralized Canada with Québec

In this scenario, we consider a more decentralized (relative to the status quo) Canada that includes Québec. Provincial governments assume most of the status quo responsibilities and powers of the federal government except in the areas of defence, territorial security, equalization, and management of the Canadian debt. Foreign policy becomes a shared provincial-federal responsibility.

The four federal programs providing transfers to persons—CPP, UI, OAS, and Family Allowances—are now undertaken by the provincial authorities. Transfers under CAP and EPF are eliminated but the program expenditures financed by these transfers are assumed to be maintained in each province at their status quo levels. Federal government revenues collected in each province to finance these programs become the property of that provincial government. We assume the federal authority retains taxing abilities sufficient to cover its obligations, especially with respect to equalization.

Alternative #3: An Independent Alberta or Western Region

An independent Alberta or Western Region is the third constitutional arrangement examined. The assumptions are the same as in the previous scenario, a more decentralized Canada, but without the equalization program. In addition, the remaining federal functions are now the responsibility of the independent governments.

Transfers to Provinces: The Status Quo

The three major redistributive programs that provide transfers to provinces currently in place are equalization and transfers under EPF and CAP.

Equalization

The equalization program is designed to transfer revenues to the provincial governments from the federal government to enable provinces to meet their expenditure responsibilities and to redistribute resources from well-endowed to poorly endowed regions. Historically, the existence of such a program has been justified on the grounds that an unequal distribution of tax bases across provinces is inequitable since all provinces face similar expenditure responsibilities.

Equalization entitlements are unconditional transfers based on an explicitly legislated formula set out in the Federal-Provincial Fiscal Arrangements and Established Program Financing Act, 1977 and its amendments. This formula is periodically reviewed every five years, with a March 1992 expiry date for the current governing formula. These unconditional transfers are not open-ended as a result of two constraints placed on entitlements. Since 1982-83, growth in total equalization payments has been constrained by the rate of growth in GNP. If this constraint is binding, each recipient's entitlement is reduced on a equal per capita basis until the overall growth in payments does not exceed the rate of growth in GNP. There is also a constraint on the extent to which any province's equalization payment can be decreased in a given year. The size of the allowable reduction is dependent on the province's revenue-raising capacity relative to the national average.

To calculate a province's entitlement to equalization under the formula, its revenue-raising capacity is first determined using the Representative Tax System (RTS). The RTS consists of 33 sources of tax revenue available in principle to the provinces. When the Representative National Average Standard formula (RNAS) was introduced in 1967, there were 16 tax sources classified for purposes of equalization. Much reclassification plus the inclusion of new revenue sources have increased the number of sources over the years to the current figure of 33. The introduction of property taxes levied for school purposes in 1973-74 and municipal revenues from the sale of goods and services in 1982 under the Representative Five Province Standard formula (RFPS) as new revenue sources were two of the most important additions. The treatment of resource revenues for the purpose of equalization has changed significantly over the years and has been the subject of much controversy. Under the RFPS, resource revenues are equalized in full. However, from 1973-74 to the introduction of the RFPS in 1982, resource revenues were divided into two categories, basic and additional, and only revenues under the former category were fully equalized.

A province's potential revenues are estimated as the revenues that could be generated if the national average tax rate for a given tax source had been applied to the province's tax base for that source. Differences in revenues generated in each province for a particular tax source reflect differences in tax bases and not differences in need or tax effort, as measured by tax rates and the elasticity of the tax base. Revenues from each of the 33 tax sources are added together to obtain total provincial revenue capacity. This total is then divided by the provincial population to arrive at a per capita measure.

A revenue standard, or benchmark, is necessary to indicate if a province's potential revenues are adequate and, if not, to determine the size of the transfer required. Under the RNAS formula, benchmark revenues were calculated as the revenues that could be generated if the national average tax rate was applied to the national average tax base for a given source. All provinces were included for the purposes of determining the average tax base and tax rate. Since 1982, the RFPS has been used. Under this new formula, benchmark revenues for each tax source are calculated using the national average tax rate and the five province average tax base for a given source. The five provinces included to estimate the average tax base are Ontario, Manitoba, British Columbia, Québec, and Saskatchewan. Summing benchmark revenues over all revenue sources yields standard total revenues, and dividing by the national population yields per capita benchmark revenue. If the per capita benchmark revenue exceeds a province's potential revenue per capita, that province qualifies for an equalization entitlement equal to this difference multiplied by its population. If potential revenue per capita exceeds the per capita benchmark measure given by the five-province standard, the equalization transfer is set equal to zero. Thus, the system of equalization payments now in place in Canada does not equalize revenue capacity across all provinces but rather gives recipient provinces a minimum capacity defined in terms of the five-province average. These equalization entitlements are financed out of the federal government's general revenue fund.

In 1986, the federal government paid a total of $5.7 billion in equalization. This figure rose to over $7 billion in 1988. Approximately 10% of all equalization paid in 1986 was generated by the transfer of tax points under the EPF program. If the equalization associated with these EPF transfers is excluded, total equalization amounts to approximately $5 billion and $6.5 billion in 1986 and 1988, respectively. Québec accounted for the largest share of total equalization, receiving 52% of all equalization paid in 1986 and 47% in 1988. This translates into a per capita entitlement of $410 in 1986 and $460 in 1988. In comparison, per capita equalization entitlements going to Atlantic Canada in 1986 and in 1988 were $820 and $1035, respectively. The combined share of the four Atlantic provinces in both years was 36%. Historically, Alberta, Ontario and British Columbia have not qualified for equalization although the western region accounted for 12% and 16% of equalization in 1986 and 1988 respectively.

EPF Grants

A substantial amount of federal government revenue is transferred to the provinces to help finance hospital and medical care and postsecondary education. Prior to 1977, the EPF transfers took the form of conditional, open-ended, cost-sharing grants with a matching rate of 50%. In 1977, the federal government shifted to block grants to finance these established programs. Entitlements and conditions are governed by the Federal-Provincial Fiscal Arrangements and Federal Post-Secondary Education and Health Contributions Act, 1977.

The 1977 block grant system consisted of a cash payment supplemented by a federal tax abatement. The cash payment was based on a common national average to ensure all provinces received the same per capita cash entitlement. The tax abatement component required the federal government to reduce taxes by a specified amount in order to give the provinces greater tax room. A four-point personal income tax transfer and a one-point corporate tax transfer were already in existence prior to 1977 under the financing arrangements for postsecondary education. Under the 1977 arrangements, the total personal income tax transfer was increased to 13.5%.[25] Moreover, growth in annual payments were constrained to the rate of growth in GNP per capita, representing a radical departure from the open-ended nature of the replaced cost-sharing grants.

In 1982, the tax abatement component of the program was combined with the cash component to ensure that the combined per capita entitlement was the same for all provinces. A province's global EPF entitlement is calculated in two steps. The combined national average per capita federal contribution under both cash payments and tax transfers for the base year 1976 determines the base per capita payment. This amount is then accelerated by the average rate of growth in national per capita GNP over the

---

25   Québec also receives an additional abatement of 8.5 personal income tax points for EPF and another 5 points for the Canada Assistance Plan under the contracting out arrangements offered in the 1960s.

three-year period directly preceding the year of payment and grossed up by the province's population. To determine the actual cash payment under EPF, the equalized value of the tax transfer is first deducted from the global entitlement and the remainder is paid in the form of a cash transfer.

The allowable rate of acceleration of the payments has been modified in more recent years. Growth in payments for postsecondary education were constrained to 6% in 1983 and 5% in 1984, with the shortfalls recovered in the 1985 payments. In the May 1985 federal budget, the rate of acceleration with respect to GNP was reduced by two percentage points (i.e., percentage growth in GNP minus two). Per capita EPF entitlements were frozen in the February 1990 budget, and the 1991 budget extended this freeze until 1994-95 when payments are then constrained to the rate of growth in GNP minus three percentage points.

Total EPF transfers including the cash, tax point, and associated equalization components equalled $15.8 billion in 1986 and increased to $18 billion in 1988. Actual cash payments accounted for about 56% of this total in 1986 and 49% in 1988. In 1986, 40% of EPF took the form of tax transfers to the provinces, with the remaining 4% paid as equalization. In 1988, tax transfers accounted for 47% of EPF while the share of EPF paid as equalization stayed at 4%. A complete description of EPF cash payments, tax point transfers, and associated equalization by province for 1986 and 1988 appears in Tables 3.1a and 3.1b.

Ontario and Québec accounted for 37% and 22% respectively of EPF in 1986, compared to Ontario's 36% share and Québec's 26% share of the Canadian population. The 9.5% and 31% shares of EPF going to the Atlantic provinces and to the western provinces respectively were roughly in accordance to their 9% and 29% shares of the total population. In 1988, the distribution of EPF across regions remained fairly stable, with Ontario's share decreasing slightly to 35% and Québec's share increasing to 25%. Alberta received 10% and 11% of all EPF transfers in 1986 and 1988, compared to its 9% share of the population.

The relative magnitudes of the transfers occurring under the EPF program can be seen most clearly when these figures are converted to per capita measures. In 1986, the highest per capita EPF payment of $667 went to the West while Québec's per capita EPF grant of $534 was the lowest. The national average was $625. In 1988, the West continued to receive the highest per capita grant under this program, equal to $742. Ontario's per capita transfer was the lowest at $674. The national average for 1988 was $697 per capita. Of the western provinces, Alberta received the highest per capita EPF grant in 1988. In 1986, however, all western provinces received approximately equal per capita grants.

TABLE 3.1a:
Payments Under Federal-Provincial Fiscal Arrangements
& Established Program Financing Act 1977
1986-87 Fiscal Year (millions of dollars)

	NFLD	PEI	NS	NB	QUE	ONT	MAN	SASK	AB	BC	CANADA
CASH TRANSFERS											
- Insured Health Services	140.61	31.11	214.93	181.48	1085.63	2002.81	262.59	254.59	515.51	779.35	5468.60
- Ext. Health Care Services	25.80	5.73	39.44	32.17	294.50	407.34	48.14	45.46	106.40	129.39	1134.37
- Post-sec. Education	60.21	13.34	92.19	75.13	434.80	809.87	112.46	109.26	207.37	311.59	2226.21
Sub-Total	226.62	50.17	346.55	288.78	1814.94	3220.02	423.18	409.31	829.27	1220.32	8829.17
TAX POINT TRANSFERS											
- Insured Health Services	51.90	12.30	111.60	78.40	960.40	1825.90	147.20	139.20	510.10	497.20	4334.20
- Post-Sec. Education	24.50	5.80	52.80	37.00	454.00	864.20	69.60	65.80	241.40	235.30	2050.40
Sub-Total	76.40	18.10	164.40	115.40	1414.40	2690.10	216.80	205.00	751.50	732.50	6384.60
Cash + Tax	303.02	68.27	510.95	404.18	3229.34	5910.12	639.98	614.31	1580.77	1952.82	15213.77
ASSOCIATED EQUALIZATION											
- Insured Health Services	47.60	9.70	40.00	45.30	176.50		37.90	35.90			392.90
- Post-Sec. Education	22.50	4.60	18.90	21.40	83.40		17.90	17.00			185.70
Total EPF Equalization	70.10	14.30	58.90	66.70	259.90	0.00	55.80	52.90	0.00	0.00	578.60
Total EPF	373.12	82.57	569.85	470.88	3489.24	5910.12	695.78	667.21	1580.77	1952.82	15792.37

Source: Cash Transfers - Public Accounts
Tax Transfers and Equalization - The National Finances, The Canadian Tax Foundation

TABLE 3.1b:
Payments Under Federal-Provincial Fiscal Arrangements
& Established Program Financing Act 1977
1988-89 Fiscal Year (millions of dollars)

	NFLD	PEI	NS	NB	QUE	ONT	MAN	SASK	AB	BC	CANADA
CASH TRANSFERS											
- Insured Health Services	138.21	31.57	218.34	176.23	959.17	1897.04	269.35	244.46	666.34	786.89	5387.59
- Ext. Health Care Services	27.40	6.29	43.20	34.77	324.79	462.85	53.40	49.47	117.46	147.23	1266.85
- Post-Sec. Education	58.01	13.25	91.69	74.09	371.05	776.48	113.19	103.07	285.38	332.80	2218.99
Sub-Total	223.61	51.10	353.23	285.08	1655.01	3136.37	435.94	396.99	1069.18	1266.91	8873.43
TAX POINT TRANSFERS											
- Insured Health Services	61.10	14.80	129.50	93.10	1732.20	2183.50	175.60	158.70	574.60	582.10	5705.20
- Post-Sec. Education	29.00	7.00	61.30	44.10	819.80	1033.40	83.10	75.10	271.90	275.50	2700.20
Sub-Total	90.10	21.80	190.80	137.20	2552.00	3216.90	258.70	233.80	846.50	857.60	8405.40
Cash + Tax	313.71	72.90	544.03	422.28	4207.01	6353.27	694.64	630.79	1915.68	2124.51	17278.83
ASSOCIATED EQUALIZATION											
- Insured Health Services	57.70	11.00	51.00	54.90	213.60		57.50	62.70			508.40
- Post-Sec. Education	27.30	5.20	24.10	26.00	101.10		27.20	29.70			240.60
Total EPF Equalization	85.00	16.20	75.10	80.90	314.70	0.00	84.70	92.40	0.00	0.00	749.00
Total EPF	398.71	89.10	619.13	503.18	4521.71	6353.27	779.34	723.19	1915.68	2124.51	18027.83

Source: Cash Transfers - Public Accounts
Tax Transfers and Equalization - The National Finances, The Canadian Tax Foundation

The Canada Assistance Plan

The Canada Assistance Plan was enacted in 1966 to assist provinces and territories in providing social assistance and welfare programs. This federal program transfers revenues to provinces on a cost-sharing basis. The exact terms of the cost-sharing agreements are specified in the Canada Assistance Plan Act. Under the plan, the federal government is responsible for 50% of the costs of provincially (or municipally) provided programs for individuals in need and 50% of the costs of provincial programs designed to improve the employment opportunities of persons who are in need of such assistance. In this form, these transfers are equivalent to open-ended, conditional matching grants available uniformly to all provinces.

In its October 1990 budget, the federal government sought to restrain the growth in CAP payments. To achieve this, a limit of 5% growth in 1990-91 and 1991-92 CAP payments was imposed on provinces not entitled to equalization payments in those years. The 1991 budget extended this capping to 1994-95. The federal government continues to share 50% of the costs of provincial programs in equalization-recipient provinces. This constraint effectively converts the transfer for nonequalization recipients to a closed-ended grant while maintaining the open-ended nature of the transfer for those provinces entitled to equalization. Additionally, it causes transfer payments under the CAP program to behave more like equalization payments in that "need" as defined by the equalization system, becomes a criterion for transfers under the CAP program.

In 1986, CAP payments totalled close to $4 billion and, in 1988, total payments rose to $4.5 billion. The Atlantic region received 9.4% of total CAP payments in 1986, which is in accordance with its share of the population. The West received approximately 34% of CAP transfers in 1986, about 4% more than its population share. Alberta's share of CAP payments in 1986 was approximately two percentage points greater than its share of population. The CAP shares of the West, Alberta, and the Atlantic provinces were unchanged in 1988. Ontario received a smaller percentage of CAP transfers than its share of population in both 1986 and 1988. The province accounted for 28% of CAP in 1986 and 33.1% in 1988 in contrast to its 36% share of the 1986 and 1988 populations. In comparison to its 26% share of the population in these years, the province of Québec received 28% and 25% of 1986 and 1988 CAP payments respectively.

As the magnitude of these transfers suggests, some provinces derive a large proportion of their total revenues from these programs. For example, these transfers comprised 43% of the Atlantic region's provincial government revenues in 1986 and 42% in 1988. Prince Edward Island and Newfoundland obtained the highest percentage of government revenues from these sources,

FIGURE 3.1: Relative Importance of Federal Transfers as a Proportion of
Provincial Government Revenues, 1988

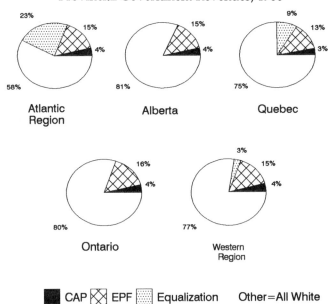

CAP ☒ EPF ▦ Equalization   Other=All White

Source: See Table 3.2 for Equalization, EPF, CAP; Provincial Economic Accounts, SC #13-213.

approximately 45% in both 1986 and 1988. As a comparison, for 1986, only
22% of Ontario's revenues and 18% of Alberta's revenues were derived from
the three transfer programs combined. In 1988, the share of Ontario's
revenues from EPF, equalization and CAP decreased slightly to 20% while
the fraction of Alberta's revenues derived from these sources increased by
one percentage point. The proportion of Québec's revenues coming from
these programs was slightly higher than that for Ontario at 25% in both 1986
and 1988. Of the western provinces, federal government transfers made the
greatest contribution in percentage terms to the revenues of the Manitoba
government. Approximately 23% of the combined revenues of the four
western provinces were derived from these three transfer programs.

Equalization is the most important of the three revenue programs as a
provincial government revenue source for the Atlantic region.
Newfoundland's dependence on revenue from this source was the greatest
in 1986 at 26%, while Nova Scotia's dependence was the lowest at 18.4%. EPF
transfers rank as the second most important transfers to this region,
accounting for 16% to 19% of Atlantic provincial government revenues.
Figure 3.1 illustrates the proportion of 1988 provincial government revenues
derived from equalization, EPF and CAP for the Atlantic provinces, Québec,
Ontario, Alberta and the West.

Table 3.2 summarizes the status quo case. The table shows each province's or region's federal government revenue contribution to the three transfer programs discussed above relative to the program expenditures made in that particular province or region. These data are useful for the analysis of redistribution under the alternative constitutional scenarios since the difference between a region's contribution to the cost of a program and the revenues it receives under the program reflects the net amount of revenue redistributed to the provincial governments of that region by the program. The redistribution of resources associated with equalization is clearly away from Ontario, Alberta and the West and in favour of the Atlantic region and Québec. The net effect of EPF and CAP appears to be a transfer of resources away from Ontario towards all other regions. In per capita terms, the Atlantic provinces receive the largest net redistributive gain for all programs.

Transfers to Provinces: Constitutional Scenarios

Alternative #1: A more centralized Canada without Québec

To examine the implications for redistribution of this constitutional arrangement for Canada, we first consider the status quo situation without Québec and ask the following question: Would the major federal transfers to provinces be more or less costly to operate, in per capita terms, at their current levels if the province of Québec opts out of Canada and there is no reassignment of powers and responsibilities for the rest of Canada? The data in Table 3.2 indicate that it is likely to be less costly for the rest of Canada to maintain the current level of transfers to all remaining provinces should Québec leave. Québec receives more in terms of program expenditures made in the province than it contributes to federal revenues to pay for the program for all three programs considered.

In 1986, Québec received a total transfer from equalization, EPF and CAP of $7278.70 million and, if these federal expenditures had been fully financed with current taxation, would have contributed $5420.28 million in federal government revenue. Accordingly, in 1986 Québec received a net inflow of $1858.42 million, or $284.16 per Québec resident. In 1988 this net inflow was $2452.05 million, or $369.23 per Québec resident. If Québec had not been part of Canada in either of these two years so that no federal transfer payments had flowed to Québec and no federal tax revenue could have been collected from it, these net flows would have been "saved" by the rest of Canada. Thus, without Québec, the rest of Canada could have maintained the same equalization, EPF, and CAP flows to the remaining provinces with a per capita expenditure by the federal government of $944.68 in 1986 and $1062.03

TABLE 3.2:
Distribution of Program Costs and Expenditures by Province/Region for Equalization, CAP and EPF

Year	Atlantic Region	Quebec	Ontario	Alberta	Western Region	Canada
Equalization						
1986-87 Distribution of Program Costs	296.20	1127.64	2416.37	519.65	1356.29	5196.65
Distribution of Program Exp	1867.70	2681.70	0.0	0.00	647.10	5196.50
Net Inflow (+) or Outflow (-) Total	1571.50	1554.06	-2416.37	-519.65	-709.19	0.00
Per Capita	689.86	237.62	-265.16	-218.80	-96.55	
1988-89 Distribution of Program Costs	383.52	1397.56	3081.14	604.53	1638.08	6500.30
Distribution of Program Exp.	2373.90	3055.40	0.00	0.00	1071.00	6500.30
Net Inflow (+) or Outflow (-) Total	1990.38	1657.84	-3081.14	-604.53	-567.08	0.00
Per Capita	867.65	249.64	-326.70	-253.05	-75.94	
Canada Assistance Plan						
1986-87 Distribution of Program Costs	227.39	865.70	1855.06	398.94	1041.23	3989.38
Distribution of Program Exp	374.75	1107.76	1132.19	427.33	1374.68	3989.380
Net Inflow (+) or Outflow (-) Total	147.36	242.06	-722.87	28.39	333.45	0.00
Per Capita	64.69	37.01	-79.32	11.96	45.40	
1988-89 Distribution of Program Costs	269.07	980.49	2161.65	424.12	1149.23	4560.44
Distribution of Program Exp.	416.60	1128.97	1510.95	487.87	1503.91	4560.44
Net Inflow (+) or Outflow (-) Total	147.53	148.48	-650.70	63.75	354.68	0.00
Per Capita	64.31	22.36	-69.00	26.68	47.50	

TABLE 3.2: (continued)

Year	Atlantic Region	Quebec	Ontario	Alberta	Western Region	Canada
Established Program Financing						
1986-87 Distribution of Program Costs	900.16	3426.94	7343.45	1579.24	4121.81	15792.36
Distribution of Program Exp	1496.42	3489.24	5910.12	1580.77	4896.58	15792.36
Net Inflow (+) or Outflow (-) Total	596.26	62.30	-1433.33	1.53	774.77	0.00
Per Capita	261.74	9.53	-157.28	0.65	105.48	
1988-89 Distribution of Program Costs	1063.64	3875.98	8545.19	1676.59	4543.01	18027.82
Distribution of Program Exp.	1610.12	4521.71	6353.27	1915.68	5542.72	18027.82
Net Inflow (+) or Outflow (-) Total	546.48	645.73	-2191.92	239.09	999.71	0.00
Per Capita	238.22	97.23	-232.42	100.08	133.88	

Sources:

(1) Distribution of program costs calculated from the distribution of federal revenue by province obtained from the Provincial Economic Accounts.

(2) Equalization data obtained from Dept. of Finance 1990 mimeo, The Fiscal Equalization Program.

(3) CAP data obtained from the Canada Assistance Plan Annual Report and the Public Accounts.

(4) EPF data obtained from The National Finances and the Public Accounts.

Note: Costs and Expenditures reported in millions of dollars. Per capita values reported as dollars.

in 1988, as opposed to the actual per capita expenditures of $988.22 and $1126.02, respectively, that occurred with Québec as a part of Canada. These per capita reductions represent an average expenditure saving of 4.5% in 1986 and 5.7% in 1988.

With the reassignment of powers in the areas of postsecondary education, health, and welfare envisaged by the increased centralization assumed in the Canada without Québec constitutional scenario, the need for EPF and CAP is eliminated. We see several issues arising from this reassignment of responsibilities that require examination. First, the assumption of provincial spending in these areas by the federal government and the elimination of EPF and CAP will cause an increase in total federal government spending. Second, federal responsibility in these areas will likely lead to a uniform provision across Canada of the goods and transfers associated with these programs, which is a departure from the current situation. Finally, the implications for the equalization system of this restructuring need to be addressed.

If the federal government were to assume responsibility for the provincial programs financially assisted by EPF and CAP, federal government spending would rise significantly. For 1986, elimination of EPF and CAP would reduce federal expenditures by $24,978 million but acquiring full responsibility for health, welfare, and postsecondary education would raise expenditures by $69,478 million, assuming the federal government chose to undertake the same level of expenditures as the provinces in aggregate. This results in a net increase in federal spending of $44,500 million. For 1988, the net increase in federal expenditures would be $49,926 million. Thus, not only would restructuring toward more centralization lead to a net increase in federal government spending, it would necessitate a substantial shifting of "tax room" from the provinces to the federal government.

In addition to the change in aggregate spending between levels of government, a move to more centralization will likely result in a more uniform provision across Canada of the goods and transfers embodied in these programs. Such a move towards uniformity may be desirable if the current diversity across provinces is simply the result of differences in abilities to finance these programs at the provincial level. However, uniformity may be an undesirable outcome if provincial diversity is the result of differences in local preferences for these programs. Finally, the issue of nominal versus real uniformity/diversity must be raised. The uniformity imposed by the federal government in Canada has usually been in terms of nominal payments (e.g., OAS payments, CPP payments) when, in fact, if uniformity is desirable it should be defined in real terms (i.e., the purchasing power of these benefits). Variation in the cost of living across provinces would be an argument favouring differences in nominal payments under these programs.

A move towards greater centralization in a Canada without Québec will also impact upon the equalization program, possibly reducing or even eliminating the need for such a program. This could occur in two ways. First, by transferring responsibility for "people" programs from the provinces to the federal government, the expenditure levels in the provinces will fall significantly so that the need for funds at the provincial level will be reduced. Second, depending upon which tax bases are transferred to the federal government to allow it sufficient tax revenue to finance these programs, the inequity in the distribution of fiscal capacity across provinces might be eliminated. For example, if the resource tax base were transferred to the federal government, a major source of disparity in fiscal capacity across provinces would disappear and the need for equalization would be reduced.

Alternative #2: A more decentralized Canada with Québec

In the constitutional scenario in which Québec remains part of a decentralized Canada, we assume that provinces obtain exclusive responsibility for the program areas partially funded by the federal government through EPF and CAP. Thus, the EPF and CAP expenditures are eliminated and the tax revenue used by the federal government to finance these programs becomes available to the provinces. We also assume that this revenue is not pooled and shared by the provinces but rather is distributed according to the amount collected in each province. Equalization continues as a federal program of transfers to the provinces.

By referring to the net inflow and outflow calculations summarized in Table 3.2, we can determine whether it is more or less costly for a given region or province to maintain its expenditures in the areas of health, welfare, and postsecondary education when EPF and CAP are eliminated and the financing of these programs becomes a pure provincial responsibility. As the data for 1986 and 1988 indicate, Ontario would have been the only province to experience a decline in per capita program costs,[26] as it is the only "net outflow" province or region under the EPF and CAP programs. Under this constitutional arrangement, net per capita costs of these programs for Ontario would have been $236.66 less in 1986 and $301.42

---

26. In this analysis we are assuming that program expenditures remain unchanged. We are, therefore, ignoring possible economies in program delivery or other cost-saving measures that might be effected with full provincial control over these programs. We examine only the impact of changes in financing responsibilities.

FIGURE 3.2: Net Redistribution Among Provinces or Regions from Equalization, EPF, and CAP, 1988 ($ millions)

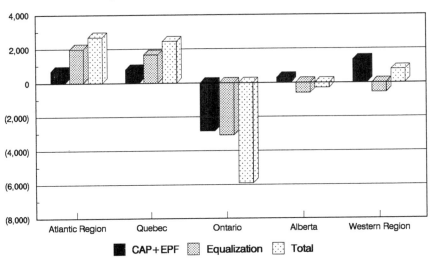

Source: See Table 3.2.

less in 1988. All other provinces or regions would have experienced a net increase in the per capita financing costs of these programs. In 1986 these increases would have ranged from a low of $12.61 per capita in Alberta to a high of $326.43 per capita in the Atlantic region. In 1988, the range of increased costs would have been from a low of $119.57 per capita in Québec to a high of $302.53 per capita for the Atlantic provinces.

The calculations discussed above serve to raise two important issues when considering the decentralization option of constitutional change. First, the redistribution of resources among provinces and regions in Canada occurs not only through equalization but also significantly through the EPF and CAP programs. Figure 3.2 illustrates the relative importance of equalization, EPF, and CAP in the interprovincial redistribution process. If the decentralization option simply eliminates EPF and CAP leaving the current system of equalization unchanged, the level of actual redistribution will be greatly reduced. Second, these calculations highlight the potential difficulties that would likely arise in an attempt to negotiate a decentralizing constitutional change like the one envisaged by this scenario. Without significant changes to the equalization system to compensate for these sizeable financial losses resulting from the elimination of EPF and CAP, many provinces would have little incentive to support such a constitutional arrangement.

Alternative #3: Independent Alberta or Western Region

In the case of an independent Alberta, we assume that the equalization program is eliminated and not replaced with a similar interprovincial scheme. The other programs are eliminated at the federal level but replaced by Alberta programs with similar levels of expenditures in the areas affected by these now defunct programs, namely health, welfare and postsecondary education. Since Alberta has not been a recipient of equalization, the discontinuation of this program represents a considerable saving had the province collected the revenue that would have been collected by the federal government to finance this program. In 1986 the net outflow from Alberta through the equalization program was $218.80 per capita and in 1988 it was $253.05 per capita. These revenues could be used to reduce tax rates or increase other provincial expenditures.

Table 3.2 shows that Alberta received a net revenue inflow with respect to both the CAP and EPF programs in 1986 and 1988. To the extent that Alberta chooses to finance expenditures in these areas at their benchmark levels, these programs will become slightly more costly to the Alberta taxpayer. However, the cost increase to Alberta residents from the elimination of EPF and CAP is less than the cost reduction effected by the elimination of equalization. Thus, a net gain of $206.19 per capita would have been available in 1986 and $126.29 per capita would have been available in 1988.

If Alberta joins an independent western region, maintaining expenditures in health, welfare, and postsecondary education will also be more costly to provide when compared to the status quo. As a region, the West received larger per capita revenue inflows under EPF and CAP than did the province of Alberta in both 1986 and 1988. In addition, the gains from the elimination of the equalization scheme are smaller for an independent western region than for an independent Alberta in per capita terms since both Manitoba and Saskatchewan received net revenue inflows under this program in 1986 and 1988.

Not surprisingly, an independent Atlantic region comprised of the four Atlantic provinces would suffer large revenue outflows from the elimination of equalization, EPF and CAP. Maintenance of spending in the areas of health, welfare, and postsecondary education would be particularly expensive since the per capita redistribution from EPF in favour of this region are substantial. In 1988, the per capita inflow under EPF was $238, in comparison to $64 under the CAP program and the $100 per capita inflow from EPF for both Alberta and Québec.

An independent Québec is also likely to suffer substantial revenue outflows from the disappearance of an equalization scheme. In addition, the

province would find it more costly to continue current expenditures in the
areas covered under EPF and CAP. In per capita terms, however, inflows
attributable to EPF and CAP are significantly lower than those accruing to
Atlantic Canada or the West.

Along with independence comes the additional spending responsibilities
in the fields occupied under the status quo situation, including defense,
customs and tariffs, and postal services. This imposes an even greater burden
on the Atlantic region and, to a lesser extent on the West and Québec, since
potential economies of scale may be lost and authorities would now have
responsibility for an even greater array of programs.

Transfers to Persons: The Status Quo

The major redistributive programs of the federal government that provide
transfers to individuals are family allowances, old age security, the Canada
Pension Plan, and UI. Family allowances and old age security are financed
out of general revenues, while UI and CPP are funded primarily through a
system of specially earmarked taxes.

Family Allowances

The family allowances program provides a monthly benefit to families on
behalf of dependent children under the age of 18 who are resident in
Canada. Under this federal program, a province may request that different
rates be paid from the federal rates on the basis of the number of children in
a family or age. Québec and Alberta are the only two provinces to have
selected this option. Québec also has its own system of family allowances
payable in addition to the federal program. Since 1986, The Family
Allowances Act allows for escalation of family and special allowances each
year for increases in the CPI index in excess of three percent.

The redistributive effect of the family allowance program occurs in two
ways. First, because the program is financed out of general revenues,
resources are transferred from taxpayers without children to those with
children. Second, since family allowance payments are taxable, there is a net
redistribution from higher income to lower income taxpayers (particularly
with the recent introduction of the "clawback" feature for high income
earners).

Total payments under this program equalled approximately $2.5 billion
in both 1986 and 1988. The distribution of these expenditures across
provinces or regions is provided in Table 3.3. In these years, Ontario received
the largest share of expenditures, about 35% of all payments. Thirty per cent

TABLE 3.3:
Family Allowance Program

Year	Atlantic Region	Quebec	Ontario	Alberta	Western Region	Canada
1986 Distribution of Program Costs	143.24	543.32	1168.55	251.30	655.89	2513.00
Distribution of Program Exp.	250.00	622.00	879.00	260.00	762.00	2513.00
Net Inflow (+) or Outflow (-) Total	106.76	76.68	-289.55	8.70	106.11	0.00
Per Capita	46.87	11.72	-31.77	3.66	14.45	
1988 Distribution of Program Costs	152.45	555.56	1224.82	240.31	651.17	2584.00
Distribution of Program Exp.	247.00	633.00	922.00	265.00	782.00	2584.00
Net Inflow (+) or Outflow (-) Total	94.55	77.44	-302.82	24.69	130.83	0.00
Per Capita	41.21	11.66	-32.11	10.33	17.52	

Source: Provincial Economic Accounts, Statistics Canada 13-213.
Notes: Program costs and expenditures are in millions of dollars and per capita values are in dollars.

of all allowances were paid to the West, while the Atlantic provinces and Québec received shares of 10% and 25% respectively. This distribution of program expenditures corresponds to the distribution of the 19 years of age and younger population across these regions. On a per capita basis, payments range from a high of $111 in Alberta to a low of $95 in Québec in 1988. The differential payments on a per capita basis are representative of the relative shares of the 19 years of age and younger population out of total population for each of the regions. The differences in the age distributions of provincial/regional populations is shown in Table 3.4.

Table 3.3 also provides calculations regarding the interprovincial or interregional redistribution effects of the family allowance program. As can be seen from these data, all provinces or regions except Ontario were net beneficiaries of this program in both 1986 and 1988. These net inflows ranged from a high of $41.21 per capita for the Atlantic provinces to a low of $10.33 per capita for Alberta in 1988.

TABLE 3.4:
Age Distribution of Population, 1988

	Atlantic Region	Quebec	Ontario	Alberta	Western Region	Canada
0-19 yrs	30.8%	27.1%	27.7%	31.3%	29.6%	28.4%
20-24	8.7	8.1	8.2	8.5	7.9	8.1
25-44	31.7	34.1	32.8	34.8	32.7	33.0
45-64	17.5	20.2	20.0	16.8	18.3	19.3
65+	11.3	10.4	11.3	8.6	11.5	11.1

Source: Postcensal annual estimates of population by marital status, age, sex, and component of growth for Canada, provinces, and territories June 1, 1988.

Old Age Security Program

This federal program consists of the OAS pension, the Guaranteed Income Supplement, and the Spouse's Allowance. The latter two types of benefits are not included as taxable income. In conjunction with the Canada Pension Plan, these programs represent the available programs designed to provide income security to Canada's older population.

OAS provides a monthly benefit payable to persons aged 65 or over who fulfil the Canadian residency requirement. The amount of the benefit is dependent on an individual's length of residency in Canada provided the 10-year minimum has been satisfied. Those with greater than 20 years of residency may reside outside the country and receive the pension indefinitely. The GIS is designed to provide income support to those pensioners with little or no income. Entitlement to the supplement must be demonstrated by application each year, and benefits are dependent on the recipient's marital status and the pension status of the recipient's spouse. With some exception, residency in Canada is required in order to receive the GIS. The Spouse's Allowance is paid to the spouse of an OAS recipient if the spouse is between the ages of 60 and 64. Widowed spouses are also eligible for the allowance except under certain limited conditions. Both the conditions for OAS and the Spouses Allowance are subject to any international social security agreements that may be relevant.

The federal government spent about $13 billion under the OAS program in 1986 and $14.8 billion in 1988. Approximately $38 million of total 1986 OAS payments were made to nonresidents. Of the payments made to Canadian residents in 1986 and in 1988, 34% went to beneficiaries residing in Ontario, 29% to the Western region, 26% to Québec, and the remaining 10%

TABLE 3.5:
Old Age Security Program

Year	Atlantic Region	Quebec	Ontario	Alberta	Western Region	Canada
1986 Distribution of Program Costs	748.64	2850.08	6107.3	1313.40	3427.97	13134.00
Distribution of Program Exp.	1423.00	3430.00	4494.00	905.00	3787.00	13134.00
Net Inflow (+) or Outflow (-) Total	674.36	579.92	-1613.31	-408.40	359.03	0.00
Per Capita	296.03	88.67	-177.03	-171.96	48.88	
1988 Distribution of Program Costs	872.32	3178.77	7008.09	1375.00	3725.82	14785.00
Distribution of Program Exp.	1535.00	3877.00	5096.00	1035.00	4277.00	14785.00
Net Inflow (+) or Outflow (-) Total	662.68	698.23	-1912.09	-340.00	551.18	0.00
Per Capita	288.88	105.14	-202.75	-142.32	73.82	

Sources: Provincial Economic Accounts, Statistics Canada 13-213.
Notes: Program costs and expenditures are in millions of dollars and per capita values are in dollars.

went to the Atlantic provinces. Residents of the province of Alberta received about 7% of OAS payments. In comparison, Ontario's 37% share of both the over-45 and the over-65 populations in 1986 corresponded to its share of the total population. The Atlantic region and the West also had shares of these sub-populations similar to their shares of the total Canadian population. Alberta accounted for 7.1% of the over-65 population in both 1986 and 1988 in contrast to its 9% share of the total population. Québec also had a slightly smaller percentage of the older Canadian population relative to its share of the total population.

The total flow and regional distribution of Old Age Security program expenditures for 1986 and 1988 are summarized in Table 3.5. Per capita expenditures on OAS in 1988 ranged from a high of $669.14 in the Atlantic region to a low of $433.24 in Alberta. This variation in per capita expenditures across regions is partly the result of differences in the age distribution of the population (e.g., Alberta's relatively low proportion of its population aged 65 and over) and partly the result of differences in the number of low-income individuals who may qualify for the guaranteed income supplement.

Included in Table 3.5 are calculated interprovincial or interregional redistributive effects of the OAS program. In both 1986 and 1988, Ontario and Alberta were net contributors of resources in this redistribution process while the Atlantic provinces, Québec and the West were net beneficiaries.

Canada Pension Plan (CPP)

The Canada Pension Plan (CPP) was established in 1965 as a federal income security program and is administered primarily by the Department of National Health and Welfare. The compulsory contributions are collected by Revenue Canada, while the CPP Account and the CPP Investment Fund are administered by the Department of Finance. The province of Québec does not participate in the CPP but has its own pension plan. Only a small fraction of CPP contributions come from Québec and this is paid by federal employees residing in the province. The plan is funded by contributions from employees and employers, contributions from self-employed individuals, and the investment earnings of the CPP Investment Fund. Contributors are individuals between the ages of 18 and 70 with annual earnings greater than a specified minimum which was $2,700 in 1989. The contribution rate of 3.6% in 1986 was evenly split between employees and employers. In 1989, the contribution rate increased to 4.2%, again evenly split between employees and employers. The federal government has indicated that continued increases in contribution rates would be necessary to meet the needs of the fund over the next 25 years.

The CPP is comprised of three benefit programs providing retirement benefits, survivor benefits, and disability benefits. All benefits under the Plan are indexed by the CPI on an annual basis. Retirement benefits are payable automatically at age 65 or as early as age 60 provided certain eligibility requirements are met. The most significant restriction is that at the time benefits begin the recipient must not be substantially employed. Three types of survivor's benefits are available under the program: surviving spouse benefits, orphan's benefits, and a death benefit. The death benefit is a lump sum payment to the estate of the deceased provided the deceased was a contributor to the program for a sufficient length of time. Orphan's benefits pay a monthly benefit to the dependent child of a deceased contributor. Under the surviving spouse's pension plan, a spouse may be eligible for a monthly pension if contributions by the deceased had been made for a sufficient period. The maximum benefit is dependent on whether the surviving spouse is over or under the age of 65. Further adjustments to the benefits may apply if the survivor is under the age of 45, has no dependent children or is disabled. Contributors who meet the criteria for the minimum CPP contribution and who suffer a disability are eligible for a disability

TABLE 3.6:
Canada and Quebec Pension Plans Revenue and Expenditure, 1988

	Canada Pension Plan						Quebec Pension Plan
	Atlantic Region	Quebec	Ontario	Alberta	Western Region	Canada	
REVENUES:							
Direct Taxes	536	5	3303	744	2131	6023	1916
Investment Income	391	14	1968	504	1512	3885	1169
Total	927	19	5271	1248	3643	9908	3085
EXPENDITURES:							
Goods & Services	5	0	112	4	13	130	46
Transfers to Persons	886	34	4221	741	2946	8155	2619
Total	891	34	4333	745	2959	8285	2665
SURPLUS (+) or DEFICIT (-):							
Total	36	-15	938	503	684	1623	420
Per Capita	15.69	-2.26	99.46	210.55	91.60	62.83	63.24

Source: Provincial Economic Accounts, Statistics Canada 13-213.
Notes: Revenues and expenditures are in millions of dollars. Per capita values are in dollars.

pension. Actual benefits paid consist of a flat rate amount plus an earnings related component dependent on the actual earnings and contributions made to CPP.

The CPP Investment Fund allows for surplus funds to be lent to provincial governments. The surplus available for loans is calculated as the difference in CPP revenues and the estimated amount of funds necessary to meet benefit and administrative responsibilities over a three-month period. This surplus is lent to individual provinces in proportion to contributions made to the plan on behalf of the residents of that province over the past 120 months. The relatively small amount available for loans to Québec reflects its share of federal employees living in the province and contributing to the pensions fund, namely members of the RCMP and the armed forces. Funds not borrowed by the provinces are invested in federal securities.

The 1988 expenditures and revenues of the Canada and Québec Pension Plans are detailed in Table 3.6. As can be seen from the data both plans were in a surplus position in that year, with the largest per capita difference between revenue and expenditure occurring in Alberta. This large surplus was the combined result of relatively low per capita transfers to recipients, due to the relatively small proportion of Alberta's population found in the over-65 age group, and a relatively high per capita receipt of direct taxes, reflecting both the age distribution of the population and the comparatively high labour force participation rate in Alberta.

Unemployment Insurance Program

The federal unemployment insurance program is governed by the
Unemployment Insurance Act of 1971 and its amendments, although the
origins of the program can be traced back to 1940 when the first federal
program was established. Approximately 96% of today's work force is
covered under the program. Entitlement to UI benefits depends on a number
of parameters relating to employment, attachment to the labour force, reason
for leaving employment, and the regional unemployment rate.

There are three main types of UI benefits: regular, extended, and special.
The basic eligibility requirement for all types of benefits is a minimum of
10-14 weeks of insurable employment during the qualifying period. The
qualifying period is defined as the 52 weeks immediately preceding the start
of the benefit period. This requirement is known formally as the Variable
Entrance Requirement, and the minimum number of weeks generally
depends on the regional unemployment rate. The Variable Entrance
Requirement was implemented in 1977. In Bill C-21, amending the
Unemployment Insurance Act of 1971, the variable range was extended to
10-20 weeks. The only exception to this occurred in 1990 when this condition
was not renewed and the minimum weeks requirement was uniformly set at
14 weeks during this year.

Regular benefits are paid out for the number of weeks of insurable
employment worked during the qualifying period or 25 weeks, whichever is
less. The benefit rate is equal to 60% of insurable earnings. An individual
who has less than the 10-14 week minimum, mainly new or re-entrants to the
labour force, are required to have 20 weeks in insurable employment to be
eligible for regular UI benefits.

Two types of extended benefits are available under certain conditions.
Labour force extended benefits pay an additional one week of benefits for
every two weeks over 25 of insurable employment during the qualifying
period up to a maximum of 13 weeks. Regional extended benefits are
payable to eligible individuals who reside in regions with unemployment
rates in excess of 4%. For every 1/2 percentage point the region's
unemployment rate exceeds 4%, an extra 2 weeks of benefits are paid. An
additional 2 weeks are paid for a fraction of less than 1/2%. The maximum
regional extended benefit cannot exceed 32 weeks.

Special benefits include maternity, paternity, adoption, sickness,
retirement, job creation, work sharing, training, and fishermen's benefits. The
first five categories are available to individuals with a significant labour force
attachment of more than 20 weeks of insurable employment and are entirely
financed by employee and employer contributions. The remaining four types
of special benefits are funded by the federal government. Paternity benefits

TABLE 3.7:
UI Contributions and Benefits by Province/Region and by Benefit Program, 1988
(millions of dollars)

	Atlantic Region	Quebec	Ontario	Alberta	Western Region	Canada
Total Contribution	815.28	2754.00	4639.20	1029.12	2997.84	11206.32
	7.28%	24.58%	41.40%	9.18%	26.75%	100.00%
Total Expenditures	2027.11	3394.21	2370.05	855.39	3018.36	10809.73
	18.75%	31.40%	21.93%	7.91%	27.92%	100.00%
Program Expenditures:						
Regular	1715.37	3064.97	1876.08	740.96	2615.88	9272.30
	18.50%	33.06%	20.23%	7.99%	28.21%	100.00%
Sickness	30.07	74.22	140.29	21.84	79.95	324.53
	9.27%	22.87%	43.23%	6.73%	24.63%	100.00%
Maternity	35.02	131.92	240.34	60.03	156.41	563.69
	6.21%	23.40%	42.64%	10.65%	27.75%	100.00%
Fishing	196.96	22.11	0.94	0.17	49.99	270.00
	72.95%	8.19%	0.35%	0.06%	18.52%	100.00%
Training Rel.	29.06	57.36	73.25	22.09	76.77	236.44
	12.29%	24.26%	30.98%	9.34%	32.47%	100.00%
Work	0.69	4.76	5.89	1.26	5.48	16.82
	4.10%	28.30%	35.01%	7.49%	32.59%	100.00%
Job Creation	18.41	35.28	21.20	6.93	27.23	102.12
	18.03%	34.55%	20.76%	6.78%	26.66%	100.00%
Other	1.52	3.58	12.06	2.11	6.65	23.81
	6.39%	15.05%	50.62%	8.86%	27.93%	100.00%

Sources: UI expenditures are obtained from Cansim series D730284-D-736418.
UI contributions are from Taxation Statistics, Individual Returns.

have only been available since the passing of Bill C-21 in October 1990. The new amendments to the UI Act also eliminate the retirement benefits category.

A repeat qualifier is defined as having received UI benefits for more than 14 weeks during the qualifying period. Until recently, a repeater was required to have up to six additional weeks of employment over the 10-14 week minimum to establish entitlement to benefits. However, if the regional unemployment rate was greater than 11.5%, no additional weeks were required. Bill C-21 eliminates this additional weeks requirement for repeat qualifiers.

The costs of the program in the past have been shared by employees, employers, and the federal government. Employee and employer, or private, contributions financed the administrative costs of the program, all regular benefits, all special benefits not covered by the federal government, and the labour force extended benefits. The federal government was responsible for benefits to fishermen and wives, training and related special benefits, and the regional extended benefits. With the introduction of the Bill C-21 amendments, employers and employees are to assume full financing responsibility for the UI program.

A detailed summary of UI contributions and program benefit expenditures for 1988 is provided in Table 3.7. Regular benefits are the primary expenditure of the program, constituting 86% of total expenditures for Canada as a whole. The relative importance of regular and other benefits differs substantially across regions and provinces. For example, in 1988 residents of the Atlantic region collected about 73% of the benefits paid out under the fisherman benefit program, reflecting the relative importance of that industry. As another example, Alberta collected about 11% of the total maternity benefits paid in Canada which is a share greater than its share of population but reflects the relatively high female labour force participation rate in Alberta and the relatively large proportion of the population in the child-rearing age groups.

The Unemployment Insurance program is a complicated program whose impacts are difficult to analyze. It contains both an insurance component and a redistributive transfer component. Resources are transferred across industries because contribution rates are not risk-rated. All workers and firms pay the same contribution rate regardless of the unemployment experience of those workers and firms. Thus, there is a transfer from industries which over time experience low levels of unemployment or small fluctuations of employment to those whose experience is more volatile. Additionally, there are significant transfers across provinces and regions. This interregional redistribution occurs through a variety of mechanisms: industrial structure differs across provinces so that the interindustry transfers discussed above translate into interregional transfers as well, the regional extended benefit program disproportionately transfers resources from low to high unemployment areas, and interregional differences in demographics and labour force characteristics lead to further transfers across regions or provinces (e.g., the maternity benefit program).

TABLE 3.8:
Distribution of UI Program Costs and Benefits

Year	Atlantic Region	Quebec	Ontario	Alberta	Western Region	Canada
1986						
UIC Contributions	681.36	2297.04	3840.00	904.32	2581.20	9399.60
General Revenues	61.29	233.32	499.96	107.52	280.62	1075.19
Total Revenue	742.65	2530.36	4339.96	1011.84	2861.82	10474.79
UIC Expenditure	1769.69	3186.19	2482.71	983.33	3036.20	10474.79
NET INFLOW (+) OR OUTFLOW (-)						
Total	1027.04	655.83	-1857.25	-28.51	174.38	0.00
Per Capita	450.85	100.28	-203.80	-12.00	23.74	0.00
1988						
UIC Contributions	815.28	2754.00	4639.20	1029.12	2997.84	11206.32
General Revenues	0.00	0.00	0.00	0.00	0.00	0.00
Total Revenues	815.28	2754.00	4639.20	1029.12	2997.84	11206.32
UIC Expenditure	2027.11	3394.21	2370.05	855.39	3018.36	10809.73
NET INFLOW (+) OR OUTFLOW (-)						
Total	1240.78	737.77	-2104.97	-136.85	126.80	0.00
Per Capita	540.88	111.09	-223.20	-57.28	16.98	0.00

Sources: Distribution of federal revenues from the Provincial Economic accounts. UIC contribution data from Taxation Statistics, Individual Returns. Employer contributions are calculated as 1.4 x employee contributions.

Note 1: For 1988, net inflows are calculated by redistributing the UI surplus back to the provinces on the basis of percentage of revenue collected from the province to obtain a "balanced-budget" adjusted revenue for each province.

Note 2: Revenue and expenditure flows are in millions of dollars and per capita values are in dollars.

The magnitude of these interregional redistributions of resources through the UI program are summarized for 1986 and 1988 in Table 3.8. The major differences between the 1986 and 1988 data is that in 1988 revenues from employer and employee contributions were sufficient to finance UI expenditures, while in 1986 they were not sufficient and a contribution from federal government general revenues was required. In both years, however, the pattern of redistribution is similar. There was a substantial net inflow of resources on a per capita basis to the Atlantic region and Québec, and this was financed primarily by an outflow of resources from Ontario and Alberta.

Transfers to Persons: Constitutional Scenarios
Alternative #1: A more centralized Canada without Québec
In this scenario we assume that family allowances, OAS, CPP, and
Unemployment Insurance all continue to exist but without any participation
from Québec. Of these, impacts on the Canada Pension Plan are the easiest to
analyze as the status quo situation is one of no Québec participation. Since
the CPP and QPP are already separate entities, a Canada without Québec
constitutional option does not appear to entail any significant impacts upon
either of these two programs (except possibly issues of individual portability
between programs and the effect this may have on labour mobility between
Canada and Québec), particularly with respect to financing and benefit
payments.

Continuation of the family allowance and old age security programs may
occur at a reduced cost for the Canada without Québec scenario. As Tables
3.3 and 3.5 show, in 1986 and 1988, Québec residents received a net inflow of
resources under these two programs (i.e., program expenditures to Québec
residents exceeded the "adjusted" general revenue collected from Québec
residents to finance these programs). The total net inflow of resources from
family allowances and OAS was about $657 million in 1986 and about $775
million in 1988. Had Québec not been part of Canada in either of these two
years, this net inflow to Québec or net outflow from the rest of Canada
would not have occurred, thus reducing the costs of these programs for the
rest of Canada. These total dollar savings represent a 5.7% reduction in per
capita costs in 1986 and a 6.0% reduction in per capita costs in 1988. Finally,
it should also be recognized that the greater centralization assumed in this
scenario could impact on these programs administratively. In particular, if
uniformity of program results from centralization, Alberta's current system
of a schedule of family allowance payments based upon children's ages
would disappear and be replaced with a uniform rate.

Assessing the impact of a constitutional change in which Québec departs
from Canada is more difficult for the case of the Unemployment Insurance
program than for family allowances, OAS, and CPP because UI is a complex
program. On a simple level we can continue our retrospective analysis of
program expenditures to determine whether this program would be more or
less costly for the remainder of Canada to operate in the absence of Québec.
As is shown in Table 3.8, residents of Québec received a net inflow of
resources through the UI program of about $656 million in 1986 and $738
million in 1988. Thus, in the absence of Québec, the Unemployment
Insurance program would have been less costly for the rest of Canada to
operate in both of these years as these transfers would not have occurred.

TABLE 3.9:
Provincial Unemployment Rates

| | Levels | | | | Deviations* | | | |
| | 1961-1989 | | 1980-1989 | | 1961-1989 | | 1980-1989 | |
	Mean	Std. Dev.	Mean	Std. Dev.	Mean	Std. Dev.	Mean	Std. Dev.
Newfoundland	13.60	4.56	17.29	2.53	6.61	2.98	7.98	1.66
Prince Edward Isl.	9.52	2.78	12.67	1.06	2.52	1.49	3.36	1.82
Nova Scotia	8.74	2.90	11.82	1.62	1.74	0.96	2.51	0.71
New Brunswick	10.15	3.23	13.32	1.50	3.16	1.47	4.01	0.70
Quebec	8.67	2.60	11.24	1.75	1.67	0.54	1.93	0.55
Ontario	5.59	2.05	7.36	1.84	-1.40	0.65	-1.95	0.78
Manitoba	5.53	1.92	7.63	1.18	-1.47	0.78	-1.68	0.98
Saskatchewan	4.55	2.02	6.85	1.35	-2.45	1.11	-2.46	1.60
Alberta	5.45	2.62	8.15	2.64	-1.55	1.37	-1.16	1.77
British Columbia	8.29	2.94	11.20	2.89	1.29	1.10	1.89	1.61

Source: Historical Labour Force Statistics, Statistics Canada 71-201.

*Provincial Unemployment Rate - Canadian Unemployment Rate.

There is a danger, however, in focusing too narrowly on the net inflows or outflows of resources under the UI program in any given year. Such a focus ignores the behaviour of program expenditures and contributions over time and, in particular, ignores the cyclical behaviour of these flows. A large part of the "insurance" component of the UI program is tied to the cyclical movement of employment and unemployment so that a point-in-time analysis will not provide a complete assessment of UI under alternative constitutional scenarios.

Table 3.9 provides some summary statistics regarding the behaviour of provincial unemployment rates for the 1961-89 period. Whether we examine the level of the provincial unemployment rate or the deviation of the provincial rate from the national rate for Canada, the data in Table 3.9 generally show that there have been, on average, relatively high unemployment provinces and relatively low unemployment provinces and that this ranking is the same whether the full 1961-89 period is examined or the sub-period of 1980-89 is examined. The higher unemployment provinces have been the Atlantic provinces, Québec and British Columbia, while the lower unemployment provinces have been Ontario and the prairie provinces. These differences in average levels of unemployment between provinces are a major source of the redistributive flows arising from the UI program and summarized in Table 3.8. Since Québec is a relatively high unemployment province, it is a net beneficiary of the UI program. Accordingly, if Québec were to depart from Canada, the average unemployment for Canada would be lower and, on average, the UI program would be less expensive for the rest of Canada to operate.

Again, we must be careful not to focus the analysis too strongly on average behaviour over time. The cyclical behaviour of expenditures and contributions depends upon the cyclical behaviour of employment and unemployment. Our analysis should also address the question of whether these cyclical fluctuations would differ significantly between the Canada with Québec and Canada without Québec scenarios. The data contained in Tables 3.10 and 3.11 provide some information on this issue. Table 3.10 summarizes the distribution of employment across broad categories of industries for the provinces and regions of Canada in 1988. As can be seen, Québec's industrial structure is not fundamentally different from the Canadian average so that a Canada with Québec, and a Canada without Québec would have very similar distributions of employment across industries. Thus, we should not expect large differences in cyclical fluctuations arising from differences in industrial composition.

The correlation matrix presented in Table 3.11 provides some rudimentary information on risk-sharing and insurance provision across provinces and regions provided by the Unemployment Insurance program. If the provinces and subregions of Canada have different cyclical behaviour of employment and unemployment over time (i.e., if the timing and magnitude of their business cycles differ), then a national unemployment insurance program which "pools" these cyclical characteristics essentially allows regions and provinces to insure each other. This is particularly so if the cycles at the subnational level exhibit negative correlations with each other (i.e., if business cycle booms in one region tend to be associated with business cycle recessions in other regions). The correlations found in Table 3.11 are for deviations of the provincial unemployment rate from the national rate and are a crude attempt to measure the relationships between provincial cycles independent of the national cycle. The main features of this correlation matrix are the relatively large and always negative correlation coefficients between Ontario and the Atlantic provinces and between Ontario and the western provinces; the positive correlations between the provinces comprising the Atlantic region; the positive correlations between the provinces comprising the Western Region; and the negative but virtually zero correlation coefficient between Ontario and Québec. These correlations provide some indication of the nature of unemployment risk sharing and insurance provided between regions and provinces by the UI program. Since there is a tendency for unemployment in the Atlantic region and the west to

TABLE 3.10:
Industry Distribution of Employment, 1988

	Atlantic Region	Quebec	Ontario	Manitoba	Saskat-chewan	Alberta	British Columbia	Canada	Canada without Quebec	Western Canada
Agriculture	2.2%	2.3%	2.3%	7.4%	17.3%	7.9%	2.8%	3.6%	4.1%	6.9%
Other Primary	5.6	1.3	1.2	2.0	2.7	5.9	4.4	2.4	2.7	4.1
Manufacturing	13.3	20.4	21.1	12.7	6.0	8.0	14.0	17.2	16.2	10.1
Construction	6.0	5.8	6.0	4.6	5.5	6.1	7.2	5.9	6.0	5.9
Transportation	8.5	7.5	6.7	9.5	7.5	7.8	9.0	7.4	7.4	8.0
Trade	19.6	17.1	17.5	17.6	17.9	18.0	21.4	17.8	18.0	18.2
Finance	4.2	5.5	6.7	5.3	5.1	5.1	7.7	6.0	6.1	5.7
Service	34.7	33.4	32.3	32.9	31.2	33.8	40.7	33.3	33.2	34.1
Public Admin.	9.4	6.6	6.1	7.9	6.9	7.3	7.0	6.7	6.7	6.9

Source: Labour Force Annual Averages, Statistics Canada 71-220.

TABLE 3.11:
Correlations of Deviations of Provincial Unemployment Rates
From Canadian Unemployment Rate, 1961-89

	NFLD	PEI	NS	NB	QUE	ONT	MAN	SASK	AB	BC
NFLD	1.00	0.16	0.53	0.82	0.36	-0.59	-0.45	-0.10	-0.09	0.22
PEI		1.00	0.51	0.38	0.07	-0.48	0.37	0.54	0.25	0.11
NS			1.00	0.68	0.39	-0.50	-0.34	-0.02	-0.06	0.17
NB				1.00	0.48	-0.52	-0.41	-0.06	-0.21	0.05
QUE					1.00	-0.02	-0.45	-0.46	-0.65	-0.46
ONT						1.00	-0.08	-0.44	-0.62	-0.70
MAN							1.00	0.78	0.51	-0.02
SASK								1.00	0.66	0.22
AB									1.00	0.74
BC										1.00

move in a direction opposite to that of central Canada, a pooling of these regions into one unemployment insurance scheme allows one region to implicitly "insure" the other. Removal of Québec from Canada, or at least Québec from the unemployment insurance plan, may adversely affect this insurance element thus offsetting some of the gains to the rest of Canada that accrue from the reduced average costs of providing UI should Québec depart from the program.

Alternative #2: A more decentralized Canada with Québec

Under this scenario, we assume that the provinces obtain responsibility for the Family Allowance program, OAS, CPP, and Unemployment Insurance and receive the federal tax room now used to finance these programs. We also assume that these status quo federal programs are replaced with provincial programs of similar structure and size.

In considering family allowances and OAS, Tables 3.3 and 3.5 reveal that only the province of Ontario would have been able to provide both programs at less cost to their taxpayers than occurred under the status quo situation of 1986 and 1988. The Atlantic region would have faced a substantial rise in per capita costs, about $330 per person in 1988, while Québec and the western region would have encountered smaller increases of about $117 and $91 per capita respectively in 1988. Alberta would have incurred an increased per capita cost of about $10 if it had assumed full responsibility for the 1988 Family Allowance program but this would have been offset by a $142 reduction in per capita costs associated with the OAS program. Considering these two programs combined, Alberta would have "saved" about $132 per capita or about $315 million in total had it operated the Family Allowance and OAS programs in 1988, made the same payments as were made by the federal government and received access to the Alberta portion of the tax revenue needed by the federal government to finance these programs.

The adverse redistribution of resources encountered by Alberta from the federal operation of family allowances and OAS arises from two sources. First, because Alberta's population distribution is such that it has a relatively small proportion of persons in the over-65 age category when compared to the rest of Canada, it receives a proportion of total OAS benefits that is smaller than its share of total Canadian population. Second, because Alberta is a relatively wealthy province, it pays a disproportionately large, relative again to population, share of the federal government general revenues used to finance these programs.

Dismantling the Canada Pension Plan and replacing it with a set of provincially administered pension plans raises a number of interesting issues. First, while CPP is currently in a "surplus" situation for all subregions or provinces, so that revenues from CPP payroll taxes exceed expenditures, the sizes of those surpluses differ dramatically. They ranged from a low of $15.69 per capita in the Atlantic region to high of $210.55 per capita in Alberta during 1988. Thus, as the size of the over 65 age category grows in importance over time and pension contribution rates must rise to finance increased total pay-outs, these rate increases will need to occur sooner and will be larger in Atlantic Canada than in Alberta. Alberta's relatively strong financial position in this regard is a function of its population distribution and its relatively high labour force participation rate so that CPP expenditures are low and revenues high. Accordingly, replacing CPP with a set of provincial pension plans will likely adversely impact on the Atlantic provinces in the short to medium term and favourably impact on Alberta, the western provinces in aggregate, and Ontario.

Second, it is likely the case that the "savings" calculated for Alberta under provincial administration of OAS and CPP are overstated. The data used to determine these savings are based upon the distribution of payments by province where these data depend upon the province of residence of the recipient of pension payments. If Alberta were a net exporter of retired persons, then under a provincially-administered plan these "exportees" would remain the responsibility of the exporting province not the importing province. In the long run, then, Alberta's total payments under OAS and a provincial version of CPP may be larger than indicated by the data on federal expenditures in Alberta under these plans.

Third, it is important to distinguish between long-run and short-run effects. While demographics are currently favourable for Alberta when it comes to providing programs such as OAS and CPP, these favourable demographics may not last in the longer term [see, for example, forecasts made by Foot (1991)]. Thus, a more appropriate method for evaluating the impact of constitutional change on programs of this nature may be to focus on the long-run characteristics of these programs rather than to examine the more short-term features that we have discussed above.

Finally, it is necessary for us to raise issues of labour mobility. If the intention of constitutional reform under the decentralized Canada with Québec scenario is to maintain at least the same amount of factor mobility, particularly with respect to labour, that currently exists in Canada, then a significant amount of interprovincial coordination will be required for the provincial versions of OAS and CPP. An important issue that must be addressed to ensure that the provincial versions of these programs do not discourage mobility is portability, or the ability to transfer accumulated claims on future benefits or eligibility between provinces. Without coordination of this type, any potential benefits that might accrue due to decentralization might easily be dissipated through labour market inefficiencies.

A major impact of replacing the national Unemployment Insurance program by a set of provincial programs will be to eliminate the significant interprovincial and interregional transfers contained within the current system. If the current package of benefits were maintained by each provincial program, the costs of providing unemployment insurance benefits would rise significantly in the Atlantic provinces and Québec, fall in Ontario and Alberta, and remain about the same for the western region in aggregate. For example, as detailed in Table 3.8, if the provinces had simply assumed responsibility for unemployment insurance payments in 1988 and had obtained unemployment insurance contributions, unemployment insurance revenues would have needed to rise by $541 per capita in the Atlantic region and by $111 per capita in Québec to finance expenditures on a balanced budget basis. In that same year, unemployment insurance revenues could have fallen by $223 per capita in Ontario and $57 per capita in Alberta. Even if the Atlantic provinces eliminated all benefits other than regular benefits, the shortfall of revenues from expenditures would have been $390 per capita. Clearly, a move to decentralization of the UI program, with no offsetting compensation of revenues from other sources, would require major restructuring of UI benefits and revenues in the Atlantic provinces and, possibly, even in Québec.

While Alberta would be a net beneficiary from eliminating the implicit transfers of resources contained in the national UI program, the establishment of a provincial UI program would not be without its difficulties. As Table 3.9 shows, Alberta has a relatively low average unemployment rate over time but its standard deviation, a measure of volatility around the average, is relatively high. Thus, on average, benefits and program costs would be low but fluctuations around this average over time may be relatively large. This creates potential problems of financing for the program, necessitating either significant changes in contribution rates over time or access to borrowed funds or the general revenues of the provincial government. This volatility problem is likely the result of Alberta's industrial structure which differs markedly from the national average. As Table 3.10 shows, relatively more of Alberta's employment is found in agricultural and other primary industries than for the national economy and relatively less employment occurs in the manufacturing sector. In addition to the volatility issue, the creation of separate provincial UI programs eliminates the interprovincial and interregional pooling and risk-sharing that occurs in a national program.

As a final comment on the decentralization scenario of constitutional change, we again raise an issue that was first discussed when examining the implications of this scenario in the system of federal transfers to provincial governments. Decentralization, with provincial governments assuming control of the family allowance program, OAS, CPP and Unemployment Insurance, will generate a substantial reduction in interprovincial and interregional transfers of resources. Thus, in the absence of any compensation for the loss of resources, it may be unreasonable to expect that all provinces would support a constitutional change that leads to the decentralization scenario outlined here.

Alternative #3: An independent Alberta or Western Region

Most of our conclusions regarding the implications of a more decentralized constitutional arrangement apply to the scenario of independent provinces or regions. Like the decentralization case, control of the programs of federal government transfers to persons would be moved to the provincial or regional level. The major difference between the decentralization scenario and the independent provinces or regions scenario lies with what can reasonably be assumed about labour mobility. Independence is likely to lead to a significant reduction in the mobility of labour resources across provinces or regions.

Reduced labour mobility is likely to impact most seriously upon the provision of an Unemployment Insurance program. For Alberta or the Western Region, less mobility should lead to an increase in average unemployment rates and their volatility over time as an historically important vehicle for westerners to deal with the unemployment problem disappears. This should raise the costs of providing UI on average and, consequently, reduce the "savings" accruing to Alberta or the Western Region from eliminating the interregional transfers contained in the current system of national Unemployment Insurance.

Conclusions

In this study, we have attempted to examine the implications of constitutional change for the conduct of the major redistributive programs currently undertaken in Canada by the federal government. We have considered both the transfer of resources from the federal government to provincial governments and the transfer of resources from the federal government to persons. We have focused on identifying the magnitude and direction of the net redistribution among provinces and regions arising from these federal transfer programs, assessing the implications of constitutional change for the future existence of these programs, and determining the financial implications for provinces and regions arising from the modification or deletion of these programs implied by different constitutional arrangements.

Our major findings are summarized by Figures 3.3 and 3.4, which outline the magnitude and direction of the net redistribution among provinces and regions arising from federal transfer programs in total and per capita terms respectively. Clearly, the impact of federal transfer programs existing in 1988 was to redistribute resources away from Ontario and Alberta and towards the Atlantic provinces and Québec. This information can be used to provide a crude assessment of the interregional impacts of constitutional change. For alternative one, where Québec departs from Canada, the net resources available to Québec will diminish, thus increasing the cost of government programs administered in Québec and decreasing them elsewhere. For alternative two, where Canada remains intact but there is a significant redistribution of powers and responsibilities from the federal government to the provinces, the distribution of resources among the provinces and their residents may be affected greatly. If the only redistributive program remaining as a responsibility of the federal government is equalization and if there is no change in the payments made under that program, there will be a significant movement of resources away from the Atlantic region and Québec and towards Ontario and Alberta. Likewise, under alternative three, where the country disintegrates into independent regions or provinces, this redistribution back towards Ontario and Alberta continues but to an even larger extent due to the termination of equalization. Under both of these scenarios, Atlantic Canada and Québec lose a significant net flow of resources both in total and on a per capita basis.

Finally, we must recognize that the conclusions summarized above are crude projections of potential impacts based upon a set of very restrictive assumptions. In particular, our analysis assumed that the distribution of population and economic activity across regions and provinces would remain the same after constitutional changes had been implemented. While

FIGURE 3.3: Net Redistribution Among Provinces or Regions from Federal Transfers to Provinces and Persons, 1988

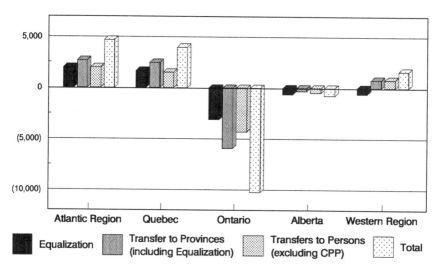

Source: See Table 3.2.

FIGURE 3.4: Per Capita Net Redistribution Among Provinces or Regions from Federal Transfers to Provinces and Persons, 1988

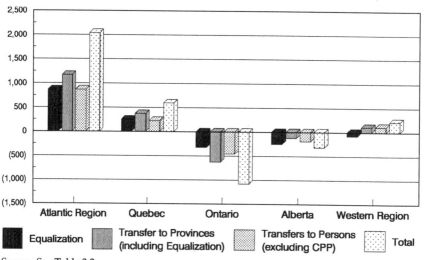

Source: See Table 3.2.

this assumption is convenient analytically, it is not necessarily realistic. In the case of Québec departing from Canada, we would expect population shifts for cultural and political reasons. In the cases of decentralization or disintegration, there may be significant population movements arising from the fiscal disparities among regions created by the termination or modification of federal transfer programs.

References

Boadway, R. & Flatters, F. (1991). Federal-provincial fiscal relations revisited: Some consequences of recent constitutional and policy developments. In M.L. McMillan (Ed.), *Provincial Public Finances: Plaudits, Problems and Prospects, Volume 2*. Toronto: Canadian Tax Foundation.

Canada. Department of Finance (1991). *The budget*, February 26, 1991. Ottawa: Supply and Services.

_____. Department of Finance (1990). *The Fiscal Equalization Program.* Mimeo, April.

_____. Department of Health and Welfare (1990). *The Canada Assistance Plan Annual Report, 1985-1986*. Ottawa: Supply and Services.

_____. Department of Health and Welfare (1990). *Family Allowances, Old Age Security and Canada Pension Plans, Report For the Year Ending March 31st, 1989*. Ottawa: Supply and Services.

Canadian Tax Foundation. (1991). *The national finances.* Toronto: Canadian Tax Foundation.

Foot, D.K. (1991). Demographic change and provincial government finances: A cause for concern?. In M.L. McMillan (Ed.), *Provincial Public Finances: Plaudits, Problems and Prospects, Volume 2*. Toronto: Canadian Tax Foundation.

Perry, J. Harvey. (1989). *A fiscal history of Canada in the postwar years.* Toronto: Canadian Tax Foundation.

Statistics Canada. (1991). *Unemployment insurance statistics annual supplement.* Ottawa: Supply and Services.

Paper prepared for the Western Centre for Economic Research conference, Alberta and the Economics of Constitutional Change, September 28, 1991, Edmonton, Alberta. This research was supported by a grant from the Western Centre for Economic Research.

Commentaries

Derek Hum, St. John's College, University of Manitoba

Bradford Reid and Tracy Snoddon focus on the pattern of redistribution among both persons and differently grouped regions under alternative constitution arrangements. They consider programs which transfer monies to provincial governments for earmarked purposes (Established Program Financing [EPF], Canada Assistance Plan [CAP]) as well as unconditionally (equalization) on the one hand, in addition to programs which directly give benefits to persons (Family Allowance [FA], Old Age Security [OAS], Canada Pension Plan [CPP], and Unemployment Insurance [UI]) on the other. They investigate, therefore, redistribution across "place" and among "persons." Three constitutional options are explored: greater centralization without Québec, greater decentralization with Québec, and finally an independent Alberta or western region, the latter comprising British Columbia, Alberta, Saskatchewan, and Manitoba. Centralization, for Reid and Snoddon, consists of assigning total financial responsibility for EPF and CAP, along with equalization, to the federal government. Decentralization assigns everything except equalization to the provinces. The sine qua non of independence is thus seen to turn on whether or not there are any equalization transfers from another order of government. This is quite logical since equalization transfers from anyone for an independent nation is tantamount to foreign aid. Within this framework, Reid and Snoddon proceed to document the extent of regional redistribution that occurs under the three alternative constitutional scenarios.

Most of the findings by Reid and Snoddon are unlikely to be challenged by all but the most fastidious nitpickers. The empirical work is informative and illuminating, and contains little that would be considered counterintuitive to those who have examined regional disparities and federal transfers before. The relative importance of federal transfers varies, as expected, by region; the Atlantic provinces being the most dependent and Alberta and Ontario being the least. Lumping all transfers together, and measuring transfers in per capita terms, the picture doesn't change much. Of special note in the present context is the fact that Québec is a net beneficiary of redistribution, while stand-alone Alberta is a net donor. This summary of results by Reid and Snoddon obviously lacks in subtlety and nuance, but given the nature of the exercise and the policy-oriented aim of the discussion, there is no sense in quibbling over the numbers. The direction and magnitude of the redistribution outlined by Reid and Snoddon is unlikely to be overturned by any reasonable reworking of the numbers.

The findings that three programs which give benefits directly to individuals (Family allowance, Old Age Security, and Canada Pension Plan) redistribute among regions is, in my judgement, less interesting or relevant to a discussion of constitutional alternatives. Reid and Snoddon assume that programs remain the same in principle and structure, and that the distribution of population and economic activity among regions also remains unaltered under different constitutional scenarios. Given this, it appears that the main determinants of redistribution in the long run have to do more with demographic factors such as the age, gender, fertility, mortality, and site of retirement of people than anything else. For example, the Family Allowance program redistributes from general taxpayers to families with children, and from higher income groups to lower income groups. Similar comments could be made for the OAS and CPP programs. Consequently, a region is a net donor to other provinces accordingly as its regional population has an above-average proportion of childless households, nonelderly individuals, above-average income taxpayers, and above-average outmigration of retirees. The authors acknowledge as much, as when they point out that redistribution for a program such as CPP is calculated on the basis of province of residence or recipient, but under either decentralized or independent regions the liability for CPP benefits would remain with the province in which the citizen earned such income and paid such premiums. In short, these programs derive their redistributive consequences from sociodemographic features and interregional mobility patterns rather than from assignment of spending responsibility to one level of government or another.

This last point is especially noteworthy since Reid and Snoddon assume that such programs would not only continue to exist under alternative constitutional arrangements but also remain constant and uniform across regions. In short, it assumes a degree of program harmonization and "national standards" that are even more stringent than presently exists. A most heroic assumption, since more decentralization and independence will inevitably lead to divergences in program design over time, even to elimination in some cases.

The Unemployment Insurance (UI) program, though still one in which transfers are directed to individuals, differs from the FA, CPP, and OAS programs in that regional economic activity levels such as unemployment and participation rates, regional growth, and the like determine redistribution rather than do demographic characteristics. Here, the issue will be the extent to which a decentralized or independent region is able to both redesign its unemployment program as well as manage its macroeconomic performance and implement an appropriate labour mobility strategy, all things well beyond the scope of Reid and Snoddon's framework. The main point is simply that UI is different in kind more than degree from FA, CPP, and OAS.

Turning to the programs involving intergovernmental transfers (EPF, CAP, and equalization) one finds again the familiar pattern of redistribution. There is a substantial net inflow of resources to the Atlantic provinces and Québec, financed primarily from Ontario and Alberta. With respect to the four western provinces, while Alberta is a net contributor, the western provinces taken together receive net inflows due to Saskatchewan and Manitoba. If one takes a narrow balance sheet approach, it is axiomatic that ridding a federation of a poorer, net recipient region (either Québec or the Atlantic provinces or both) must necessarily increase financial benefits to the remaining richer regions (Ontario, Alberta, British Columbia). Accordingly the gains to the rest of Canada are equally captured with separation by Québec or the Atlantic region, and any argument valid for Alberta on this basis holds equally for Ontario and British Columbia. More puzzling would be why an independent Alberta would want to combine with Saskatchewan and Manitoba. (Other than the wisecrack that every country should have its own Maritimes.) Reid and Snoddon certainly did not intend their careful empirical work to carry this interpretation, and neither do I. The point is that such calculations as these provided by Reid and Snoddon must be interpreted with care and common sense. They illustrate certain salient features about the current pattern of redistribution; they cannot be taken to be clinching arguments implying any constitutional arrangement.

For one thing, Reid and Snoddon are scrupulous in asserting that they are considering only certain programs, and that they are confining their examination to the years 1986 and 1988. This should alert us to the significance of other redistributive programs and the pattern of regional distribution over time. For example, Alberta (and the West) has in the past been a major beneficiary of Confederation through such devices as debt forgiveness in the thirties, the Crows Nest rates, and regulations of the oil industry before the seventies. Similarly, the point can be made that a region will benefit or contribute to its federal partners as economic circumstances change (albeit sometimes slowly), and this surely must be uppermost when considering the financial gains and redistribution patterns involved with economic confederation. The Reid and Snoddon paper is an auspicious beginning to getting the facts before the Canadian public in what promises to be an interesting debate to come.

Kenneth Norrie, University of Alberta

This paper is an interesting and useful contribution to the constitutional debate in Canada. It sets out clearly and succinctly how major federal government programs redistribute income among provinces currently and how this reallocation would be affected by each of three alternative constitutional arrangements. I will not discuss the paper in detail in these brief comments, but rather will make some general points that are suggested by their analysis.

The paper reminds us forcefully that, among its many other features, Confederation is about interregional sharing. Some of this sharing is overt and deliberate, equalization and the regionally differentiated features of unemployment insurance being the most obvious examples. But much of it is implicit, an inevitable consequence of funding national programs through a broadly progressive tax structure. Reid and Snoddon give us an indication of the extent of the implicit transfer in EPF, CAP, OAS, CPP, and the main part of the UI scheme.

The authors draw the important implication from these calculations: major constitutional change will necessarily affect both types of programs, so reconsideration of our commitment to sharing is inevitable. The point is obvious with respect to equalization, which explains why this program has been a prominent feature of most reform proposals. But little or no attention has been paid to implicit sharing, and to what is to happen to it under alternative constitutional arrangements. As this paper makes clear, the magnitudes involved are large enough to warrant serious consideration.

The implications of this point for the option of a more decentralized Canada with Québec are of particular interest. Are we prepared to accept the greater inequality among provinces that will necessarily result from complete federal government withdrawal from the major social programs? Or do we think, as some of the advocates of decentralization have suggested, that we can offset the loss of implicit redistribution by an enhanced equalization program? Do those who accept this solution really believe that a federal government that taxed Canadians mainly to pay off the national debt and make large unconditional transfers to other governments would long retain political legitimacy?

It is important to note that we face a debate about the commitment to sharing even in the absence of formal constitutional reform. Current fiscal arrangements are very much the hostage of federal government budgetary pressures. EPF is the most obvious example. With total entitlements frozen and the value of the tax point transfers increasing annually, it will not be long before federal cash transfers to provinces decline to zero. At that point, the social programs covered under EPF will be purely provincial ones, intended or not. The bite of the equalization ceiling moves that scheme further from its objective of offsetting differences in provincial fiscal capacity. The cap on CAP reduces the federal government's share of welfare spending in the three wealthiest provinces, and the sheer magnitude of the "snap back" for Ontario at least suggests it will likely never be returned to the 50% level.

The third point follows from the first two. The authors are careful to point out that they ignore the adjustments to any changes in fiscal arrangements. They are correct in doing so, given the complexity of the task they set themselves. But it is important to remember that these adjustments are potentially quite important. Capital and labour make decisions about where to locate on the basis of expected net returns. We know from a decade or more of work in the area that fiscal variables matter in these decisions. A change in interregional redistribution will affect the location of economic activity. Some reallocation may be socially efficient (that following reform of unemployment insurance is an example), but some of it (that responding to changes in net fiscal benefits) will come at a cost. It is important not to lose sight of these general equilibrium consequences.

The final set of comments concerns the apparent inequity in the conclusion that, outside the equalization program, the main redistribution appears to be from Ontario to everyone else. This is an important point to make in the West, given the perception here that Alberta and British Columbia pay for everything. But Ontario's contribution in this respect must be put against the benefit it probably receives from a number of federal government trade and industrial policies. A full-blown calculation of redistribution would take these other balances into account as well. The connection between transfers and other economic policies is important since, as Tom Courchene among others has pointed out repeatedly, Ontario's willingness to finance interregional transfers may well wane as continental and international economic ties replace internal ones.

Taxation under Alternative Constitutional Arrangements

by Bev Dahlby

Introduction

This paper is concerned with the effects of alternative constitutional arrangements on taxation in Canada. The primary focus is on the allocation of federal and provincial tax powers. The paper contains an overview of the Canadian tax system and outlines the normative economic analysis of the allocation of revenue sources in a federal system of government. The final section of the paper considers how the tax system might evolve under three constitutional scenarios—a more centralized Canada without Québec, a more decentralized federal system which includes Québec, and an independent Alberta. The constitutional changes are considered in terms of their impact on the residents of Alberta.

I do not reach any conclusions regarding the relative merits of the three constitutional scenarios. There are a number of reasons for adopting an agnostic stance. First, each of the scenarios would involve changes in the level of taxation in Alberta, the proportion of revenue collected from each of the major taxes, and changes in the design of the various taxes. Individual Albertans would be affected in different ways by these tax changes depending their income levels, the sources of the income, and how they spend it. Thus, the endorsement of a particular scenario must involve some value judgements, which I am not qualified to make. Second, in assessing any new constitutional arrangement, the allocation of taxation powers must be considered along with the allocation of expenditure and regulatory powers as well as its effect on the economic union, the protection of civil liberties, and the promotion of peace, order, and good government. Some, but not all, of these issue are dealt with in the other papers presented at this conference. Third, the scenarios which are considered in the papers presented at this conference were selected because they involve different directions for constitutional reform, and it is hoped that by discussing some concrete cases we can provoke thought and discussion about our constitutional options. However, the actual constitutional arrangements that will emerge for serious consideration in the next year will likely depart from these scenarios in number of ways. It seems pointless to devote a great deal of energy to weighing the pros and cons of these scenarios when they probably will not be serious contenders when the constitutional negotiations begin in earnest. Hopefully, the sections of this paper which contain the overview of the current system of taxation and the discussion of the economic principles regarding the allocation of tax powers will serve as useful background for the analysis of whatever constitutional changes are eventually proposed.

How important is the allocation of tax powers between the federal and provincial governments in the overall question of constitutional reform? Judging from the lack of attention that it has received in the official documents and the academic papers that have emerged since the failure of the Meech Lake Accord, one would conclude that taxation is not perceived to be very important. For example, the Allaire report devotes considerable attention to the division of expenditure responsibilities between the federal government and the province, but has very little to say on the division of tax powers.

Should more attention be paid to the issue of taxation in the current round of constitutional negotiations? Obviously, I have a biased opinion on this matter, but I would like to make three points. First, the historical importance of taxation in constitutional reform is evident, especially when one recognizes that constitutional reform in other societies has frequently coincided with major political revolutions. Taxation figures prominently in the list of causes of the English civil war, the American Revolution, and the French Revolution. It was Mirabeau, one of the leaders of the French Revolution, who concluded that:[27]

> in the final analysis the people will judge the [French] revolution by this fact alone—does it take more or less money? Are they better off? Do they have more work? And is that work better paid?

---

27. Quoted in Schama(1989, p. 537).

If the French Revolution, which marked the end of feudal privileges and obligations and produced emotional declarations concerning the equality of men and their inalienable rights, was judged as a success or failure by the "sans culotte in the street" on the basis of whether his taxes went up or down, then is it not possible that our own constitutional reforms will be judged by the same criterion? Second, the public's increasing concern about the level and distribution of the tax burden is evident in the rise of such groups as the Alberta Federation of Taxpayers and the Taxpayers Coalition of Ontario. The public may see taxation as a major constitutional issue even if most politicians and academics do not. Third, it seems clear that under any new constitutional arrangements in which Canada remains a federal country there are going to be major federal-provincial conflicts over tax policy in the years ahead as all governments struggle with reducing their chronic deficits.

An Overview of Taxation in Canada

International Comparisons of the Level and Composition of Tax Revenues
Some international comparisons help to put the level of taxation in Canada in relation to the size of the Canadian economy in some perspective. Figure 4.1 shows tax revenues as a proportion of Gross Domestic Product (GDP) for Canada and the other G7 countries in 1988. Note that Canada's ratio of tax revenues to GDP, 34.0%, exceeded that of Japan and the United States, but was below the European G7 countries and the OECD average of 38.4%. (The highest ratio of taxes to GDP in the OECD in 1988 was Sweden at 55.3%.) Thus, Figure 4.1 indicates that taxpayers in many other OECD countries are surrendering a higher proportion of their incomes to their governments.

Figure 4.2 shows the percentage of tax revenues collected from various sources for the G7 countries and the OECD average. While the proportion of tax revenues collected on the basis of personal income is relatively high in Canada, social security contributions—such as pension, unemployment, and health insurance contributions — are relatively low. In particular, note that when personal income and social insurance contributions are combined, the Canadian percentage of 49.9 is below the OECD average of 55.0%. Note also that the United States obtains a much larger proportion of revenues from social security contributions and a correspondingly smaller share from taxes on goods and services. Canada's reliance on taxation of goods is similar to that of the European G7 countries and the average for OECD countries. The share of tax revenues obtained in Canada from taxes on corporations is almost the same as in the United States and slightly higher than the OECD average. The one area where the Canadian tax structure appears to depart

FIGURE 4.1:
Tax Revenue: Percentage of GDP in 1988

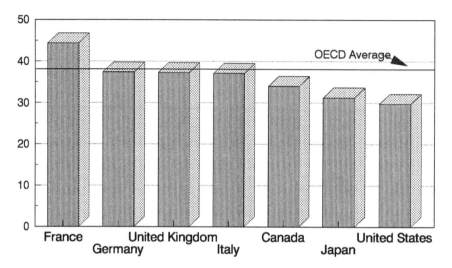

Source: Table 1, Perry (1990).

FIGURE 4.2:
International Comparisons of the Composition
of Tax Revenues in 1988 (percent)

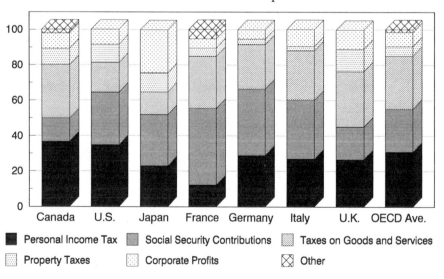

Source: Table 2, Perry (1990)

significantly from the OECD average is with regard to taxes on property. Our greater reliance on property taxation reflects the fact that local governments play a more important role in Canada than in many European countries. Overall, Figure 4.2 indicates that the Canadian tax mix is similar to the OECD average, except that we rely more heavily on property taxation and finance social insurance programs to a greater extent with the personal income tax.

Federal and Provincial Government Revenues

The BNA Act gave the federal government the power to raise revenue "by any mode or system of taxation." The provinces were empowered "to levy direct taxation within the province." The distinction between direct and indirect taxation has been interpreted according to the definitions propounded by J.S. Mill:

> A direct tax is one which is demanded from the very person who it is intended or desired should pay it. Indirect taxes are those which are demanded from one person in the expectation and intention that he shall indemnify himself at the expense of another; such are the excise or customs.[28]

At the time of Confederation, most tax revenues were from excises and customs duties, and therefore the provinces were restricted to the minor and relatively "unpalatable" tax revenue sources. However, the importance of the income taxes has increased dramatically in this century and, as LaForest (1967, p. 161) has noted, judicial interpretation of the concept of direct taxation has expanded the tax powers of the provinces to include "almost every type of tax except customs duties and taxes having primary impact outside the taxing province."

The composition of federal and provincial-local government revenues are shown in Tables 4.1 and 4.2.[29] From Table 4.1, note that the personal income tax (PIT) has become an increasingly important source of tax revenue for the federal government in recent years, and generated almost half of its tax revenues in 1989. Consumption taxes, comprised of general sales taxes, excise taxes, and customs duties, were the second largest source of federal tax revenue. These revenues declined in importance over the period 1975-1985, but then rapidly increased in importance in the 1985-1989 period.

---

28. J.S. Mill, *Principles of Political Economy*, 5 vols. (Toronto: University of Toronto Press, 1965), 2. Quoted by LaForest(1967, p. 63).

29. For more comprehensive discussions of federal government and provincial government revenues, see Canadian Tax Foundation(1990, 1991), Ip(1991), and McMillan(1991).

TABLE 4.1:
The Composition of Federal Government Revenues

	1975	1980	1985	1989
Personal Income Taxes	38.85%	39.60%	39.82%	43.90%
Corporation Income Tax	16.04%	15.34%	12.02%	10.71%
Tax on Payments to Non-Residents	1.42%	1.74%	1.31%	1.44%
Consumption Taxes	22.70%	21.28%	18.53%	24.05%
Social Insurance Levies	5.54%	6.17%	9.76%	10.28%
Petroleum and Natural Gas Taxes	0.00%	2.54%	7.86%	0.10%
Other Miscellaneous Taxes	5.56%	0.90%	0.59%	0.62%
Natural Resource Revenue	0.07%	0.08%	0.23%	0.05%
Privileges, Licences, and Permits	0.08%	0.14%	0.15%	0.20%
Sales of Goods and Services	3.20%	3.88%	3.01%	2.61%
Return on Investments	6.25%	7.52%	5.80%	5.09%
Other Revenue	0.30%	0.83%	0.91%	0.90%
Total Gross General Revenue	100.00%	100.00%	100.00%	100.00%

Notes: Calculations based on Cansim Matrix 2777.

TABLE 4.2:
The Composition of Provincial-Local Revenues in Canada

	1975	1980	1985	1989
Personal Income Taxes	16.60%	17.66%	18.41%	21.19%
Corporate Income Taxes	5.40%	4.80%	3.40%	4.12%
Property Taxes	14.73%	13.00%	13.17%	13.08%
Consumption Taxes	14.76%	12.40%	14.80%	15.97%
Social Insurance Levies	4.56%	4.88%	5.76%	6.02%
Miscellaneous Taxes	1.10%	1.49%	1.97%	2.79%
Natural Resource Revenues	6.72%	9.79%	6.50%	3.47%
Privileges, Licences, and Permits	2.74%	2.31%	2.04%	2.23%
Sales of Goods and Services	4.43%	5.44%	5.48%	5.14%
Return of Investment	6.94%	8.42%	9.01%	8.30%
Transfers from the Federal Govt	20.82%	17.72%	17.81%	16.07%
Transfers from Govt Enterprises	0.27%	0.39%	0.54%	0.51%
Other Revenue	0.93%	1.71%	1.13%	1.10%
Total Revenue	100.00%	100.00%	100.00%	100.00%

Notes: Calculations based on Cansim Matrix 3146.

The share of revenue from the payroll taxes and premiums used to finance social insurance programs doubled over the 1975-1989 period and in 1989 were almost as large as corporate income tax revenues which declined in importance over this period.[30] Finally, the petroleum and gas revenue tax, which was cancelled in October 1986, was a significant source of tax revenue for the federal government in the early 1980s.

Table 4.2 shows the composition of revenues for provincial and local governments. Since we are principally concerned with the division of powers between the two orders of government in Canada, the provincial and local government revenues have been combined. This consolidation is also important for the interprovincial comparisons of taxation that are made in some of the subsequent tables. As in the case of the federal government, the personal income tax and consumption taxes were the largest sources of tax revenue for the provincial-local government sector in 1989. The main differences in the composition of revenues of the two orders of government are that the provincial-local sector obtained a substantial amount of revenue from transfers from the federal government and from the property tax. Note that as a percentage of provincial-local government revenue, transfers from the federal government declined from over 20% in 1975 to 16% in 1989. The trends in the composition of provincial-local tax revenues are broadly similar to those of the federal government with the personal income tax, consumption taxes and social insurance levies becoming more important and the corporate income tax and the property tax becoming less important.[31] It is also interesting to note that the sale of goods and services is a more important component of total revenue for the provincial-local government sector than it is for the federal government. Whether this indicates a greater willingness, or a greater opportunity, to employ user charges to finance expenditures is difficult to say.

With the exception of the property tax, the main sources tax revenue for the federal and provincial governments are shared, i.e. their tax bases overlap. Table 4.3 shows the provincial-local government sector's share of total government revenues from the various tax sources. Note that in 1989 the provincial-local sector received just under two-thirds of total government revenues while only imposing about 48% of the taxes. The difference between these percentages is primarily due to the federal transfers to the provincial governments. The provincial-local sector received about 38% of

---

30. Douglas(1990) has concluded that the primary reason for the relative decline in corporate income tax revenues was a decline in profitability. A similar conclusion was reached by Auerbach and Poterba(1987) in their analysis of U.S. corporate income tax.

31. See Smith(1990b) for a discussion of trends in property taxation.

TABLE 4.3:
The Provincial-Local Government Sectors' Share of Taxes and Revenues

	1975	1980	1985	1989
Personal Income Tax	33.59%	38.35%	38.57%	38.63%
Corporate Income Tax	26.68%	30.70%	30.46%	34.43%
Total Consumption Taxes	44.58%	46.16%	50.40%	47.00%
General Sales Taxes	51.07%	53.36%	55.60%	51.39%
Motive Fuel Taxes	78.13%	80.43%	80.92%	57.26%
Alcohol and Tobacco	19.04%	33.97%	41.21%	40.01%
Social Insurance Levies	47.55%	52.39%	43.75%	47.57%
Total Taxes	43.23%	46.31%	47.62%	48.31%
Total Revenue	62.43%	66.15%	66.09%	63.90%

Notes: Calculations based on Cansim Matrices 3146 and 3159.

personal income taxes in 1989, which was about the same share that it received in 1980. It received about one third of the corporate income tax revenues in 1989, and its share of this revenue source increased by about eight percentage points over the 1975-1989 period. Consumption tax revenues and social insurance levies were almost evenly divided between the federal and the provincial-local government sector in 1989. It is interesting to note the divergent trends in the provincial-local government's shares the motive fuel and alcohol and tobacco taxes. Its share of the former decreased dramatically over the 1985-1989 period while its share of the latter increased, especially over the 1975-1985 period.

Interprovincial Comparisons of Per Capita Revenues and Fiscal Capacity
Indices of the per capita revenue obtained from the personal income tax (PIT), consumption taxes (CT), property taxes (PT), social insurance (SI) levies, corporate income tax (CIT), natural resources (NR), by the provincial and local governments in each of the provinces in 1989 are shown in Figures 4.3 (a) to 4.3 (f). The figures indicate that there were substantial variations in the per capita tax yields collected in different provinces. For example, with the national average per capita revenue equalling 100:

- the PIT index varied from 54 in Newfoundland to 119 in Québec,

- the CT index varied from 23 in Alberta to 120 in Newfoundland,

- the CIT index varied from 34 in Newfoundland and PEI to 156 in Ontario,

- the NR revenue index varied from a value of 1 for PEI to 601 for Alberta.

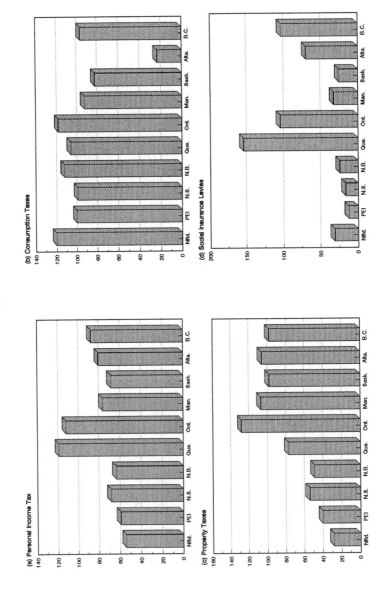

FIGURE 4.3: Indexes of Provincial Per Capita Revenue in 1989 (National Average = 100)

FIGURE 4.3 (continued): Indexes of Provincial Per Capita Revenue in 1989 (National Average = 100)

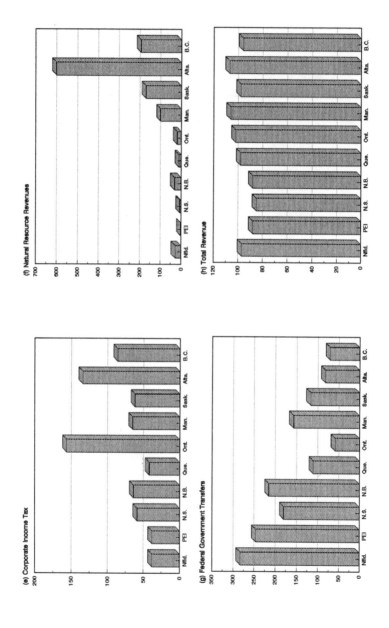

Figure 4.3(c) indicates that revenues from property taxes were relatively high in Ontario and the western provinces, and Figure 4.3(d) indicates that SI levies were especially high in Québec and relatively low in Atlantic Canada, Manitoba, and Saskatchewan.

Figure 4.3(h) indicates that there was relatively little variation in per capita total revenue, with Alberta having the highest index at 107 and Nova Scotia registering the lowest at 85,[32] in spite of the substantial variation in tax yields because of the equalizing effect of the federal government's transfers (FGT) to the provinces which are shown in Figure 4.3(g). While all of the provinces received some transfers from the federal government, especially through the Established Program Financing (EPF) and Canada Assistance Plan (CAP) grants, Figure 4.3(g) indicates that Atlantic provinces, Manitoba, and Saskatchewan received substantially larger amounts in per capita terms. The federal equalization grants which Québec and the other "have-not" provinces receive are one of the main factors in narrowing the range of per capita revenues among the provinces. Note that Québec's per capita federal transfer in 1989 was only slightly above the national average. This is slightly misleading because Québec receives some additional implicit transfers through the transfer of "tax room" in lieu of grants for health services under EPF, CAP payments, and youth allowances.[33]

The variations in per capita tax revenues shown in Figure 4.3 are the result of variations in tax bases (or fiscal capacity) and tax rates (or tax effort). For example, Newfoundland had the highest index for consumption tax revenue because of its relatively high rates of taxation, and not because its sales and excise taxes bases are high.[34]

Figure 4.4 shows indices of fiscal capacity for the provinces based on their own revenue sources. Alberta had the highest fiscal capacity in 1987-88 with an index of 145.6 and Newfoundland had the lowest with an index of 60.4, with the national average fiscal capacity having a value of 100.

The remainder of this section of the paper will focus on the PIT tax and CIT. Particular attention is paid to these taxes because the PIT is the largest source of tax revenue for the federal and provincial governments and because the CIT has potentially important effects the allocation of investment among the provinces. Particular attention is paid to the tax sources in Québec and Ontario because if Québec separates part of the current tax base of the

---

32. The Alberta index was much higher in earlier years. For example, in 1980 the index of total revenue per capita in Alberta was 172.

33. See Canadian Tax Foundation (1991, Table 16.1).

34. Only in the area of beer sales does Newfoundland appear to have an above average fiscal capacity.

FIGURE 4.4:
Indexes of Fiscal Capacity, 1987-88
(National Average = 100)

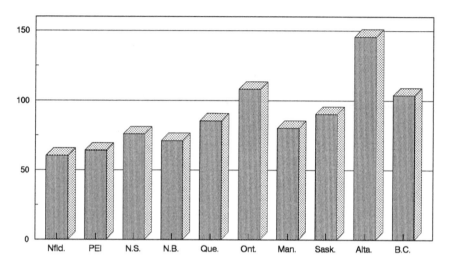

Note: Fiscal capacity based on provincial own source revenues.

Source: Dept. of Finance (1990)

federal government will be eliminated, and this will affect the rates of
taxation that will be required to cover federal expenditures in the rest of
Canada. Attention is also paid to the Ontario tax base because, under the
scenario of Québec independence, Ontario will account for about half of the
population, and it will have a dominant influence on tax policy.

The Personal Income Tax

The PIT Rates
The federal government administers the collection of the personal income for
all of the provinces, except Québec which maintains its own personal income
tax collection system.[35] This system has resulted in a high degree of tax
harmonization because the other nine provinces use the federal defined PIT
base in levying their personal income taxes. The provinces that are part of the
tax collection agreement set their tax rates as a percentage of the basic federal
tax levied on a taxpayer. The provincial rates for 1991 are shown in Table 4.4.

35. See Courchene and Stewart(1991) for a discussion of the PIT collection agreements.

TABLE 4.4:
Provincial Tax Rates, 1991

	Personal Income Tax	Retail Sales Tax	Corporate Income Tax
Newfoundland	62.0	12.0	17.0
Prince Edward Island	57.0	10.0	15.0
Nova Scotia	59.5	10.0	16.0
New Brunswick	60.0	11.0	16.0
Quebec	—	8.0	6.3
Ontario	53.0	8.0	15.5
Manitoba	52.0	7.0	17.0
Saskatchewan	50.0	7.0	15.0
Alberta	46.5	0.0	15.5
British Columbia	51.5	6.0	14.0

Source: Government of Alberta, Budget Address, 1991.

In addition, individual provinces impose surcharges and flat taxes as well as provide tax reductions, deductions, and credits that are administered by the federal government for a fee which covers the additional collection costs. The existence of these additional tax measures, which vary from province to province, means that the PIT rates shown in Table 4.4 may be misleading, and they can also change the progressivity of the provincial taxes because the tax reductions are directed to low income taxpayers and the surcharges are imposed on high income taxpayers.

Figure 4.5 shows the federal and provincial PIT rates as a percentage of total assessed income in 1988.[36] The average federal income tax rate varies from 13.7% in Ontario to 10.6% in PEI because the progressivity of the federal PIT rate structure means that higher average tax rates are imposed in provinces with higher average incomes. The average provincial tax rates reflect the provincial tax rate on basic federal tax payable plus the surtaxes and flat taxes levied by the provinces. Note that the highest average provincial PIT rates were imposed by Manitoba and Saskatchewan, in spite of the fact that they had the fifth and seventh highest basic rates in 1988, because they imposed relatively high flat taxes.

36. Total assessed income is equal to the total income figure on the income tax return. It does not include certain types of income such as workers' compensation, social assistance, guaranteed income supplement, and lottery winnings. Dividend income is gross-up to include 125% of the actual amount paid to the taxpayer and capital gains include only 66.67% of the gain realized.

FIGURE 4.5:
PIT Rates as a Percentage of Assessed Income, 1988 (percent)

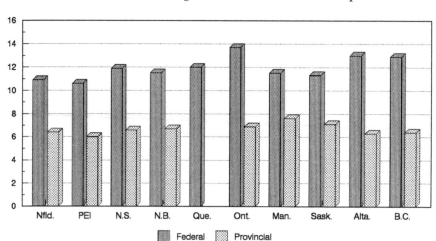

Note: The Quebec provincial tax rate is not shown.

Source: Table 8, Perry (1991)

The PIT Bases

Figure 4.6 shows that Québec accounted for 22.73% of total assessed income under the federal PIT in 1988 while its population share was 25%. Ontario's share of total assessed income was 42.78%, Alberta's share was 9.17%, and the combined share of the other provinces was 25.32%. In the absence of Québec, Ontario would have about 50% of the population and about 55% of the federal government's PIT base.

Labour income accounted for around 75% of total assessed income under the federal income tax in Québec, Ontario, and Alberta in 1988. Income from transfers was relatively more important in Québec, and capital income was somewhat more important in Ontario, but overall the composition of the PIT base was very similar in the three provinces.

Figure 4.7 shows how the distribution of assessed income varied by income group in Québec, Ontario, and Alberta in 1988. The proportion of returns with incomes less than a given amount was higher in Québec than in Alberta and higher in Alberta than in Ontario. In other words, Ontario had a higher proportion of well-to-do taxpayers than Alberta which, in turn, had a higher proportion of well-to-do taxpayers than Québec.

FIGURE 4.6:
The Shares of Total Assessed Income under the Federal PIT

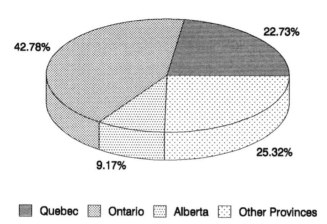

42.78%

22.73%

9.17%

25.32%

■ Quebec ■ Ontario ▦ Alberta ▦ Other Provinces

Source: Revenue Canada, Taxation Statistics, 1988

FIGURE 4.7:
Cumulative Proportion of Returns by Income Group, 1988
(cumulative proportion of returns)

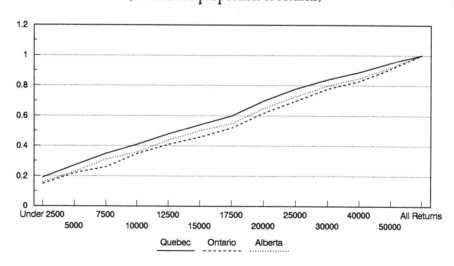

The Corporate Income Tax

The CIT Rates
The federal government receives approximately two-thirds of the total corporate income tax revenues. It collects the CIT levied by seven of the ten provinces. The corporate income tax bases of the three provinces that administer their own corporate income tax—Alberta, Ontario, and Québec—are very similar to the federal CIT base, and therefore the Canadian CIT displays a relatively high degree of tax base harmonization.[37] Table 4.4 shows the standard provincial corporate income tax rates.[38] However, the federal government and the provinces impose lower rates of taxation for small businesses and firms in manufacturing and processing. Figure 4.8 shows the combined federal and provincial CIT rates for small business, manufacturing and other. Note that the rates in Québec for small business and manufacturing are quite a bit lower than in the other provinces and that (excluding Québec) the variation in rates within each category is relatively small.

The effective tax rates on corporate profits depend not only on the statutory rates which were shown in Table 4.4, but also on the capital cost allowance, investment tax credits, and other provisions of the CIT system. The average effective rate of taxation for 10 industrial categories is shown in Figure 4.9. Note that the lowest rate of taxation in 1987 was in agriculture, forestry, and fishing (AFF) at 14.7% and the highest was in transportation, communications and other utilities (TCU) at 33.5%. Note that the average effective rate of taxation in the mining sector (which includes the oil and gas industry) was one percentage lower than the average effective rate in manufacturing.

The CIT Bases
Table 4.5 shows the distribution among the provinces of taxable corporate income by industry in 1986-87. Ontario had relatively large shares of corporate taxable income arising from manufacturing, the wholesale industry, and finance. Alberta accounted for just over 70% of the total taxable corporate income in the mining sector and a relatively large share of taxable corporate income from transportation, communications and other utilities. Québec's share of taxable corporate income was below its population share for all industries except construction, the wholesale and retail sector, and manufacturing. In 1986-87, Ontario accounted for 43.6% of total taxable corporate income. Excluding Québec, Ontario's share was 56.6%.

---

37. See Bossons(1991) on the provincial corporate income tax systems.

38. Québec imposes a higher rate for inactive business income.

FIGURE 4.8:
Federal and Provincial CIT Rates, 1990 (percent)

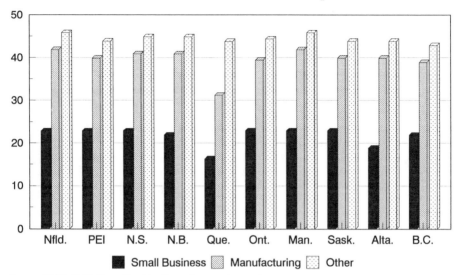

Source: Table 7.25, Canadian Tax Foundation, National Finances (1991)

FIGURE 4.9:
Combined Federal and Provincial CIT as a Percentage of Book Profit
Before Tax in 1987 (percent)

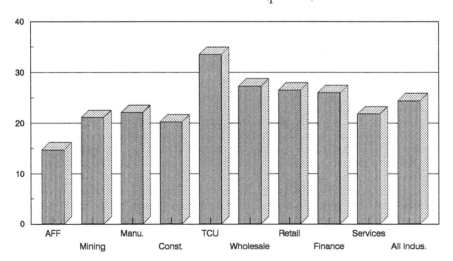

Notes: For corporations reporting positive book profits.

Source: Table XVII, Corporate Tax Statistics (1987).

TABLE 4.5:
The Shares of Taxable Corporate Income by Industry in 1986-1987

	Quebec	Ontario	Alberta	Other Provinces
Agriculture, Forestry, and Fishing	19.08%	27.10%	12.42%	41.40%
Mining	2.74%	9.73%	71.07%	16.46%
Manufacturing	25.48%	51.13%	7.81%	15.58%
Construction	29.82%	44.15%	8.63%	17.40%
Transportation, Communication, and Other Utilities	19.73%	35.46%	21.08%	23.73%
Wholesale	28.41%	46.14%	7.86%	17.59%
Retail	27.53%	39.49%	9.80%	23.18%
Finance	21.43%	47.91%	9.25%	21.41%
Services	22.56%	43.56%	14.84%	19.04%
Total for all Industries	22.99%	43.62%	14.36%	19.03%

Notes: Calculations based on *Corporation Taxation Statistics*, 1987, Table 5, pp. 88-107.

Assigning Tax Revenue Sources in a Federal System

Functions to be Performed by the Tax System
Before discussing the principles underlying the assignment of tax revenue sources in a federal state, it is useful to review the functions that we want the tax system to perform. The main functions of the tax system are:

- to generate revenue so that governments can purchase the resources necessary to provide the goods and services for the public;

- to generate revenue so that governments can make income transfers to those individuals who are judged to be in need of assistance; and

- to alter the allocation of resources in the economy if the market fails to perform this task adequately.

Governments can obtain command over resources by other means, such as by borrowing funds, expanding the money supply, conscripting resources, or charging for the use of public services. The first **three** methods of finance are used by governments to some extent, but they are generally inferior to taxation on efficiency and equity grounds and cannot be relied on to finance all government activities for an extended period. While user charges are an attractive way of financing government programs, they cannot be utilized to finance all government expenditures because:

- some public services, such as defence and public health measures, are pure public goods which cannot be sold because everyone in a particular area benefits from these goods whether or not they pay for them, and

- user charges cannot be used to pay for welfare services and other government programs which are aimed at the redistribution of income.

One of the major responsibilities of government is the redistribution of income. The provision of a social safety net is an essential activity of government because private voluntary charitable activity will almost invariably fail to provide adequately for the poor because of the free rider problem. In the absence of government transfers of income to the least well-off groups in our society, there is no strong ethical foundation for the private ownership of property and a free market economy. The social safety net provides the "glue" which holds our society together and makes democracy compatible with free markets.

Income transfers can either be made through expenditure programs, such as social assistance or family allowance payments, or through the tax system, such as occurs with the child tax credit or the sales tax credit. The combination of an income transfer program and the taxation of benefits under the PIT, such as occurs with respect to Old Age Security Payments, permits greater targeting of transfers. The integration of transfer programs and the personal income tax system, such as occurs under a negative income tax scheme, would make possible a comprehensive income redistribution program that would help the "working poor" as well as those who are unable to earn income. The tax system provides a potent tool for redistributing income.

The tax system can also be used to alter the allocation of resources if it is felt that private markets do not allocate resources properly. For example, the tax system provides incentives for charitable activity, research and development, investment, regional development, and pollution abatement. However, unless there is strong evidence to the contrary, most economists feel that the private sector allocates resources in an efficient manner, and under these circumstances, the tax system should minimize its impact on the allocation of resources in the economy.

Criteria for Evaluating Tax Systems

The criteria that economists normally use to appraise the merits of a tax system are the following:

- the tax system should promote economic efficiency;

- the tax system should be fair;

- taxes should be visible; and

- tax collection and compliance costs should be low.

The first criteria implies that the allocation of resources should not be distorted by the tax system except where there is good reason to think the allocation of resources by the private sector will be unsatisfactory. Equity in taxation means that the tax burden should rise at an appropriate rate as the taxpayers' ability to pay rises, and that taxpayers who are otherwise equal should pay equal amounts in taxes. The first characteristic is called vertical equity and relies on value judgements concerning the appropriate degree of progressivity. The second characteristic is called horizontal equity and requires judgements concerning situations when two taxpayers are sufficiently similar that their tax payments should be the same. Visibility helps taxpayers know how much they are paying in taxes. This permits taxpayers to make informed judgements about what the tax mix should be and to weigh the cost of additional taxation against the gain from additional government expenditures. Low tax collection and compliance costs mean that the tax system should be kept as simple as possible with the various governments coordinating their tax collection measures.

These four characteristics provide the basis for normative evaluations of alternative tax assignments in a federation. Each characteristic is intrinsically desirable. Unfortunately, there are conflicts in achieving these goals, and it is frequently necessary to give up, to some extent, one characteristic in order to achieve more of another.

Efficient Taxation and The Marginal Cost of Public Funds

Most of the discussion about the optimal assignment of taxation powers in a federation revolves around questions of economic efficiency, and therefore I will discuss in some detail the efficiency issue.

Taxes have efficiency costs when they cause firms to change their production techniques or product mix, or when they cause households to alter their consumption, savings, or labour supply decision relative to what they would be under an equal yield lump-sum tax. The more the tax system distorts the pattern of production and consumption, the greater the efficiency loss from taxation.

We can think of the total value of the goods and services and leisure consumed in an economy as the private-consumption economic pie. When the government imposes taxes, it reduces the size of the economic pie that is available for private consumption. For every dollar collected, the private sector's economic pie will normally shrink by more than one dollar because of the distortions in consumption and production decisions that the taxes induce. Economists call the difference between the shrinkage of the private-consumption economic pie and the tax revenue collected the deadweight loss from taxation.

Two important aspects of the deadweight loss from taxation should be stressed. First, the deadweight loss increases with the square of the tax rate. Therefore, to collect a given amount of revenue, it is generally better to impose taxes at low rates on broad range of goods and services than to impose high rates of taxation on a small range of goods and services (assuming that all goods and services have the same elasticities of demand and supply). In other words, broad-based taxes are generally more efficient than taxes with narrower bases. One of the reasons why governments throughout the world have, in recent years, broadened their income tax bases and lowered their income tax rates is to reap the efficiency gains that come from collecting the same revenue at lower tax rates.

There are two other interesting implications of the fact that the deadweight loss from taxation increases with the square of the tax rate. The first is that there may be gains from tax rate harmonization. Keen(1987) has shown that if two regions start with different arbitrary sets of commodity taxes, there will be a net efficiency gain if each region adjusts its tax rates toward a weighted average of the initial tax rates. This results because the average efficiency loss incurred by each region at the initial arbitrary set of tax rates exceeds the efficiency loss that each region would sustain at the average tax rate. The implications of this result for tax harmonization in a federation are less obvious if the pre-harmonization tax rates are not arbitrary and have been set in response to local economic conditions in order to diminish the deadweight loss from taxation.

The second implication has to do with the desirability of running a counter-cyclical budget deficit. If a government is faced with fluctuations in its expenditure requirements or in its tax bases, it may be desirable to maintain a relatively constant tax rate, instead of varying the tax rate to maintain a balanced budget, because the deadweight loss incurred at the average tax rate required to finance expenditures over the cycle may be less than the average deadweight loss that would be incurred if tax rates were varied to maintain a balanced budget. This argument for "tax rate smoothing," which has been developed by Barro(1979, 1989), implies a counter-cyclical fiscal policy which is often associated with Keynesian economics, although the justification in this case for it is quite different.

It should also be noted that the deadweight loss per dollar of revenue becomes larger as more revenue is raised because the deadweight loss from taxation increases with the square of the tax rate, whereas tax revenues do

not increase in proportion to tax rate increase because the tax base is usually
smaller at a higher tax rate. This has obviously important implications for the
amount of public expenditures that a government should undertake.

A second important characteristic of the deadweight losses from taxation
are that they are smaller when the demand and supply responses to taxation
are smaller. Those commodities with relatively inelastic demand and supply
should be taxed at higher rates if the efficiency loss from taxation is to be
minimized. Since many necessities, such as food and housing, have relatively
inelastic demands, and since luxuries, which are mainly consumed by the
rich, generally have high elasticities of demand, minimizing the efficiency
loss from taxation would imply high tax rates on necessities and low tax
rates on luxuries. This would obviously lead to a regressive tax system. Thus,
policy-makers are frequently faced with a trade-off between a more efficient
tax structure and a less progressive distribution of the tax burden.

One way of measuring the efficiency cost of obtaining tax revenue from
different sources is to calculate the cost to the economy of raising an
additional dollar from that revenue source. This is called the marginal cost of
public funds (MCPF) and can be defined in terms of the following
equation:[39]

$$MCPF \quad = \quad \frac{\Delta E}{\Delta R}$$

where ΔE is the change in private expenditure, and ΔR is the change in
revenues, as a result of a small tax rate increase. By way of illustrating the
concept of the MCPF, consider the following results from a study by
Hamilton and Whalley(1989) which calculated the MCPF for three different
types of sales taxes using a model of the Canadian economy in 1980:

		MCPF
•	Comprehensive Sales Tax	1.07
•	Retail Sales Tax	1.16
•	Manufacturers Sales Tax	1.34

The lower MCPF for the comprehensive sales tax compared with the
retail sales tax or the manufacturers sales tax indicates that it is the most
efficient of the three taxes, and there would be a net efficiency gain by

---

39. The negative sign is included in the expression in order to define the MCPF as a positive
    number because the change in private expenditures will normally be negative and the
    change in revenue will normally be positive.

switching to that form of taxation (assuming that the collection costs were similar). The MCPF from comprehensive sales tax was lower than for the other two taxes because its broader base means that it could be applied at a lower rate. It also distorted the relative prices of services and other products, or manufactured goods and other products, to a lesser degree than the retail sales tax or the manufacturers sales tax.

The concept of the MCPF provides a convenient way of characterizing an efficient tax system in a federation. The following efficiency conditions are those which a "benevolent dictator" would try to satisfy if the dictator could set all of the tax rates and expenditure levels by all of the governments in the federation and regarded all individuals as equally deserving of an additional dollar of income:

- each government should set its tax rates such that the MCPF is the same for all of its revenue sources;

- each government should extend its public services until the marginal benefit from spending tax revenue equals its MCPF;

- intergovernmental transfers should be made until the MCPF is the same for all governments in the federation.

The first condition ensures that each government has the optimal tax mix such that the cost of raising a given level of tax revenue is minimized. The second condition ensures that optimal mix of public and private sector outputs is obtained. The third condition ensures that a fiscal balance prevails in the federation. Without it, there may be "too much" government expenditure in one jurisdiction and "too little" expenditure in other jurisdictions, or "excessive" taxation in one jurisdiction and "overly lenient" taxation in another jurisdiction. To achieve this fiscal balance, it will generally be necessary to have a system of intergovernmental transfers because different governments will have tax bases of differing sizes with different degrees of responsiveness to taxation, have different demographic characteristics which will affect the marginal benefit from public expenditures, or have different costs of providing public services.

Fiscal Externalities and the Marginal Cost of Public Funds

The preceding discussion shows how an efficient tax system can be characterized using the concept of the marginal cost of public funds derived from taxation. It assumed a coordinated approach to public sector decision-making since a benevolent dictator sets all tax rates and expenditure levels, and it assumed that the optimal assignment of tax bases to the various governments in the federation had been made. In this section, the problems that may arise from uncoordinated tax policy in a federal system of government are discussed. Then in the next section, the optimal assignment of taxation powers will be considered.

Uncoordinated tax policy can create problems in a federal system of government because of the interaction of the governments' tax bases. When the tax policy of one government impinges on the well-being of taxpayers in another jurisdiction or affects the tax revenues of another government, then a fiscal externality is said to exist. Problems in the application of tax policy occur if, as will be assumed, each government is only concerned with the additional cost to its own taxpayers in raising an additional dollar of revenue for itself. By ignoring the impact of its tax policies on the well-being of taxpayers outside its jurisdiction or the tax revenues received by other governments, the MCPF that a government uses to set its taxation and expenditure policies will generally be different from its actual MCPF. In other words, governments may misconstrue either the numerator or the denominator of the expression for the MCPF in equation (1). If this is the case, the governments' tax and expenditure policies will not satisfy efficiency conditions.[40]

The three general types of fiscal externality are noted as follows:[41]

- tax exportation

- tax base mobility

- tax base overlap

Each type of externality will be discussed below.

Tax exportation occurs when some, or all, of the burden of a tax is borne by individuals or firms who do not reside in the jurisdiction which imposed the tax. Examples of tax exportation are hotel taxes which are borne by tourists from another jurisdiction or payroll taxes which cause the price of an exported product to increase. For this type of tax shifting to occur, the export demand for the industry's product must not be completely elastic. Another way in which tax exportation can occur is if the taxes that are imposed by one government are a deduction or a credit in calculating the taxes due another government. Consequently, increases in the revenues of one

---

40. An analogous problem exists in the private sector when firms pollute the environment. The market mechanism may not force them to take into account the costs that they impose on others in making their production and investment decisions.

41. A fourth type of fiscal externality which is not dealt with in this paper is the benefit spillover from public expenditure programs.

government come at the expense of another government and will oblige it to raise its taxes to compensate for its loss of revenue. An example of this type of tax exportation occurs when a province imposes a capital tax which is deductible from the federal corporate income tax.

Tax exportation causes governments to underestimate the total MCPF because they either neglect part of the cost of their taxes (since they are borne outside of their jurisdiction) or they overestimate the change in revenue from a tax increase because they neglect the decline in revenues incurred by other governments. Thus, tax exportation may result in excessive utilization of this form of taxation. It may lead to excessive expenditures by that government if the revenue sources that have this characteristic are significant. Tax exportation is a potential problem with provincial and local government taxes.[42]

The second type of fiscal externality arises when taxes distort the location of economic activity. For example, an excise tax may cause consumers to purchase the taxed commodities in another jurisdiction. Personal income tax rates may cause mobile workers to move to another jurisdiction. Property taxes or corporate income taxes may induce firms to shift production and investment to regions with lower taxes. In such cases, a government is confronted with a mobile tax base.

In general, smaller jurisdictions will face more mobile tax bases because it is easier to avoid the tax by relocating economic activity outside a small jurisdiction. The more mobile the tax base is, the more responsive the tax base is to a tax increase, and the higher the MCPF. Tax base mobility may cause a vertical imbalance in a federation because the provinces may face a higher MCPF than the federal government which imposes a nation-wide tax on the same base.

A coordinated tax increase by all of the subnational governments would not alter the incentives to change the location of economic activity and would have a relatively low efficiency cost for these governments. The same objective could be achieved by a tax increase on the geographically mobile tax base by the federal government and the transfer of the revenue to the subnational units of government.

Tax base mobility may cause subnational governments to overestimate the total cost of raising revenue from mobile tax bases and to underestimate the cost of providing tax incentives to attract economic activity to their jurisdiction. Tax competition puts downward pressure on the revenues of subnational governments, and some view this as leading to the inadequate provision of public services by these governments.[43] Alternatively for those,

---

42. See Thirsk(1982) on the exporting of the nonresidential property tax.

43. See Wildasin(1989), Wilson(1986), and Zodrow and Meiszkowski(1986).

such as Brennan and Buchanan(1980), who view all governments as biased in favour of excessive public expenditures, tax competition is one of the few effective restrains on these Leviathans.

The third type of fiscal externality, tax base overlap, occurs when two governments tax the same base. Tax base overlap creates problems for tax policy when governments ignore the impact of their tax rate changes on the revenues of the other government that taxes the same base. For example, both the federal and the provincial governments in Canada levy taxes on cigarettes. When either level of government raises its tax on cigarettes, it reduces the consumption of cigarettes which lowers the tax revenues that the other level of government can collect at its existing tax rates. This leads to a situation where both levels of government may underestimate the actual MCPF from their taxes because they neglect the revenue losses incurred by the other government which taxes the same base. This leads to excessive reliance on the shared tax bases.

Tax base overlap is an important feature of the Canadian tax system because, as we have seen, the major tax bases are utilized by the both the federal and provincial governments. One solution to this problem would be to eliminate tax base overlap by assigning each unit of government a distinct tax base. For example, the provinces might be assigned consumption taxes and the federal government might be assigned income taxes. While this might ameliorate the problem to some degree, it would not completely eliminate it because there will always be interactions among the major tax bases. Consumption tax increases by a provincial government can have disincentive effects for the supply of labour, which would reduce personal income tax collections by the federal government. Conversely, personal income tax increases by the federal government, by reducing disposable income and consumer expenditures, will diminish consumption tax revenues by the provincial governments.

Principles for Assigning Tax Powers in a Federal System

The assignment of tax revenue sources to the various levels of government in a federation has received relatively little treatment by economists. The most comprehensive discussion of this issue is contained in a book edited by McLure(1983). Federal-provincial relations in the field of taxation have generated some literature concerned with the question of tax harmonization, including contributions by Huggett(1977) and Thirsk(1980, 1983, and 1984); and Canada's current constitutional crisis has generated a few papers dealing with the tax assignment issues, notably those by Boadway(1991), Mintz and Wilson(1991), and Winer(forthcoming). I will begin by reviewing some of the contributions to the literature on how the tax powers in a federation should be allocated. Then, I will provide some comments on the relevance of this literature for the contemporary Canadian situation.

Richard Musgrave(1983, p. 11) has presented the following list of general principles for the assignment of tax powers in a federation:

1. middle and especially lower-level jurisdictions should tax those bases which have low inter-jurisdictional mobility;

2. personal taxes with progressive rates should be used by those jurisdictions within which a global base can be implemented most efficiently;

3. progressive taxation, designed to secure redistributional objectives, should be primarily central;

4. taxes suitable for purposes of stabilization policy should be central, while lower-level taxes should be cyclically stable;

5. tax bases which are distributed highly unequally among sub-jurisdictions should be used centrally;

6. benefit taxes and user charges are appropriate at all levels.

Some specific suggestions concerning the assignment of tax powers are noted below. Charles McLure(1983, p. 101) has concluded that "severe conceptual faults, as well as troublesome administrative defects, render the corporate income tax not a proper source of revenue for jurisdictions as "open" as the American states." Robin Boadway(1990, p. 12) has indicated that his ideal assignment of tax bases would be the following:

The provinces would have sole responsibility for indirect (sales) taxes, licences and fees, property taxes, and would have some access to direct taxes on residents (personal income and payroll taxes). The federal government would have sole access to corporate taxes, resource taxes and wealth taxes, and would have access to personal income and payroll taxes. They would not occupy indirect tax fields. For the purposes of achieving equity and of maintaining a system of income tax harmonization, the federal government would need to be [sic] occupy a predominant position in the income tax field.

J.M. Mintz and T.A. Wilson (1991, p. 4) have outlined their preferred allocation of tax powers as follows:

Some tax powers would be solely allocated to the federal government (wealth taxes, tariffs, capital taxes and most of the corporate income tax field). Other powers would be given solely to provincial or municipal governments (sales and excise taxes, property taxes and resource taxes). Environmental taxes and the personal income tax (and, perhaps the corporate income tax base) would be co-occupied.

Although differing to some degree, the assignments of tax powers that are preferred by McLure (1983), Boadway (1990), Mintz and Wilson (1991) are very similar and for the most part consistent with the principles outlined by Musgrave (1983). Central governments are to be assigned exclusive control, or a dominant share, of the taxes on the mobile tax bases in order to avoid tax induced distortions in the location of economic activity. Since the CIT and wealth taxes are usually considered the most fiscally mobile tax bases, control of these tax base is assigned to the central government.

Because the personal income tax base is also mobile and because these authors think that the central government should have the primary responsibility for income redistribution, most would assign exclusive, or dominant, control of the PIT to the central government.

Property taxes are viewed as suitable tax bases for local governments because this tax base is relatively immobile, although it is generally recognized that the capital component of the property tax base is highly mobile.

Excise taxes and sales taxes collected on a destination basis are considered suitable taxes for provinces because it is felt that these taxes will not be exported. Sales and excise taxes are not considered suitable for local government because cross-border shopping would be a major problem given their relatively small geographic areas. Tariffs are assigned to the central government to prevent provinces from engaging in protectionism and erecting trade barriers.

Musgrave (1983) and Boadway (1990) would assign natural resource revenues to the central government because these revenues are not uniformly distributed across subnational governments and because the central government is viewed as having the responsibility for maintaining an equitable distribution of income.[44] Boadway acknowledges, however, that the provinces in Canada have been assigned the ownership of the natural resources within their boundaries and that these historical rights would have to be maintained in any new assignment of federal and provincial tax powers.

---

44. The inefficiency caused by fiscally induced migration is also frequently cited as a reason for assigning resource rents to the central government.

The main problems with applying the Musgravian model of the assignment of tax powers in the Canadian context are the following:

- the assignment of tax powers is not considered within the context of the governments' expenditure responsibilities or the system of the intergovernmental grants;

- the need to link expenditure decisions and taxation decisions to ensure an appropriate balance between public and private sector claims on the economy is not stressed;

- assigning the responsibility for income redistribution to the central government may be inappropriate if taxpayers' concern for the well-being of the poor is largely focussed on those who reside in the same community;

- history matters: the provinces have responsibility for social welfare and the ownership of natural resources, and any new assignment of taxation powers will be constrained by these historical "anomalies";

- concentrating tax powers with the federal government reduces the scope for regional variations in tax policy to deal with widely varying economic conditions;

- the argument that the federal government needs substantial tax powers in order to conduct stabilization policy is not compelling because many real economic shocks are region-specific;

- the federal government may be in a better position to impose a comprehensive sales tax and handle the problem of cross-border shopping in the United States than the provinces;

- there is little empirical evidence on the cost of departing from any of the six principles outlined by Musgrave, making it difficult to assess the trade-offs that are inevitably required in assigning the tax bases in a federation.

The literature on the assignment of tax bases in a federation provides a useful framework for discussing the implications of alternative Constitutional arrangements, but it does not provide neat and tidy solutions for these problems.

Three Constitutional Scenarios

Canada Without Québec

In the absence of Québec, the federal government's fiscal position should improve with the elimination of the net fiscal transfer to Québec. If all of the adjustment occurred in terms of a reduction in federal taxation, it would be on the order of 4%.[45] To the extent that the federal government used the improvement in its net fiscal position to reduce its deficit more quickly or to increase its expenditures, or to the extent that adverse economic conditions developed because of an uncertainty investment climate in the transition to an independent Québec, the reduction in federal tax revenues would be less than 4%. A further qualification concerning the extent of any reduction in taxation would be the division of the debt.[46]

Québec's independence may have implications for provincial taxation to the extent that federal transfers to the provinces may be altered. With its improved fiscal position, the federal government could afford to make more generous transfers to the provinces. It has been argued, however, that in the absence of Québec, the political pressures to continue making transfers to the "have-not" provinces through the equalization grant program would be greatly diminished. This, of course, would not have any direct impact on taxation by the provincial governments in the "have" provinces such as Alberta. However, the federal government might use its improved fiscal position to make more transfers to the provinces in order to influence the provincial governments' taxation and spending decisions. For example, with more generous grants to the provinces, the federal government might shift the interest of the provincial governments away from the administration of their PIT. The upshot of this might be that part of the improvement in the federal government's net fiscal position might be transferred to the provinces, and this improvement might be especially beneficial for the "have" provinces—Alberta, British Columbia, and Ontario.

From an Alberta perspective, the improvement in the federal government's fiscal position is the favourable aspect of the Québec separation scenario. However, there will likely be other consequences of the separation of Québec which are not as appealing. The most important of these is a greater tendency for increased centralization of political and economic power. The characteristics of the Canadian federation that make it unique and which have resulted in greater powers for the provinces vis-a-vis

---

45. Calculations based on estimate of the federal fiscal balance with Quebec in 1988 contained in Mansell(1991) and data in Cansim matrix 2777.

46. See Boothe and Harris (1991) on the implications of dividing the debt.

their counterparts in Australia, Germany, or the United States, is largely due to the important role that Québec has played in safeguarding and promoting the powers and responsibilities of the provinces.[47] If Québec had not joined Confederation in 1867, Canada would probably have evolved into a more centralist state. In a new federation without Québec, the balance of the forces would be tilted in favour of increased centralization.

This centralizing tendency would likely manifest itself in terms of a greater propensity for Ottawa to impose uniform standards in areas of provincial jurisdiction, such as education, using Section 36(1) of the Constitution Act, 1982, which commits the federal and provincial governments to:

a) promote equal opportunity for the well-being of Canadians;

b) further economic development to reduce disparity in opportunities;

c) provide essential public services of reasonable quality to all Canadians.

With greater federal responsibilities would come an increase in federal taxation.[48]

Another aspect of this centralizing tendency would be a greater tendency for the federal government to tax natural resource rents. There would be immense pressure on the federal government to capture a larger share of the profits from oil and natural gas production if we again enter a period when world energy prices are very high. In such an event, the redistribution of the energy resource rents from Alberta and the other producing provinces, would likely occur through federal taxation of the energy sector rather than through pricing policies because of the energy pricing provision of the Free Trade Agreement (FTA) with the United States and perhaps because the application of "made in Canada" energy prices of the 1970s and early 1980s is now widely regarded as a futile and counter-productive policy. Albertans should remember that during the conflicts with the federal government over the National Energy Program, Québec backed the Alberta position while Ontario supported the federal government's taxation, pricing, and regulatory strategy. Support for the FTA in Québec was critical for its adoption by Parliament. In the absence of Québec, the federal government would encounter less resistance from the other provincial governments if it tried to take a larger share of oil and gas revenue profits generated in Alberta.

Thus, as regards the taxation of natural resources, the separation of Québec would be a mixed blessing for Alberta. In the absence of Québec,

---

47. See Bird(1986) for a comparative analysis of federal states.

48. Recent proposals for enacting a social charter "with teeth," which seem to be unacceptable to Quebec, are an indication of the forces in favour of centralization.

there would be a greater likelihood that the federal government would try to absorb a larger share of energy resource rents, especially in the event of an upswing in world energy prices, but there would be a 25% smaller population over which the federal government would distribute these rents. If one views Québec as a rather ineffective, and possibly ambivalent, ally in the last conflict with the federal government over energy rents, then the separation of Québec would not be calamitous.

In considering other changes in federal policies that might be expected to occur if Québec separates, it should be borne in mind that Ontario, with at least 50% of the population, would dominate the new federation and have an even greater influence on tax policy than it does in the current federal system. How would tax policy be affected? In the absence of Québec, Ontario would represent approximately 55% of the PIT base, 57% of the CIT base, 50% of the CT base, and 52% of the SI tax base. Given that Ontario's shares of these major tax bases are very similar, there would likely be little impact on the tax mix if Ontario's influence on tax policy significantly increased.

However, more subtle changes in tax policy might occur. One effect might be a reduction in the progressivity of the federal PIT. As shown in Figure 4.8, Ontario has the highest proportion of high income taxpayers. With the progressive rate structure under the PIT, this implies that the average PIT rate is higher in Ontario than in other provinces (see Figure 4.4). One might expect that without Québec, which had a smaller proportion of high income taxpayers and paid a lower average rate than Ontario, the federal tax structure would change to reflect this realignment of political interests and become less progressive. This change would, of course, benefit high income taxpayers in all provinces, including Alberta, at the expense of middle and, possibly, low income taxpayers.

In terms of the administration of the tax system, one might expect that the existing tax collection agreements would continue with the federal government collecting the PIT for all of the provinces. With Québec as a independent country, one might expect some reduction in the mobility of labour and capital between Québec and the rest of Canada, reducing to some extent the pressure on the provinces to react to tax competition on the part of Québec. Québec has been in the forefront of attempts to use the tax system to attract investment to the province as witnessed by its introduction of its stock saving plan, which a number of the other provinces subsequently introduced, and its low corporate income tax rates, especially for small business and for manufacturing and processing industries. (See Figure 4.9.)

A More Decentralized Canada

An alternative constitutional scenario is one in which Québec is induced to remain within Canada through a restructuring of the federation which gives more powers to the provinces. Although this restructuring could take many forms, I will adopt for the purposes of this discussion the re-alignment of expenditure responsibilities which is contained in the Allaire Report.[49] That report envisages a substantial increase in the areas of exclusive authority for the Québec government. (See Allaire Report, p. 38.) It will be assumed that this expansion in provincial jurisdiction would apply to all provincial governments, not just Québec.

Three aspects of the division of powers are particularly important with regard to tax policy. First, the provinces' areas of exclusive authority would include income security and unemployment insurance so that the federal government's role in income redistribution would be severely curtailed. Second, taxation and revenue would be matters of "shared authority" because, as the Report notes, there would be need for the "harmonization of tax policies," but no specifics are discussed. Third, customs and tariffs and equalization would still be areas of exclusive federal jurisdiction. The Allaire Report (p. 40) also argues that the nature of the equalization program must change

> to place greater emphasis on improving the conditions of production in recipient regions. The focus of the support provided will shift from maintaining public services of comparable quality to investment assistance in physical infrastructures, communications, transportation, etc.

These comments are intriguing but no further details are provided concerning the type of equalization program which is envisioned.

Some calculations of the changes in federal and provincial expenditures which would have occurred if the Allaire Report's recommendations had been in effect in 1989-90 have been made by Mintz and Wilson(1991, Table 2). They estimate that the provinces' net financial requirement would have been $33.7 billion dollars higher and the federal government's financial requirements would have been reduced by that amount.[50] The additional revenue requirements of the provincial governments could be satisfied either

---

49. Some proposals which would also lead to a more decentralized federation are contained in "Some Practical Suggestions for Canada" a Report of the Group of 22.

50. The transfer in expenditures to the provinces would have been about $45.4 billion including unemployment insurance benefits. The transfer of the UI contributions to the provinces of about $11.7 billion reduces their net additional financial requirement to about $33.7 billion.

by an increase in grants, or by a transfer of tax room, from the federal government to the provinces. The Allaire Report clearly desires the latter because it argues that "decisions must be brought closer to the citizens they affect" (p.18) and that there be "a new distribution of taxation powers reflecting [Québec's] greater autonomy" (p.27). No indication is given in the Allaire Report as to which taxation powers would be reallocated.

The Mintz and Wilson Assignment of Sources of Tax Revenue
for a Decentralized Canada
Mintz and Wilson(1991) have noted that the increase in the net financial requirements of the provinces envisaged in the Allaire Report could have been accomplished in 1989-90 if the federal government had withdrawn from the sales and excise tax field and if the provinces' share of the PIT revenues had been increased to 50% from around 38%. The authors note that "with equal sharing of the PIT and no change from existing arrangements for the CIT, the federal government could continue to play a major role to ensure adequate harmonization of these two important taxes." (p.30) Essentially, the Mintz and Wilson proposal implies that the PIT field would be equally shared between the federal government and the provinces; the CIT field would be co-occupied (with the federal government having the larger share); and the CT, PT, and SI tax fields would be the exclusive domain of the provinces.

The transfer of tax room in the Mintz and Wilson (1991) proposal could be accomplished if the federal government eliminated the GST and removed its various excise taxes so that the provinces could replace them with their own sales taxes and excises. The reallocation of the PIT would be accomplished through a reduction in the federal PIT rates which would allow the provinces to increase their rates by a corresponding amount.

The Mintz and Wilson (1991) proposal is an attractive solution because it is a relatively simple readjustment of the existing allocation of taxation powers which preserves the net fiscal balances of the two levels of government. There are, however, some potential problems with the proposal. One problem, which they acknowledge, is that the new assignment of tax revenues would meet the additional financial requirements of the provinces as a group, but have very different impacts on individual provinces. Specifically, the "have-not" provinces' financial position would deteriorate because their increased expenditure responsibilities would not be matched by their additional CT and PIT revenues. Mintz and Wilson (p. 33) claim that this problem could be resolved by reducing transfers to the "have" provinces and increasing them to the "have-not" provinces. The "have-not" provinces would become even more dependent on federal transfers than they are currently.

A second problem with the proposal is that while the federal government would have an equal share of the PIT (at least at the time when the re-alignment of expenditure responsibilities took place), the provinces would have, according to the Allaire Report, exclusive jurisdiction in the area of income security. There are many interactions between the transfer system and the PIT system, and there may be substantial gains from integrating or coordinating the transfer system in each province with its PIT system. The federal presence in the PIT might make it very difficult for the provinces to achieve this.

Third, with the federal and provincial governments as "equal rivals" in the PIT field, the stage would be set for serious conflicts between the two orders of government over income tax policy, and the provinces would likely demand greater control over the administration of the PIT. Whether the PIT system would continue to exhibit a high degree of harmonization, when the role of "price leader" in the "PIT cartel" would be contested by the two orders of government, is debatable.

Another important implication of the Mintz and Wilson (1991) proposal is that it would involve the elimination of the Goods and Services Tax.[51] It would be difficult for the provinces to adopt the GST if the provinces imposed different tax rates because the collection of the tax on a destination basis is extremely complicated.[52] With a common tax rate and tax base, a provincial GST would be feasible, but the provinces would lose the autonomy and flexibility that they now have with the retail sales tax. Alternatively, the provinces could simply increase their retail sales taxes instead of adopting the GST. The problem with this is it might exacerbate the cross-border shopping problem and the taxation of some capital goods which are included in the retail sales tax base.

The impact of the Mintz and Wilson (1991) proposal on Alberta is difficult to assess. In order to take advantage of the federal government's withdrawal from the sales tax area, the Government of Alberta would have to introduce a provincial sales tax, a tax measure which it has eschewed in the past. The transfer to the provinces of tax points under the PIT would be advantageous to Alberta, but the cuts in federal transfers to the "have" provinces which are envisioned by Mintz and Wilson could largely offset the gain from more access to the PIT in the province.

---

51. Whether one views this as a merit or a flaw in the Mintz and Wilson proposal depends on whether or not one regards this tax as a useful addition to the set of tax revenue instruments.

52. Boadway(1991, p. 109) argues that "the complexities of operating a value-added tax in a multi-jurisdictional economy . . . really requires virtually complete federal dominance in the field." See also Johnson (1991, p. 331). Some of the problems with the attempts by Quebec and Saskatchewan to "harmonize" their provincial sales taxes with the federal GST are discussed in the Globe and Mail, "Report on Business," Sept. 1, 1991.

A Direct/Indirect Assignment of Tax Powers for a Decentralized Canada
Given the above discussion of the Mintz and Wilson tax assignment for
decentralized federation, an alternative assignment can be envisaged in
which the provinces would have exclusive jurisdiction over the personal and
corporate income taxes and the federal government would have exclusive
jurisdiction in the sales tax field. With exclusive responsibility for income
security assigned to the provinces, it can be argued the PIT should be under
the exclusive control of the provinces in order to allow them to integrate their
PIT system with their income security programs. If the PIT is assigned to the
provinces, then it can be argued that the CIT should also be assigned to the
provinces in order to maintain the integration of the PIT and the CIT. If the
federal government did not levy a PIT, but shared the CIT with the
provincial governments, then the federal government could suck funds out
of the provincial treasuries by increasing its CIT rate if the provinces
provided dividend tax credits under their PIT. One solution to this problem
would be to assign the exclusive control of the CIT to the provinces.[53] It
could be argued, however, that the integration of the PIT system with the CIT
system is not a necessary feature of a CIT system. (See Boadway and Kitchen
(1984, p. 184).) In that case there would be a strong case for assigning the CIT
to the federal government because the CIT base is highly mobile and
provincial tax competition would either be highly distortionary or drive rates
to very low levels. In the following discussion, it is assumed that the CIT is
assigned to the provincial governments although it is recognized that this is
the most contentious aspect of this alternative assignment of tax powers.

The direct/indirect assignment of taxes was contained in a proposal by
the Government of British Columbia in constitutional discussion in 1969
which suggested that:

> The capacity of each government to tax must be sufficient for each
> government to effectively discharge its constitutional obligations.
> Accordingly, the Federal government should leave exclusively to the
> provinces the direct tax fields of personal and corporate income taxes
> and succession or estate taxes. Having done that, the Constitution
> should restrict the spending power of the Federal government to
> those matters under its jurisdiction.[54]

53. It can be argued, see Boadway and Kitchen(1984, p.184), that the integration of the PIT
    system with the CIT system is not a necessary feature of a CIT system and should be
    assigned to the federal government because the CIT base is highly mobile and provincial tax
    competition would either be highly distortionary or drive rates to very low levels.

54. Quoted in Bayefski (1989, p. 141). The withdrawal of the provinces from estate taxation in
    the 1970s is an indication of the potential effect of tax competition involving a highly mobile
    tax base.

The ideas proclaimed in this quotation are of course very similar to the sentiments expressed in the Allaire Report. This assignment of tax sources corresponds to that which prevails in Switzerland where direct taxes are imposed by the cantons and indirect taxes on consumption are imposed by the Confederation.[55]

What would be the financial consequences of a direct/indirect assignment of tax revenue sources? If it had occurred in 1989, the provincial governments would have received an additional $41.6 billion in tax revenues while the federal government's revenues would have declined by this amount. Recall that Mintz and Wilson estimate that the change in expenditure responsibilities would have added only $33.7 billion to the provinces' spending, leaving them with a net gain of about $7.9 billion and the federal government with a net loss of this amount. To preserve a fiscal balance, either the federal government would have to increase the rates on its assigned CT base (while the provinces reduced their PIT and CIT rates) or some additional expenditure responsibilities would have to be transferred to the provinces. I think that it is interesting to consider the latter option, and the particular function that I think should be transferred to the provinces is the payment of equalization grants. If the federal government had been relieved of the obligation of making the $8.2 billion in equalization payments, and these payments had been made directly to the "have-not" provinces by the "have" provinces, then the transfer of expenditure responsibilities would have matched the transfer in revenues for each order of government and the fiscal balance within the federation would have been maintained.

Transferring the responsibility for funding the equalization grant system from the federal government to the "have" provinces should be considered for its intrinsic merit and not just because it would help maintain the fiscal balances of each level of government. Such an equalization grant system could be based on the representative national average standard (RNAS) formula which could be used to calculate each province's fiscal capacity deficiency or surplus.[56] Provinces with a fiscal capacity surplus would contribute to a central fund, and provinces with a fiscal capacity deficiency would draw from the fund. There would be no need for the federal

---

55. See Duss and Bird(1979). The title of their paper, "Switzerland's `Tax Jungle'," indicates their assessment of the Swiss system.

56. The RNAS formula was employed to calculate the equalization grant entitlements before 1982. See Courchene(1984). Other methods for calculating equalization entitlements and contributions would be possible, and the RNAS system is not necessarily the preferred system for calculation of equalization grants. See Dahlby and Wilson (1991) on the properties of an "optimal" equalization grant system.

government to be involved in the financing of the equalization grants, except perhaps to guarantee that payments were made by the provinces with surplus fiscal capacity.[57]

One reason why provincial funding of equalization grants should be seriously considered under a decentralized constitutional scenario is that it links the taxes which are used to finance equalization with the sources of above-average fiscal capacity. Under the existing equalization program, the federal government finances these grants out of general tax revenues. If increased equalization grants are to be paid to the "have-not" provinces because of an increase in fiscal capacity in, say, Ontario, it makes little sense for federal tax rates to be raised in all provinces, including the "have-not" provinces, in order to finance these payments. One of the major problems with equalization system in the 1970s was that the federal government was supposed to finance increased equalization grants arising from increased oil and gas revenues in Alberta even though the federal government's share of these revenues, before the NEP, was relatively small, and much of the additional revenue from an increase in federal taxation came from Ontario.[58] Many of the federal-provincial conflicts may have been avoided if the equalization grant system had involved direct transfers from Alberta to the "have-not" provinces.

A second reason why provincial funding of equalization grant program would be desirable is that it would help to internalize some the fiscal externalities that a province may impose on other provinces. For example, consider a "have" province which adopts a "beggar thy neighbour" strategy and through its tax, expenditure, or regulatory policies tries to attract jobs or investments that would have occurred in other provinces. Under the current system with federal financing of equalization, a "have" province bears few of the costs of increasing its fiscal capacity at the expense of the other provinces. Under a system with provincial funding of equalization grants, a "have" province would find that its payments to the equalization program would go up if it transferred fiscal capacity from the other provinces to itself. Thus, in a decentralized federation, an equalization system funded directly by provincial tax revenues would reduce the incentives of provinces to engage in the fiscal competition.[59]

---

57. See Meyers (1990) for an analysis of the voluntary equalization payments by provincial governments in a model with fiscally induced migration.

58. See Courchene and Copplestone(1980) on this problem. They proposed a two tier equalization scheme which included provincial funding of equalization grants with respect to resource revenues.

59. To put this in more concrete terms, would the headquarters of the lottery corporation been transferred from Manitoba to Alberta if Alberta had to compensate Manitoba for the loss of its tax base?

The implications for Alberta of a direct/indirect division of tax powers between the provincial governments and federal government are summarized below:

- there would be a closer link between expenditures and taxes perhaps leading to better fiscal management;

- there would be less tax base overlap;

- there would be more scope for tailoring the tax system to the particular needs of each province;

- there would be more scope for tax competition, leading to lower rates of taxation on the mobile sources of income and perhaps a less progressive distribution of the tax burden;

- the increase in tax competition might be offset by a reduction in expenditure competition;

- fiscal policy decisions might be constrained by a provincially funded equalization scheme.

In conclusion, a division of tax powers which confers indirect taxes on the central government and direct taxes on the provincial governments is the antithesis of the "accepted" theory, but it may be the preferred allocation of tax powers for a decentralized federation in which the provincial governments have exclusive jurisdiction over income security.

An Independent Alberta

It is difficult to predict the tax policy implications of independence for Alberta because, of the three scenarios considered in this paper, independence would involve the most radical changes in the structure of government in Alberta. The tax policy issues for an independent Alberta would be qualitatively different from those in the other scenarios because all of the tax powers which are now wielded by the federal government in Ottawa would be exercised by a government in Edmonton. These new tax powers of an independent Alberta would primarily be in the field of indirect taxation and tariffs.

How independent would an independent Alberta be? While an independent Alberta would have all of the tax powers of an sovereign state, its ability to utilize those tax powers would be constrained by its relatively small size and the relative openness of its economy. Alberta would be even more dependent on foreign investment in resource development projects. With independence, our trading links with the other former Canadian provinces would probably atrophy, and the pressure to harmonize with the United States tax policy would become even greater than it is today.

Independence for Alberta would presumably reduce labour mobility more than it would reduce capital mobility. One might expect changes in tax policy which would shift the burden of taxation from capital income to labour income. This might occur through PIT incentives for capital income, such as favourable treatment of capital gains, or through changes in the tax mix in favour of greater use of payroll taxes or sales taxes. Overall, a less progressive distribution of the burden of the tax might be expected.

Independence would also affect tax policy because it would lead to:

- a decline in the net fiscal transfer from Alberta; and

- an increase in the volatility of the Alberta economy.

The decline in the net fiscal transfer could lead to lower taxes in Alberta. The greater economic instability could lead to greater use of the tax system to diversify the economy, and the problem of revenue instability which would afflict the government of an independent Alberta might affect its choice of the tax mix. These issues will be addressed in more detail below.

The analysis in Mansell (1991, Table 2) indicates that the net per capita federal fiscal transfer from Alberta in 1988 was $737 (in 1990 dollars). While the one might expect the total tax burden in Alberta to decline with the elimination of this fiscal transfer, the reduction in taxes might be lessened by increases in expenditures by the Government of Alberta if it undertook some of the defence, diplomatic, and regulatory services which the federal government now performs outside the province. Alberta might also decide to continue making some transfers to the other former provinces of Canada. In addition, there would be pressure on the government to increase expenditures especially in response to the desire for economic stabilization/diversification programs, and this would further limit the extent of any tax rate reductions.

The analysis in Mansell and Percy(1990, Chapter 4) indicated that the Alberta economy is subject to much greater fluctuations than the other provincial economies because of its dependence on energy and agriculture and because there have been wide fluctuations in output prices of these industries in the last two decades. A survey of Albertans by Mansell and Percy(1990, p.89-90) found that 73.6% of the respondents thought that Alberta's specialization in these industries was undesirable because it has produced a less stable economy. However, only 41.5% of the respondents indicated that they were willing to have their taxes increased to finance tax breaks and subsidies to promote new industries which would stabilize the economy, and the average tax increase that these respondents were prepared to support was about 7.5%.

I expect that the public's willingness to pay for diversification policies would be considerably greater in an independent Alberta if the stabilizing linkages with the Canadian economy, especially with regard to the labour market, were less effective or no longer function. High unemployment rates during slumps and severe labour shortages during booms would put tremendous pressure on the government of an independent Alberta to diversify the economy by promoting employment in more "stable" manufacturing industries. Such industries would require government grants, low interest loans, tax breaks, or protection from foreign competition. Tariffs on Alberta's manufactured goods might be a response to the strong desire for a more stable, albeit less productive, economy. However, I think that it is unlikely that protectionism, under the guise of diversification, would take the form of a high tariff wall because these measures are relatively visible and therefore subject to retaliation. Diversification would probably involve more subtle policy measures which would include tax subsidies to specific industries and grants and subsidies from the expenditure side of the budget as well as regulatory measures. Anticipating the use of tax measures to diversify the economy does not mean, of course, that I would necessarily recommend these policies.

Economists usually stress the desirability of a stable tax system, with some stressing tax rate stability and others stressing revenue stability.[60] Note that there is an inherent conflict between these two objectives. Faced with fluctuations in natural resource revenues and economic activity in response to fluctuations in world oil prices, revenue stability in Alberta would require higher tax rates when world oil prices are low and lower tax rates when world oil prices are high.

The desirability of tax rate stability was discussed previously. An efficient allocation of the tax burden over time may require constant tax rates, causing a government to run deficits during slumps and surpluses during booms.[61] In the context of the Alberta economy, this would imply that resource revenues during a boom should be placed in the Alberta Heritage Trust Fund and utilized during a slump.

---

60. See Jamieson and Amirkhalkhali(1990) for an empirical study of tax revenue stability in Alberta.

61. Greater economic instability may also affect income tax policy if it increases the attractiveness of measures to "smooth" the tax liabilities of individuals and corporations. See Mansell and Percy(1990, pp. 110-113) on the use of income averaging under the PIT and the use of a cash-flow tax base under the CIT as policy responses to economic instability in Alberta.

It has been argued by Boothe (1991), Smith (1990a) and others that Alberta's savings rate from its natural resource revenues has been too low. An independent Alberta would be even more dependent on resource revenues and subject to wide fluctuations in economic activity, and therefore the government's policy with regard to the Alberta Heritage Trust Fund and saving rate on natural resource revenues would become even more important than they have been in the past. Democratic governments, with mandates of less than five years, may have difficulty making the appropriate long-term saving decisions, and this would have serious consequences in an independent Alberta.

The main case for trying to achieve a high degree of revenue stability is that instability in the government's revenues makes the government's expenditure decisions more difficult. If government expenditures are pro-cyclical, with more spending during booms when revenues are plentiful and cut-backs during slumps when revenues decline, the fluctuations in economic activity would accentuated. Consequently, if one thinks that the government of an independent Alberta would be unable to resist the temptation to engage in pro-cyclical spending, then policy measures which promote greater revenue stability, such as changing in the tax mix in favour of the more stable revenue sources (e.g., a sales tax), and reducing reliance on the relatively unstable revenue sources (e.g., the corporate income tax), may be desirable.

Determining the appropriate tax rates and tax mix in an independent Alberta would be even more difficult than it has been in the past because of the instability of the economy and the uncertainty concerning future natural resource revenues. The potential for making serious mistakes would be very great.

I would like to thank Mel McMillan, Joe Ruggeri, Roger Smith, and Wayne Thirsk for their comments. They are not responsible for, and do not necessarily agree with, the opinions expressed in this paper.

References

Allaire, J. et al. (1991). A Québec Free to Choose. *Report of the Constitutional Committee of the Québec Liberal Party Submitted to the 25th Party Convention.*

Auerbach, A.J. & Poterba, J.M.(1987). Why have corporate tax revenues declined? In L. Summers (Ed.), *Tax policy and the economy*. Boston, MA: MIT Press.

Barro, R.J. (1979). On the determination of public debt. *Journal of Political Economy*, 87 (October), pp. 940-971.

_____. (1989). The neoclassical approach to fiscal policy. In R.J. Barro (Ed.), *Modern business cycle theory*. Cambridge, MA: Harvard University Press.

Bayefski, A.F. (1989). *Canada's Constitution Act 1982—Amendments: A documentary history*. Toronto, ON: McGraw-Hill Ryerson Ltd.

Bird, R. (1986). *Federal finance in comparative perspective*. Toronto, ON: Canadian Tax Foundation.

Boadway, R.(1990). *Constitution design in a federation: An economic perspective*. Paper prepared for The Business Council on National Issues Symposium on Canada's Post Meech Lake Constitutional Options, Toronto.

_____. (1991). *The constitutional division of powers: An economic perspective*. Kingston, ON: Queen's University, Department of Economics.

Boadway, R. & Kitchen, H. (1984). *Canadian tax policy* (2nd ed.). Toronto, ON: Canadian Tax Foundation.

Boothe, P. (1991). *Public sector saving and long-term fiscal balance in a resource-Based economy: Alberta 1969-1989*. (Discussion Paper 90-13.) Edmonton, AB: University of Alberta, Department of Economics.

Boothe, P. & Harris, R. (1991). *The economics of constitutional change: Dividing the federal debt*. Edmonotn, AB: University of Alberta, Faculty of Business, Western Centre for Economic Research. (Discussion Paper 91-1.)

Bossons, J. (1991). Provincial taxes on corporations. In M.L. McMillan (Ed.), *Provincial public finances: Provincial surveys (pp. 301-314), Vol. 2*. Toronto, ON: Canadian Tax Foundation.

Brennan, G. & Buchanan, J. (1980). *The power to tax: Analytical foundations of a fiscal constitution*. Cambridge, MA: Cambridge University Press.

Canada. Department of Finance (1990). *The equalization program*. Ottawa, ON: Supply and Services.

Canadian Tax Foundation. (1990). *Provincial and municipal finances*. Toronto, ON: Canadian Tax Foundation.

_____.(1991). *The national finances*. Toronto, ON: Canadian Tax Foundation.

Courchene, T.J. (1984). *Equalization payments: Past, present, and future*. Toronto, ON: Ontario Economic Council.

Courchene, T.J. & Copplestone, G.H.(1980). Alternative equalization programs. In R.M. Bird (Ed.), *Fiscal Dimensions of Canadian Federalism* (pp. 8-45). Toronto, ON: Canadian Tax Foundation.

Courchene, T.J. & Stewart, A.E. (1991). Provincial personal income taxation and the future of the tax collection agreements. In M.L. McMillan (Ed.), *Provincial public finances: Provincial surveys* (pp. 266-300), Vol. 2. Toronto, ON: Canadian Tax Foundation.

Dahlby, B. & Wilson, S. (1991). *Fiscal capacity, tax effort, and optimal equalization grants*. Edmonton, AB: University of Alberta, Department of Economics.

Douglas, A.(1990, January/February). Changes in corporate tax revenue. *Canadian Tax Journal*, 38, pp. 66-81.

Duss, R. & Bird, R.M. (1979). Switzerland's "Tax Jungle". *Canadian Tax Journal*, 27 pp. 46-67.

Group of 22. (1991). *Some practical suggestions for Canada*. Montreal, PQ: c/o Le Groupe Columbia Inc.

Hamilton, B. & Whalley. J. (1989, August). Reforming indirect taxes in Canada: Some general equilibrium estimates. *Canadian Journal of Economics*, 22, No. 3, pp. 561-575.

Huggett, D.R.(1977). Tax base harmonization. In *Intergovernmental Relations*. Toronto, ON: Ontario Economic Council.

Ip, I. (1991). Big spenders: A survey of provincial government finances in Canada. *Policy Study 15*. Toronto, ON: C.D. Howe Institute.

Jamieson, B. & Amirkhalkhali, S.(1990, November/December). Revenue stability in Alberta. *Canadian Tax Journal*, 38, pp. 1503-1518.

Johnson, J.A. (1991). Issues in provincial sales and excise taxation. In M.L. McMillan (Ed.), *Provincial public finances: Provincial surveys, Vol. 2* (pp. 315-343). Toronto, ON: Canadian Tax Foundation.

Keen, M. (1987, June). Welfare effects of commodity tax harmonisation. *Journal of Public Economics*, 33, pp. 107-114.

LaForest, G.V. (1967). *The allocation of taxing power under the Canadian Constitution*. Toronto, ON: Canadian Tax Foundation.

Mansell, R. & Percy, M. (1990). *Strength in adversity: A study of the Alberta economy*. Western Studies in Economic Policy. Edmonton, AB: University of Alberta, Western Centre for Economic Research, University of Alberta Press.

Mansell, R.(1991). *The economics of Canadian federalism*. Paper presented to the New Brunswick Commission on Canadian Federalism.

McLure, C.E. (1983). *Tax assignment in federal countries*, Canberra, Australia: Australian National University, Centre for Research on Federal Financial Relations.

_____. (1983). Assignment of corporate income taxes in a federal system. In C.E. McLure (Ed.), *Tax Assignment in Federal Countries* (pp. 101-124). Canberra, Australia: Australian National University, Centre for Research on Federal Financial Relations.

McMillan, M.L. (Ed.). (1991). *Provincial public finances: Provincial surveys* (Vols. 1 & 2). Toronto, ON: Canadian Tax Foundation.

Meyers, G.(1990). Optimality, free mobility, and the regional authority in a federation. *Journal of Public Economics*, 43, pp. 107-121.

Mintz, J.M. & Wilson, T.A.(1991). *The allocation of tax authority in the Canadian federation (Policy Study 91-7)*. Toronto, ON: University of Toronto, Institute for Policy Analysis.

Musgrave, R.A. (1983). Who should tax, where, and what? In C.E. McLure (Ed.), *Tax assignment in federal countries* (pp. 2-19). Canberra, Australia: Australian National University, Centre for Research on Federal Financial Relations.

Perry, D. (1990, September). International tax comparisons. *Canadian Tax Journal, 38*, pp. 1326-1336.

Schama, S. (1989). *Citizens: A chronicle of the French revolution.* New York: Knopf.

Smith, R.S. (1990a). *Spending and taxing: The recent record of Western Canadian provincial governments* (Information Bulletin No.1). Edmonton, AB: University of Alberta, Western Centre for Economic Research.

_____. (1990b, March/April). Why the Canadian property tax(payer) is not revolting. *Canadian Tax Journal, 38*, pp. 298-327.

Thirsk, W.R. (1980). Tax harmonization and its importance in the Canadian federation. In R.M. Bird (Ed.), Fiscal dimensions of Canadian federalism. Toronto, ON: Canadian Tax Foundation.

_____. (1982). Political sensitivity versus economic sensibility: A tale of two property taxes. In W.R. Thirsk and J. Whalley (Eds.), *Tax Policy Options in the 1980s.* Toronto, ON: Canadian Tax Foundation.

_____. (1983). Tax assignment and revenue sharing in Canada. In C.E. McLure (Ed.), *Tax assignment in federal countries* (pp. 234-250). Canberra, Australia: Australian National University, Centre for Research on Federal Financial Relations.

_____. (1984). Policies toward tax harmonization. In D.W. Conklin (Ed.), *Aseparate personal income tax for Ontario* (pp. 339-364). Toronto, ON: Ontario Economic Council.

Wildasin, D.E. (1989). Interjurisdictional capital mobility: Fiscal externality and corrective subsidy. *Journal of Urban Economics, 25*, pp. 193-212.

Wilson, J. (1986). A theory of inter-regional tax competition. *Journal of Urban Economics, 19*, pp. 296-315.

Winer, S. (in press). Taxation and federalism in a changing world. In R. Bird & J. Mintz, *Tax policy to the year 2000 and beyond.* Toronto, ON: Canadian Tax Foundation.

Zodrow, G.R. & Meiszkowski, P.M. (1986). Pigou, property taxation, and the under-provision of local public goods. *Journal of Urban Economics, 19*, pp. 356-370.

Commentaries

Melville L. McMillan, University of Alberta

My thank you to the organizers of the conference for inviting me to comment upon Bev Dahlby's interesting paper. After a year outside of Canada, this has provided me the opportunity to better acquaint myself with the more recent constitutional developments.

Perhaps somewhat surprisingly, taxation matters have received little attention in the constitutional discussion thus far. More attention is likely, especially if a reallocation of federal and provincial responsibilities that differ more from the existing arrangements and from the modest (federal at least) variations currently on the table were to assume a greater probability. Even if they were not, a careful examination of the merits of the existing arrangements and of potential alternatives is warranted as part of the search for improvement. The paucity of treatment to date makes Bev Dahlby's thorough and fundamental examination of the issue an even more important and valuable contribution.

Bev Dahlby divides his study into three topics; an overview of Canadian taxation, a discussion of the tax assignment problem in a federation, and the application to three constitutional scenarios. My comments follow a similar pattern. However, my comments will range rather broadly while I leave the more specific points to my partner in this exercise, Wayne Thirsk.

Following an approach used by Richard Bird (1982), I begin by contemplating what a taxpayer's view might be of the fiscal efficacy of the three levels of government. I consider the ratio of what could be the taxpayer's perceived benefits and perceived costs. Primarily, I consider perceived benefits to consist of a government's expenditures on those items that provide relatively direct or obvious benefits to broad groups such as education, health and social welfare including direct transfers to individuals or families such as family allowance. Large items omitted from this category are interest payments on the public debt and intergovernmental transfers that support the expenditures of other levels of government. Obvious major costs include the personal income taxes, sales and excise taxes, and property taxes. Important government revenues not included are the corporate income tax and natural resource revenues.

From some back-of-the-envelope calculations, I estimate that the ratios of obvious taxpayer benefits to obvious taxpayer costs are 0.7 for the federal government, 1.4 for the provincial governments and 1.8 for the local governments. That is, the Canadian taxpayer sees benefits of 70 cents from each dollar of federal tax, $1.40 for each dollar of provincial tax, and $1.80 for each dollar of local tax. For the Alberta taxpayer the estimated ratios are 0.6, 3.1, and 1.9. Although this simple and uni-dimensional perspective ignores many other important factors, perhaps it is not surprising that surveys (e.g., Auld, 1979) find that more taxpayers feel that they are getting their money's worth from the lower levels of government. Does such a (distorted) perception of the fiscal efficacy of the different levels of government exist and, if so, does it bias our constitutional preferences?

The table below shows the recommended assignments of three major tax sources between the federal and provincial governments from three studies (Boadway, 1990; Mintz and Wilson, 1991; and Dahlby's).

	Boadway		Mintz-Wilson		Dahlby	
	Fed	Prov	Fed	Prov	Fed	Prov
PIT	X	x	x	x	X	
CIT	X	X	x	X		
Sales and excise	X		X	X		

The large Xs show the jurisdiction assigned the tax source and the smaller Xs indicate more and less responsibility where the tax is shared. In recommending that the personal and corporate income taxes rest with the provinces entirely while the sales and excise taxes become the field of the federal government, Dahlby's recommendations differ strikingly from those of Boadway and of Mintz and Wilson. This occurs despite the fact that they all start from the same Musgravian principles. Dahlby's logic is that if the provinces assume full responsibility for income security, it is appropriate to put the income taxes in their hands. The thinking underlying the Mintz and Wilson reallocation is less clearly defined. No doubt, the differences of opinion result in large part because, in the absence of significant empirical evidence, we are left to our own judgement as to the importance of the consequences of departing from the criteria. Furthermore, different federations sometimes exhibit rather wide variations in their assignment of tax authority. Compare, for example, Australia, Canada, and Switzerland.

On one issue, however, economists seem to have reached some consensus. That is that regional (i.e., provincial) taxation of (net) resource rents tends to distort factor allocation and reduce national efficiency. Now, when resource rents are relatively modest and broad constitutional issues are before us, it seems an opportune time to put this item on (or at least keep it in mind for) the agenda. Though well entrenched with the provinces and probably non-negotiable in many minds, being mute on this issue will forego the even small opportunity for reconsideration of a potentially important tax matter. Again, however, a lack of strong empirical evidence leaves the question of the magnitude of the potential benefits of change debatable. Indeed, some estimates suggest that the welfare gains may be quite small (e.g. Mieszkowski, 1983).

In the consideration of constitution scenarios, the Canada without Québec possibility is expected to result in a fiscal saving to the federal government. Bev Dahlby estimates this to be 4% of federal taxes; elsewhere in this volume, Reid and Snoddon estimate it to be slightly larger. The implication is that we in the rest of Canada (ROC) would realize some saving as a result. Although most of us probably consider the amount relatively modest in the context of the whole issue, it deserves consideration. How much tax Albertans would save (as Bev Dahlby mentions) or whether they would realize any saving at all depends upon the division of the national debt; both between Québec and Canada and among the ROC. Although potential allocation formulae using reasonable criteria (see Boothe and Harris, 1991, for examples) and 1989 data suggest some variation around the (say) 4% value, if one used GDP shares from even 1985 (or if similar values reoccurred from a moderate increase in resource rents to the province), Albertans could find themselves losing rather than saving as a result.

Although debt-sharing is not considered, it appears to me that it is important in even the intermediate case of a more-decentralized Canada. Both the Dahlby and the Mintz and Wilson studies assume that the devolution (to all provinces) of responsibilities proposed in the Allaire report would be accompanied by a fully compensating transfer of revenue-raising capacity. That is, the provinces would be transferred additional taxes equalling the extra costs. Federal and provincial debts, however, are left unchanged. I question whether this is a reasonable assumption. The reason for my doubt is that the resulting erosion of the federal tax base and tax revenues would cause debt charges to consume one half rather than the current one third of federal own revenue. Provincially, debt charges would shrink to about one-tenth rather than one-sixth of provincial own revenue. More detailed numbers are reported in the accompanying table based on 1989-90 data. Reference to own tax revenue changes the specific figures and demonstrates more clearly the difference between the Dahlby and the Mintz and Wilson approaches.

Relative Burden of Government Debt Charges Under Selected Alternatives

	Current fiscal arrangements	M Mintz and Wilson (Allaire)	Dahlby
Debt charges as % of total own revenue, 1989-90			
federal	33.0%	52.1%	51.5%
provincial	15.7%	11.1%	11.2%
As % of own tax revenue			
federal	40.5%	61.3%	72.6%
provincial	20.4%	14.6%	13.4%

Is it reasonable to assume that the federal government would permit the burden of federal debt to become so large relative to its revenue and revenue raising capabilities? I think not. Because it can be argued that a portion of the debt is due to the transferred programs, one could expect an effort to transfer some of the debt with the responsibilities and the revenue sources. This is to say, the federal position would not be, "Here is the farm free and clear," but "If you want the farm you will have to assume the mortgage also."

Allow my comments to range even further. When faced with the proposals of the Allaire report and the frequently heard requests for expanded provincial authority from certain other provinces, more attention could have been paid in the volume to the issue of an appropriate (re)assignment of federal-provincial responsibilities—especially the health, education, social welfare, and unemployment insurance functions highlighted—and the linking of that with the tax assignment issue. That is, I see a case for a paper spanning but building upon the Boothe and the Dahlby papers. That exercise could have examined in detail and from a broad economic and political perspective the pros and cons of selected important reassignments. For example, what I may simplistically refer to as national programs with provincial delivery may have done much to strengthen the economic union and shared responsibilities may have served to expand political representation. Furthermore, such an exercise could have assessed whether the proposed constitutional structure would have the flexibility to serve the country as well as the existing structure by being able to adapt (or be adapted) to changes as dramatic as those witnessed over the past century. Such considerations seem to have been bypassed and the independent discussions to have defaulted to an acceptance of a layer-cake model of federalism with little consideration of the marble cake alternative. I believe that the packaging is not quite as neat as depicted in their individual treatments and, even within the narrow context of the assignment of expenditures and revenues, the two issues are much more intertwined than is suggested here.

As a concluding comment, permit a final reflection on the Canada without Québec possibility. Should that situation occur, the ROC will be a Canada with an Ontario-dominated federal government. Westerners certainly would regard that as an unattractive consequence and be pursuing avenues to protect regional interests. Employing a perspective similar to Bev Dahlby's, Roger Smith (1991) considers the fiscal circumstances of a Western Canada union (independent, or as a region in a confederation of regions) and concludes, purely from this relatively narrow approach, that that option would not be without some appeal. An alternative may be for the provinces to attempt to constrain Ottawa's fiscal power by limiting it to (what might be hoped to be the less popular) sales and excise taxes while the provinces assumed the income taxes in total; that is, the Dahlby tax assignment. Thus, Bev Dahlby's tax assignment may have some political as well some economic appeal.

References

Auld, D.A.L. (1979). Public sector awareness and preferences in Ontario. *Canadian Tax Journal 27*, pp. 172-183.

Bird, Richard. (1982). Closing the fiscal scissors: Or the public sector has two sides. *The National Tax Journal XXXV*, pp. 477-481.

Boadway, Robin. (1991, January). *Constitution design in a federation: An economic perspective*. Paper prepared for The Business Council on National Issues Symposium on Canada's Post Meech Lake Constitutional Options, Toronto.

Boothe, Paul & Harris, Richard. (1991). *The economics of constitutional change: Dividing the federal debt*. Edmonton: University of Alberta, Western Centre of Economic Research (Information Bulletin 91-1).

Dahlby, Bev. (1991, September). *Taxation under alternative constitutional arrangements*. Paper prepared for and presented at the Alberta and the Economics of Constitutional Change Conference, Western Centre for Economic Research, University of Alberta.

Mieszkowski, Peter. (1983). Energy policy, taxation of natural resources, and fiscal federalism. In Charles E. McLure (Ed.), *Tax Assignment in Federal Countries*, pp. 129-145. Canberra: Centre for Research on Federal Financial Relations.

Mintz, J.M. & Wilson, T.A. (1991). *The allocation of tax authority in the Canadian federation*. Paper presented at the Economic Dimensions of Constitutional Change Conference, John Deutsch Institute for the Study of Economic

Policy, Queen's University, Kingston, Ontario.

Reid, Bradford & Snoddon, Tracy. (1991). *Redistribution under alternative constitutional arrangements for Canada*. Paper prepared for and presented at the Alberta and the Economics of Constitutional Change Conference, Western Centre for Economic Research, University of Alberta.

Smith, Roger. (1991). *Constitutional reform and the structure of government: Fiscal residuals in the West—A reason for getting together*. Edmonton: University of Alberta, Western Centre for Economic Research (Information Bulletin 91-2).

Wayne Thirsk, University of Waterloo

Bev Dahlby's paper appears in three parts: a description of the current Canadian tax system, a discussion of the problem of how to assign taxes to different levels of government in a federal system and, finally, a speculative portion which explores the probable consequences of three alternative policy scenarios for the Province of Alberta. The three potential states of the world include an independent Alberta, a Canada without Québec, and a highly decentralized Canada. While I agree with most of Dahlby's predictions about the fiscal impacts of different constitutional outcomes, I would have preferred to have seen the arguments cast in a slightly different form which would be both more illuminating and more consistent with the conventional literature in this area.

I believe it is frequently useful to catalogue all taxes into two distinct groups, residence-based and source-based taxes. Residence-based taxes tax income and wealth where the income recipient and wealth owner reside and tax sales at the point at which consumption occurs. Source-based taxes, on the other hand, tax income at the site where the income is earned and tax wealth at the location where wealth is employed. Source-based sales taxes, often referred to as origin taxes, impose their burden at the point of commodity production. Personal income taxes, retail sales taxes, and residential property taxes are the primary examples of residence-based taxes. Corporate income taxes, capital taxes, natural resources taxes, and the nonresidential property tax are the major illustrations of source-based taxes.

Compared to source-based taxes, residence-based taxes in a small open economy environment are much less likely to be exported to foreigners and are much less susceptible to the pressures of tax competition. Within a federation, therefore, residence-based taxes are the most suitable instrument for subfederal units of government to employ. This position echoes the assignment choices of Boadway (1991) and Mintz & Wilson (1991) that are mentioned in the paper by Dahlby. Although my view contrasts somewhat with Dahlby's main prescription—to give the federal government the more mobile tax bases, it also fits in much better with what economists have to say about the expenditure side of the budget.

Contrary to Dahlby's assertion that public expenditures have played no role in the tax assignment debate, Flatters et al. (1974) and Boadway and Wildasin (1984) have shown that residence-based taxes will induce inefficient labour migration when they are used to pay for the provision of pure public goods. Source-based taxes are more appropriate in this case. However, as my co-discussant, Mel McMillan, and others have demonstrated in their empirical work, subfederal governments appear to supply private-type goods and services, such as health and education, for the most part. When this is the case, residence-based taxes are needed to internalize the fiscal internality associated with interjurisdictional labour mobility.

As for the rest of Dahlby's paper, I find only two points that provoke some mild disagreement. First, if Québec severs its connection with the rest of the country, I have no doubt that a reconfederated Canada would be anything other than a highly decentralized country. Provinces other than Ontario would insist on decentralized political structure as a necessary part of any constitutional marriage with Ontario. Secondly, I am dubious about the economic payoff to a concerted diversification strategy in a newly independent Alberta. This strategy gives too much priority to place prosperity and not enough to people prosperity. It might be far better to bank the public's share of the economic surpluses obtained from oil and gas exploitation and use the proceeds to upgrade the human capital of Alberta residents to the point where many could qualify for high-paying jobs anywhere in the world. Finally, the design of tax policy in an independent Alberta requires an entirely different mind set than the one given in Dahlby's paper. Why not export Alberta taxes to the rest of the world if a new "national" tax policy can arrange for this to happen?

References

Boadway, R. & Wildasin, D. (1984). *Public sector economics* (2nd Ed.). Toronto and Boston: Little, Brown and Co.

Flatters, F.R., Henderson, J.V., & Mieszkowski, P.M. (1974, May). Public goods, efficiency and regional fiscal equalization. *Journal of Public Economics 3*, pp. 99-112.

Structural Characteristics of the Alberta Economy: Implications for Constitutional Scenarios

5

by Edward J. Chambers and Michael Percy

Introduction

The collapse of the Meech Lake constitutional accord has prompted a period of intense evaluation within Canada of the political and economic underpinnings of Confederation. Unfortunately, solutions to the Meech Lake debacle are often cast in political terms, with proposals for alternate allocations of functions between levels of government or for various groupings of provinces being assessed in terms of their conformity with the required political dimensions of a potential new constitutional configuration. Terms such as asymmetrical federalism and disentangling have become part of the lingua franca of the debate. When the economic dimensions of alternate constitutional scenarios are discussed, it is often in the context of Québec's vision of a more decentralized economic union juxtaposed against the more centralized entity perceived in tune with the aspirations of the rest of Canada.

Our paper eschews this approach and focuses on a far more narrow but easily more tractable issue—that of the implications of alternate constitutional scenarios for Alberta in light of its distinctive economic structure.[62] Three

---

62. This paper draws heavily on work presented in Edward J. Chambers and Michael Percy, Western Canada in the International Economy, Western Studies in Economic Policy 2 (Edmonton: Western Centre for Economic Research, forthcoming); idem, and "Natural Resources and the Western Canadian Economy: Implications for Constitutional Change," in *From East and West: Regional Views on Reconfederation, Canada Round Series*, C.D. Howe Research Institute, (1991).

constitutional scenarios are assessed: an independent Alberta, a more centralized economic union without Québec, and a more decentralized Canada including Québec with functions allocated between the federal government and the provinces along lines suggested in the Allaire Report. However, since an Alberta in an independent West is also a possibility, we cast our discussion of the structural characteristics of the Alberta economy in the context of Western Canada where feasible.

We do not directly deal with how changes in federal-provincial fiscal relations impinge on the economy as this topic is covered extensively in the other papers of the Conference. However, for sectors such as agriculture and transportation where direct federal subsidies are important, we will assess the structural adjustments which might emerge under alternate constitutional scenarios.

In the first section of the paper, we assess the potential benefits to Alberta of participation in an economic union like Confederation. The essential issue dealt with in this section is the nature of the benefits of the current structure and those benefits that would not be available to an independent Alberta or to different regional groupings of current members of the economic union. The next section reviews the outstanding structural features of the Alberta economy which include its continued reliance on natural resources and agriculture and the high degree of economic variability which characterizes many economic variables. The last section ranks the constitutional options in terms of their effects on the sources of economic surplus from integration and the ability of the Alberta economy to accommodate trade shocks emanating in the international economy.

The Gains from Economic Integration

One of the difficulties in trying to assess the economic benefits of the Canadian economic union to its participating members is casting the discussion in terms of tangible factors. Precisely what benefits of Confederation are specific to its current spatial configuration and would not be available through other forms of economic integration? One approach to this question has been to employ the notion of an economic surplus to Confederation, first introduced by Maxwell and Pestieau (1980), as a means of cataloguing potential benefits.[63] In essence, one compares the level of real income of the observed integrated economy to the sum of the real incomes

---

63. The notion of an economic surplus to Confederation has been employed extensively in work undertaken for the Royal Commission on the Economic Union and Development Prospects for Canada. See Norrie, Simeon, and Krasnick (1986), and Whalley and Trela (1986).

that would exist if the individual economic units were independent. The difference between the observed and hypothetical incomes represents the gains from integration or the economic surplus.

The usefulness of this exercise is that it forces one to define the possible sources of economic gain from integration in an economic union as opposed to those available to a region by means of greater integration in international markets. Maxwell and Pestieau (1980, pp. 14-15) set out four elements of the surplus:

1. sharing of overheads;

2. gains from trade;

3. enhanced international market power; and

4. the gains from insurance and stabilization.

Gains from Regional Specialization

In the context of Confederation today, two of these factors are likely to have a small or even negative contribution to the economic surplus. In an economy where autarky (no trade) prevails, the move to economic integration would yield significant economic gains from trade through exploiting economies of scale in production and from increased productivity from greater regional specialization. However, autarky is not a reasonable next-best alternative for evaluating the surplus of Confederation. The international economy has made significant strides to eliminating tariff barriers and to setting out rules for promoting greater trade liberalization under the auspices of GATT. The Free Trade Agreement with the United States has secured access to the American market for Canadian producers. Even were the Agreement abrogated in the event Canada fragmented, it is likely that separate agreements with the new political units would be negotiated. It remains a moot question whether the terms would be as favourable as under the current agreement. Nonetheless, the basic point is that international trade is a substitute for interregional trade as a means of capturing any of the gains from trade.[64]

---

64. Interprovincial trade may in fact be a costly alternative to international trade to the extent it represents trade diversion within the economic union. Canadian tariff and non-tariff barriers may lead to increased trade within Canada but it is at the expense of imports of lower cost goods and services from countries not part of the economic union. The costs arise in the form of foregone production and consumption.

Sharing of Overheads

The sharing of overhead expenses is also unlikely to be an important gain specific to the current Canadian economic union. These overheads include investments in transportation infrastructure and defence. There are several reasons why the gains in this area are modest. First, the increasing importance of service industries and the declining importance of goods production means that in general, the demand for transportation investments to carry high-bulk, low-value goods is declining. Although tradeable services are increasingly important, they are handled electronically and do not require transportation per se. Second, much of the existing transportation network is configured for East-West interregional trade. The reality is that free trade with the United States and the possibility of a continental free trade agreement including Mexico has made the current East-West transportation grid a high cost alternative to North-South feeder lines connecting with the United States transportation network. Defence remains an area where the benefits to sharing of overheads are important. The fact remains, however, that defence expenditures by Canada, or whatever political entities emerge after constitutional reforms go the course, will continue to be lower than for most countries by virtue of the American defence umbrella—a public good from Canada's perspective.

Insurance and Stabilization

The two remaining components of the economic surplus—insurance and stabilization and market power—are significant in contributing to a real income gain from Confederation. The Canadian economic union is characterized by a significant degree of regional specialization determined by proximity to markets and regional resource endowments. Economic specialization, while efficiency enhancing, can also be accompanied by undesirable side-effects. A region with a highly specialized industrial structure whose narrow range of exports are geographically concentrated may be prone to cyclical instability. An economic union permits the pooling of risks across such specialized regional economies operating through the budget of the federal government. A boom in one region of the country generates personal and corporate tax revenues which help fund programs such as unemployment insurance and equalization in regions undergoing slumps and where own-source tax revenues might not be sufficient to fund stabilization programs. In an economic union in which there are distinct regional differences in industrial structure—resources vs manufacturing—the inherent (at least in theory) self-financing and counter-cyclical nature of federal stabilization expenditures suggests the possibility of significant gains from the insurance component of

Confederation. The potential costs of economic specialization can be offset by the pooling of risks made possible because of differences in economic variability across regions.

An economic union also offers participating regions the ultimate insurance should the resource base be depleted or should there occur a permanent shift in demand away from the region's exports. Tastes do change, and technological change can abruptly make the export base of a region less valuable through providing lower cost alternatives. Interregional labour mobility for the residents of a region in secular economic decline is the alternative to absorbing the fall in living standards required for balance of payments equilibrium. In the face of a permanent decline in earnings from its export base (and in the absence of sustained long-term capital inflows), the basic options open to a region require adjustments which lead to either a reduction in the value of imports or an increase in exports, or a combination of the two. Both options require a reduction in domestic absorbtion of goods and services by residents—hence a decline in real consumption levels.

Two important features of the insurance and stabilization component of the economic surplus should be emphasized. First, the objective of insurance and stabilization policies for regions in the federation is to accommodate cycles or random shocks in economic activity; it is not to offset the economic adjustments required of a region in secular decline. If the latter function dominates fiscal federalism, the potential economic surplus from Confederation can easily be dissipated. Second, even if the risks associated with the economic variability of a region are reflected in the wages of labour and returns to capital, the role of efficiency enhancing government programs at aimed at risk sharing remains.[65] Instability, while less of an issue if it is reflected in the product and factor prices which signal resource allocation within the economy does warrant government attention.

Bargaining Power in International Markets

In a global economy where a region is but one of many exporters to a variety of countries, none of which accounts for a sufficient share of exports to influence price, market power would not be an issue. The contemporary reality of global trade is that some countries do import a sufficient share of world exports of a particular commodity that they possess monopsony power—that is, their volume of purchases do influence the price of the good in question. In this case, the importing countries, or trading block, have every incentive to use market power to reduce prices and redistribute

65. Purvis and Mintz (1990) discuss the role of government policy in unstable economies and emphasize the need to intervene only in instances where market failure exists.

income from producers in the exporting country to government and/or producers in the importing country. Imposition of an import duty or countervailing duty are examples of efforts consistent with the exercise of monopsony power. Conversely, the exporting country may account for a sufficiently large share of global exports or exports to a particular market that it possesses market power. Incentives in this case lead firms or government in the exporting country to adopt policies which increase export prices and redistribute income from consumers in the importing country to government and producers in the exporting country. In this case the imposition of an export tax or restrictions on the volumes exported are consistent with the exercise of monopoly power. In a trading environment where exporting and importing countries both possess market power, the potential for trade conflicts are very high, and economic clout becomes a key determinant in the magnitude of income redistribution between the two countries.

Economic size (in terms of gross domestic product) and a multiplicity of trade linkages are both important factors for countries coping with international market power issues. The ability of a country to protect its exporters from the exercise of monopsony power of large trading partners is clearly linked to economic size and linkages. A larger economy is capable of making more credible threats since it has the economic wherewithal to withstand the potential costs of trade disputes. While income in a region may depend very much on exports of a particular good, this would not be true for the country as a whole. A multiplicity of trade linkages also makes it easier for the participants to negotiate agreements which include face-saving trade-offs in other areas. A country will have an array of trade links that transcend those of any one region. Conversely, a larger country will find it easier to provide the institutional framework to project market power for its exporters in the international trading environment. In part, this arises from the virtue of being large. But it also stems from the fact that trade policies specific to one sector in this context are simply part of a whole array of rules governing trade for the entire country.

The softwood lumber dispute has been analyzed extensively in the context of a dispute over the exercise of monopsony power by the United States and market power by Canadian exporters.[66] The initial outcome of the 1986 episode of the dispute set out in the Memorandum of Understanding (MOU) increased revenues accruing to the producing provinces relative to the status quo, or the imposition, of a countervail duty. The federal government levied an export tax and remitted the revenues to producing

---

66. Papers examining this dispute include Boyd and Krutilla (1987), Anderson and Cairns (1988), Percy and Yoder (1987), and Constantino and Percy (1990 and 1991).

provinces in proportion to their exports of softwood lumber. The alternative was for the United States Treasury to impose and collect an equivalent countervailing duty. From the perspective of the forest industry, both outcomes were equally costly as the effect of each on producer prices is roughly the same (Constantino and Percy, 1990). British Columbia, acting alone as the single largest exporter of softwood lumber, probably would not have been able to achieve the 1986 resolution of the dispute nor move to abrogate the MOU as has the federal government recently.[67] A case can be made that Canada "won" the dispute and that no single province alone would have been able to negotiate a comparable deal.

Mechanisms of Regional Adjustment

There is another important element of the economic surplus of Confederation not explicitly identified by Maxwell and Pestieau but which is very important in the Canadian context. It is far easier for a region to adjust to shifts in its terms of trade or to other shocks affecting its balance of payments when it is part of an economic union than as an independent entity. On one hand, a regional economy would appear to lack fewer mechanisms of adjustment than an independent country. The region lacks its own exchange rate and has no control over the money supply; the need to harmonize other regional economic policies with those of the central government further reduces regional economic policy autonomy. Nonetheless, the "avenues of adjustment" open to regions within an economic union are likely less disruptive and operate over a longer time frame than those facing a nation.

A region such as a nation cannot maintain expenditures in excess of production (or vice versa) indefinitely, at least not in the absence of offsetting financial transfers. If the nominal currency value cannot fluctuate, what are the factors which permit long-run convergence between expenditures and production within a region? An array of impressive papers has dealt with this issue in the Canadian context.[68] The ease of regional adjustment arises from a variety of factors. It is easy within a national banking system to accommodate regional trade imbalances because, at least in the short-run, it merely involves notional asset transfers. Interprovincial migration is also an important adjustment mechanism; it reduces the magnitude of per capita real

---

67. With the exception of Alberta and Ontario, the Canadian provinces alleged to have underpriced timber used in the softwood lumber industry have increased stumpage prices so that all or a portion of the export tax had been removed.

68. Among the most widely cited are Courchene (1978) and Norrie et al. (1986).

income shifts required within a region to accommodate trade imbalances. Similarly, the insurance and stabilization features of an economic union preclude, or at least ameliorate, adjustments that occur in response to cyclical or short-term shocks.

The importance of regional adjustment mechanisms to resource-based economies such as Alberta's cannot be over-emphasized. The evidence regarding the adjustment of oil exporting economies to the 1973 and 1979 price shocks is replete with disaster stories.[69] An array of oil producing economies emerged from the years of rising oil prices and their consequent slump in 1986 with very heavy foreign debt burdens and their traditional export (mainly other primary products) and import-competing manufacturing sectors in absolute and relative decline. Rising terms of trade, driven by escalating oil prices, had led to rapid exchange rate appreciation. Traditional export sectors were no longer competitive in international markets and domestic manufacturers were displaced by lower cost imports. The income effects of rising oil prices also led service sector prices to rise relative to other prices in the economy. Service sector prices in this context refers to prices of goods set within the region (non-traded) as opposed to tradeable goods whose prices are set outside the region. These relative price movements within the domestic economy further exacerbated the loss of traditional export industries and manufacturing. Rising non-traded prices and the pressure this put on nominal wages led to a cost-squeeze on those industries facing competition in export markets or from imports.

When one assesses the economic development of oil producing regions within economic unions—Alberta in Canada, Texas and Alaska in the United States—the extent of deindustrialization accompanying the oil booms is indeed modest. The ability of these regional economies to draw upon interregional labour flows meant that some of the cost pressures that induced structural changes in oil-rich national economies were avoided. Booming resource sectors were able to draw upon labour from the rest of the country rather than have to bid it away from competing uses within the region. Similarly, the expansion of activity in the non-traded sector, especially the accompanying increase in non-traded prices relative to traded prices, was accommodated in the longer term through interregional labour flows. The relative ease with which Alberta accommodated the large swings in its terms of trade during the 1970s and 1980s is detailed in the second section of this paper.

---

69. Gelb (1986) provides an overview of the experience of several economies experiencing oil income windfalls. Neary and Wijnbergen (1986) provide a detailed analysis of the economic underpinnings of this process of "deindustrialization" accompanying booming resource sectors.

Structural Characteristics of the Alberta Economy

The industrial structure of most industrialized economies differs little as the service sector usually accounts for around two-thirds of economic activity. Table 5.1 demonstrates that the service sector dominates economic activity in both Canada and Alberta. Yet within goods-producing sectors, significant differences do exist. Manufacturing in Alberta accounts for less than half the share of income the sector generates nation-wide. Conversely, mining, which includes energy, accounts for more than four and one-half times the share of income in Alberta that it does for Canada as a whole.

Industrial structure has shifted differentially over the period 1971-86 nationally and in Alberta as shown in Table 5.2. Both economies display a shift away from goods production, although the decline is 1.2 percentage points smaller in Alberta than Canada. In Alberta, the rise in the relative price of energy has led the mining sector to increase its share of economic activity by 3.6 percentage points. The decline in the share of gross domestic product arising from manufacturing in Alberta has been less than half that for the country as a whole. Provincial development strategies aimed at promoting further processing of energy in primary manufacturing probably account for the smaller decline in Alberta.

Relative Importance of Exports

Alberta is the epitome of an export-led economy. Trade with other provinces and the international economy constitutes a significant proportion of economic activity in the province. Figure 5.1 shows that "out of province" exports of goods accounted for between 45 to 50% of provincial gross domestic product over the period 1975-86 and for approximately 40% from 1986 to 1988.[70] Net exports, the difference between exports and imports, varied considerably more in relative importance over the period, ranging from 20% of gross domestic product in 1975 and 1985, to only 5% in 1988. Throughout the period Alberta ran a substantial positive trade balance with its domestic and international trading partners.

Distribution of Goods Exports, 1984

Table 5.3 provides a breakdown of the exports of goods by category and destination for 1984, the most recent year for which these more detailed data

---

70. Out of province exports include both interprovincial and international exports.

TABLE 5.1: Distribution of Provincial and National
Gross Domestic Product (current prices) at Factor Cost, 1986

	Canada	Alberta
Goods-producing industries	36.2	39.0
Agriculture	2.5	3.4
Fishing and trapping	0.2	0.0
Logging and forestry	0.7	0.2
Mining	3.9	18.1
Manufacturing	19.2	7.2
Construction	6.3	6.7
Other utilities	3.5	3.3
Service-producing industries	63.8	61.0
Other	48.1	47.5
Non-market services[1]	15.7	13.5

1.   Non-market services include provincial and local government services, educational
services, and health and social services industries. Federal government services are included
in other services.

Source: Quarterly Economic Review, March 1991. (SC #15-203)

TABLE 5.2: Change in Composition of
Gross Domestic Product: 1971-1986[1] (percentage change)

	Canada	Alberta
Goods-producing industries	-4.3	-3.1
Agriculture	-0.8	-3.1
Fishing and trapping	0.0	0.0
Logging and forestry	0.0	0.1
Mining	0.4	3.6
Manufacturing	-3.5	-1.7
Construction	-1.3	-3.7
Other utilities	1.2	1.2
Service-producing industries	4.3	3.1
Other	3.5	3.8
Non-market services[2]	0.8	-0.8

1.   Percentage share in 1986 minus percentage share in 1971.

2.   Non-market services include provincial and local government services, educational services,
and health and social services industries. Federal government services are included in other
services.

Source: Quarterly Economic Review, March 1991. (SC #15-203)

FIGURE 5.1:
Share of Exports in the Current Account of Alberta, 1970-88 (percent)

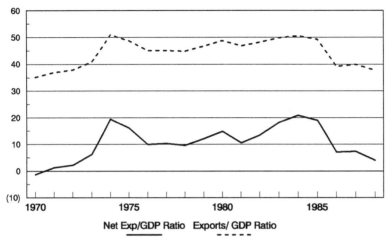

Net Exp/GDP Ratio   Exports/ GDP Ratio

Source: Alberta Economic Accounts (1988)

TABLE 5.3:
Export of Goods from Alberta by Destination 1984
(as percent of total exports)

	Atlantic	Quebec	Ontario	Other Prairies	BC	Foreign	Total Value ($Billions)
Goods	0.32	11.35	26.98	10.40	10.20	38.92	29.7
Primary	0.12	14.08	33.60	4.53	7.36	38.98	20.2
MFRG	0.75	5.29	12.71	23.00	16.33	38.96	9.4
Other	0.00	52.13	36.63	11.24	0.00	0.00	0.5

Source: Quarterly Economic Review, March 1991, Table 11.A4, revised data. Rows may not add
to 100 because of exports to Yukon and Territories.

are available.[71] In addition to manufacturing exports, Table 5.3 contains values and destinations for primary exports (agricultural, fishing and trapping, logging and forestry, mining, and construction goods), and other utilities (those industries engaged in the generation, transmission, and distribution of electricity; distribution of natural gas; treatment and distribution of water).[72] International exports constitute approximately 39% of the province's total goods exports and this share holds for both the primary and manufacturing categories. Ontario is the dominant "rest of Canada" trading partner, taking fully 27% of total goods exports and nearly 34% of primary exports.

The Atlantic region is clearly not an important export destination for Alberta firms; the region absorbs less than 1% of Alberta's goods exports. Québec is more important than either the rest of the prairies or British Columbia considered separately. But the West (British Columbia and the prairies) accounts for almost 40% of Alberta's manufacturing exports and about 21% of over-all goods exports. Proximity thus appears to be an important element in the strength of interprovincial trade linkages.

More Detailed Breakdown on Interprovincial Manufacturing Exports, 1984

The potential for trade diversion (sourcing from a higher cost domestic producer than a lower cost external supplier) is greater for interprovincial manufacturing exports than for primary goods exports. The latter likely reflect trade arising from genuine comparative advantages, unlike the former where Canadian tariff and non-tariff barriers might play a greater role. Primary products destined to rest of Canada markets could be redirected to the international markets and remain competitive in terms of prices. Interprovincial trade arising from trade diversion, however, would find it difficult to survive unrestricted international competition in the domestic market because it would be high cost in comparison to rest of world imports.

Chart 5.1 provides estimates of the contribution of interprovincial manufacturing exports to provincial gross domestic product in each of the Western provinces. These data, unlike those of Table 5.3, are for manufactured goods alone. It is clear that, with the exception of Manitoba, interprovincial manufacturing exports are not important relative to provincial income. Even in the case of Manitoba, interprovincial exports

71. These data are derived from the 1984 Provincial Input-Output accounts compiled by Statistics Canada. The data reported here differ slightly from those found in *Quarterly Economic Review* (March 1991), Economic Linkages Among Provinces. The data contained in the QER have been subsequently updated in light of revisions to the input-output data. We have used the revised data supplied to us by the Department of Finance.

72. *Quarterly Economic Review* (March 1991), "Economic Linkages Among Provinces," p. 42.

CHART 5.1:
Share of Interprovincial Manufacturing Exports in Provincial GDP, 1967-84
(% Share in GDP)

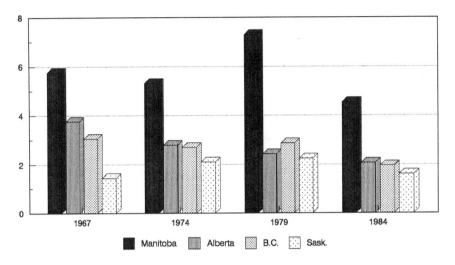

Source: Canadian Economic Observer, MFRG, Industries of Canada (31-203).

account for only slightly more than 4% of gross domestic product. Moreover, the manufacturing exports underlying Chart 5.1 arise in part from the processing of natural resources, including agricultural products induced by transportation costs and regional cost advantages. Hence, the potential disruption of interprovincial trade in manufactured goods possible under various constitutional scenarios does not appear to pose a significant problem overall to Alberta or other Western provinces.

More detailed data on interprovincial manufacturing does, however, indicate some specific products where the potential for disruption may be greater. For example, in 1979 slaughtering and meat processors in Alberta exported $448 million of products to Québec out of total shipments in the industry originating in the province of $1,610 million (Statistics Canada, 31-530, 1979 [revised], p. 64). The dependence of Alberta's slaughtering and meat processors on the Québec market appears to have lessened somewhat by 1984 although the data are not strictly comparable between the two years.[73] In 1984, the total value of food industry exports (which includes slaughtering and meat processors) from Alberta to Québec was $251 million out of total food industry shipments originating in the province of $3,581

---

73. Unlike 1979, the value of slaughtering and meat processors exports from Alberta to Quebec are not available for 1984 because of confidentiality (Statistics Canada, 31-530, 1984, p. 76).

million (Statistics Canada, 31-530, 1984, pp. 77-78).

In 1984, three industries involved in the further processing of natural resources and agricultural commodities—food (SIC 10), refined petroleum & coal (SIC 36), and chemical and chemical products (SIC 37) accounted for $9,994 million (or 65.4%) of total manufacturing shipments of $15,288 originating in Alberta (ibid., pp. 76-83). For these three industries, 59.8% (or $5,973 million) of shipments were destined for use in Alberta. Unfortunately, the Statistics Canada data do not permit a more detailed examination by destination out of the province for shipments of these large industries.

Of Alberta's total manufacturing shipments, 27% were destined for other provinces in 1984. Of this share, 10 percentage points are accounted for by shipments destined for Saskatchewan and Manitoba, 7.5 percentage points by British Columbia, 6.4 percentage points by Ontario, 3.0 percentage points by Québec, and less than 0.1 percentage points by the Atlantic region.

These data, like the input-output data underlying Table 5.3, indicate that the Atlantic region and Québec account for very modest shares of Alberta's exports. Taken together, the data on interprovincial trade linkages thus suggest that the loss of these markets—Québec and the Atlantic region—would have a minor impact on the Alberta economy and probably could be made up by diversion of exports to markets in other provinces or to the rest of the world, albeit in some cases, such as slaughtering and meat processors, with lower prices to producers.

The Structure of Alberta's International Trade

Alberta's exports to international markets are characterized by both a narrow concentration in natural resource and agricultural products and a geographic concentration of these exports. Table 5.4 shows the five leading commodity exports for each of the Western provinces for 1986 and 1987. The data for Alberta clearly indicate that unprocessed natural resources account for almost 62% of its total international exports in each of the two years. A similar pattern holds for Saskatchewan and British Columbia. Exports for the three most Western provinces remain resource-based. Only for Manitoba is there evidence of both further processing in the leading export commodities and greater diversification in the composition of exports, as only a small share of total exports is accounted for by the five leading exports.

Table 5.5 illustrates the geographic markets for exports from the Western provinces. Alberta's dependence on the United States market is similar to the national average, unlike the other Western provinces where it is a less important destination. British Columbia has the strongest export links with Japan, and dependence on this export market declines as one moves from west to east across Western Canada.

TABLE 5.4: Leading Five Commodity Exports by Province,
as a Per Cent of Total Exports (1986-1987 Averages)

Alberta		
Commodity Exports	% Total Exports	
	1986 (%)	1987 (%)
Crude petroleum	27.16	30.26
Natural gas	21.51	19.26
Sulphur	5.33	4.78
Wheat	4.62	4.52
Coal	3.19	3.07
Total	61.81	61.89

British Columbia		
Commodity Exports	% Total Exports	
	1986(%)	1987(%)
Sawn and planed lumber	23.38	25.72
Woodpulp	13.99	17.08
Coal	11.37	7.83
Newsprint	6.52	5.90
Copper ores and conc.	3.41	3.63
Total	58.67	60.16

Saskatchewan		
Commodity Exports	% Total Exports	
	1986(%)	1987(%)
Wheat	28.31	26.50
Crude petroleum	16.96	20.04
Potash	13.08	13.08
Canola (rapeseed)	3.76	3.56
Woodpulp	2.81	3.38
Total	64.92	66.56

Manitoba			
Commodity Exports	1986(%)	% Total Exports	1987(%)
Wheat	23.55	Wheat	14.20
Flaxseed	4.84	Nickel and alloys	6.12
Electricity	4.51	Aircraft parts	4.05
Lumber products	3.55	Motor vehicle parts	3.73
Canola	3.29	Canola	3.17
Total	39.74	Total	31.27

Source: Exports by Country (65-003).

Western Canada's Market Power in International Markets

Table 5.6 provides estimates of Western Canada's share of world production and exports. These data are somewhat surprising in that the region appears to possess market power in a range of important commodity exports by virtue of its large share of world exports. The perception of the region as a price-taker for all of its international exports is not borne out by these data. Even where the market shares are small, such as for natural gas and oil, the potential for market power by both sellers and buyers remains. An important aspect of Alberta's trade with the United States is that it is regionally concentrated within a few states. Alberta's natural gas exports, for example, account for a significant share of the California market. Dedicated transmission facilities, such as pipelines, create a market structure in which disputes over price or other contractual issues are likely since both buyer and seller have a degree of market power.

The Price Volatility of Western Canada's Commodity Exports

A major consequence of Western Canada's specialization in natural resource and agricultural products is the high degree of price volatility which accompanies it.[74] Table 5.7 provides estimates of the price volatility of Western Canada's major exports, aggregate primary product prices, consumer prices, and industrial product price index (IPP). The industrial product price index is a proxy for movements in the price of imports to Western Canada. These data clearly indicate an extremely high absolute and relative level of price volatility for Western Canadian exports, especially agriculture. The two export mainstays of the Alberta economy—agriculture and energy—display the largest absolute and relative volatility of the sectors assessed.

Export Volatility and the Domestic Economy

Export price volatility would not be an issue were it not transmitted to the rest of the economy through income effects and shifts in derived demands for inputs. The evidence clearly indicates that export price volatility is associated with regional economic instability. Charts 5.2, 5.3, and 5.4 depict the variability of provincial gross domestic product, total and per capita personal income, and population. Those provinces in Western Canada whose export prices are most variable also display the greatest degree of economic

---

74. The measure of volatility used throughout this paper is the standard deviation of the annual percentage changes of the variable in question. This definition permits us to compare the volatility of different goods directly.

TABLE 5.5: Geographic Markets: Per Cent Share for the
Four Western Provinces, from 1986-1988 Export Value Averages

Market	Alberta	BC	Manitoba	Sask.	Western Canada	Canada
US	71.55	44.97	57.07	39.74	54.06	75.30
Japan	6.54	26.30	7.63	10.63	15.93	5.78
Pacific Rim	4.68	7.19	2.36	4.64	5.59	2.72
W. Europe	2.59	13.40	10.45	6.23	8.50	8.33
LatinAmerica	1.65	1.36	2.00	3.79	1.86	0.82
CentralAmerica	1.16	0.66	2.73	3.34	1.36	1.26
USSR, EastEurope	2.87	0.20	6.16	10.75	3.13	1.07
China	2.94	1.61	5.87	11.41	3.82	1.36
Middle East	1.34	0.25	2.84	4.25	1.40	0.43
Africa	2.31	0.35	0.96	2.60	1.38	0.78
Other Asia	0.74	0.66	1.02	1.66	0.86	0.72
Australia, NZ	1.60	2.97	0.88	1.01	2.09	1.12
Total*	100.0	100.0	100.0	100.0	100.0	100.0

*Totals may not add to 100.0 because of rounding.

Source: Exports by Country (65-003).

instability. The provinces of Western Canada are more unstable than other provinces and Alberta exhibits the greatest instability for all variables depicted in the three charts.

A high degree of volatility in major economic variables appears to be endemic to Alberta and, to a lesser extent, other provinces in the region. Capital formation is an important component of regional demand. The level of capital formation is responsive to current levels of economic activity and to expectations regarding future demands. In an economic environment characterized by significant volatility, it is highly likely that variables contingent on expectations might also display volatility.

Table 5.8 provides estimates of the volatility of real fixed capital formation from 1972 to 1988 for selected regions and provinces in Canada. In terms of total real fixed capital formation, Alberta displays the greatest volatility. The West is almost twice as volatile as the rest of Canada (excluding the West) in terms of real investment. Disaggregation of the total real investment series into public and private components does little to change the results. Alberta continues to display the greatest degree of volatility, especially in public sector investments.

TABLE 5.6: Western Canada's Share of World Production and Exports,
Selected Commodities, Volume Basis

Commodity	% Share of Production	% Share of Exports
Copper ores and conc.	5	9
Natural gas	5	5*
Crude oil	2	8*
Sawn and planed lumber	10	38
Paper and paperboard	1	4
Woodpulp	3	14
Sulphur (all forms)	12	45
Zinc ores and conc.	11	11
Potash	25	40
Wheat	5	20
Rapeseed	17	43
Barley	8	24

*Represents percent share of the US market.

Sources: **Copper**: Data on Canadian and world production and exports of copper ores and
concentrates from UNCTAD. *Commodity Yearbook 1987*, and the U.S. Bureau of Mines, *Minerals
Yearbook, 1987;* Western Canada production from Energy, Mines and Resources, *Statistical
Summary of the Mineral Industry in Canada 1987*, Table 5; Western Cdn. exports from Statistics
Canada, *Exports by Country* (65-003). **Crude Oil**: Data on Cdn. and world production from
OECD, *Annual Oil and Gas Statistics, 1985, 1986*, and *U.S. Import Data from OECD*, Imports by
Commodity, 1986 and 1987. **Natural Gas**: Data on Cdn. and world production, and on imports
from Canada as a share of the U.S. market from OECD, *Annual Oil and Gas Statistics, 1985, 1986*.
Sawn and planed lumber (coniferous): Data on Cdn. and world production and exports from
FAO, *Yearbook of Forest Products 1984*; Western Cdn. production estimated from Stats. Canada,
Sawmills and Planing Mills and Shingle Mills 1984 (35-204): Western Cdn. exports from Stats.
Canada, *Exports by Country* (65-003). **Newsprint**: Data on Cdn. and world production and
exports from FAO, *Yearbook of Forest Products 1984*; Western Cdn. production estimated from
Stats. Canada, Pulp and Paper Industries 1984 (36-204); Western Cdn. exports from Stats.
Canada, *Exports by Country* (65-003). **Woodpulp**: Data on world and Cdn. chemical woodpulp
production from FAO, *Yearbook of Forest Products 1984*; Western Cdn. production estimated from
Stats. Canada, *Pulp and Paper Industries 1984* (36-204). Western Cdn. exports from Stats. Canada,
Exports by Province (36-204). **Paperboard**: Data on Cdn. and world production and exports from
FAO, *Yearbook of Forest Products 1984*; Western Cdn. exports estimated from share of Western
Cdn. value added in Cdn. paperboard production in Statistics Canada, *Pulp and Paper Industries*
1984 (36-204). **Sulphur**: Data on Cdn. and world production and exports from Stats. Canada,
Exports by Country (65-003). **Zinc**: Data on world and Cdn. production of ores and concentrates
and alloys from U.S. Bureau of Mines, *Minerals Yearbook 1987*. Data on Western Cdn. exports
from Stats. Canada, *Exports by Country* (65-003). **Potash**: Data on Cdn. and world production and
exports from U.S. Bureau of Mines, *Minerals Yearbook 1987*, Volume I. **Wheat**: Data on Cdn. and
world production and exports from FAO, *Yearbook of Agricultural Production, 1988* and FAO,
Yearbook of Trade and Commerce in Agricultural Products 1988. **Rapeseed/Canola**: Data on Cdn.
and world production and exports from FAO, *Yearbook of Agricultural Production 1988*, and FAO,
Yearbook of Agricultural Trade and Commerce 1988.

TABLE 5.7:
Volatility of the Prices of Main Export Groups, and of Finished Goods

Sector Price Index	Volatility (1)	Multiple[1] of CPI (2)	Multiple[2] of IPP (3)
Agricultural	10.6	11.8	7.9
Forestry	4.8	5.3	3.5
Energy	5.4	6.3	4.0
Metals	5.1	6.0	3.9
Aggregate PrimaryProduct Index (APPI)	3.6	4.0	2.6
Consumer Price Index (CPI)	0.9	—	0.7
Industrial ProductPrice Index (IPP)	1.3	1.5	—

Notes:
1. Column (2) is derived by dividing column (1) by measure of CPI volatility.
2. Column (3) is derived by dividing column (2) by measure of IPP volatility.

Sources:
1. Commodity price index coefficients from price series constructed at Western Centre for Economic Research.
2. CPI coefficient from Cansim D 484000.
3. IPP coefficient from Cansim D 694000.
Quarterly, 1972(1) - 1988(2).

TABLE 5.8:
Volatility of Real Fixed-Capital Investment,
Selected Regions and Provinces, 1972-1988

Investment by Province/Region	Private Sector Volatility (%)	Public Sector Volatility (%)	Total Volatility (%)
British Columbia	12.25	10.45	11.11
Alberta	14.17	16.29	13.41
Saskatchewan	11.51	9.23	10.45
Manitoba	10.23	8.74	9.04
Western Region	10.66	8.88	9.65
Rest of Canada	5.33	5.96	4.90
Canada	6.25	4.10	5.44

Source: Provincial Economic Accounts, SC 13-213; National Income and Expenditure Accounts, SC 13-001; Implicit Price Indexes, SC 13-351.

CHART 5.2:
Variability of GDP, 196-1985 (instability index)

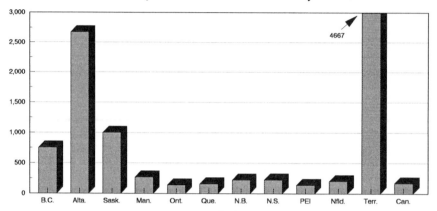

Index is REI (index of regional economic instability) = $\sum\limits_{t=1}^{N} \left(\dfrac{X_t - \hat{X}_t}{(N-3)\bar{X}^2} \right)^{1/2}$

where X=actual value of variable

$\hat{X}$=trend value of X

$\bar{X}$=mean value of X

N=number of observations

Source: Statistics Canada (61-510) and CANSIM (D20031).

CHART 5.3: Variability of Total and Per Capita Personal Income by Province,
1961-1985 (instability index)

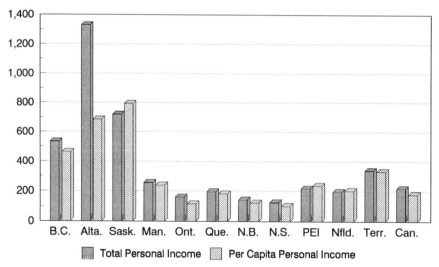

Source: Statistics Canada (13-201).

CHART 5.4: Variability of Population, 1961-1985 (instability index)

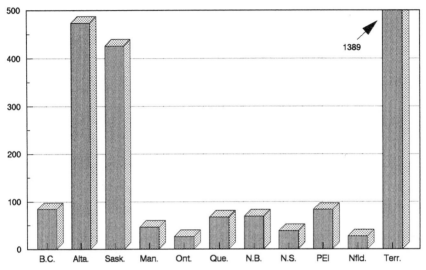

1389

Source: Statistics Canada (91-210).

Table 5.9 focuses on the volatility of land prices for selected Canadian cities from 1976 to 1987. Land prices can be thought of as a crude proxy for non-traded prices and their movements can reflect the adjustment of the economy to terms of trade changes. However, land prices also capture a number of other effects including changes in taxes and their incidence, and zoning regulations. Regardless of how specific the link of land prices is as a proxy for non-traded prices, these prices also reveal how variable wealth is within a region. For most individuals, the value of housing reflects the major component of their wealth. Housing structure prices tend to reflect the prices of the traded goods used in building the house; one would expect relatively little variation in these across regions. Land prices on the other hand will tend to vary and this variability will have corresponding effect on the wealth of home-owning individuals. Vancouver land prices are more than three times more volatile than those in Toronto or the Canadian average, while those in Edmonton are slightly more than twice as volatile. In light of the over-all instability exhibited by the Saskatchewan economy in variables such as gross domestic product, personal income, and population, the evidence of below national average volatility in Regina land prices is surprising.

TABLE 5.9:
Volatility of Land Prices, Selected Cities and Canada, 1976-1987

City/Region	Volatility
Canada	4.80
Toronto	4.57
Winnipeg	4.78
Regina	4.18
Edmonton	10.44
Vancouver	16.14

Source: Construction Price Statistics, SC 62-007. IPP from Industry Price Indexes (d55000).

Terms of Trade and Regional Adjustment

The price at which a region trades with the rest of the world—the terms of trade—is given by the ratio of export prices to import prices. An increase in the terms of trade for a region will increase aggregate real income as each unit of exports now purchases more in terms of import goods. An improvement in the terms of trade also stimulates the export sector and leads to increases in its demands for capital, labour, and intermediate inputs. For an economy such as Alberta's, shifts in the terms of trade are of fundamental importance given the share of exports in gross domestic product shown in Figure 5.1. Oil prices remain the best single indicator of perceptions regarding the strength of the Alberta economy.

Figure 5.2, panel A, depicts the time path of key export and import prices for Alberta. The path of import prices is proxied by the industrial product price index. The sharp rise in energy prices accompanying the exercise of market power by OPEC in late 1973 is clearly evident as is the rise accompanying the Iranian crisis in 1979. The collapse of oil prices in 1986 is also apparent. Import prices have risen steadily through the period although at a slower rate in the 1980s and 1990s than in the 1970s. Panel B of Figure 5.2 illustrates movements in the terms of trade—an index of crude oil prices in Alberta at the well-head divided by the index of industrial product prices. In 1985 the terms of trade were 53% above their 1981 level; the following year they had fallen to only 84% of the 1981 level.

The large swings in the terms of trade shown in Figure 5.2, panel B, pose serious problems of economic adjustment for regional economies. These dramatic swings induce corresponding swings in other variables and ensure that a high degree of volatility across economic variables becomes a

FIGURE 5.2:
Panel A: Key Export and Import Price Indexes (1981 = 100)

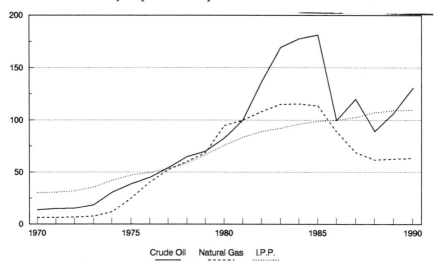

Panel B: Terms of Trade for Alberta (1981 = 100)

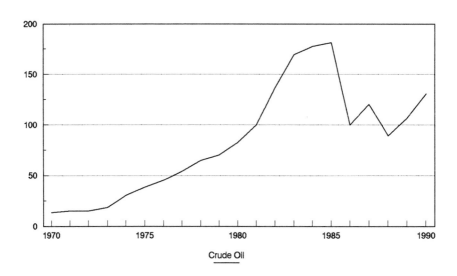

Source: Canadian Petroleum Assc. Statistical Handbook, Table 2, Section VI.

Statistics Canada #62-011 (matrix 20001)

structural characteristic of the economy. Charts 5.2, 5.3, and 5.4 suggest that this is so for Alberta.[75]

Volatility per se is not a problem if economic agents can diversify their sources of income and spread the risks associated with income streams in the volatile economy. Unfortunately, while firms can engage in market diversification and also rely on other mechanisms such as futures markets to hedge against unanticipated outcomes, workers often cannot. In most instances, workers have only their own labour income to rely upon. Moreover, wage rates may not embody risk premia to compensate workers for the greater risk of job loss they face in volatile economies. Hence market failure especially in labour markets may accompany the high degree of volatility observed in an economy such as Alberta's.

Despite the magnitude of the swings in the terms of trade depicted in Panel B of Figure 5.2, the shifts in sectoral employment are quite modest. Figure 5.3, Panel A shows the share of employment in mineral fuels, services incidental to mineral fuels, and food and beverages. Employment peaks in the mineral fuels industry at slightly over 3.5% in 1986 and then falls. While employment is services incidental to mining surges from 1975 onwards, it peaks at slightly more than 2.5% of total employment in 1981 and subsequently does not does not reach this level again. Given the capital intensive nature of the mineral fuels sector, these employment trends are that surprising.

However, the food and beverage industry, illustrative of a traditional export sector, does not appear to be "squeezed" to any extent. Employment declines from approximately 2% in the mid-1970s to less than 1.5% in 1990. Panel B of Figure 5.3 shows that the share of employment in manufacturing declined from around 9% in the mid-1970s to approximately 8% in 1990. In light of the secular decline in employment in manufacturing in most industrialized economies, the modest decline evident for Alberta is, in light of the terms of trade improvements in the late 1970s to 1986, surprising.

The share of employment in construction peaks in 1979 at approximately 11% of total employment and by 1990 accounts for about 7% of employment. Employment in this sector really does serve as a bell-weather for the relative expansion of non-traded activity in the province, but variations in its share do not appear to reflect any "crowding out" of employment in traditional export sectors in manufacturing or in manufacturing as a whole.

---

75. Mansell and Percy (1990, p. 79) found that employment in all sectors but one in the Alberta economy moved in the same direction (i.e. the covariance between sectors was positive) over the period 1961-85.

FIGURE 5.3:
Share of Employment of Selected Industries of Alberta, 1975-1991
Panel A (percent)

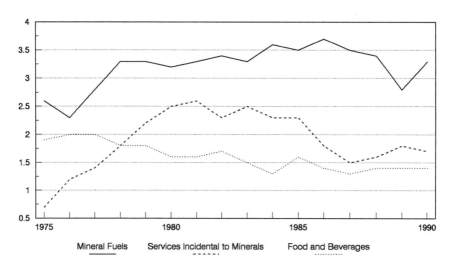

Mineral Fuels   Services Incidental to Minerals   Food and Beverages

Panel B (percent)

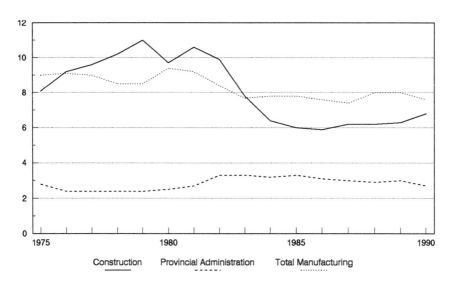

Construction   Provincial Administration   Total Manufacturing

Source: Estimates produced by Labour Force Survey, Sub-Division, Household Survey.

Migration and Regional Adjustment

Migration for a regional economy is a key mechanism of adjustment to swings in economic activity. Figure 5.4 illustrates the interaction between net migration to Alberta and the terms of trade. What is very surprising in this figure is the indication that swings in net migration lead, rather than follow, movements in the terms of trade in the period from 1975 on. In part this can be explained by the regulation of crude oil prices from 1973 to their deregulation under the Western Accord in June of 1985. The various regulatory regimes in this period set out the increases in oil prices and the degree to which domestic prices would converge on international ones. Thus, migrants knew with some degree of certainty the extent of the increase in oil prices and hence the numerator of the terms of trade. Likely firms also transferred workers in response to these anticipated increases in wellhead crude oil prices in Alberta. However, even after 1985 and deregulation, net migration appears to continue to lead the terms of trade.

Figure 5.5 looks at the links between the components of gross migration to the province and the terms of trade. The pattern of movements in the terms of trade and gross interprovincial migration is similar to that of net migration. The population variable leads rather than lags movements in the terms of trade. In part the introduction of the NEP in early 1981 confuses the picture as this regulatory regime had a very significant negative effect on the Alberta economy, especially investment levels, despite the rise in the terms of trade in this period.

While the links between the timing of terms of trade shifts and net migration may not be as straightforward as anticipated, the evidence does suggest migration has ameliorated some of the mechanisms by which booming resource sectors deindustrialize an economy. Figure 5.6 illustrates movements in the terms of trade and nominal weekly wages. Nominal wages, not real wages, were chosen because it is the former which firms pay, and which affect their ability to compete in price with imports or with out of province markets. Booming resource and non-traded sectors would offer higher nominal wages as one means of attracting labour and could afford to do so because their output prices were rising relative to other prices in the economy. Although nominal wages rise throughout most of the period, they do not track the swings in the terms of trade. Had firms in the booming resource sectors and non-traded sectors such as construction been forced to rely solely on the labour force within Alberta, nominal wages probably would have risen far more than shown in Figure 5.6. The outcome of such a scenario would have been a far more dramatic decline in manufacturing employment than is evident in Figure 5.3.

Figure 5.7 looks at the movement in relative nominal average weekly wages in Alberta and Canada and the terms of trade. The relative nominal

FIGURE 5.4:
Net Migration to Alberta and Terms of Trade, 1973-1990

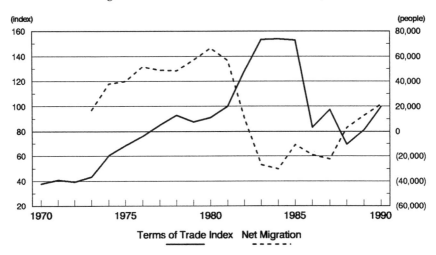

Terms of Trade Index   Net Migration

Source: Canadian Petroleum Association, Statistical Handbook, Table 2.
Statistics Canada (62-011).
Net migration from: Alberta Statistical Review

FIGURE 5.5:
Gross Interprovincial and International Migration to Alberta
and Terms of Trade, 1973-1990

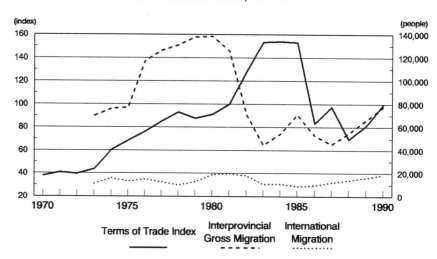

**Terms of Trade Index   Interprovincial   International
Gross Migration   Migration**

Source: Canadian Petroleum Association, Statistical Handbook, Table 2.
Statistics Canada (62-011)
Migration: Statistics Canada (D269465)

FIGURE 5.6:
Nominal Average Weekly Wages in Alberta and the Terms of Trade,
1974-1989 (1981 = 100)

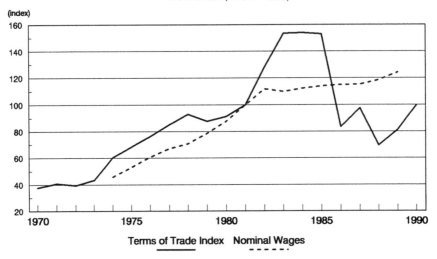

Source: Canadian Petroleum Association, Statistical Handbook, Table 2.
Statistics Canada (62-011).

FIGURE 5.7:
Relative Wages and the Terms of Trade 1974-1989 (1981 = 100)

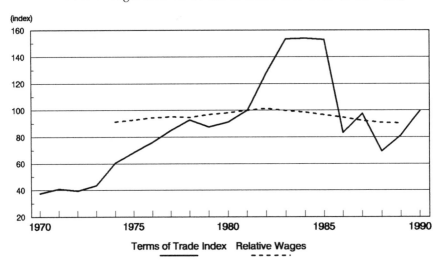

Source: Canadian Petroleum Association, Statistical Handbook, Table 2.
Statistics Canada (62-011)

wage series is calculated as the ratio of nominal weekly wages for Canada divided by the corresponding estimate for Alberta. Again, what is apparent from this figure is that despite the dramatic terms of trade shifts, the net impact on nominal wages in Alberta was slight. We argue that this is because shifts in the volume of migration, as well as the other avenues of regional adjustment, ameliorated wage pressures and the extent of relative price movements in the Alberta economy. The ratio of total migrant inflows to Alberta (interprovincial and international) to population increase for the period 1981-86 was 2.1, the largest for Western Canada after Manitoba at 2.3 (*Quarterly Economic Review*, March 1991, p. 46). Thus while booming oil sectors may have deindustrialized a number of oil exporting national economies, this effect is not evident for Alberta.

Destinations and Origins of Interprovincial Migrants

Chart 5.5 presents the spatial dimension of interprovincial migration to and from Alberta. Panel A contains the evidence for interprovincial migration from Alberta. British Columbia is the destination of choice for most migrants from Alberta. From 1975 to 1982, it received 41.2% of the 504,000 individuals leaving the province over that eight-year period. The share fell to 31.4% of the 337,000 who left the province from 183 to 1986. From 1987 to 1990, British Columbia was the destination of 44.8% of the total interprovincial outflow of 278,000 people. Québec and the Atlantic region (the rest of Canada—ROC) are the destination for only a small share of persons leaving the province. The largest share—16.4%—occurred in the period 1983-86. Ontario is the most important destination next to British Columbia in all periods except 1979-82. The share of interprovincial migrants leaving Alberta for the other Prairie provinces ranges from a low of 16.2% in the period 1987-90 to a high of 26.5% in 1975-78. Western Canada generally captures anywhere from approximately 50% of individuals leaving Alberta to two-thirds of the flow.

A roughly similar pattern holds with respect to migration to Alberta from other provinces as shown in Panel B of Chart 5.5. The major difference is that the share of migrants from other Prairie provinces to Alberta is on average greater than the corresponding figure in Panel A. British Columbia and the other Prairie provinces account for anywhere from 45% to 61% of interprovincial migrants going to Alberta in the sub-periods from 1975 to 1990. The largest share coming to Alberta from the rest of Canada is 20.2%, between 1979-82.

Although the degree of factor market integration between Alberta and Québec/ Atlantic region exceeds the importance of the corresponding trade flows (see the section Insurance and Stabilization) it is still not very large.

CHART 5.5:
Panel A: Migration from Alberta to Other Provinces, 1975-1990 (percent)

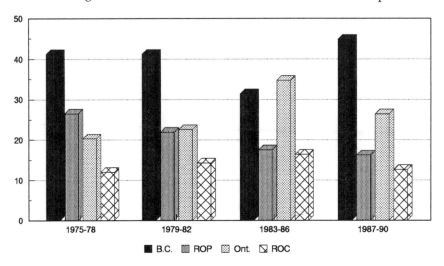

Panel B: Migration to Alberta from Other Provinces, 1975-1990 (percent)

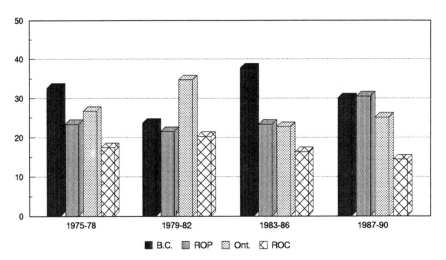

Source: 1975-78, Interprovincial Migration in Canada by Alberta Bureau of Statistics, 1979-90, Alberta Statistical Review.

The Implications of Competing Constitutional Scenarios for the Alberta Economy

The focus of our paper is to assess how the economic underpinnings of the various constitutional scenarios relate to the structural characteristics of the Alberta economy. The impact of reallocating federal and provincial tax and expenditure functions between levels of government, and the implications that this has for tax effort, government revenues, expenditures and deficits at the provincial level is beyond the scope of our discussion. Hence we cannot cast our conclusions regarding constitutional change in terms of the overall economic well-being of Albertans. Instead, we return to the questions that initially motivated our study. What are the gains to the economic union and to what extent can they be achieved under the constitutional scenarios considered? What are the key structural characteristics of the Alberta economy and how do they relate to the constitutional scenarios?

The evidence provided in the paper suggests that the Alberta economy remains highly specialized in a relatively narrow range of resource-based products destined for international markets and the rest of Canada. The province relies heavily on the United States market for exports but also engages in a large volume of trade with other provinces in Western Canada and Ontario. The economy is characterized by a high degree of economic variability which emanates from the export sectors and price variability therein. This economic variability appears to be an outstanding structural characteristic of the Alberta economy and is reflected in volatility of a wide range of economic variables.

Not unexpectedly, proximity appears to be a key determinant of the degree of product and factor market integration between Alberta and the other provinces and regions of Canada. Over all, commodity trade with the Atlantic region is extremely modest while migration is somewhat larger but still small in comparison to that with Western Canada and Ontario.

These structural characteristics suggest the following factors are important in evaluating the potential impact of alternate constitutional scenarios on the Alberta economy. First, the degree of insurance and stabilization afforded by the constitutional option is important. An economic union that spans regions whose economic structures differ from Alberta's and whose economic fluctuations, at least in response to terms of trade shocks, are out of phase with the province is important. The insurance and stabilization benefits of an economic union are important to a volatile economy especially if there are distinct differences in the level of regional variability and the phases of cycles.

Enhanced market power is also important. Alberta and the other Western provinces are vulnerable to trade harassment from major international trading partners. The narrow industrial base, geographic concentration of exports, and large share of some of these exports in world trade, leaves the region vulnerable to the exercise of market power by the United States. The Free Trade Agreement does provide some insulation from the extreme cases of trade harassment. However, the regulatory environment is still receptive to well-organized industry pressure groups seeking protect domestic markets. Bigger is better when it comes to international negotiations over trade issues and market access.

The ease of regional economic adjustment afforded by the constitutional options is also important. Relative to the magnitude of the terms of trade shifts experienced by the Alberta economy since the 1970s, the structural shifts in employment and output occurred in the province are modest. This outcome is quite different that experienced by a variety of oil-exporting nations which ultimately appear to have been made worse off by their booming resource sectors. The constraints on the provincial economy arising from factor mobility in the Canadian economic union, and variety of channels of adjustment to deal with regional trade balance surpluses and deficits, made the terms of trade shocks less disruptive than they otherwise might have been.

When assessing the scenarios it is assumed, perhaps unrealistically, that the international trading environment inclusive of the Free Trade Agreement is unchanged.[76] This assumptions ensures that the estimate of anticipated gains for "independence" scenarios for Alberta or the West are upper-bound in nature. That is, the potential losses arising from a less favourable Free Trade Agreement are neglected. Also, the political units are assumed to adopt fixed exchange rate regimes under the various scenarios. We assume that in the short-term, labour markets adjustments consist of intraprovincial labour migration between sectors but that in the longer term, labour remains freely mobile among the provinces which currently constitute Canada.

Competing Scenarios

There are three constitutional scenarios to be assessed: an independent Alberta, a more decentralized Canada along lines of the Allaire Report, and a more centralized Canada without Québec. Again, it should be emphasized that the major distinctions between a more centralized Canada vs a less centralized one, hinge on factors related to the structure of fiscal federalism,

---

76. Lipsey (1991) provides a convincing argument that were Québec to leave Confederation the rest of Canada and Québec each would have to negotiate new Free Trade Agreements with the United States. His perspective is that the new agreements if successfully negotiated would be less favourable than the current one.

a topic not considered in our paper, but examined by others in the conference. We now turn to the task of assessing the various scenarios in order of increasing desirability.

An Independent Alberta

The least attractive of the three core scenarios is that of an independent Alberta. The problems do not arise from the disruption in the province's trade with other regions of Canada. There probably is only a small share of exports from Alberta that require the tariff and non-tariff barriers afforded by the economic union, most of which arise from supply management in the agricultural sector. It is also difficult to conceive of an independent Alberta restricting labour flows from the rest of Canada, especially from other provinces in the West.

Structural Adjustments in Agriculture

The real problems arise from three sorts of structural issues. The first has not been discussed and relates to federal transfers targeted at specific sectors and the structural change that would be forced to occur in their absence. Grains in 1989 received a total commodity subsidy of $1.1 billion, a figure equivalent to 15.39% of the purchaser price (*Canadian Economic Observer*, May 1991, p. 3.6). Live animals, other agricultural products, and dairy products received total commodity subsidies amounting to $785 million, in the neighbourhood of 2.5% of the purchaser price of these commodities on average. No allocation is provided for the shares of federal and provincial subsidies. In aggregate, the federal government provided 49.5% of the $11.0 billion dollars of subsidies to business in 1989 (ibid., p. 3.2). The transportation and storage sector received government commodity subsidies of $2.3 billion in 1989, a figure equivalent to 6% of the purchase price of transportation and storage services.

Although Alberta has the most diversified of the agricultural sectors in the Prairie provinces, the grains sector is a large-scale recipient of subsidies. Furtan (1991, p. 7) has estimated that were Canada to move to freer trade in agricultural products and eliminate subsidies perhaps as many as one-half of existing farms would disappear. In 1988/89 federal government agricultural expenditures on a per capita and per farm basis for Alberta were $411 and $17,065, respectively. The corresponding Canadian averages were $184 and $16,868, respectively (Furtan, 1991, p. 10). Would an independent Alberta have the fiscal capacity to maintain this level of subsidy in addition to already high provincial transfers to the sector? It seems unlikely to us that an independent Alberta could. Even if it did so, could it escape targeted retaliation by the United States and ECC?

The issue of transportation subsidies also looms large. A recent study by Agriculture Canada (Klein et al., 1991) assessed the consequences of moving to compensatory freight rates and eliminating the Western Grain Transportation Act (WGTA). That is, grain farmers would have to pay full compensatory rates for freight services under the existing rate determination structure of the National Transportation Agency. Among the provisions of the WGTA is the payment of $658 million by the federal government to the railroads. The authors find agricultural net margins would decline by about $680 with more than 35% of this loss occurring in Alberta (Klein et al., 1991, p. 110). Removal of the WGTA subsidy paid to producers does lead to an expansion of the livestock and hog sectors. The rise in freight rates leads to a fall in regional feed grain prices with a positive effect on the ranching and hog sectors. However, the gains in these sectors are more than offset by losses in the grains sector. It must be borne in mind, that at the same time the agricultural sector would be adjusting to the loss of some or all of the federal subsidies, Alberta's existing red meat trade with Québec would likely diminish significantly in an independence scenario.

Another study by Agriculture Canada (Townshend et al., 1991) assessed the competitiveness of the beef industry in Canada and beef imports. It did so in the context of the existing array of agricultural and transportation subsidies. Its conclusions with regards to Alberta were favourable. The authors concluded that "Alberta is the only major cattle producing province in Canada with a high growth potential for producing feeder cattle and a packing industry infra-structure with any hope of long-term viability" (ibid., p. 4.4). Whether this optimistic assessment would withstand the removal of the existing structure of federal transfers and no corresponding increase in support by an independent Alberta is moot.

Agriculture contributed only 6.94% of provincial GDP in Alberta in 1989 unlike Saskatchewan where the figure was 22.34%. Among the Prairie provinces, the adjustment to the removal of federal agricultural and transportation subsidies is least difficult in Alberta and virtually insurmountable in Saskatchewan.

Insurance and Stabilization
All of the evidence provided in the second section of this paper pointed to the Alberta economy being highly volatile across most economic variables. It is difficult to see how an independent Alberta would be any less unstable; it is likely to be even more volatile. The issue of the exchange is a case in point. Say Alberta has a petro dollar pegged to the United States dollar. In the face

of an oil price increase, the key mechanism of adjustment would have to be a shift in relative prices within the independent Alberta economy. In particular, non-traded prices would have to rise relative to traded prices to ensure that the trade surplus would be reduced. Non-traded price increases and concurrent nominal wage increases would reduce exports especially in traditional export industries such as agriculture. Imports would also increase as Alberta's import-competing goods industries would become high-cost producers relative to imports. If an independent Alberta allowed the petro dollar to float, the same structural effects would come into play but now directly through movements in the nominal exchange rate. An independent Alberta would find its industrial structure far more locked into terms of trade shifts than is the case currently. Oil prices are still viewed by many contemporary observers of the Alberta economy as the single best predictor of performance. One could debate the merits of this perception in the context of Confederation today. In the case of an independent Alberta, there is no doubt that it would be true.

The long-term insurance argument also takes on greater weight when considering the independence option. Non-renewable resource revenues still constitute 25.6% of the estimate of 1991-92 provincial government revenues. Transfers from the federal government make up 11.8%. The latter transfer would disappear and the former derives from a non-renewable resource. A recent study suggests that savings from this resource base by the provincial government have been too low and inconsistent with ensuring a sustained flow of revenues from this asset base (Smith, 1991). Thus, in the absence of a significant gain from reducing the net flow of tax revenues to the government (and abstracting from the issues of dealing with the federal debt as addressed by Boothe and Harris, 1991) it is difficult to see how the government of an independent Alberta could provide stabilization in the short-term and insurance in the long-term for the economy.

What of the role of labour mobility? This issue is addressed in more detail in the discussion of an independent West. But one very important consideration should be emphasized. In the independent Alberta scenario, there would be significant fiscal incentives for residents in what used to be the rest of Canada to migrate to Alberta. No longer would federal transfers serve to reduce outmigration from regions in secular decline. What should Alberta do? If it restricts immigration from the rest of Canada, it precludes outmigration from Alberta should the terms of trade turn against the region permanently. Yet if it does not do so, migration to the rest of Canada may place fiscal burdens on the government and possibly dissipate real income to the extent migration was induced by differences in net fiscal capacity.

Market Power

The gains from enhanced market power in an economic union in comparison to that possessed by independent regions was stressed in the second section. The structure of Alberta's export trade and its concentration in specific regions in the United States market make it highly vulnerable to trade harassment. There is no guarantee that it will not happen in the current economic union. However, the ability to withstand the costs of such harassment is greater for Alberta in some form of economic union than it is for the province in isolation.

Is an Independent West the Solution?

The degree of economic integration among the provinces of Western Canada is significant as the evidence of the first section demonstrated. The high degree of labour mobility within the region certainly suggests that the West meets the requirement for an optimum currency area. However, the structural factors which make an independent Alberta unappealing also hold true for an independent West. The issue of structural adjustments in the agricultural sector in the absence of federal subsidies to the sector and transportation also remain. The insurance and stabilization in an independent appear none too different from those facing Alberta.

Another important issue that pertains to the notion of an independent West relates to the structure of government for such an entity. The late transfer (1930) of remaining Dominion Lands to provincial jurisdiction has meant that in Western Canada, Crown ownership of the resource base remains important. The transfer of ownership to the private sector has not occurred to the same extent as in the rest of Canada. Significant differences exist among the Western provinces in revenues captured by government from the resource base although the magnitude of potential rents today are likely nowhere near as high as estimated by the Economic Council (1982) when real energy prices were far higher. Smith (1990) provides estimates of resource revenues actually captured by provinces on a per capita basis and these are provided in Table 5.10. Substantial variation in the level of these revenues exist for a given province through time and across provinces at a point in time. A similar variation exists in the relative contribution of these revenues to provincial expenditures.

A substantial body of literature exists that argues that interprovincial migration is responsive to fiscal incentives and demonstrates that such migration is inefficient. The empirical literature lends weak support to the existence of fiscally induced migration. It is clear that the net fiscal benefits differ significantly across the West and have the potential to influence both interregional and intraregional migration within the West.

TABLE 5.10:
Provincial and Local Government Per Capita Spending
and Natural Resource Revenues, in 1981 Dollars

	1976/7	1982/3	1987/8
Expenditures:			
Ontario	$3235	$3234	$3722
Manitoba	3295	3449	4128
Saskatchewan	3418	3908	4080
Alberta	4097	5711	5043
British Columbia	3422	3800	3767
Nat.Res. Revenues:			
Ontario	21	14	21
Manitoba	44	33	42
Saskatchewan	516	527	300
Alberta	1915	2049	805
British Columbia	173	193	152

Source: Provincial and local government expenditures are from financial data found in Statistics Canada financial management series as adjusted by Irene Ip of the C.D. Howe Institute. Population data are from the same source as in Table 1, and the price index used is that for government current expenditures in goods and services in Appendix II of Statistics Canada, Provincial Economic Accounts: Annual Estimates, 1984-88 (Ottawa: Ministry of Supply and Services, March 1990), p. 133.

Smith (1990) also provides estimates of tax effort and tax capacity for Canadian provinces in 1988 that are presented in Table 5.11. These data show that variations between tax effort and capacity for Western provinces are large. The design of a stand-alone Western regional grouping would, with current provincial configurations, face the identical problems which currently confound the federal government with equalization, EPF, and CAP programs.

The logic of these data suggest that only a unitary state would make sense in an independent West. The alternative—the existing configuration of provinces and a Western central government with a significant redistributive role would be a high cost institutional structure to maintain with the relatively small population base of the region. It would be unrealistic to presume that the residents of the West would want to replicate a central government with many of the functions held by the current federal government yet on a smaller economic base.

TABLE 5.11:
Indices of Tax Effort (a), and Provincial-Local Fiscal Capacity for All Own-Source Revenue (b), Plus the Federal Equalization Transfer (c), Plus All Federal Transfers (d)

	Tax Effort Index (1988)		Fiscal Capacity Indexes (1988/89)	
Newfoundland	102	61.8	92.8	95.1
Prince Edward Island	95	65.0	92.8	95.0
Nova Scotia	92	76.6	92.8	94.4
New Brunswick	95	72.2	92.8	96.2
Quebec	120	86.8	92.8	93.5
Ontario	98	108.7	101.9	100.3
Manitoba	113	81.7	92.8	94.7
Saskatchewan	103	90.2	92.8	95.3
Alberta	77	137.0	128.4	125.9
British Columbia	95	104.5	98.0	99.9

Source: Tax effort indices have been calculated by David Perry of the Canadian Tax Foundation, based on data provided by the Department of Finance in April 1989. Fiscal Capacity Indices are from Historical Summary of Provincial Indices of Fiscal Capacity, 1972-73 to 1988-89 (Ottawa: Department of Finance, March 31, 1989), mimeo.

Centralized vs Decentralized Economic Unions

In terms of the issues addressed in this paper, it is hard to choose among these two options. However, the centralized option—a stronger central government in an economic union spanning the West, Ontario, and possibly the Atlantic region—offers many of the current benefits potentially available in Confederation, possibly with fewer of the costs associated with the decentralized option. There is the diversity in regional economic structure which permits risk-pooling. The market power of the West is certainly enhanced in an economic union which includes Ontario and long-run insurance options are preserved. But both of these features are also available in the decentralized option.

A Canada without Québec would probably see strong support for protectionist agricultural policies diminish. Furtan (1991, p. 7) argues that the UPA, one of the most powerful farm groups and one based solely in Québec, has been very successful in promoting protectionist trade policies in agriculture. Would a more centralized economic union continue to bear the costs of maintaining an agricultural sector which is too large in light of foreseeable agricultural prices? In the decentralized option could the provinces afford to contribute more to agriculture and transportation were the federal contributions to diminish?

It is also difficult to assess the degree to which policies that currently dissipate the potential surplus in the economic union would differ between the two options without detailed study of specific programs. This review is precisely the objective of the other papers. However, one could argue that an economic union consisting of the West and Ontario alone would be sufficient to realize the potential gains from economic integration. An additional benefit would be the absence of much of the pressure to introduce federal transfer programs whose intent is primarily to finance economic activity in regions in secular decline and thereby dissipate the surplus from integration.

What About the Status Quo?

A revitalized economic union would also have to address the issue of the distribution of the potential economic surplus. A study undertaken for the Royal Commission on the Economic Union indicated that the current structure of Confederation generated a negative economic surplus (Whalley and Trela, 1986) and discriminated significantly against resource-producing regions. While the conclusions of this study reflect its choice of a 1981 base year and the distortions introduced into the energy sector by the since dismantled NEP, an array of federal policies remain which continue to dissipate portions (or all) of the gains from the economic union.

Data available on regional net fiscal balances (federal revenues in a province less disbursements) also indicate that on equity and insurance grounds one can fault federal policies especially in terms of their effects on the Alberta and British Columbia economies (Mansell and Schlenker, 1990). The study of federal revenues and disbursements by Horry and Walker (1991) also highlight disparities in net federal spending in provinces that seems inconsistent with equity considerations or which could be justified on efficiency grounds.

What are the simple punch lines that emerge from this study? First, Western Canada, and Alberta are different from other regions and provinces in Canada in terms of some fundamental structural characteristics. Alberta and the West remain very much resource based and characterized by a high degree of volatility. These characteristics make the insurance/stabilization, and market power potential gains of an economic union an important consideration. Second, shifting the focus of the institutions of Confederation from maintaining the status quo in the spatial distribution of economic activity and population in Canada to dealing with the consequences of economic volatility would improve the well-being of all residents of Canada, not just those in Western Canada, and it would contribute to a larger surplus of the economic union.

References

Anderson, F. & Cairns, R. (1988). The softwood lumber agreement and resource politics. *Canadian Public Policy, XIV*, pp. 186-196.

Boothe, Paul & Harris, Richard. (1991). The economics of constitutional change: Dividing the federal debt (Information Bulletin, Economics of Constitutional Change Series No. 1). Edmonton, AB: University of Alberta, Western Centre for Economic Research.

Boyd, R. & Krutilla, K. (1987). The welfare impacts of U.S. trade restrictions against the Canadian softwood lumber industry: A spatial equilibrium analysis. *Canadian Journal of Economics*, XX(1), pp. 17-35.

Chambers, E.J. & Percy, Michael. (forthcoming). *Western Canada in the international economy* (Western Studies in Economic Policy 2). Edmonton, AB: University of Alberta Press.

Chambers, E.J. & Percy, Michael. (forthcoming). Natural resources and the western Canadian economy: Implications for constitutional change. In John McCallum (Ed.), *Canada Round Series*. Toronto, ON: C.D. Howe Research Institute.

Constantino, L. & Percy, M.B. (1990) The softwood lumber dispute and its impact on the economy of British Columbia: A general equilibrium analysis. Vancouver, BC: University of British Columbia, Forest Economics and Policy Analysis Research Unit.

Constantino, L. & Percy, M.B. (Eds.). (1991). The political economy of Canada-U.S. trade in forest products. In *Canada-United States trade in forest products*. Vancouver, BC: University of British Columbia Press.

Courchene, Thomas J. (1987). Avenues of adjustment: The transfer system and regional disparities. In *Canadian confederation at the crossroads: The search for a federal-provincial balance*. Vancouver, BC: Fraser Institute.

Economic Council of Canada. (1982). *Financing Confederation*. Ottawa, ON: Supply and Services Canada.

Paper prepared for the Western Centre for Economic Research conference, Alberta and the Economics of Constitutional Change, September 28, 1991, Edmonton, Alberta. The views expressed in this paper are our own. This research was supported by a grant from the Western Centre for Economic Research.

Furtan, W.H. (1991). *Agriculture in a restructured Canada* (Information Bulletin, The Economics of Constitutional Change Series No. 3). Edmonton, AB: University of Alberta, Western Centre for Economic Research.

Gelb, Alan H. (1986). Adjustment to windfall gains: A comparative analysis of oil-exporting countries. In J. Peter Neary & Sweder Van Wijnbergen (Eds.), *Natural Resources and Macroeconomy*. Oxford: Centre for Economic Policy Research, Basil Blackwell Ltd.

Horry, I. & Walker, Michael. (1991). *Government spending facts*. Vancouver, BC: The Fraser Institute.

Klein, K.K., Fox, G., Kerr, W.A., Kulshreshtha, S.N. & Stennes, B. (1991). *Regional implications of compensatory freight rates for prairie grains and oilseeds*. (Working Paper 3/91, Agriculture Canada, Policy Branch, Grains and Oilseeds Branch.)

Lipsey, Richard G. (1991). *Trade issues involved in Québec separation*. Paper presented at the meeting of Western Economists on the Constitution, Simon Fraser Harbour Centre, Vancouver, March 20-21, 1991.

Maxwell, Judith & Pestieau, Caroline. (1980). *Economic realities of contemporary confederation* (Accent Québec 14). Montreal, PQ: C.D. Howe Research Institute.

Mansell, Robert L. & Percy, Michael B. (1990). *Strength in adversity: A study of the Alberta economy* (Western Studies in Economic Policy 1). Edmonton, AB: University of Alberta Press, Western Centre for Economic Research.

Mansell, Robert L. & Schlenker, Ronald C. (1990). *An analysis of the regional distribution of federal fiscal balances: Updated data*. (University of Calgary Research Paper). Unpublished manuscript.

Neary, J. Peter & van Wijnbergen, Sweder. (1986). *Natural resources and the macroeconomy*. Basil Blackwell Ltd., Centre for Economic Policy Research, Oxford.

Norrie, Kenneth, Simeon, Richard, & Krasnick, Mark. (1986). *Collected research studies of the Royal Commission on the Economic Union and Development Prospects for Canada* (Macdonald Royal Commission 56). Toronto, ON: University of Toronto Press.

Percy, Michael B. & Christian Yoder, Christian. (1987). *The softwood lumber dispute & trade in natural resources*. Halifax, NS: Institute for Research on Public Policy.

Mintz, Jack & Purvis, Douglas D. (1990). Risk and Economic Policy. *Canadian Public Policy*, XVI, 3, pp. 298-307.

Smith, R.S. (1990). *Spending and taxing: The recent record of western Canadian provincial governments* (Information Bulletin 1). Edmonton, AB: University of Alberta, Western Centre for Economic Research.

Smith, R.S. (1991). *Income growth, government spending, and wasting assets: Alberta's oil and gas.* Edmonton, AB: University of Alberta, Faculty of Business, mimeo.

Townshend, Jim, Martin, Larry, van Duren, Erna, & Reenstra-Bryant, Robin. (1991). *Competitiveness of the beef industry in Canada and beef imports* (Working Paper 8/91). Agriculture Canada, Policy Branch.

Whalley, John & Trela, Irene. (1986). *Regional Aspects of Confederation. Collected Research Studies of the Royal Commission on the Economic Union and Development Prospects for Canada* (The Macdonald Royal Commission 68). Toronto, ON: University of Toronto Press.

Commentaries

Wendy K. Dobson, University of Toronto

Although the purpose of this paper is to examine the interaction between Alberta's structural characteristics and constitutional options, this topic provides the only opportunity at this conference to consider the international economic context in which Canadians must consider their constitutional options. For this reason, I will begin by viewing what I see as five key characteristics of the international environment. In discussing those, however, it is useful to recognize that our overriding goal must be to insure steady rise in per capita living standards for all Canadians.

I see five characteristics in the international environment. First, for the foreseeable future, I believe we will be living in a world of low inflation. This means that commodity prices are unlikely to rise much. Second, we will live in a world in which production in key industries takes place globally. Coupled with that development will be the increasing importance of information technologies to make possible, for example, computer-integrated manufacturing. This world will also be one that is less materials-intensive, which has also negative implications for commodities. The third characteristic of this world will be one of increasing interdependence; one in which policies implemented by one government or legislative jurisdiction will have an impact on the economic performance of other countries or jurisdictions. The economic linkages of trade and investment that influence this interdependence mean that there will be more pressures on national governments, in particular, to co-ordinate their policy to promote international goals, which will mean there will be less room for discretion in domestic economic policy making. The fourth characteristic is that we are likely to live in a world of slower growth than we became accustomed to in the 1980s. With the economic pie growing more slowly, and related problems of higher unemployment, trade conflicts are likely to increase, as is the possibility of managed trade. In a world of managed trade, for example, large governments, such as the United States and Japan, are likely to solve some of their conflicts in a cooperative way by carving up market shares based on their political clout. Third-country producers such as Canadians will suffer even though they may be more efficient producers. The fifth characteristic of the international economic environment will be one of continental integration resulting from the negotiation of an enlarged free trade area that includes Canada, the United States, and Mexico. An associated development that will be particularly significant for the western

regions of the North American continent will be the economic dynamism of
the East Asian economies. Increased flows of trade and investment, in both
directions, will increase integration across the Pacific. Therefore, I do not
believe we can assume, in thinking about the future, that the characteristics
of the Canada-United States Free Trade Agreement will remain unchanged.

This brings me to the paper before us. What we have here is a very
useful and insightful empirical analysis that casts light on Alberta's structure
of production and its linkages with the rest of Canada and the external
environment.

There are two areas, however, in which I think the analysis flowing from
the empirical work could be vastly strengthened. The first has to do with the
structure of the constitutional options. As I see it, there are two main
economic scenarios under consideration here: one of economic integration,
the other of economic *disintegration*. In other papers in this conference, the
focus has been on centralization versus decentralization. But when we come
to economic structure, the issues really relate more closely to degree of
integration. By this reasoning, I would like to see the paper restructured to
focus on the two options, with Alberta standing alone and Canada minus
Québec as two "cases" of the larger disintegration scenario. Neither can be
considered without realizing that they involve the horrendous costs of a
break-up of Canada's economic union. The other scenario involves muddling
on in an unbroken economic union.

The other important question in the structure of the paper relates to its
fundamental assumptions. The authors have chosen to assume that under
any scenario the Canada-United States Free Trade Agreement would remain
unchanged. I believe this assumption contributes to an incomplete analysis
of the scenarios. In those cases in which the economic union is broken, I
believe the new entities would have to renegotiate free trade arrangements
with the United States. Much is known about the kinds of demands
Americans would make, given the opportunity of a renegotiation. Examining
these likely demands and their implications would enrich the analysis.

Finally, I would like to make a few comments about the way the
scenarios are treated. First, I consider the Alberta stand-alone option as a
thought experiment—nothing else. As the authors have clearly demonstrated
in their empirical work, the narrowness of the economic structure in Alberta
and the volatility of its economy means that, even if it survived the costs of
Canada breaking up, it would face huge costs of volatility. To the extent that
separatism is an option, Alberta would have to join other Western
provinces—particularly British Columbia to release its land-locked
constraint—or seek absorption into the north-south economic geography in
order to diversify its options and reduce economic volatility. This is a

widely-ignored set of constraints; too many people seem to assume breakup is costless.

With respect to the Canada-minus-Québec scenario, as I have said, I do not think we can assume that Canada in that scenario will be the same entity we know now. The FTA will have to be renegotiated; the economic union would not exist. In addition I do not find it helpful to assume that because the empirical evidence indicates few linkages between Alberta and Québec and the Maritimes, that the issue stops there. If we look at the table on exports of goods from Alberta by destination in 1984 in a different way, by lumping together Ontario and Québec, we get a very different story than if we treat them separately. I think they should be lumped together because of the integration of the two economies. It is wrong to assume that Ontario will not be damaged by Québec's separation. And that damage is bound to affect the western provinces as well.

Things brings me to what I consider to be the only viable option—maintenance of the economic union (at the very least). This option has clear advantages which must be brought out in any analysis. First, we preserve the Canadian Common Market. Second, with the federal proposals of September 24, 1991, we see some promise of a concerted attack on interprovincial trade barriers. These developments would contribute to increased efficiency, lower factor prices, and would hold the promise of better adjustment options for Alberta because people could still move during the downturn periods. In this way, the cost of specialization would be reduced. Incidentally, the authors refer to a number of programmes that might be continued under this scenario that dissipate the economic surplus. It would be a service to spell out which programmes these are.

A final observation on the tone of this and the other papers in this volume. All tackle the scenarios in a remarkably "surgical" fashion, focusing on the "letter" of each scenario instead of the "spirit." I doubt that any of the authors would dispute the suggestion that it is essential they take more into account the very large costs, in terms of uncertainty, length of time, and fractiousness that would be involved in breaking apart the economic union. This I believe they, like all Canadians, must factor into their analysis. Otherwise, they run the risk of ignoring the most obvious—and important—dimension of choosing Canada's constitutional and economic future.

Richard G. Harris, Simon Fraser University

This is a useful and important paper on the structural aspects of Alberta's economy, with particular focus on factor markets and commodity prices. It is an important paper in the context of the current constitutional debate because arguments about factor mobility figure importantly in discussions of economic union and the common market aspects of Canada, yet surprisingly little evidence has been provided on these questions. The Chambers and Percy paper takes us a long way to providing a more detailed picture on the significance to the West, and to Alberta in particular, of the "insurance" argument for a common market. This is the well-known idea that a region facing volatile terms of trade and a highly specialized pattern of production and export can stabilize its level of economic activity through recourse to moving factors of production into, and out of, the region in response to shocks in the terms of trade. Other arguments regarding economic integration are also raised, such as sharing of overheads and the exercise of market power in international trade, but it is the insurance argument that receives the most attention. I will divide my comments into two parts. The first part concerns some aspects of the insurance argument, and the second concerns the constitutional scenarios and conclusions drawn in the Chambers and Percy paper.

Chambers and Percy leave the impression that the insurance argument for economic union hinges on the presence of imperfect capital markets, particularly imperfect markets for human capital. This is not quite correct. Imperfections in the market for human capital imply that workers cannot insure perfectly against fluctuations in their income stream, and this certainly enhances the case for a common market with labour mobility. Workers who face low incomes in one region due to adverse terms of trade changes can self-insure in this imperfect world by moving from one region to another. True enough, and highly relevant to the Alberta experience! But suppose capital markets were perfect. It would still be the case that there would be efficiency gains to labour mobility which would result in a higher than otherwise permanent income stream to workers. Insurance and capital markets would provide consumption smoothing to workers, but by moving labour into and out of volatile sectors average levels of real income would be higher. Unfortunately the paper does not provide direct evidence on these gains, but the observed factor movements illustrated in charts 5.4 and 5.5 lead us to believe these gains must be large.

The arguments on the volatility of commodity prices are important but, in my view, too simplistic. Recent work on the time series structure of economic activity (see Nelson and Plosser [1982] for the seminal paper) have taught us that we must be very careful to distinguish between fluctuations about a linear trend and so-called stochastic trends. The most prominent example of the latter is a random-walk model of GNP. These arguments are highly relevant to commodity prices and have been recently applied to oil prices to give one example. Any movement in a commodity price has a quite different interpretation if it represents a fluctuation about a trend, which is expected to revert to a mean, compared to a situation in which a commodity price change represents a permanent shift in the trend. To be more specific, do current low oil prices represent a temporary blip which is expected to be eradicated, or do they represent a new lower trend path in oil prices?

From the insurance perspective these two views have fairly different implications, particularly when one considers that any decision to move resources between regions is likely to be fairly costly. If commodity prices can always be expected to revert to the mean trend, the case for moving resources in response to price changes is certainly less compelling than if any change is expected to be permanent.

This brings me to my next point: measuring the true welfare gains to factor mobility. The insurance principle tends to focus on the risk aversion motive for insurance; i.e. to stabilize a consumption stream brings certain benefits to risk-averse individuals. This must be distinguished from the option benefits of factor mobility which exist even if all individuals are risk-neutral. To have an option to move within a common market creates benefits beyond those provided by simple income stabilization.[77] If a worker can move from a low wage region to a high wage region as a matter of choice, the presence of this option creates economic benefits. In the case of workers who live in regions with volatile income levels, we expect these option benefits to be large. Harris and Purvis (1991) provide one example of how large these benefits can be. Consider the black market price for a green card which gives access to the United States labour market. The price runs into the ten- to thirty-thousand dollar range. If you lived in an independent Alberta, facing restrictions on emigration to other regions of Canada, ask what you would be willing to pay to give your children rights to work in British Columbia or Ontario? The answer is clearly a very large sum, and both examples provide some indication of what these mobility option values might be worth.

This brings me to the section of the paper dealing with constitutional options. The authors note that economic union amongst the western provinces offers little net economic benefit on grounds of the insurance principle, given that all western provinces face volatile terms of trade and are

---

77. The Heritage Fund is the prominent example of a public policy which provides welfare gains through consumption smoothing.

undiversified; the region as a whole would be highly dependent on
commodity exports. I would concur in their assessment, but would tend to be
more cautious as to the future economic potential of an independent
West—whether a centralized federation or unitary state. The past may not be
a particularly good guide to the future. First, large scale growth in the
developing countries may ultimately put pressure on the demands for raw
materials, such that the trends observed in commodity prices over the last
decade may be reversed. Second, the economic growth of the western
American states has been substantially above that of the American East and
the Pacific Rim countries have the highest growth rates of all countries. The
natural economic integration on a continental basis is north-south and, given
the growth in the American west and in the Pacific Rim regions, Western
Canada is likely to do fairly well over the long haul. The question becomes
one of politics: how does one secure those economic benefits of Western
North America integration but at the same time secure the degree of political
independence that people living in the region would like? If Canada becomes
a highly decentralized economic federation, or confederation, Western
Canadians must ask themselves the question as to what the long term
implications such an arrangement might have. In my own view, there is a
strong possibility that a highly decentralized Canada may ultimately reduce
economic mobility within Canada.[78] If this turns out to be the result of the
current constitutional round, Western Canada might wish to re-think its
strategy, and a strong Western Canadian Political and Economic Union may
not be a silly idea.

References

Nelson, C.R. & Plosser, C.I. (1982). Trends and random walks in
    macroeconomic time series. *Journal of Monetary Economics 10*, pp. 139-162.
Harris, R. & Purvis, D. (1991). Some economic aspects of political
    restructuring. In R.W. Boadway et al. (Eds.), *Economic dimensions of
    constitutional change, Vol. 1*. Kingston: John Deutsch Institute for the
    Study of Economic Policy, Queen's University.

---

78. These arguments are elaborated upon in Harris and Purvis (1991).

A Regional Analysis of Fiscal Balances under Existing and Alternative Constitutional Arrangements

by Robert L. Mansell and
Ronald C. Schlenker

Introduction

Background

There has always been an important economic dimension to the regional dissonance that represents such a distinctive feature of Canada. Indeed, the alienation commonly observed in the peripheral regions is almost entirely economic in nature. As noted by Norrie (1976), Anderson and Bonsor (1986), and others, the usual complaints are that general federal monetary, expenditure, and tax policies, along with specific policies in areas such as transportation, trade, energy, and regional development, have prevented the regions from achieving their potential in terms of diversification, stability, growth, and prosperity.

The economic grievances in the peripheral regions and the links to Constitutional structure have not gone unnoticed by external observers. Brimelow (1990, p. 22), for example, has suggested that the political economy of Canada can be summarized simply, if crudely, as:

> A Central Canadian elite, extracting "rents" from a rich, resource-based economy, struggles to quieten peripheral protest by coercion—voting down regional opposition in Parliament, as with the National Energy Programme; by bribery—extensive regional

transfer payments, under rubrics such as "Welfare" or Economic Development"...; and by conning—persuading the regions of the legitimacy of the rent-seeking activity.

These economic complaints are not restricted to the peripheral regions. In Québec, where the grievances typically have distinct nationalistic and cultural overtones, there is nevertheless a strong economic undercurrent. Some of these economic complaints have been summarized by Ethier (1986). They concern federal monetary, fiscal, tariff, and energy policies, as well as the overall benefits and costs of Confederation to Québec. It is also revealing that economic concerns relating to such things as development, international competitiveness, monetary policy and federal fiscal management permeate the recent reports by Allaire (1991) and Bélanger and Campeau (1991).

There have even been rumblings of discontent from Ontario despite that province's dominance in the national economy and federal policy making. One of the more common complaints emanating from the province is that Ontario has always subsidized the other regions or, in other words, has been the "milch cow of Confederation." This theme also includes the view, perhaps best expressed by Stothart (1988), that provinces like Alberta and British Columbia have not made a fair contribution and have become the "spoilt children of Confederation." While these assessments may not accord with reality, they probably capture the gist of perceptions that are widely held in Ontario.

There is probably no better example than Alberta in terms of the breadth and long history of the economic grievances in the country. It would be misleading to suggest that there have not been any significant changes in the list of complaints since the early 1900s. Clearly, the list has been shortened as a result of changes such as the dismantling of the National Energy Program (NEP) and the implementation of the Free Trade Agreement (FTA). Yet, one is struck by the similarities between the general concerns today and those expressed in the Province's submission to the Rowell-Sirois commission over 50 years ago which included the following: the problems associated with the high variability of income arising from the vagaries in the price and yield of wheat and other products; the disparity between the growth of required public expenditures in Alberta in areas of provincial jurisdiction and the revenues available to the province; the imprudence of transferring more power to the central government than was intended by the Fathers of Confederation; and, the importance of following the principle that responsibility should be left to that government which can most readily perform that function. In addition, it was noted (Government of Alberta, 1938, p. 8) that "Successful confederation cannot continue where the benefits and burdens of national policies are unequally distributed. The benefits of policies instituted for the general good should not in practice be restricted to particular groups or areas."

A common theme in these economic grievances emanating from the various regions is that federal policies, taken as a whole, have too often conflicted with fundamental regional development and stabilization objectives and with notions of equity in terms of the regional distribution of the benefits and costs of Confederation. In the western provinces, and particularly in Alberta and British Columbia, these complaints are amplified. Relatively few can identify federal policies that historically have directly and visibly increased the economic welfare of the residents but many can list numerous policies that have directly and visibly reduced their welfare. A key issue, of course, is the extent to which these views are based on myths and perceptions and the degree to which they are based on facts.

Objectives

While the failure of the Meech Lake Accord has created considerable uncertainty and unease, it has also provided the opportunity to address many of these regional grievances. A first step in this process must involve an examination of the implications of various Constitutional changes for these areas of regional concern. The analysis presented here is intended as a small part of this evaluation process.

This study focuses on the regional distribution of federal fiscal balances (or the difference between federal government revenues and expenditures) when all policies involving taxation, transfers, and expenditures are taken into account. The specific objectives are as follows:

1. to estimate the regional distribution of fiscal balances under existing and selected alternative constitutional arrangements, and

2. to evaluate the implications of the distributions under the various arrangements in terms of: regional economic adjustment and stability; the allocation of population and economic activity across the regions; and, notions of regional fairness or equity.

The general objective of this paper is to determine the extent to which regional grievances concerning equity, stability, adjustment, and distribution might be alleviated or amplified under various types of changes in the allocation of powers.

While the emphasis is on the significance of these changes for Alberta, it is recognized that the ramifications for other provinces and regions are equally important and will have an important bearing on the range of viable alternatives. Consequently, the fiscal balances and implications for the other regions are also discussed.

The cases analyzed include the status quo, Québec independence, greater decentralization along the lines proposed in the Allaire report (1991), and an independent Alberta. The case of existing arrangements is used for two purposes. First, it allows an examination of the validity of regional complaints about the effects of federal tax, expenditure, and transfer policies in terms of regional distribution, stability, and equity. Second, it provides a benchmark against which the implications of the other cases can be assessed.

It must be emphasized that the alternative arrangements employed for the analysis were not selected because they were thought to be desirable, probable, or realistic. Rather, they were selected to reflect the broadest possible range of circumstances and, as such, to reveal the general nature of the relationships between constitutional arrangements on the one hand and regional distribution, stability, and equity on the other.

Qualifications and Limitations

There have been numerous Canadian studies dealing with the regional impacts of federal fiscal policies taken as a whole. They embody wide variations in scope (and quality), but they are all generally referred to as "balance sheet exercises." References for seven of the earlier studies that were frequently used in the Québec-Ottawa debates during the 1970s can be found in C.D. Howe (1977). A sampling of other such analyses includes: Hollinshead and Blackman (1975); Banks (1977); Leslie and Simeon (1977); Hazeldine (1979); Glynn (1979); Whalley and Trela (1986); and, Mansell and Schlenker (1988, 1990). In spite of the inclusion of proper qualifications, at least by some of the authors, considerable confusion as to the meaning of the results has emerged. In particular, there is the common perception that they provide an overall measure of the costs and benefits of Confederation to the various regions. However, for a number of reasons, this view is invalid.

First, there are many intangibles that cannot be quantified. It is impossible to put a value on such things as patriotism, notions of national purpose and identity, the reduction in regional power and control that federation entails, or the gain in market power achieved by regions acting together under a national policy. Second, it is not possible to make unequivocal statements about the relative costs and benefits of Confederation to any particular region unless a realistic next-best alternative can be clearly defined. However, as noted by Whalley and Trela (1986, p. 189), such a benchmark is not easy to establish. Unless and until a region actually withdraws from Confederation, it is impossible to know the outcome of negotiations concerning the sharing of debts and assets, the nature of trade agreements, monetary arrangements, and the like. Without such information, the next-best alternative used as the basis for evaluating benefits and costs will fall mostly within the realm of speculation.

In practice then, what we are left with are much more narrowly defined balance sheet exercises. Rather than measure the costs and benefits of Confederation, they indicate the regional economic impacts associated with the policies that capture the main economic dimensions of Confederation. If properly computed, the results might also provide some indication of the regional distribution of the relative net costs associated with some policy or group of policies. It must be emphasized that the balances presented in this study are to be used for the latter two purposes and should not be interpreted as measures of overall costs and benefits of Confederation to various regions.

Within this class of impact studies, it is also important to keep in mind two further distinctions. One involves the difference between the fiscal and "other" effects of policies. The dominant regional macroeconomic impacts of federal policies occur via taxation, expenditures, and transfers. In some cases, however, the main effects are more structural in nature and arise through other avenues. For example, the regional impacts of tariff policies primarily involve changes in prices and locational economics. Although numerous studies have been done to establish these non-fiscal effects for trade and other selected policies, taken individually, with the exception of Whalley and Trela (1986), they have not estimated the combined regional impacts. It will suffice to note that the results obtained by Whalley and Trela indicate that, relative to overall fiscal and energy policy effects, these other impacts are not large but do generally work against the peripheral regions.

Also within this group of "other" policies that have important non-fiscal effects are national monetary and banking policies. There have been few attempts to quantify the regional impacts of monetary policy. However, qualitative analysis, such as that by Reeves and Kerr (1985), does suggest that the regional effects are significant and do not generally favor the peripheral regions. Laidler (1991), who has also considered this issue, argues for better regional representation in the design of Canadian monetary policy. There have been relatively few studies on the regional aspects of banking policy. A recent study by Dow (1990, p. 160) which addresses this topic concludes that:

> Much of Canada's particular experience of uneven regional development, therefore, can be attributed to the centralised financial system with the implications for the regional pattern of credit creation and the means by which attempts are made by the non-bank sector to satisfy liquidity preference.

Another distinction is between total (or direct plus indirect) impacts and direct impacts. The direct impacts associated with some particular policy are those which occur in the "first round." The indirect effects arise through regional multipliers which, in turn, depend on interregional linkages via trade, migration, and flows of funds. Because of the size and complexity of the general equilibrium models required to capture these indirect effects, most of the analyses have been restricted to measuring only the direct regional impacts. The results from the few empirical studies which have attempted to measure the total regional impacts of fiscal policies indicate that the indirect effects mostly favor the two central provinces (for example, see Economic Council of Canada [1977]).

Finally, it should be emphasized that, even if the analysis is restricted to the fiscal and regional economic dimensions, there are numerous issues beyond those discussed in this study that must be considered in any evaluation of Constitutional alternatives. These include such things as economies of scale in the provision of public services, regional differences in preferences for public goods, spillover effects, program duplication and transitional problems. A survey of these and other relevant economic considerations can be found in Boadway, Purvis, and Wen (1991). Also, see Courchene (1991), the other papers prepared for the John Deutsch Institute for the study of Economic Policy (presented at the conference on the Economic Dimensions of Constitutional Change, Kingston, June 4-6, 1991), and the other papers in this volume.

In summary, the analysis presented in this study focuses on the direct fiscal effects of policies and, further, it concentrates on the implications in terms of regional distribution, stability and, equity. While these considerations are undoubtedly important in assessing Constitutional alternatives, it has to be kept firmly in mind that, even from a purely economic perspective, numerous other factors must be taken into account.

Outline

The paper is presented in the following order: the general analytical framework, along with an outline of key concepts and an overview of the relevant literature; an historical and a forward-looking view of the allocation of fiscal balances and the implications for regional distribution, stability, and equity under the status quo; the results of a similar analysis for the cases of Québec independence, greater decentralization, and an independent Alberta; and, a summary and overall assessment of the results and their implications for Constitutional change.

General Framework

Why Regions Matter

The impacts of tax, expenditure, and transfer policies on the economic welfare of individuals or groups of individuals are clearly an important consideration. Since income is an important element of economic welfare, it makes sense to examine the impacts on groups distinguished according to income class. It is perhaps less obvious why one must also be concerned about the distribution of impacts across groups arranged according to province of residence.

One very important reason is that in a federal system, as opposed to a unitary system, regions are a fundamental part of the Constitutional arrangement. Canada is, and is likely to remain, a federation of provinces (and territories) and, as such, provincial governments are independent constitutional units which are assigned specific responsibilities. Two of the overall responsibilities amplified in the Canadian case are the protection and promotion of the economic interests of the residents in the region. That is, unlike the federal systems in most other industrialized democracies, Canada does not have any serious form of regional representation at the federal level to counterbalance the concentration of power in Parliament that arises from large regional differences in population size Consequently, it is the provincial governments, especially those in the peripheral regions, that must provide this counterbalance.[79]

There are also reasons from a purely economic perspective. So long as there are immobile factors of production and/or costs to adjustment, there will be important regional welfare effects of national policies. For example, a policy such as the NEP, that imposes special taxes on oil and gas production, is also a special tax on the individuals who happen to live in the petroleum-producing provinces. Even though they pay the same federal personal income tax rates as residents in other regions with similar incomes, they are, in effect, subjected to additional taxes in the form of adjustment costs or changes in asset values. The former include the psychic, out-of-pocket, and opportunity costs arising from the changes in incomes and jobs or the regional relocation that would otherwise not have been required. The changes in the value of land, infrastructure, or natural resources owned by residents of the region are examples of the latter. In any case, it is readily apparent that geographical space and distance are

---

79. That is, under the existing system, the interests of people in the peripheral regions can only be protected by provincial governments. In the case of the heavily populated provinces, on the other hand, the interests of the residents are protected by their provincial governments and by the federal government since they will control both.

particularly important economic dimensions in any country as large and diverse as Canada. It is therefore imperative that analyses of national tax, expenditure, and transfer policies consider the regional impacts.

Types Of Federal Fiscal Balances

The federal fiscal balance for a particular region is defined as the total federal revenues collected in the region minus total federal expenditures in and transfers to the region. There are, however, two fundamentally different ways of computing this balance. One is the *financial flow* or *cash-flow approach* which is appropriate for analyses dealing with the regional economic impacts of combined federal taxation, expenditure and transfer policies. The other is the *benefits approach* which is more suitable for evaluating the regional distribution of the tax burden relative to the distribution of the benefits accruing from federal government expenditures.

A simple example similar to that in C.D. Howe (1977) may be helpful to illustrate the key differences between the two approaches. Suppose that the federal government collects $2 billion in revenues from region A and uses it to purchase $2 billion worth of military hardware produced in region B. The financial flow approach would show a transfer of $2 billion in purchasing power from region A to region B. The initial impact of this would be to increase B's Gross Domestic Product (GDP) and decrease A's. Beyond this point there would be numerous indirect effects, such as those arising from region B's purchase of raw materials from region A.

With the benefits approach, on the other hand, the expenditure of the $2 billion is viewed as producing consumption (or defense) benefits of an equal amount and some proportion of these would be credited back to region A. Assuming that this is the only transaction and that each region, with 50% of the national population, is allocated 50% of the benefit, this approach would show a net burden of $1 billion for region A and -$1 billion for region B.

Strengths and Weaknesses

There are many federal tax, expenditure, and transfer programs and it is likely that the majority will have effects that vary widely across the regions. Some, such as support for grain producers, may favor the West while others, like industrial development expenditures, may primarily benefit Central Canada or the Atlantic region. As a result, piecemeal evaluations of the many programs can give a very distorted picture of the overall regional impacts, benefits, and burdens. Even if all federal expenditures and revenues are tallied for each region, it may be difficult to make meaningful regional comparisons because not all provinces work under the same federal-provincial fiscal arrangements. For example, Québec has for many years operated under the "opting-out" arrangements whereby both tax room and expenditures for certain programs are transferred to the provincial government. As a result, simple provincial comparisons of per capita federal expenditures might suggest that Québec is disadvantaged when in fact they just reflect this transfer of revenues and expenditures to the Québec government.

Perhaps the greatest strength of exercises involving the calculation of overall federal fiscal balances for each region is that they avoid both types of problems. By focusing on the difference between revenues and expenditures, the special federal-provincial fiscal arrangements can be taken into account. Further, since they involve the aggregate fiscal impacts of all policies taken together, it is possible to obtain a more accurate picture of the regional distribution of the effects.

There are, however, definite limitations and weaknesses. One which has already been noted is that the balances only indicate the "first-round" impacts. In order to determine the overall macroeconomic effects for each region, these results would need to be fed into a model designed to capture the many complex interregional linkages. Another is that it is very difficult to estimate accurately the regional incidence of some revenue and expenditure items as is required in the benefits approach. Examples here include the incidence of federal sales taxes and the federal debt. Still other limitations arise from the inability to take into account regional differences in costs and preferences with respect to the provision of public goods. The methods used to address these problems are outlined in the section entitled Fiscal Balances, Economic Impacts and Equity Under Existing Arrangements.

Fiscal Balances and Regional Macroeconomic Impacts

The objective here is to outline briefly the main mechanisms through which the federal fiscal balance for a region affects regional adjustment and the distribution of economic activity. In this context the relevant balances are those calculated using the cash-flow approach.

It is useful to distinguish among the various types of impacts of fiscal balances. First, there are the impacts that are fairly direct and those that occur via effects on the manner and extent to which a regional economy adjusts to shocks of various types. The adjustment impacts can be further broken down according to the temporal dimension. Those involving adjustments to cyclical or random shocks will be referred to as stabilization-related; those associated with secular shifts will be indicated by the term "long run adjustment impacts" or simply "long run impacts."[80]

Ignoring interregional linkages for the moment and using a simple Keynesian framework, federal fiscal balances will affect GDP in a given region directly via impacts on government investment and/or government expenditures on goods and services. The tax and transfer elements of the balance will also have effects by altering disposable income, and thereby affecting consumption expenditures, and by changing returns on investment which will modify total investment expenditure. Other impacts may occur through direct effects on the regions exports and/or imports. In the case of a federal fiscal surplus, which constitutes a net withdrawal from the regional economy, there would be a multiplied contraction of GDP. The opposite would occur in the case of a fiscal deficit.

In terms of the significance of the impacts, the effects on total income and per capita received by residents of the region will generally be more important than the changes in GDP. It will be recalled that GDP is a measure of value-added within the region's geographical boundaries and not a measure of income received by those residing within these boundaries. Although there is usually a close relationship between GDP and income measure, there can be substantial variations. In the case of Alberta, for example, GDP varies significantly in relation to income received because a large portion of the resource rents, which vary with resource prices, are collected by the government and, at least in the first instance, do not become part of personal income.

The effects in terms of per capita income will depend on many factors. For reasons outlined in Mansell and Copithorne (1986, p. 5), these effects of federal fiscal balances will be governed by how they affect these outcomes: the gap between transfers and taxes; capital intensity; industrial structure; the age, education, and skill structure of the labour force; the size of the population (via migration) and agglomeration economies; and, labour force participation and unemployment rates. To put it simply, a sophisticated model is required to determine the overall effects on per capita income even within this simple Keynesian framework.

Many of the impacts of federal fiscal balances will occur through linkages involving interregional flows of people, commodities, and funds. For example, in addition to the Keynesian and Leontief multiplier effects within the region, there is also a population multiplier impact as people migrate based on relative income and employment opportunities and carry with them demands for private and public goods and services.

---

80. The implications in terms of seasonal instability are not considered in this study.

Perhaps the most frequently overlooked adjustments occur via the regional balance of payments or, in other words, by shifts involving interregional flows of commodities and funds. Detailed explanations of these mechanisms have been provided by, among others, Thirsk (1973), Scott (1978), Courchene (1978), and Thirlwall (1980). To highlight some of the key elements, consider the case of a region that, as a result of some external shock, experiences a decline in its exports. Without the possibility of a change in the exchange rate (since for interregional trade the exchange rate is fixed at one), and assuming for the moment no offsetting financial flows via federal fiscal balances, there are several possible outcomes. First, in a Keynesian world with rigid prices and wages there would be a (multiplied) decline in the region's income which would result in a reduction in imports to restore balance, along with higher unemployment and outmigration. Alternatively, economic agents in the region could sell real or financial assets to those in other regions and the resulting capital account surplus could offset the current account deficit. This redistribution of wealth might restore balance in the case of a temporary downturn in exports but would likely result in a decline in the region's income and imports if it were a secular shift.

Other possibilities exist if one moves to a Neoclassical framework where there are flexible wages and prices. In such a case prices would decline and this, along with some combination of reduced wages and outmigration, would restore the competitiveness of the region's exports, encourage import replacement and create an incentive for capital to move into the region. In practice these types of adjustments are limited by wage and price rigidities related to institutional factors and government policies.

It can be argued on both efficiency and equity grounds that for short run variations in a region's exports it is better to prevent or ameliorate these types of adjustments through offsetting changes in federal fiscal balances. Indeed, this is viewed as a major source of the economic gain associated with a federal system. That is, it provides a mechanism whereby a region can specialize in its areas of comparative advantage without suffering the instability that specialization usually entails. Since the main federal taxes and many of the federal expenditures and transfers are sensitive to income and unemployment, they provide an important element of automatic stabilization. In addition, discretionary policies such as those involving capital assistance, can be used to further offset cyclical or random variations in the region's economy.

While there is general agreement on the merits of federal tax, expenditure and transfer policies to smooth out short run variations, there is no consensus with respect to secular or long run shifts. In the case of a secular decline in the region's exports, Buchanan (1970), for example, has argued that by running a fiscal deficit with the region it may be possible to improve the resources in situ and that migration in such cases would be inefficient and actually subvert the required adjustment. Another view is that in the absence of such policies both capital and labour will relocate to regions with the lowest fiscal pressure and this will lead to economic inefficiency. Other arguments, such as those associated with Myrdal (1957), are that, for the region experiencing outmigration, there are backwash effects in the form of reductions in the quality of labour, in demand and in the scope for agglomeration economies and these outweigh any equilibrating effects.

An opposing view that has gained considerable acceptance is one associated with Courchene (1978, 1981). The general argument is that, by preventing required adjustments and creating transfer dependencies, large fiscal injections of the place-oriented (vs. people-oriented) types lead to inefficiencies in the trade-deficit regions and in those regions where the federal government runs a fiscal surplus. The end result is no significant improvement in per capita incomes in the deficit regions and heavy fiscal burdens which reduce output and productivity in the surplus regions.

If, as is widely accepted, there is an important role for federal government fiscal policy in reducing random and cyclical variability in the regions, the question remains as to what constitutes the appropriate fiscal response. The narrow view is that, regardless of whether the initial fiscal balance was positive or negative, the stabilization objective will be served if it declines when the regional economy turns down relative to the national average and increases in the case of an upturn. In fact this will almost always be the case because of the operation of stabilizers in the form of income taxes, welfare expenditures, unemployment insurance, and so forth which respond automatically to changes in economic conditions.

However, it can be argued that a broader view embodying the notion of regionally differentiated fiscal policy is more appropriate. For example, consider the case where a region with an income level equal to the national average experiences an economic downturn relative to the other regions as a result of a random or cyclical decline in the price of its key exports. Further, suppose that prior to this event the federal government was running a fiscal surplus with that region. Effective stabilization would require not just that the size of this surplus fall, but that it shifts from a surplus to a deficit so as to provide a net injection to the region's economy. In other words, it is important to judge the effectiveness of the stabilization in terms of both the change in and sign of the fiscal balance.

Following the seminal work in this area by Engerman (1965), the Economic Council of Canada (1977) has analyzed the feasibility of regionally differentiated fiscal policy. After evaluating the usual concerns, such as the leakages arising from interregional trade which cause the fiscal impacts to spill over into other regions, it concluded that such policy would be both desirable and feasible.

Fiscal Balances and Regional Equity

Differences in federal fiscal balances across regions produce redistribution which has implications for regional fairness or equity. Before one can determine whether a particular structure of fiscal balances is consistent with this important objective, it is necessary to define regional equity. However, such a definition involves value judgements and, therefore, it is difficult to get broad agreement.

One approach might be to appeal to the various Constitution Acts. As noted by Cumming (1986), Section 118 of the 1867 Constitution Act set out the equality of treatment among provinces but this was immediately followed, in Section 119, by provisions for an additional per capita subsidy for New Brunswick because of special circumstances. Over the years these types of transfers became an accepted feature of Confederation and, in 1957, were formalized with the introduction of the fiscal equalization program. The general intent was to ensure some reasonable equity across provinces in terms of the level of public services provided. The issue of equity is also addressed under the "Equalization and Regional Disparities" section (Part III, Section 36) of the 1982 Constitution Act. Subject to the division of powers, it commits the Government of Canada and the provincial governments to:

a.   promoting equal opportunities for the well-being of Canadians;

b.   furthering economic development to reduce disparity in opportunities; and,

c.   providing essential public services of reasonable quality to all Canadians.

It will suffice to note that a wide range of federal fiscal balances for any given region could be consistent with equity as defined by these broad objectives.

Alternatively, one can turn to the large public finance literature for a definition. There, a distinction is made between vertical and horizontal equity. Vertical equity concerns the change in net fiscal benefits (the difference between the value of public services received and the taxes paid) across individuals or groups that vary in terms of economic circumstances. In general it requires net fiscal benefits (NFBs) to decrease in going from low income groups (regions) to high income groups (regions), but the amount of decrease will depend on societal values.

Horizontal equity is defined as the equal treatment of equals. This principle would require that, with respect to federal tax, expenditure, and transfer policies, individuals who are equally well-off are treated the same, regardless of the region in which they reside. In practice, "equally well-off" is usually taken to mean "having the same level of taxable income."

In the standard theoretic treatments within a fiscal federalism context, horizontal inequities arise from variations in provincial budgetary policies that produce regional differences in NFBs. For example, it is argued that, in the absence of other fiscal transfers, federal taxes which are applied equally to residents in all regions will result in horizontal inequity because other determinants of real economic welfare may not be fully reflected in the calculations for taxable income. As explained by Boadway (1986), broad-based horizontal equity would require interregional transfers to equalize fiscal capacities and thereby take account of these other factors. On the other hand, according to the narrow-based definition of horizontal equity, residents of a province are viewed as having full property rights to the NFBs generated by their provincial government. Consequently, horizontal equity does not require equalization of fiscal capacities.

In one of the most balanced discussions of these issues, the Economic Council of Canada (ECC, 1982) has suggested that a hybrid definition is most appropriate for Canada. That is, the narrow-based approach should be used for net fiscal benefits (NFBs) originating from such things as resources which, under the Constitution, are clearly owned by the provinces. However, for other NFBs, including those related to Crown corporation profits, the broad-based definition and, hence, full equalization should be applied.

The analyses of equity typically found in the literature are subject to many serious limitations that diminish their usefulness in an applied context. First, they focus on mechanisms such as fiscal equalization transfers and various types of federal grants. But, in practice, these may often account for a relatively small portion of total interregional transfers. In fact, by far the largest of such transfers in Canada in recent decades have been those associated with special energy taxes and regulated energy prices. As noted by Robinson (1967), unless the distributional effects of the full range of policies are considered it is doubtful that regional equity can be defined in any meaningful way.

Second, in most cases the items selected as being important in terms of NFBs are rather arbitrary and lead to numerous inconsistencies. Cumming (1986), for example, lists a number of reasons why Alberta's oil and gas rents should be distributed across all regions: that is, redistributed to a greater degree than what naturally occurs through federal direct and indirect taxes. In addition to overlooking the issue of provincial ownership, this view ignores the fact that there are rents in most regions which are not subject to federal taxes or other types of redistribution. There are, for example, sizable hydroelectric rents in Québec and Ontario and locational rents in the "golden triangle." The only difference is that Alberta collects the rents and distributes them via the tax expenditure system while the hydroelectric rents are not collected but are distributed via artificially low prices for electricity. It is surely inequitable to select the items that are to be subject to redistribution simply on the basis of the degree of visibility. Further, since it is easily demonstrated that the distribution of rents via artificial, low prices violates the principle of vertical equity and leads to inefficiency, redistribution of only the rents which are collected by provincial governments creates an incentive for both inequity and inefficiency.[81]

In this context it is also interesting to note the selective way in which the efficiency implications of NFBs associated with oil and gas rents have been addressed in this literature. The usual arguments are that the visible, energy-related NFBs in provinces such as Alberta lead to greater levels of in-migration than is warranted by the efficiency requirement which involves the equalization of the marginal product of labour across regions. Not only is the evidence on NFB-driven migration tenuous, to put it mildly, but the implicit assumption is that the potential inefficiency arising from any such migration is important, and the inefficiency (and inequity) associated with the distribution of other rents by non-tax/expenditure methods is unimportant.

A third problem is that these discussions typically assume that taxable income is an adequate measure of economic welfare. Accordingly, it is argued that, all other things equal, so long as individuals with the same taxable income levels are subject to the same federal tax rate regardless of province of residence, regional equity is achieved. However, consider the case where a policy such as the NEP is introduced. Since the subsidy to individuals in the main consuming provinces is, at least in part, in the form of energy prices which are lower than they would otherwise be, this gain is not reflected in taxable income. Nor are the additional costs to individuals in the net producing regions who are hurt by the policy. There is no account taken of such things as the loss in potential income, the adjustment costs for those forced to relocate or the reduction in wealth as the prices of immobile assets such as housing fall, all as a result of the policy.

---

81. For example, the distribution of energy rents via artificially low prices is said to be inequitable (in a vertical sense) because energy consumption is highly correlated with income level and, hence, those who benefit most are likely to be those who need the subsidy least. The distribution via artificially low prices leads to inefficiency because the price does not reflect the true opportunity value of the resources.

After reviewing the extensive public finance literature on equity and efficiency within a federal system, Wiseman (1987, p. 383) reaches the conclusion that it is "easier to discover significant questions than agreed answers" and that there are many aspects of "federal equity" which should be considered in practice. These include:

> equity in the (tax and benefit) treatment of individuals by the federal and regional fiscs; equity in the federal treatment of the different (political) regions; equity in the formulation of policies for economic stability; equity in the use of public finance to improve regional growth rates; equity in the equalization of (federal) standards of provision of particular types of service; and, equity in the derivation sense—the distribution of federal expenditures, by reference to the (regional) origin of federal tax revenues. (p. 406).

In this study we employ a similar, broad definition of regional equity. An attempt is made to incorporate all of the fiscal policies that are significant in terms of regional redistribution and not just those, such as equalization payments and federal grants, which serve as the focus in much of the literature.

Fiscal Balances, Economic Impacts and Equity Under Existing Arrangements

General Approach

In this section we outline the regional distribution of federal fiscal balances for Canada and discuss the implications with respect to regional economic impacts and equity. It will be recalled that the impacts include the effects on the regional distribution of economic activity and population (or the long run adjustment impacts) and the effects on regional economic stability (or the stabilization-related impacts).

We begin by focusing on the structure of fiscal balances over the period 1961-1989. This historical analysis is not motivated by a belief that the future balances under existing constitutional arrangements will be the same as those observed in the past. Rather, the purpose of this focus is threefold. First, such an analysis can be useful in evaluating some of regional complaints that have no doubt helped shape provincial positions on constitutional reform. Second, it can be helpful in uncovering any systematic linkages between economic impact and equity issues on the one hand and the division of powers on the other. Third, this analysis provides a useful benchmark against which the changes under alternative constitutional arrangements can be assessed. This historical evaluation is supplemented, at the end of the section, with a look ahead at the types of changes that might exist under a status quo constitutional scenario.

Data and Methodology

For the reasons presented earlier, two basic types of fiscal balances are required for the analysis. Balances computed on a financial or cash-flow basis are needed to assess the regional macroeconomic impacts, while a benefits approach must be used for regional equity evaluations. For both types of balances, the foundation is the Provincial Economic Accounts (PEA). These include federal revenues and expenditures by province (and territory), estimated using National Accounts conventions and procedures. The main categories are as follows:

Federal Revenues (R)

Direct Taxes (DT). These consist of income taxes on individuals, corporate income taxes, succession and estate duties, contributions to public service pensions, contributions to UIC, and withholding taxes.

Indirect Taxes (IT). These consist of indirect taxes on banks and insurance companies, customs import duties, excise duties, excise taxes, the oil export charge, the Petroleum Compensation Fund levy, the Canadian Ownership charge, air transportation taxes, and miscellaneous indirect taxes.

Investment Income (IY). This is made up of interest on government-held public funds and on loans, advances and investments plus remittances from government business enterprises.

Federal Expenditures/Transfers (E)

Government Expenditure (G). Included here are the expenditures on goods and services associated with government operations.

Transfer Payments (TR). This consists of transfer payments to individuals, to businesses, to nonresidents and to provincial and municipal governments. See Tables 13, 14 and 15 in the PEA for a detailed breakdown.

Interest on the Public Debt (IOPD). This includes the interest on the federal debt which is paid to residents and nonresidents.

Two additional items should be noted: these are Capital Consumption Allowances (CCA) and Investment in Fixed Capital and Inventories (I). The net federal balance for each region is then computed as R-E+CCA-I.

There are a number of adjustments to these data that are required under both the cash-flow and the benefits approach. The two most significant changes concern IOPD and the fiscal transfers associated with regulated oil and gas prices. In assembling the PEA, the IOPD which is paid to residents of other countries is allocated among the provinces in proportion to that paid to provincial residents. The first adjustment involves removing the IOPD paid to nonresidents by a reverse operation and putting it in the "outside Canada" region.[82]

As noted by Whalley and Trela (1986, p. 192), the interregional effects of energy policies, especially the price controls, dominate the interregional effects of all other policies. While the PEA do include the explicit oil and gas taxes and transfers, they do not incorporate the much larger implicit taxes and subsidies associated with regulated oil and gas prices. For example, if region X is required to sell its oil to region Y (as well as within region X) at $6/bbl. when the market value is $10/bbl., this is the same as a federal tax of $4/bbl. on all oil produced by region X for domestic markets and a subsidy of $4/bbl. on all oil consumed in the two regions. Failure to take these transfers into account would lead to severely biased results. As an example, the unadjusted PEA data would show that Québec and the Maritimes gained during the period when domestic prices were fixed below market levels but Ontario did not. That is because both of the former regions imported significant amounts of off-shore oil and, consequently, received payments from the Petroleum Compensation Fund (PCF), while Ontario purchased domestic crude at the lower domestic price and therefore did not receive PCF payments. Yet it is clear that the effective subsidy per unit of oil at the blended Canadian price would essentially be the same and full accounting should reflect this.

To arrive at the net federal transfers associated with regulated energy pricing, the differences between the actual domestic price and the market (export) price, netted back to each region, for both oil and natural gas was multiplied by the regional production of each product destined for Canadian markets. This represents the implicit tax on production associated with regulated pricing. Next, this price differential was multiplied by the domestically produced oil and gas consumed in each region. This is the implicit subsidy to oil and gas consumers. For each region the implicit subsidy is subtracted from the implicit tax to arrive at the net fiscal transfer due to regulated pricing.

For the period 1961 to 1972 this shows net transfers to Alberta of $1.7 billion (in 1990 dollars) and $0.6 billion to Saskatchewan and net transfers from British Columbia, Manitoba, and Ontario equal to $0.3 billion, $0.2

---

82. Estimates of interest payments to non-residents are from Statistics Canada, Cat. No. 67-001.

billion, and $1.8 billion respectively. It might be recalled that during this period the National Oil Policy provided a protected market for Western Canadian crude, and oil consumers in Ontario and west of Ontario paid slightly higher prices than would have otherwise been the case. After 1972 the situation reversed. Over this period the prices were kept below market values and this produced a net transfer of $65.7 billion (in 1990 dollars) from Alberta and $1.5 billion from Saskatchewan and net transfers to the other regions. The net gains to these other regions are as follows: British Columbia, $7.6 billion; Manitoba, $2.4 billion; Ontario, $42.5 billion; Québec, $14.4 billion; and the Atlantic provinces, $0.5 billion. It should be noted that these gains shown for Québec and the Atlantic region are in addition to those from explicit energy subsidies that are already incorporated in the PEA.

The fiscal balances incorporating these adjustments are provided in Table 6.1. As shown there, for the period 1961-1989 as a whole there was a net outflow from Alberta and Ontario and net inflows to the other regions. If a sufficiently sophisticated interregional model existed it would be possible to simply input these numbers to arrive at estimates of the regional impacts. That is, such a model would take into account things such as the regional effects of federal deficits and debt, the regional leakages via interregional trade and all of the factors which determine the ultimate incidence of federal taxes and expenditures.

Unfortunately, this type of model does not exist and even the closest thing to it, such as the general equilibrium model used by Whalley and Trela (1986), would be extremely difficult and expensive to apply if the analysis involves more than one time period. The "second best" approach which is adopted here is to make adjustments to reflect the incidence of taxes, the federal debt, and so on, so as to at least establish the range of values for relative impacts.

Before outlining these additional adjustments, it may be useful to consider the nature of the indirect impacts via interregional trade in relation to the direct effects which we will focus on. Table 6.2 shows the results of an exercise to compare the direct and total (direct plus indirect) impacts for each region that are associated with federal government investment expenditures. This involves the use of the regional leakage/distribution matrix for construction expenditures found in ECC (1977, p. 106). It can be observed that the indirect effects arising from interregional trade generally favor Ontario and Québec relative to the other regions. For example, the indirect effects result in gains of 35% and 8%, respectively, for Ontario and Québec while for all other regions there are reductions. Similar effects can be shown for federal taxes. However, the total effects will depend on the composition of both revenues and expenditures.

TABLE 6.1:
Total and Per Capita Federal Fiscal Balances as Shown in PEA
with Energy Price Adjustments, 1961-1989

Region	Total Balances (billions of 1990 dollars)				Annual Per Capita Balance (1990 dollars)			
	1960s	1970s	1980s	Total	1960s	1970s	1980s	Avg.
Nfld	-6.5	-16.6	-27.1	-50.3	-1485	-3033	-4762	-3149
PEI	-2.3	$-4.9	-6.8	-14.0	-2338	-4218	-5362	-4029
NS	-14.2	-29.0	-41.5	-84.6	-2080	-3534	-4790	-3516
NB	-7.7	-18.4	-28.1	-54.3	-1400	-2761	-3974	-2757
Que	17.3	-35.6	-91.3	-109.6	342	-567	-1403	-574
Ont	36.8	22.3	-19.8	39.4	592	293	-243	201
Man	-6.1	-12.6	-27.6	-46.3	-708	-1240	-2602	-1545
Sask	-7.6	-9.2	-18.9	-35.7	-892	-993	-1881	-1268
Alta	-3.0	45.9	$75.0	117.9	-241	2455	3322	1917
BC	2.9	5.2	-14.6	-6.4	161	237	-506	-43
Terr	-2.9	-4.9	-16.1	-23.9	-7685	-8011	-21552	-12579
Reg. Sum	6.7	-57.8	-216.7	-267.8	35	-246	-859	-370
Outside								
Canada	-11.2	-20.4	-62.4	-94.1				
Canada	-4.5	-78.2	-279.1	-361.9	-29	-336	-1119	-489

TABLE 6.2:
Estimates of Indirect Effects on Federal Investment for 1976

Item	Total Effect on Fiscal Balance (billions of 1990 dollars)									
	Nfld	PEI	NS	NB	Que	Ont	Man	Sask	Alta	BC
Federal Investment (PEA)	31	3	83	20	248	274	54	103	128	115
Federal Invest. Adj. for Indirect Effects	17	3	52	15	268	369	49	77	114	96C
Adj. Investment less PEA Investment	-14	0	-31	-5	20	95	-5	-26	-14	-19
Percent Difference	-47	-6	-38	-26	8	35	-8	-25	-11	-16

Other Adjustments

Approximately 65% of federal revenues and about 80% of federal expenditures/ transfers in the PEA are allocated across regions in the manner required for both the cash-flow and benefits approaches. For the remaining amounts a number of adjustments are necessary. The most important of these are outlined below.

1. Indirect Taxes (IT).

In the PEA these are allocated on the basis of the location of production or, in the case of import duties and the like, on the basis of the region of entry. However, except in situations such as those where the domestic price of oil and gas was regulated, it is generally agreed that these taxes are primarily shifted forward to consumers. Consequently, it is argued that allocating indirect federal taxes among regions on the basis of consumption or some combination of consumption and production will give a better indication of regional incidence. On the basis of theory and the results from studies of tax incidence, the most defensible method, which is used here, involves a combination of approaches. Specifically, custom import duties, excise taxes and miscellaneous indirect taxes (excluding the NGGLT—Natural Gas and Gas Liquids Tax) are reallocated according to the provincial distribution of consumption and investment; the NGGLT, which is allocated on the basis of consumption in the PEA, is redistributed according to the production of natural gas for domestic use; excise duties are reallocated on the basis of consumption expenditures; and, the Oil Export Charge is reallocated on the basis of oil exports from each province.

The changes in federal fiscal balances, relative to those shown in Table 6.1, resulting from these adjustments are shown in Table 6.3. The largest increase is for Alberta, where the balance is raised by $30 billion, and the largest decrease is for Ontario, where the balance is reduced by $59 billion. These adjustments are fairly representative of the results using other reasonable allocation methods.

2. Corporate Taxes (CT).

The method used to allocate these taxes in practice is outlined in Sheppard (1986). This is basically the derivation method and is used in the PEA. It is the proper approach for certain types of analysis such as that undertaken in the following section. However, for evaluations of equity issues where incidence is important, some adjustments are warranted.

In general, corporate taxes can be shifted forward to consumers or backwards to shareholders, to owners of immobile resources, and, via reduced wages and/or employment, to employees. There is no consensus in

TABLE 6.3:
Overall Magnitude of Adjustments to PEA Balances

Adjustment	Total Effect on Fiscal Balance (billions of 1990 dollars)									
	Nfld	PEI	NS	NB	Que	Ont	Man	Sask	Alta	BC
Indirect Taxes	8	2	6	5	-33	-59	9	13	30	16
Corporate Taxes	2	1	4	3	13	-2	3	2	-33	6
IOPD by Population	-6	-1	-3	-6	-22	77	-5	-8	-15	-13
IOPD by Personal Taxes	-2	0	0	-2	3	47	-2	-5	-19	-18
Exclusion of IOPD	3	1	11	5	79	214	12	7	19	29
NCR by Population	-3	-1	-4	-3	-16	55	-5	-4	-9	-11

the literature concerning the relative importance of these various types of shifts. The usual approach is to use a range of estimates derived using different allocation methods. Glynn (1978), for example, used two approaches: one with 50% of corporate profits (and corporate income taxes) distributed according to consumption and 50% allocated on the basis of the regional distribution of dividends and, the other, with these weights changed to 25% and 75%. The largest change occurs when corporate income taxes are distributed strictly on the basis of consumption. As shown in Table 6.3, the major change is a decrease of $33 billion in Alberta's balance and a $13 billion increase in Ontario's. For a province such as Alberta where most of the corporate taxes are paid by resource companies on profits earned in large part from export sales it is probably difficult to argue that incidence will be accurately reflected by allocations employing regional consumption patterns.

3.   Interest on the Public Debt (IOPD) and Federal Deficits.
The regional distribution of the domestic portion of IOPD as estimated in the PEA probably mostly reflects the distribution of wealth but could also capture some regional differences in asset preferences (recall that the portion going to non-residents has already been removed). In any case, this item has become very large in recent years as a result of the rapid increase in the size of the national debt.

For the benefits approach, it is important to reallocate these interest payments. One method is to view these as repayments for the benefits previously financed by increasing the federal debt. Using the "indivisibility" principle, it is assumed that these benefits were distributed equally on a per capita basis and, hence, the IOPD is allocated in proportion to regional population. Another approach is to adjust for the annual federal deficits (and surpluses) directly by increasing the federal revenue collected in each region in proportion to the actual revenue collected such that there is a balanced budget in every year and, therefore, no IOPD to be distributed.

The problem of how to take account of the regional impacts of federal deficits and IOPD also arises in the cash-flow approach. There are a number of mechanisms through which accumulated deficits can affect the regional economies. For example, these might be via effects on taxes, on interest rates or on the exchange rate. A common view is that the burden falls disproportionately on the "have" provinces, those which have the most capital intensive economies and those where the exports are most sensitive to changes in the exchange rate. Unfortunately, to this point there have not been any studies which have tested this hypothesis or quantified the regional impacts. Given this lack of information, two methods might seem reasonable. One is to assume the burden is "indivisible" and, as before, allocate the IOPD and the federal debt in proportion to regional population or, in other words, on an equal per capita basis. Another might be to allocate these items in proportion to some measure such as total personal taxes paid which, at least in part, reflects the distribution of the general tax burden.

The effects on regional balances, relative to those shown in Table 6.1, of excluding IOPD, allocating it by population and distributing it according to federal income taxes paid by individuals are indicated in Table 6.3.

4. *Indivisible Expenditures.*

For the benefits approach, it can be argued that items such as federal expenditures outside Canada or in the National Capital Region (NCR) produce indivisible benefits and, therefore, if they are to be allocated it should be on a constant per capita basis. This is the basic method used here. In the next section federal expenditures outside of Canada are not allocated but, rather, left in an "outside Canada" category. In Section 4 where cases of independent regions are considered, they are allocated strictly in proportion to population. The expenditures in the NCR are reallocated in proportion to population. The effects of this adjustment are shown in Table 6.3.

An Evaluation of the Economic Impacts

Distribution Impacts

The net financial flows by province (territory) for the period 1961-1989 and by decade are shown in Table 6.4. The comparable results under the most extreme assumptions (that is, excluding interest on the federal debt and reallocating corporate taxes strictly on the basis of consumption) are given in Appendix Tables 6A.1 and 6A.2 to provide an indication of the range of values.

In every case these show a large net financial outflow from Alberta. For the entire period, this amounts to about $148 billion (1990 dollars) or roughly $2500 per person annually. Although federal policies also generated net outflows from Ontario during the period 1961 to 1974 and after 1986 (see Appendix 6B for annual values), these were offset by large net inflows from 1975 to 1985. British Columbia was the only province besides Alberta to have a net outflow over the full period. In the case of Québec there was a net outflow from 1961 to 1969 but this reversed sharply in subsequent years. There were net inflows to all of the other provinces. For the 1961-1989 period this ranges from approximately $12 billion for Prince Edward Island to about $140 billion for Québec. The range for net inflows on a per capita basis is from $11,000 for the Yukon and Northwest Territories, to $50 for Ontario.

The relative importance of these balances in terms of the various provincial economies is indicated in Table 6.5. The province with the largest net outflow as a result of federal policies was Alberta. In that case the annual net outflow amounted to about 12% of Alberta GDP during the 1970s and 1980s, and roughly 9% for the full period. For the regions experiencing net inflows, the largest relative impacts occur in the Yukon and the Northwest Territories and in the Atlantic provinces. During the 1980s, for example, the net inflows relative to GDP were about 60% for the Yukon and the Northwest Territories, roughly 30% for the Atlantic provinces, about 12% for Manitoba, around 8% for Québec, about 7% for Saskatchewan, and between 1% and 2% for British Columbia and Ontario.

It is apparent from these figures that federal policies have had very significant impacts in terms of the regional distribution of GDP, population, and employment. In particular, they have reduced the size of Alberta in terms of GDP, population, and employment compared to what it would otherwise be.[83] At the same time, they have resulted in much larger amounts

---

83. For example, by shifting aggregate demand from Alberta to other regions, there is a corresponding shift in income, output and employment. Since the extensive literature on migration shows that interregional migration in Canada is primarily determined by relative regional income and employment opportunities, the effect is also a shift in population.

TABLE 6.4:
Total and Per Capita Federal Fiscal Balances, Cash Flow Basis,* 1961-1989

	Total Balances (billions of 1990 dollars)				Annual Per Capita Balance (1990 dollars)			
Region	1960s	1970s	1980s	Total	1960s	1970s	1980s	Avg.
Nfld	-4.7	-14.0	-23.9	-42.6	-1076	-2545	-4201	-2660
PEI	-1.8	$-4.3	-6.1	-12.2	-1858	-3651	-4829	-3501
NS	-11.9	-27.1	-39.3	-78.3	-1747	-3295	-4537	-3243
NBS	-6.1	-16.5	-26.7	-49.3	-1107	-2468	-3769	-2494
Que	5.6	-46.7	-101.1	-142.2	111	-748	-1553	-759
Ont	22.5	3.7	-45.8	-19.6	360	62	-530	-50
Man	-3.2	-9.7	-24.3	-37.3	-374	-958	-2294	-1238
Sask	-3.2	-4.8	-14.4	-22.5	-380	-520	-1433	-792
Alta	3.6	55.1	89.1	147.7	267	2965	3929	2460
BC	8.7	10.6	-9.2	10.1	509	466	-322	208
Terr	-2.6	-4.1	-14.9	-21.7	-6858	-6715	-20013	-11345
Reg. Sum	6.7	-57.8	-216.7	-267.8	35	-246	-859	-370
Outside Canada	-11.2	-20.4	-62.4	-94.1				
Canada	-4.5	-78.2	-279.1	-361.8	-28	-336	-1104	-505

*Data as in Table 6.1 but with additional adjustments to reflect incidence of indirect taxes.

TABLE 6.5:
Federal Fiscal Balances as a Percentage of Provincial GDP

	Percentage of GDP											
Period	Nfld	PEI	NS	NB	Que	Ont	Man	Sask	Alta	BC	Terr	Can
1960s	16.0	28.7	20.9	14.0	-1.0	-2.3	3.2	3.5	-1.8	-3.4	49.5	-0.2
1970s	24.8	36.8	27.3	20.7	4.4	-0.4	5.8	3.6	-11.5	-2.6	29.1	1.2
1980s	31.2	37.0	29.7	25.8	7.9	2.4	11.6	7.1	-12.3	1.4	60.5	3.8
Average	24.3	34.3	26.1	20.4	3.9	0.0	7.0	4.8	-8.7	-1.5	46.2	1.7

of economic activity and population in the Yukon and the Northwest Territories and in the Atlantic provinces than would have been observed in the absence of these policies. Similarly, the Québec, Manitoba and Saskatchewan economies are larger than they would otherwise have been. No attempt has been made here to quantify the size of the effects on economic activity and population for each region. It will suffice to note that, particularly in the case of Alberta, the effects would be highly dependent on the assumptions about the use of the funds in the alternative. If, for example, funds which were transferred out of the province by federal policies were assumed to accumulate in a fund such as the Alberta Heritage Savings Trust Fund, the effects would be much different than if it were assumed that they would be distributed via market mechanisms.

While the general impacts of federal policies on the regional distribution of population and economic activity are fairly clear, the same cannot be said about the effects on per capita incomes. It will be recalled from the discussion in the general framework section that there are two conflicting views about the ultimate effects of interregional transfers on per capita incomes. The traditional view is that they have resulted in smaller income disparities. In the context of the flows outlined above, this would primarily mean that per capita incomes in Alberta have been reduced significantly by these policies while those in the North and the Atlantic regions have been increased significantly. The main difference under the opposing view, which is associated with Courchene, is that, when all of the effects are taken into account, it is unlikely that the net inflow regions have a higher average real per capita income than would otherwise have been the case.

It is not likely that this debate will be resolved in the near future. Nevertheless, it is still possible to reach the conclusion that, in the case of Alberta, federal policies have not worked to raise per capita income levels but, rather, have reduced them. The unanswered question is "how much of a reduction?" Based on indirect evidence concerning such things as the responsiveness of migration patterns to changes in relative income and employment opportunities, it is likely that the major effects have been of the extensive rather than the intensive variety (for example, see Mansell and Wright, 1978). That is, the percentage decrease in Alberta's per capita income is probably small relative to the decrease in the province's GDP, population, and employment.

Stabilization Impacts
In order to draw conclusions concerning the implications for short run stabilization, it is necessary to compare, for each region, the changes from year-to-year in the net flows (as shown in Appendix Table 6B.1) and the

year-to-year fluctuations in relative per capita market income. (See Appendix Table 6B.6; market income is defined as personal income less government transfers.) For most regions these data do show the operation of automatic stabilizers. That is, when relative income drops the federal fiscal deficit increases (or surplus decreases) and the opposite occurs when relative income rises. It is also possible to see the operation of discretionary initiatives by the federal government in some cases to offset particularly large regional shocks. For example, the large increase in the net inflow to Saskatchewan that occurred between 1986 and 1987 reflects, in part, the federal injections to the grains industry designed to help counteract the effects of sharp declines in international wheat prices.

It is possible to observe in the case of Alberta the same general directional relationships between variations in fiscal balances and variations in relative market income. For example, as the Alberta economy collapsed in the early 1980s, the fiscal surplus which the federal government was running with Alberta declined from about $23 billion in 1981 to around $7 billion in 1984. This led Carmichael (1986) to conclude that federal policies have in fact worked to stabilize the Alberta economy. This may be true in the narrow sense that the very large deflationary effects which federal policies were having on the Alberta economy were reduced as the province's economy declined. However, simply looking at the direction of change in the fiscal balances and ignoring the absolute magnitudes and signs can give a very distorted picture and, indeed, this is the case with respect to Alberta. First, as summarized in Mansell and Percy (1990, pp. 30-43), various inquiries and evaluations have clearly shown that it was the federal policies that produced the extremely large net outflows that were mainly responsible for the very deep and prolonged recession in Alberta. Having been a major cause of the instability, it is difficult to argue that stability was promoted because the net outflow was decreased. Second, one would expect that, in light of the severity of the downturn in Alberta, the appropriate response would be changes so as to move from a net outflow to an inflow and thereby stimulate the province's economy (rather than just decrease the size of the outflow). In fact, this did not occur even though federal policies served to dramatically increase the net inflows or injections to all other regions, including those such as Ontario which by the end of 1983 were already in a strong recovery phase. To make matters worse, the continuing large federal fiscal surplus with Alberta served to neutralize the fiscal deficits which the provincial government was running in an attempt to stimulate the Alberta economy.

As noted by Mansell and Percy (1990), the Alberta economy has the distinction of being the most variable regional economy in Canada. Consequently, from an Alberta perspective, effective stabilization via proper

federal policies should be one of the most important sources of economic
gain from Confederation. There have been aspects of federal policies that
have no doubt been helpful in this regard, especially in recent years under
the fiscal stabilization arrangements and agricultural assistance programs.
However, on balance over the past three decades federal policies taken as a
whole have been more a source of economic instability in the case of Alberta
than a source of stability.

One can only speculate about the amount of stabilization which could
have been achieved had there not been the federal policies which generated
such large outflows from Alberta. It is, however, reasonable to expect that a
substantial portion of these would have otherwise ended up in the Alberta
Heritage Savings Trust Fund. This provides a mechanism to convert unstable
provincial government revenues (that is, oil and gas rents) into a stable flow
of interest and dividends that can transferred into general revenues. As such,
it is highly likely that the provincial government would have had the
capacity to reduce greatly the instability arising from highly variable energy
and agricultural prices and there would not have been the added instability
originating from perverse federal policies.

An Evaluation of the Implications for Regional Equity

It will be recalled that, for discussions of regional equity, it is necessary to
shift from fiscal balances measured on a cash-flow basis to balances
measured on a benefits basis. In general, this involves additional adjustments
to reflect the fact that, regardless of which region the expenditures are
actually made, many of the federal expenditures generate outputs which are
indivisible. For example, using this approach "overhead" expenditures in the
National Capital Region are viewed as producing the same per capita
benefits for all Canadians rather than just benefitting people in Ontario and
Québec. For similar reasons, the IOPD can be viewed as a measure of the
benefits previously received by all Canadians from federal expenditures that
exceeded taxes paid. Put differently, this is equivalent to saying that the
burden of the accumulated federal deficits cannot be accurately apportioned
on a regional basis so they are simply allocated on an equal per capita basis.

Table 6.6 shows the federal fiscal balances calculated on a benefits basis.
(The corresponding balances for each year are given in Appendix 6D).
Appendix Tables 6C.1 and 6C.2 are provided to indicate the sensitivity of the
results to different allocation methods. A comparison of the results shows
that the largest changes occur when federal revenues by region are adjusted
in proportion to the incidence of actual revenues such that the federal budget

TABLE 6.6:
Total and Per Capita Federal Fiscal Balances,
Benefit Basis,* 1961-1989

Region	Total Balances (billions of 1990 dollars)				Annual Per Capita Balances (1990 dollars)			
	1960s	1970s	1980s	Total	1960s	1970s	1980s	Avg.
Nfld	-6.0	-16.6	-28.7	-51.3	-1367	-3022	-5038	-3204
PEI	-2.1	-4.7	-6.9	-13.7	-2100	-4014	-5510	-3936
NS	-13.1	-28.9	-42.4	-84.5	-1928	-3521	-4899	-3502
NB	-7.3`	-19.0	-31.8	-58.1	-1324	-2843	-4490	-2940
Que	1.2	-60.1	-120.8	-179.7	25	-964	-1852	-963
Ont	40.0	43.5	28.7	112.3	645	551	286	489
Man	-4.7	-12.5	-29.4	-46.6	-543	-1234	-2769	-1549
Sask	-5.2	-8.1	-21.8	-35.1	-618	-870	-2169	-1240
Alta	0.8	48.9	74.6	124.3	55	2624	3315	2065
BC	5.8	3.8	-23.4	-13.8	333	185	-813	-113
Terr	-2.6	-4.2	-14.8	-21.6	-6884	-6780	-19837	-11315
Reg. Sum	6.7	-57.8	-216.7	-267.8	35	-246	-859	-370
Outside Canada	-11.2	-20.4	-62.4	-94.1				
Canada	-4.5	-78.2	-279.1	-361.8	-28	-336	-1104	-505

*Includes adjustment to reflect incidence of taxes and indivisibility of IOPD.

is balanced in each year and, consequently, there is no IOPD. The largest effects are substantial increases in the surpluses for British Columbia, Alberta, and, especially Ontario, and a substantial decrease in the deficits with Québec. However, on a per capita basis there are no changes in the rankings. It might also be noted that, as a practical matter, the balances shown in Table 6C.2 will give a more accurate representation of the distribution of the burden of federal deficit financing if the effects from higher taxes and reduced expenditures resulting from the accumulated deficits fall disproportionately on the "have" provinces. Further, it is likely that distributing National Capital Region (NCR) expenditures in proportion to population overstates the benefits to Alberta where per capita federal spending has been the lowest in Canada. It could be argued that allocating these expenditures in proportion to federal spending in each region would give a more accurate picture of the distribution of benefits. In any case, it will suffice to note that the method used here means that the net contributions for Alberta as indicated in Tables 6.6, 6C.1, and 6C.2 will be underestimated.

FIGURE 6.1:
Relative Market Income and Federal Relative Contributions

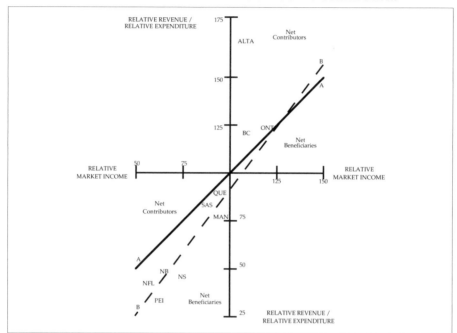

In reaching conclusions about regional equity, it is important to take a long view since other considerations, such as stabilization efforts, would produce short run variations that may not be indicative of inequity. Further, the balances must be in per capita form to take account of regional differences in population size. In addition, regional differences in per capita market income must be taken into account. As outlined in the general framework section, equity would normally require transfers from the "have" to the "have-not" regions.

Figure 6.1 represents a fairly simple way of incorporating these factors. The balances or net fiscal contributions from Table 6.7 are expressed in ratio form: that is, as the ratio of federal revenue contributed by each region (based on incidence) and federal expenditures on behalf of the residents of each region (or fiscal benefits). These ratios, which are given in Table 6.7, are plotted against relative market income: that is, market income in the region relative to the national average. The line AA is one possible definition of vertical equity. It requires a one-to-one relationship between increases in relative income and increases in net contributions (or decreases in net benefits). However, a better approach is to fit a line such as BB which reflects vertical equity as revealed by the observed patterns for relative income and net contributions. In any case, the exact position of the line is not critical

TABLE 6.7:
Relative Per Capita Market Income and
Relative Revenue/Relative Expenditure Index (Canada = 100)

Region	Market Income Index				Relative Revenue/Relative Expenditure			
	1960s	1970s	1980s	Total	1960s	1970s	1980s	Avg.
Nfld	53	55	57	55	44	39	38	40
PEI	55	61	64	60	35	35	40	37
NS	72	73	76	74	43	46	50	46
NB	64	67	68	67	49	47	47	48
Que	90	91	91	91	101	78	75	84
Ont	120	115	113	116	131	127	129	129
Man	94	91	90	92	76	75	66	72
Sask	84	86	85	85	71	82	79	77
Alta	98	102	109	103	101	183	192	160
BC	111	109	104	108	114	114	100	109
Terr	100	103	116	107	33	52	35	40
Sum	100	100	100	100	100	100	100	100

since the focus is on horizontal equity. Horizontal inequities will be indicated by large deviations from the line or, in other words, inconsistencies where, for example, a lower income province makes a larger net contribution than a higher income province.

The position of each province in terms of these two measures is indicated in Figure 6.1. The positions for the Yukon and the Northwest Territories are not shown because the rankings for these two regions would likely be meaningless in terms of this type of analysis. That is, their very large negative net contributions will mostly reflect the fact that the costs per person for delivering federal services are very high for small and widely dispersed populations.

For the most part, the relationships shown are encouraging in that there seems to be a fairly consistent relationship between net contributions and relative income position. Also, all of the provinces with above-average per capita market incomes are net contributors and all of the below average provinces are net beneficiaries. However, there are some inconsistencies, the largest and most obvious of which involves Alberta. For example, over the period as a whole Alberta's per capita market income was 3% above the national average while Ontario's was 16% above the national average. Yet, on a per capita basis Albertans made net contributions which were over four times as large as those by residents of Ontario. In fact, the disparity is even larger if, as argued earlier, NCR expenditures are more properly allocated on the basis of federal spending.

Other inconsistencies are evident in the third quadrant but they are relatively minor. For example, it is not clear why residents of Newfoundland receive smaller net benefits than residents of Prince Edward Island, given that per capita market income in the former region is significantly lower.

While this analysis quite clearly demonstrates that Albertans have been subjected to substantial inequities under federal policies, a variety of justifications are often heard. One is that Albertans were at one time major beneficiaries, particularly in the depression years. Although the sparse data for earlier periods would suggest that, at least in certain years, Albertans were in fact net beneficiaries, the size of the per capita net benefits were minuscule in relation to the net contributions over recent decades. Moreover, it is useful to remember that the policies associated with large-scale federal fiscal intervention and redistribution simply did not exist in the earlier era.

Another argument is for broad-based horizontal equity. However, for reasons outlined in the general framework section, such arguments cannot be supported. In fact what they amount to are poorly disguised arguments for discrimination against some regions and some types of rents. If one accepts that natural resources are owned by the provinces, only the narrow-based definition of horizontal equity applies to energy rents and, consequently, it is impossible to escape the conclusion that federal policies have resulted in very inequitable treatment of Albertans.

Before leaving this section, it might be useful to discuss briefly the sources of the inequities. From an accounting perspective, the sources are fairly clear. The single most important factor has been the federal government's energy policies from the early 1970s to the mid-1980s. Through a host of special taxes, including taxation through price regulation, these policies produced unprecedented levels of interregional transfers. Other effects, such as those from the severe restrictions on exports, were also large and are still being felt.

While the very high levels of federal revenues extracted from Alberta represent the major source of inequity, it would appear that the customary, low levels of federal spending in Alberta are also an important factor. For example, over the 1961-1989 period, federal government annual operating expenditures in the province were $654 per capita (in 1990 dollars) compared to a regional average of $893. A similar imbalance shows up when all categories of federal spending are included. For the same period, per capita federal spending in Alberta associated with operating expenditures on goods and services, statutory items (pension plan payments, family and youth allowances, health grants, etc.), economic assistance (unemployment insurance benefits, energy and agricultural subsidies, etc.), economic development (scholarships, research funds, regional and industrial development grants, etc.), and the taxation agreements amounted to $2404 per person per year, the lowest of any region in Canada. The comparable average for Canada over the same period was $2953.

A Look Ahead

There are certain advantages to historical analyses of the type presented above. One is that, instead of dealing with projections and hypothetical situations, it is possible to observe and measure the interrelationships and the outcomes in actual situations. But there is the disadvantage that it is by no means clear that history is a good predictor of the future. The purpose here is to address this weakness by incorporating some general trends and expectations.

The annual figures in Appendix Tables 6B.2 and 6D.2 reveal that in recent years there have been substantial reductions in the net outflows associated with federal policies and in the fiscal inequity measures. One explanation of this is purely political: that is, for one of the very few times in history, Albertans are strongly represented in the governing party and the Cabinet and, as a result, at least their biggest grievances (such as the NEP) have been addressed. Another explanation is that, since the collapse of the Alberta economy and energy prices in the 1980s, there is simply less available for federal policies to extract.

In any case, whether there is a repeat of these types of policies in the future will depend on a number of factors. First, a common perception is that the Free Trade Agreement (FTA), assuming it remains in effect, would generally make it more difficult for the federal government to reimpose NEP-style policies. However, as noted by Plourde (1991), many of the most controversial and, from an Alberta perspective, the most damaging measures could in fact be implemented under the FTA. These measures include price controls and production taxes. Second, it is sometimes argued that oil and gas price and market deregulation offers some protection against anything like an NEP II. While it is true that re-regulation would be extremely expensive, disruptive, and destabilizing, there is probably nothing to prevent a federal government committed to such a program from actually carrying it out. The third factor concerns the motivating circumstances. Even though NEP-style policies may still be possible within a new environment as shaped by the FTA and deregulation, one would not expect such policies actually to be introduced so long as energy prices and rates of return in the oil and gas sector remain low. Thus, an important issue is whether energy prices are likely to rise significantly in the foreseeable future.

Most projections of oil prices show relatively small increases in real terms, while natural gas prices are expected to recover sharply by the mid-1990s and thereafter to continue to rise in real terms at a modest rate. However, past experience demonstrates that energy prices are often very unpredictable and, consequently, one cannot rule out the possibility of rapid increases. In such a case there is almost certain to be strong support in Central Canada for major federal interventions again and this is likely to result at some point in another round of NEP-style policies. Simply put, under existing arrangements there is no protection at the federal level for the economic interests of individuals in regions such as Alberta no matter how justified they may be in terms of regional stability and equity. If it comes down to the interests of people in Ontario versus the interests of people in Alberta, it is almost a certainty that in forming federal policy the latter would be sacrificed. Ironically, the major threat to stability and equity for Albertans in the future will likely be the possibility of sharp increases in oil and gas prices.

Another potential problem concerns the large federal debt. This is likely to remain a substantial burden over the foreseeable future and has serious implications in terms of both stabilization and regional equity. As noted earlier, an important potential benefit of Confederation, especially for a region such as Alberta with a highly variable economy, is the element of insurance in the event of large cyclical or random downturns. Although Albertans have paid heavily into Confederation in recent decades and, on that basis alone, should be able to expect to be able to draw on this "insurance policy," it is unlikely that it will be able to. Quite simply, the large federal debt and the huge costs of servicing it will make it increasingly unrealistic to count on large federal injections to help offset downturns in the province's key industries or in the provincial government's revenues. In other words, the provincial governments will likely have to play a larger role in stabilizing their regional economies.

Similarly, in the absence of reforms, it is difficult to see any long term, structural changes to address the remaining fiscal inequities and perverse economic impacts. In fact, the pressure to reduce substantially federal deficits may well result in even more measures, such as the capping of federal transfers to the "have" provinces, the introduction of the large corporations tax, and the capping of federal tax rebates to private utilities, which have disproportionately large, negative impacts on the Alberta economy.

In summary, the factors which in the past have led to policies that have destabilized the Alberta economy and have led to such a high degree of regional inequity are not likely to be as dominant over the near future. However, the fundamental problems remain and, in the absence of reforms, it is probably only a matter of time until there is a replay of the types of heavy-handed and discriminatory federal policies that, until fairly recently, have been a major source of economic alienation in the province.

Fiscal Balances and Their Implications Under Other Arrangements

General Approach

The objective here is to examine the types of issues addressed in the previous section under different types of constitutional arrangements. In order to cover as broad a range as possible, the latter include a separate Québec, greater decentralization, and a separate Alberta. In each case our analysis is limited to an evaluation of the implications for the regional distribution of economic activity, for regional economic stability and for regional equity. These are measured in relation to the status quo as outlined in the preceding section and involve the same data and general methodology.

There are, however, some important differences. First, the effects under each scenario are calculated for only two years, 1986 and 1988. These particular years were selected because the focus is on the implications for Alberta and they cover the spectrum of a poor year in terms of economic conditions in the province and a year in which there was very strong growth. For each of these years, it is assumed that the particular alternative existed in that year. In other words, we completely ignore any transitional problems in going from one set of arrangements to another. Also, an historical period is used for the analysis simply to avoid the problems associated with reliance on projected or forecast values for the key variables.

Second, a number of additional assumptions are necessary in order to define the structure of the cases sufficiently to be able to compute the fiscal balances. These are summarized below.

1. *Common Currency.* In the scenarios involving separation, it is assumed that the regions which become independent continue to use the Canadian dollar as currency.

2. *Trade Policy and Patterns.* In all cases it is assumed that there would be no change in interregional or international trade policy or trade patterns. This assumption is probably unrealistic. For example, it is hard to imagine Québec being allowed to keep the same (regulated) share of the national

dairy market if it became independent. The purpose of this assumption is simply to isolate the fiscal implications.

3. *Division of Federal Assets and Liabilities.* For the purposes of our analysis, it is assumed that, in the case where a region separates, federal assets and liabilities would be divided up on an equal per capita basis. As outlined by Boothe and Harris (1991), other methods of division exist and can be defended. For example, on a benefits basis it can be argued that an independent Québec's share of federal liabilities should be greater than its per capita share and that an independent Alberta's share would be much smaller than its per capita share. Further, as a purely analytical device, it is assumed that all existing assets and liabilities remain with the federal government and that the region separating would pay its per capita share of interest on the public debt (IOPD) and would receive its per capita share of investment income (IY) from federal assets.

4. *Government Programs and Delivery Costs.* In our analysis we keep the total amount and the mix of federal revenues from and expenditures in each region constant, even in the region which separates. The only difference is that upon separation these are administered by the existing provincial government. Also, we assume no changes in per unit program costs or in overhead costs. For example, it is assumed that the separating region's per capita share of National Capital Region (NCR) expenditures are essentially moved to the new independent region without requiring additional infrastructure expenditures or affecting the per capita NCR expenditures for the remaining regions.

5. *Distribution of Powers.* In the case of greater decentralization, it is assumed that the powers would be allocated in the manner set out in Allaire (1991). That is, jurisdiction over defence and territorial security, customs and duties, currency and common debt, and fiscal equalization would remain with the federal government. Jurisdiction over the following would be shared: Native affairs, taxation and revenue, financial institutions, justice, fisheries, foreign policy, post office and telecommunications, and transport. Jurisdiction over all other areas would go to the provincial governments. These areas include: social affairs, municipal affairs, agriculture, unemployment insurance, communications, culture, regional development, education, energy, environment, housing, industry and commerce, language, recreation and sports, manpower, family policy, research and development, natural resources, health, public security, income security, and tourism.

It must be emphasized that the assumptions outlined above are intended primarily to hold "all other things equal" so that the fiscal implications can be isolated. They are not selected because they were felt to reflect fairly the overall situation if a region separates or powers are reallocated. Clearly, we are abstracting from some of the key issues such as economies of scale in the delivery of public services, regional differences in preferences for government programs, duplication of government services, shifts in trading patterns, and, what are likely to be major problems, the costs and risks, associated with the transition period. These other issues must be considered in any overall evaluation of alternative arrangements. Some of them are dealt with in the other papers in this volume.

The Case of an Independent Québec

Economic Impacts
It might be recalled that to assess the economic impacts, the fiscal balances are calculated on a cash-flow basis. Here, we calculate the changes in these balances, relative to the status quo, for all regions for a hypothetical case where Québec was independent in 1986 and for a case where it was independent in 1988. In the status quo case, the only change from the analysis presented in the third is that a "proceeds from the sale of bonds" category is added. For each region this amounts to its per capita share of the federal deficit in that year and it is used to take into account of the effects of various arrangements on the size of fiscal balances.

In addition to the assumptions outlined above, the following are used for the case of Québec independence. First, Québec gets its per capita share of federal investment income and federal revenue from outside Canada and pays to the federal government its per capita share of interest on the public debt and its share of expenditures outside Canada. Second, Québec's per capita share of NCR expenditures are shifted to Québec. Third, corresponding adjustments are made for the remaining regions and the remaining total. For example, without Québec, NCR expenditures by those remaining are lower (by about 25%), federal revenues are reduced by the amount previously paid by residents of Québec, and federal expenditures and transfers are reduced by the amount previously going to residents of Québec. Fourth, the new federal budget balance is calculated and distributed across the remaining regions on an equal per capita basis using the "proceeds from the sale of bonds" account. Finally, in the event that the revenues in the independent Québec are insufficient to cover the same level of expenditures previously made by the federal government, it is assumed that an amount of bonds equal to the revenue shortfall would be issued and

TABLE 6.8:
Changes in Fiscal Balances with Québec Independence
Relative to the Status Quo, Cash Flow Basis, 1986 and 1988
(Total change in millions of 1990 dollars; per capita change in 1990 dollars)

Period	Nfld	PEI	NS	NB	*Que*	Ont	Man	Sask	Alta	BC	Terr
86 - Total	117	26	181	147	*-854*	798	222	209	488	603	16
86 - Per Capita	206	206	206	206	*-130*	86	206	206	206	206	206
88 - Total	212	48	329	267	*-1489*	2494	403	373	899	1134	29
88 - Per Capita	371	371	371	371	*-222*	260	371	371	371	371	371

this amount would be entered under the "proceeds from the sale of bonds account for Québec.[84]

The net flows for the case with and without Québec are shown in Table 6.8. As indicated there, for 1986 the net flows for the remaining regions improve by between $16 million for the Yukon and Northwest Territories and $798 million for Ontario. On a per capita basis these gains are equal to $206 for all regions except Ontario. Ontario's per capita gain is reduced to $86 because it loses a sizable part of the NCR expenditures. With independence under these assumptions, Québec loses $854 million (that is, it goes from a net inflow of $354 million in 1986 to a net outflow of $500 million). The impacts in 1988 are larger. The gains to the remaining regions are roughly double those for 1986 and the loss for Québec increases to about $1.5 billion per year from $0.9 billion in 1986.

In general, abstracting from other important factors such as changes in trade patterns and transitional impacts, it would appear that the main effect of Québec separation would be a redistribution of economic activity away from that province and towards the other regions, especially Ontario, British Columbia, and Alberta.

Based on these results it might be tempting to conclude that, all other things equal, Alberta would gain economically. However, all other things are unlikely to remain equal and a number of these could have quite dramatic ramifications for Alberta. One of these is the political dimension. It is useful to recall that federal energy policies have been most damaging to Alberta in

---

84. Note, however, that this account for Québec would no longer include bonds to finance the federal deficit.

terms of redistribution of economic activity, destabilization, and inequity. In the past, Québec's interests in the area of federal resource policies have generally coincided with Alberta's. Consequently, Alberta would lose an important ally in the protection of provincial resource rights. Without Québec, Ontario's interests would be even more dominant and this could well mean a much higher probability of NEP-style policies in the future, with all of the attendant costs to Albertans in terms of lost opportunities, instability, and inequity. Depending on the type of political structure assumed for the rest of Canada (ROC) in the absence of Québec, much the same arguments could be made with respect to other policies.

Another particular concern should be the instability during the transition phase. Instability and uncertainty are the enemies of investment. The Alberta economy is very capital intensive, highly dependent on foreign capital, and very sensitive to interest rates. As a result, it could be seriously affected by higher interest rates or disruptions to capital flows that are almost a certainty, at least for a period of time, if Québec separated.

Equity Implications

To assess the impacts with respect to regional equity, the procedure described in the previous section is repeated but using a benefits rather than a cash-flow approach. It will be recalled that to put the balances on a benefits basis additional adjustments are required. The major ones involve reallocating IOPD, NCR expenditures, and expenditures outside Canada on an equal per capita basis. In addition, each region is allocated its per capita share of federal revenue from outside Canada and "proceeds from the sale of bonds" equal to its per capita share of the federal deficit for that particular year (that is, 1986 or 1988).

The change in net benefits between the status quo case and the case of Québec independence for each region and for each of the two years is shown in Table 6.9. Alberta's net fiscal contribution (or the difference between what residents of the province contribute to the federal government minus the federal expenditures on their behalf) falls from $2.4 billion (1990 dollars) to $1.9 billion in 1986, for a gain (or reduction in the fiscal burden) of $0.45 billion. The gain for 1988 is slightly larger. For other regions which make a negative net fiscal contribution (or receive a positive net benefit), the numbers have a similar interpretation. For example, in 1986 New Brunswick's net contribution is -$2.5 billion with Québec and -$2.6 billion without Québec, for a gain of $0.14 billion. Residents in the rest of Canada (ROC) gain by about $200 per person annually. On the other hand, residents of Québec lose about $3 billion per year in total, or approximately $450 per person annually.

TABLE 6.9
Changes in Fiscal Balances with Québec Independence
Relative to the Status Quo, Benefits Basis, 1986 and 1988
(Total change in millions of 1990 dollars; per capita change in 1990 dollars)

Period	Nfld	PEI	NS	NB	*Que*	Ont	Man	Sask	Alta	BC	Terr
86 - Total	107	24	166	135	*-2806*	1760	204	193	450	556	15
86 - Per Capita	190	190	190	190	-425	190	190	190	190	190	190
88 - Total	120	27	186	151	*-3258*	2013	228	211	509	642	16
88 - Per Capita	210	210	210	210	-486	210	210	210	210	210	210

The same qualifications as noted above must be attached to these estimates. If anything, the increase in the burden to residents of Québec, assuming they wished to maintain the same level and type of government services, would likely be larger than that indicated. At the same time, the gains to a province like Alberta may well be considerably smaller, or even negative, when the transitional risks and greater regional imbalance in political power is factored in.

The Case of an Independent Alberta

Economic Impacts
This is the polar case to that of an independent Québec. The basic assumptions and procedures parallel those outlined in the preceding analysis.

The economic impacts are set out in Table 6.10. As indicated there, the gain to Alberta varies between $2.6 billion (1990 dollars) in 1988 to $3.8 billion in 1986. All of the other regions are negatively affected. The per capita loss for Ontario and Québec is largest because it is assumed that Alberta's share of NCR expenditures would shift to Alberta. Consequently, these two provinces lose the economic impacts arising from those expenditures, as well as the associated provincial taxes. The relatively large gain for Alberta, on the other hand, occurs partly from this shift. However, it is mostly related to the fact that, after separation, the federal revenues which then remain in the province are more than sufficient to cover the same level of total expenditures in Alberta and the increased outflows associated with the

TABLE 6.10
Changes in Fiscal Balances with Alberta Independence
Relative to the Status Quo, Cash Flow Basis, 1986 and 1988
(Total change in millions of 1990 dollars; per capita change in 1990 dollars)

Period	Nfld	PEI	NS	NB	Que	Ont	Man	Sask	*Alta*	BC	Terr
86 - Total	-67	-15	-103	-84	-865	-1491	-127	-119	*3818*	-345	-9
86 - Per Capita	-118	-118	-118	-118	-131	-161	-118	-118	*1608*	-118	-118
88 - Total	-38	-9	-59	-48	-536	-1028	-73	-68	*2644*	-205	-5
88 - Per Capita	-67	-67	-67	-67	-80	-107	-67	-67	*1090*	-67	-67

province's per capita share of IOPD without having to borrow the amount
equal to its per capita share of the federal deficit under the status quo.

It is fairly clear that, considering only the fiscal impacts, an independent
Alberta would have a significantly larger economy. Whether it would have a
larger population would depend on its (hypothetical) immigration policies.
The latter would also be an important determinant of the change in the level
of per capita income.

In theory, an independent Alberta would be less stable. Although the
larger government sector associated with the shift of Alberta's share of the
NCR to the province would have a stabilizing influence, it is doubtful that
the economy would be significantly more diversified, at least in a free trade
environment. Further, there would be no potential to gain stability via
countercyclical federal transfers financed by a much more stable and
diversified national economy and tax base or through the greater market
power of the nation in combating destabilizing trade policies of other
nations.

However, as demonstrated in the third section, the experience over the
last three decades suggests that there is a large gap between theory and
practice. If the benchmark is the degree of stabilization which federal policies
have provided for the provincial economy, it is almost certain that an
independent Alberta would be able to achieve a higher degree of stability.
First, as shown in Mansell and Percy (1990), the provincial government has
had a much better record than the federal government in terms of running a
fiscal policy consistent with the stabilization requirements of the Alberta
economy. Second, the previously observed tendency for federal fiscal
balances to offset or neutralize provincial countercyclical policies would be

TABLE 6.11
Changes in Fiscal Balances with Alberta Independence
Relative to the Status Quo, Benefits Basis, 1986 and 1988
(Total change in millions of 1990 dollars; per capita change in 1990 dollars)

Period	Nfld	PEI	NS	NB	Que	Ont	Man	Sask	*Alta*	BC	Terr
86 - Total	-59	-13	-91	-74	-685	-964	-112	-105	*2360*	-304	-8
86 - Per Capita	-104	-104	-104	-104	-104	-104	-104	-104	*994*	-104	-104
88 - Total	-29	-7	-45	-36	-340	-487	-55	-51	*515*	-155	-4
88 - Per Capita	-51	-51	-51	-51	-51	-51	-51	-51	*212*	-51	-51

eliminated. Third, federal policies such as the NEP which have been such a large source of instability would not be possible.

These potential gains in terms of stability would, however, depend to a large degree on market conditions for the province's main exports. If separation occurred in a period characterized by market conditions similar to those in the 1970s, such that the possibility existed to gain stability by "banking" resource rents and using the interest to provide a stable flow of interest income, there could be major improvements in terms of stability. But, if it occurred at a time when market conditions were similar to those that exist today it is questionable as to whether there would or could be any significant gains.

Equity Implications
The balances calculated on a benefits basis for the case of an independent Alberta are shown in Table 6.11. In general it indicates that the effect would be to reduce the net fiscal burden for Albertans while still maintaining the same mix and level of government services as that under the status quo. At the same time, the net fiscal benefits in ROC are reduced.

It is unclear what the equity implications of these balances are, if only because notions of regional equity lose meaning once the region that is the focus becomes a nation. About all that can be said is that the net fiscal burden for residents of Alberta decreases. This, of course, assumes that the unit cost of supplying government services equivalent to those provided by the federal government would not be higher. As for the ROC, it is doubtful that there would be any significant ramifications since, as shown earlier, aside from the case of Alberta, there do not appear to be any major regional inequities under the status quo.

In summary, one cannot conclude from these results, and those concerning the economic impacts, that Albertans would be better off if the province were independent. Indeed, they probably say little about the relative desirability of that alternative but say much about the problem areas under existing arrangements.

The Case of Greater Decentralization

The third scenario considered in this study involves greater decentralization along the lines suggested in Allaire (1991). As outlined at the beginning of this section, under this proposal areas of strict federal jurisdiction would include: defence and territorial security, customs and duties, currency and common debt, and, fiscal equalization. Areas of shared jurisdiction would include: Native affairs, taxation and revenue, financial institutions, justice; fisheries, foreign policy, post office and telecommunications, and, transport. All other areas would fall under provincial jurisdiction.

It is important to note that the allocation of powers under a constitution does not necessarily indicate the effective distribution of powers in practice. For example, according to the allocation of jurisdictions under the existing Constitution there would appear to be a much higher degree of decentralization in Canada than in federations such as the United States or Australia. However, the reality is quite different. First, there has been a trend over time of increasing intrusions by the federal government in areas of provincial jurisdiction. This has taken place through the use of the federal government's superior taxation and spending powers and involves areas such as health, education, and social services. Second, unlike the situation in other federations, the exercise of federal power in Canada is based almost entirely on representation by population. There is no democratic or effective regional representation at the federal level to reflect the very uneven distribution of population. As a result, federal power is effectively concentrated in just two provinces, Ontario and Québec. Third, Canada is not only distinguished by this regional concentration of federal power, but also by the very high degree of centralization of the federal decision-making apparatus. For example, the concentration of federal civil servants in Canada's national capital is about three times higher than is the case in the United States.

In this context it is clear that there remains considerable room for decentralization in Canada. Further, effective decentralization must typically involve more than just changes in the allocation of jurisdictions. For example, it can be accomplished by one or a combination of the following: the addition of effective regional representation in federal decision making; the reduction of the degree of federal intrusion in areas which are already under provincial jurisdiction; a change of the sharing arrangements under areas of shared jurisdiction; and, the redistribution of taxation power to reflect the relative federal and provincial spending responsibilities under the existing allocation of jurisdictions.

These points are particularly critical in terms of the calculation of fiscal balances under the decentralization scenario. For this purpose it is insufficient to know simply the distribution of areas of jurisdiction. It is also necessary to know the degree of regional representation in federal policy making, how the expenditures at each level of government are financed (that is, the sharing of taxation powers) and the precise sharing formulas for expenditures in areas of joint jurisdiction. With the exception of programs like UIC, CPP/QPP, and fiscal equalization, there are no direct links between program expenditures and revenues. Moreover, the regional redistribution under these programs where there is a direct revenue-expenditure link is but a small part of the total regional redistribution in Canada. For example, as demonstrated earlier, by far the largest interregional transfers since 1961 have occurred via energy policy.

Since the Allaire proposals concern only the allocation of jurisdictions, and not these other important determinants of the effective degree of decentralization, it is not possible to do a quantitative assessment of the type undertaken for the status quo, Québec independence, and Alberta independence cases. Rather, we are limited to a general qualitative evaluation. In what follows, the assumption is that, along with the distribution of powers as outlined in Allaire (1991), there is a redistribution of taxation powers/taxation sharing to reflect the federal/provincial distribution of program spending, a genuine shift towards regional decision making in areas under shared jurisdiction and the introduction of a serious form of regional representation at the federal level to counterbalance strict representation by population. These changes will be referred to as "effective decentralization."

Economic Impacts
If effective decentralization had existed over the historical period analyzed in the section on existing arrangements, it is almost certain that the amount of redistribution of income, jobs, and people away from Alberta would have been much less than that which actually took place. With energy and natural resources more securely under strict provincial jurisdiction and with some form of effective regional representation in federal policy making, it would

have been considerably more difficult for the federal government to impose the types of energy policies which resulted in such massive transfers from Alberta to (primarily) Central Canada. Further, with this decentralization case the most significant redistributive program remaining under federal jurisdiction would be fiscal equalization. As shown by Reid and Snoddon (1991), there would continue to be a redistribution from Ontario, Alberta, and British Columbia under this program. However, in the case of Alberta this amount would be very small relative to that under the other fiscal programs and under energy taxation and pricing policies. In general, the provinces that would stand to lose the most under these arrangements would be those in the Atlantic region and the province of Québec.

A general view of the redistribution associated strictly with expenditures/transfers under federal programs (excluding those involving energy) is presented in Table 6.12. Note that the values for Québec are not shown. In the case of Québec, there are opting-out and other special fiscal arrangements which would need to be taken into account in order to allow meaningful comparisons with the other provinces.[85] As shown, per capita expenditures related to the operating presence of the federal government have been below the national average in Alberta, as well as in Saskatchewan and Newfoundland. For the period 1961 to 1990, these per capita expenditures in Alberta averaged 73% of those for the other regions. It would be reasonable to expect this disparity to diminish under decentralization. The provinces that stand to suffer the largest reductions in federal government operating expenditures as a result of decentralization include Nova Scotia, Prince Edward Island, New Brunswick, and Ontario.

The Statutory category in Table 6.12 consists of all statutory expenditures/transfers. It includes such things as federal payments under the CPP, family and youth allowances, pensions for veterans and government employees, medicare and official languages.[86] The Assistance category includes federal payments under UIC, disabled allowances, CAP

---

85. That is, per capita federal expenditures in Québec under many programs are lower than the national average simply because the service is provided by the Government of Québec and it has received tax points from the federal government as compensation. As noted in the section on existing arrangements, the use of net balances or a ratio of revenues and expenditures avoids this problem of regional comparability.

86. The expenditures/transfers included under the Statutory category include: Canada Pension Plan current expenditure; Family and Youth Allowances; Pensions (WWI and WWII); War Veterans' Allowances; Pensions to Government Employees; Old Age Security Payments; ; Miscellaneous and other Transfer Payments to Persons; Statutory Grants; Payments to Yukon and Northwest Territories; Health Grants; Contributions Under the Hospital Insurance;Diagnostic Services Act; Health Resources Fund; Medicare; Official Languages; Miscellaneous Transfers to Provincial Governments; and Transfers to Local Governments.

TABLE 6.12
Average Annual Real Per Capita Federal Expenditures/
Transfers by Category for Each Province (all values in 1990 dollars)

Region	Federal Government				Statutory			
	1960s	1970s	1980s	Overall	1960s	1970s	1980s	Overall
Average	703	896	1061	893	617	1112	1667	1149
Nfld	366	614	939	649	656	1182	1683	1191
PEI	890	1257	1939	1378	956	1529	2075	1539
NS	1380	1959	2488	1962	804	1385	2087	1447
NB	742	959	1373	1035	749	1304	1919	1344
Ont	862	1078	1111	1022	648	1135	1613	1149
Man	719	904	1176	940	752	1319	1988	1374
Sask	361	591	756	577	709	1272	1916	1319
Alta	524	670	756	654	623	1049	1340	1017
BC	595	738	835	727	761	1214	1785	1270
Terr	5630	3658	5186	4797	1209	6236	12464	6823

Region	Assistance				Education/Development			
	1960s	1970s	1980s	Overall	1960s	1970s	1980s	Overall
Average	229	495	825	526	88	188	207	164
Nfld	354	858	1409	891	149	297	250	235
PEI	315	872	1469	905	86	661	316	363
NS	347	566	867	602	128	302	270	237
NB	270	746	1203	756	124	333	315	262
Ont	196	423	593	411	79	145	188	140
Man	248	448	866	530	59	191	238	166
Sask	391	688	1485	871	59	174	279	174
Alta	231	374	859	497	100	161	203	156
BC	206	526	846	537	73	121	198	133
Terr	146	642	990	608	407	154	483	346

Region	Taxation Agreements			
	1960s	1970s	1980s	Overall
Average	110	255	286	221
Nfld	429	901	1371	916
PEI	423	968	1372	938
NS	314	719	921	663
NB	331	716	1028	704
Ont	19	39	5	21
Man	150	383	633	397
Sask	133	258	161	186
Alta	58	95	84	80
BC	29	29	3	20
Terr	0	11	14	8

Source: Statistics Canada Catalogue 13-213, Provincil Economic Accounts

(Canada Assistance Plan), and various agricultural programs.[87] The federal expenditures under the Education/Development grouping include those related to postsecondary education, technical, vocational and occupational training, local initiatives and regional economic development.[88] Finally, the taxation agreements category is primarily comprised of fiscal equalization payments but also includes public utility rebates, recovery of youth allowances, reciprocal taxation agreements, and so forth.

As indicated, per capita expenditures, in or transfers to, Alberta under all of these programs have typically been below the average for the other regions. The largest deviation occurs in the case of taxation agreements;[89] for the others the per capita amounts for Alberta are between 89% and 95% of the average for the other regions.

Within this historical setting it is likely that a greater degree of effective decentralization would have led to policies more consistent with stability of the Alberta economy. As noted in the third section, federal fiscal balances have on balance tended to accentuate the variability of the province's economy rather than to reduce it. Indeed, policies such as the NEP and the associated fiscal transfers have tended to be a significant source of instability. Further, it can be argued that with decentralization the probability of such policies would have been much lower and, consequently, it is likely that considerably more resource revenues could have been accumulated in the Alberta Heritage Savings Trust Fund. This would have added a considerable degree of stability to the provincial government's revenues and would have allowed it to implement even more aggressive countercyclical fiscal policies and policies aimed at broadening the industrial base. In addition, there would not likely have been as many instances where the federal fiscal balance was not only out of step with that required for stability of the Alberta economy, but also where the federal balance was serving to defeat the countercyclical policy stance of the provincial government.

If one takes a forward rather than a backward look in assessing the economic impacts associated with effective decentralization, the conclusions

---

87. The items under the Assistance category include: Unemployment Insurance Benefits; Prairie Farm Assistance Act; Subsidies; Old Age and Blind Persons' Allowances; Disabled Persons' Allowances; Unemployment Assistance; Canada Assistance Plan; and Contributions under the Crop Insurance Act.

88. The items under the Education/Development category include: Scholarships and Research Grants; Occupational Training; Local Initiatives Program; Capital Assistance Program; Post-Secondary Education Grants; Trans Canada Highway; Technical and Vocational Training; and Regional Economic Expansion Payments.

89. A large proportion of the amounts transferred to Alberta under fiscal equalization represents refunds of taxes paid by Alberta's privately-owned utilities. In most provinces the utilities are owned by provincoal governments and therefore not subject to federal tax.

are much the same. As argued in the third section, NEP-style policies are
likely in the event that there are significant increases in resource prices and
rents. However, even if such conditions in resource markets do not
materialize, there are other economic concerns that would be at least partly
addressed through greater decentralization. One of these is the reality that,
given the fiscal position of the federal government, the responsibility for
economic stabilization will, over the foreseeable future, increasingly fall to
lower levels of government. Second, there is a high probability that, as the
federal government's fiscal position worsens, the burden will be
disproportionately shifted to provinces such as Alberta that have average
or above-average income positions and do not have the population size (or
the number of federal seats) to protect against regionally discriminatory
policies. This trend is perhaps evidenced by programs such as those: which
dramatically reduce federal funding for provinces such as Alberta in the
areas of education and health care; which cap federal funding for social
services and primarily impact provinces such as Alberta with
above-average growth rates; which cap federal income tax rebates for
privately-owned utilities and therefore discriminate against provinces such
as Alberta where utilities tend to be privately owned rather than owned by
the provincial government; and, which impose special taxes such as the
large corporations or capital tax that disproportionately fall on provinces
such as Alberta that have a very capital intensive economy. In general,
effective decentralization would serve to reduce the degree to which a
province such as Alberta can be subjected to regionally discriminatory
federal policies of these types.

Equity Implications
For much the same reasons as those discussed above, effective
decentralization is more likely to lead to regional equity. It will be recalled
that this type of equity involves the application of narrow-based horizontal
equity for net fiscal benefits originating from such things as resources
which, under the Constitution, are owned by the provinces. For other net
fiscal benefits, the broad-based definition and, hence, full equalization
would apply.
    As was demonstrated in the existing arrangements section, Alberta
stands out as the only clear case where the net federal fiscal contributions
have been greatly out of line with the region's relative income position. For
example, in spite of per capita market incomes well below the average in
Ontario, Albertans made per capita net fiscal contributions to the federal
government over the 1961-1990 period which were over four times as large
as those made by residents of Ontario. By making it more difficult to

discriminate against resource-rich peripheral regions, decentralization would reduce the likelihood that Albertans would be treated in such an inequitable manner in the future.

Conclusions

The main objective in this study was to examine the implications of federal tax, expenditure and transfer policies for regional distribution, stability and equity under existing and selected alternative constitutional arrangements. The basic approach involved the calculation of federal fiscal balances by region on both a cash-flow and a benefits basis. The former are used to assess the redistribution of economic activity and regional stabilization, while the balances computed on a benefits basis are employed in the evaluation of regional equity. One of the advantages of this approach is that it allows an examination of the net regional effects when all federal tax, expenditure and transfer policies are considered. (Other analyses typically focus on just a few programs or policies and, as such, cannot give an accurate picture of the total net regional effects.) A significant weakness of this approach is that it does not take into account such things as transitional costs or changes in trade patterns. For these and other reasons emphasized at the beginning, the results from the analysis should not be interpreted as overall measures of the benefits and costs of Confederation under existing or alternative constitutional arrangements.

The main conclusions of this study are summarized below.

It is clear that, over the period 1961 to 1989, the fiscal effects of federal policies have resulted in a substantial redistribution of economic activity and population away from Alberta, and to a lesser extent, away from British Columbia and toward the other regions. Although the federal government has run a sizable fiscal surplus with Ontario over some periods, there has not likely been any major redistribution away from Ontario. This is because the surpluses have been largely offset by deficits through most of the 1970s and up to the mid-1980s and because most of the indirect effects associated with the balances for other regions work to Ontario's advantage.

The net effects of this redistribution in terms of regional disparities in per capita income are unclear. Under the Courchene view, the main effect has been to pull down per capita incomes in the fiscal surplus regions compared to what they would otherwise be, while preventing any real improvement in the deficit regions. This is because the transfers have prevented many of the required adjustments and, in general, have created a "transfer dependency."

On balance, federal policies have been more of a destabilizing than a stabilizing factor for the Alberta economy. Much of this instability can be traced to energy policies and to the lack of coordination between federal and provincial fiscal policies.

Contrary to common perceptions, there seems to be little evidence in most cases of any large or systematic regional inequities. There is generally a fairly close fit between relative income levels and relative net federal fiscal contributions. The only major exception is the case of Alberta. For most of the historical period the net contributions by residents of Alberta have been many times larger than one would expect given their relative income levels and any reasonable definition of equity. This result has also been observed in other analyses of fiscal balances. Over this period at least, the term "milch cow of Confederation" is more appropriately applied to Alberta than it is to Ontario or any other region. Further, the results for most of the years between 1961 and 1989 would seem to support the general conclusion by Whalley and Trela (1986, p. 199) that "Confederation appears to be substantially unbalanced both against resource rich and higher-income provinces."

This inequity is not related to the particular design of fiscal equalization programs so much as it is to other policies which are typically not even considered in the literature on equalization. For example, by far the largest interregional transfers have been those arising from federal energy policies. Along with the inexplicably low levels of federal spending in the province in most areas, some programs such as UI contribute to the inequity through hidden transfers. For example, UI will almost always generate a net transfer out of Alberta because, even with large negative shocks to the economy, the high degree of mobility and adjustability of the provincial labour force will prevent large or lasting increases in the province's unemployment rate. Viewed differently, such programs essentially penalize the regions which encourage efficient adjustment and reward those which discourage adjustment.

In recent years there have been substantial improvements. This is no doubt partly due to the fact that there are fewer rents to be extracted from Alberta today, but also, perhaps even more important, this is one of the very rare periods when Albertans have been well represented in the governing party. In any case, this should not lead to the conclusion that the fundamental causes of the problems have been dealt with and that, in looking ahead, there are no reasons for concern. In fact, given the right energy price environment, for example, it is highly likely that a different government at the federal level would have little difficulty in imposing NEP-style policies that have in the past been so destabilizing and inequitable for Alberta. Moreover, it is reasonable to expect that, even in a depressed energy price environment, there will be a disproportionate off-loading of problems associated with federal deficits/debt to provinces such as Alberta in the absence of significant constitutional change.

An analysis of fiscal balances using the cash-flow approach for the hypothetical case of Québec independence indicates that, abstracting from important factors such as shifts in trade patterns and transitional impacts, the main effect would be a distribution of economic activity away from that province and primarily towards Ontario, Alberta, and British Columbia. It is questionable, however, whether Alberta would gain significantly since Québec independence would mean the loss of an important ally in the protection of provincial resource rights. To the extent that Québec separation also resulted in a more centralized distribution of power in what would remain of the federation, Alberta would almost certainly lose. Further, with its very capital intensive economy and reliance on external capital, Alberta would be vulnerable to the higher interest rates and disruptions to capital flows that would likely occur during the transition. The same general assessment applies to the analysis of balances using the benefits approach.

In the polar case of an independent Alberta, there is a fairly large gain for the province in terms of net financial flows and the overall size of the economy, assuming all other factors remained constant. Further, although in theory the Alberta economy would be less stable, in practice, given the destabilizing effects of federal policies in the past, it is likely that it would be less variable. At the same time, the results suggest a significant reduction in the fiscal burden on Albertans. However, the size of this gain, as well as that related to stability, would depend heavily on the market conditions for primary products during the period when this hypothetical separation occurred.

The third alternative considered involves effective decentralization. Contrary to the popular view, there is a high degree of centralization of power in the Canadian federation. Although the provincial governments have many areas of jurisdiction, power tends to be highly concentrated at the federal level. This occurs through federal intrusions in areas of provincial jurisdiction, through the superior taxation and spending powers of the federal government, through the lack of any serious form of regional representation at the federal level and through the concentration of population and federal power in just two provinces. In light of this, there is considerable room for decentralization. In general, it is concluded that effective decentralization would be particularly beneficial for Alberta in terms of regional economic distribution, stability and equity.

The overall ranking of the alternatives for Alberta strictly on the basis of these three economic criteria is as follows. The best is a higher degree of effective decentralization. Next best is the case of an independent Alberta.

The third best is an independent Québec but with a higher degree of effective decentralization of power for the regions remaining in the federation. The status quo represents the fourth best (or second worst) alternative. The worst alternative is a greater degree of centralization with or without Québec.

The general conclusion is that, in order to deal with the major economic problems from an Alberta constitutional perspective, attention can be usefully focused on the following types of reforms.

1. Effective and equal regional representation at the federal level. While the introduction of something like a triple-E Senate may not be the panacea, it would certainly help reduce the likelihood of federal policies that systematically discriminate against the economic interests of those who reside in the resource-rich peripheral regions.

2. A reallocation of taxation power or a shift in taxation sharing to reflect better the relative federal-provincial spending responsibilities even under the existing constitution.

3. A Council of the Federation. As suggested by Wiseman (1987) and, more recently by Smith (1991), it is critical that coordination of federal and provincial policies takes place in a systematic and on-going basis. As demonstrated in this study, there have been numerous cases where this lack of coordination has resulted in substantial instability and avoidable costs to Albertans and, no doubt, to other Canadians. The entrenchment of such a process in the Constitution could be an important step in resolving these problems. In addition, such a body could be effective in ensuring that, when all federal policies with important fiscal effects are considered, regional equity objectives are served. Further, consideration should be given to amending the "regional equity" section of the Constitution so that it is clear that broad-based horizontal equity is only to be applied to those areas which do not fall under exclusive provincial jurisdiction. Other amendments to reduce the likelihood of federal policies which clearly contravene provincial powers, such as in the area of natural resources, might also be considered.

4. Other changes outside of the Constitution. Perhaps some of the most effective changes in terms of the economic problems outlined in this study can be introduced without Constitutional amendments. One example would be more effective and balanced regional representation on important federal boards and commissions. As suggested by Laidler (1991), this principle should also be extended to the Bank of Canada. Another example would be a more even regional distribution of federal government operations and operating expenditures.

In conclusion, from the admittedly narrow economic perspective adopted in this study, it would seem that rather modest reforms of this type are likely to go a long way in resolving the most serious problems concerning the effects of federal policies in terms of regional economic distribution, stability, and equity.

References

Allaire. (1991, January). *A Québec Free To Choose.* Report presented at the Constitutional Committee of the Québec Liberal Party.

Anderson, F.J. & Bonsor, N.C. (1986). Regional economic alienation: Atlantic Canada and the west. In K. Norrie (Ed.), Disparities and interregional adjustment, Vol. 64, *Research studies for the Royal Commission on the Economic Union and Development Prospects for Canada.* Toronto: University of Toronto Press.

Banks, Irene. (1977). The provincial distribution of federal government expenditures, 1972-73, 1973-74 and 1974-75. *Study Prepared for the Economic Council of Canada.* Ottawa: Supply and Services.

Bélanger, M. & Campeau, J. (1991, March). *Rapport de la Commission sur l'avenir politique et constitutionnel du Québec.* Québec.

Boadway, Robin. (1986). Federal-provincial transfers in Canada: A critical review of existing arrangements. In M. Krasnick (Ed.), *Fiscal Federalism, Vol. 65, Research studies for the Royal Commission on the Economic Union and Development Prospects for Canada.* Toronto: University of Toronto Press.

Boadway, Robin W., Purvis, Douglas S. & Wen, Jean Francois. (1991). Economic dimensions of constitutional change: A survey of the issues. In R. Boadway, T. Courchene and D. Purvis (Eds.), *Economic Dimensions of Constitutional Change,* John Deutsch Institute for Economic Policy, Kingston.

Boothe, Paul & Harris, Richard. (1991, June). Alternate divisions of federal assets and liabilities. In R. Boadway, T. Courchene and D. Purvis (Eds.), *Economic Dimensions of Constitutional Change,* John Deutsch Institute for Economic Policy, Kingston.

Brimelow, Peter. (1990). *The maple leaf forever: A short guide to Canada.* Encounter, v, pp. 18-24.

Buchanan, James M. and Richard E. Wagner. (1970). An Efficiency Basis for Federal Fiscal Equalization, in J. Margolis (Ed.), *The Analysis of Public Output,* New York: National Bureau of Economic Research.

Carmichael, Edward A. (1986). *New stresses on confederation: Diverging regional economies.* (Observation No. 28). Toronto: C.D.Howe Institute.

264   R o b e r t   L .   M a n s e l l   a n d   R o n a l d   C .   S c h l e n k e r

C.D. Howe Institute. (1977). *Why do the balances differ on federal receipts and expenditures in Québec?* (Accent Québec Series). Montreal: C.D. Howe Institute.

Courchene, Thomas J. (1978). Avenues of adjustment: The transfer system and regional disparities. In M. Walker (Ed.), *Canadian Confederation at the Crossroads.* Vancouver: Fraser Institute.

Courchene, Thomas J. (1981). A market perspective on regional disparities. *Canadian Public Policy, 7,* pp. 506-518.

Courchene, Thomas J. (1991). Canada 1992: Political denouement or economic renaissance. In R. Boadway, T. Courchene and D. Purvis (Eds.), *Economic Dimensions of Constitutional Change,* John Deutsch Institute for Economic Policy, Kingston.

Cumming, Peter A. (1986). Equitable fiscal federalism: The problems in respect of resources revenue sharing. In M. Krasnick (Ed.), *Fiscal Federalism, Vol. 65, Research studies for the Royal Commission on the Economic Union and Development Prospects for Canada.* Toronto: University of Toronto Press.

Dow, Sheila C. (1990). *Financial markets and regional economic development.* Aldershot, UK.: Athenaeum Press.

Economic Council of Canada. (1977). Towards regionally differentiated stabilization policy. In *Living together: A study of regional disparities.* Ottawa: Supply and Services.

Economic Council of Canada. (1982). *Financing Confederation, today and tomorrow.* Ottawa: Supply and Services.

Engerman, S. (1965). Regional aspects of stabilization policy. In R.A. Musgrave (Ed.), *Essays in Fiscal Federalism.* Washington: The Brookings Institution.

Ethier, Mireille. (1986). Regional grievances: The Québec case. In K. Norrie (Ed.), *Disparities and Interregional Adjustment, Vol. 64, Research studies for the Royal Commission on the Economic Union and Development Prospects for Canada.* Toronto: University of Toronto Press.

Glynn, A. (1979). The net provincial expenditures associated with federal government expenditures and fiscal autonomy. In *Institute of Intergovernmental Relations and the Economic Council of Canada, The political economy of Confederation,* Ottawa: Supply and Services.

Government of Alberta. (1938). *The case for Alberta: Dominion provincial relations.*

Hazeldine, T. (1979). The economic costs and benefits of the Canadian federal customs union. In *Institute of Intergovernmental Relations and the Economic Council of Canada, The political economy of Confederation.* Ottawa: Supply and Services.

Hollinshead, Michael J. & Blackman. W. (1975, October). The cost of Confederation: An analysis of costs to Alberta, Part II. In *Intergovernmental Transfer of Funds*. Mimeo.

Laidler, David, E.W. (1991). *How shall we govern the governor?* (The Canada Round: A Series on the Economics of Constitutional Renewal—No. 1.) Toronto: C.D. Howe Institute.

Leslie, Peter & Simeon, Richard. (1977). The battle of the balance sheets. In Richard Simeon (Ed.), *Must Canada fail?* Montreal/London: McGill-Queen's University Press.

Lesage, Jean. (1965). *La part du Québec dan les dépenses et les revenus du gouvernement fédéral, 1960-61, 1961-62 et 1962-63.* Québec: ministere des Affaires fédérales-provinciales.

Macdonald, Hon. Donald S. (1977, June). Statement by Mr. Macdonald on the provincial economic accounts. Ottawa, ON.

Mansell, Robert L. & Copithorne, Lawrence. (1986). Canadian regional disparities: A survey of the issues. In K. Norrie, (Ed.), *Disparities and Interregional Adjustment, vol. 64, Research studies for the Royal Commission on the Economic Union and Development Prospects for Canada.* Toronto: University of Toronto Press.

Mansell, R.L. and R.W. Wright. (1978). A Neoclassical Model for Evaluating Large-Scale Investment Impacts in the Regional Economy. *Growth and Change*, Vol. 9, No. 1: pp 23-30.

Mansell, Robert L. & Schlenker, Ronald C. (1988 & 1990). *An analysis of the regional distribution of federal fiscal balances* and *An analysis of the regional distribution of federal fiscal balances: Updated data.* (University of Calgary Research Paper.) Unpublished manuscript.

Mansell, Robert L. (1990). The regional economics of Confederation. *Parliamentary Government*, v, pp. 11-14.

Mansell, Robert L. & Percy, Michael B. (1990). *Strength in adversity: A study of the Alberta economy.* (Western Studies in Economic Policy, Western Centre for Economic Research and C.D. Howe Institute.) Edmonton: University of Alberta Press.

Myrdal, Gunnar. (1957). *Economic theory and underdeveloped regions.* London: G. Duckworth.

Norrie, K.H. (1976). Some comments on prairie economic alienation. *Canadian Public Policy*, 2, pp. 211-224.

Plourde, Andre. (1991). The NEP Meets the FTA, *Canadian Public Policy*, XVII, No. 1, pp. 14-24.

Reeves, M.A. & Kerr, W.A. (1985). The regional implications of the increasing emphasis on monetary policy. *The Canadian Journal of Regional Science*, 8, 1, pp. 75-84.

Reid, Bradford & Tracy Snoddon. (In publication). Redistribution under alternative constitutional arrangements for Canada.

Robinson, A.J. (1967). Is equity a viable policy objective? *Canadian Tax Structure and Economic Goals.* Toronto: York University Press.

Scott, A.D. (1978). Policy for declining regions: A theoretical approach. In N.H. Lithwick (Ed.), *Regional economic policy: The Canadian experience.* Toronto: McGraw-Hill Ryerson.

Sheppard, Anthony F. (1986). Taxation Policy and the Canadian Economic Union, in *Fiscal Federalism, Vol. 65, Research studies for the Royal Commission on the Economic Union and Development Prospects for Canada.* Toronto: University of Toronto Press.

Smith, Melvin H. (1991). *The renewal of Confederation—A British Columbia perspective.* Victoria: Ministry of Provincial Secretary.

Stothart, Paul. (1988). Exploding Alberta Myths, *Policy Options Politiques,* Vol. 9, No. 9, November 1988, pp 3-7.

Thirsk, Wayne. (1973). Regional dimensions of inflation and unemployment, (Prices and Incomes Commission). Ottawa: Information Canada.

Thirlwall, A.P. (1980). Regional problems are balance of payments problems. *Regional Studies,* 14, pp. 419-425.

Whalley, John & Trela, Irene. (1986). *Regional aspects of Confederation, Vol. 68, Research studies for the Royal Commission on the Economic Union and Development Prospects for Canada.* Toronto: University of Toronto Press.

Wiseman, J. (1987). *The political economy of federalism: A critical appraisal. Environment and Planning: Government and Policy,* 5, pp. 383-410.

Appendix Tables

TABLE 6A.1
Total and Per Capita Federal Fiscal Balances, Cash Flow Basis, 1961-1989
Sensitivity Case: Corporate Taxes Allocatedon the Basis of Consumption

Region	Total Balances (billions of 1990 dollars)				Annual Per Capital Balance (1990 dollars)			
	1960s	1970s	1980s	Total	1960s	1970s	1980s	Avg.
Nfld	-4.5	-13.0	-22.7	-40.2	-1026	-2371	-3986	-2510
PEI	-1.7	-4.0	-5.8	-11.5	-1733	-3417	-4640	-3316
NS	-11.0	-25.6	-37.3	-73.9	-1615	-3115	-4302	-3059
NB	-5.5	-15.4	-25.3	-46.2	-1001	-2307	-3573	-2339
Que	6.3	-41.4	-93.6	-128.7	125	-664	-1437	-686
Ont	19.0	2.0	-42.1	-21.2	303	40	-487	-60
Man	-2.9	-9.0	-22.4	-34.3	-334	-889	-2111	-118
Sask	-2.3	-4.1	-13.5	-20.0	-275	-445	-1343	-702
Alta	3.6	45.9	64.8	114.4	1269	2476	2884	1932
BC	8.4	11.3	-3.8	15.9	492	493	-134	277
Terr	-2.6	-4.3	-15.0	-22.0	-6812	-7047	-20131	-11486
Reg. Sum	6.7	-57.8	-216.7	-167.8	35	-246	-859	-370
Outside Canada	-11.2	-20.4	-62.4	-94.1				
Canada	-4.5	-78.2	-279.1	-361.8	-28	-336	-1104	-505

TABLE 6A.2
Total and Per Capita Federal Fiscal Balances, Cash Flow Basis, 1961-1989
Sensitivity Case: Interest on the Public Debt Excluded

Region	Total Balances (billions o f 1990 dollars)				Annual Per Capita Balance (1990 dollars)			
	1960s	1970s	1980s	Total	1960s	1970s	1980s	Avg.
Nfld	-4.5	-13.4	-22.1	-40.0	-1027	-2440	-3889	-2501
PEI	-1.7	-4.0	-.5.5	-11.2	-1760	-3431	-4360	-3233
NS	-10.8	-24.1	-32.4	-67.4	-1588	-2938	-3749	-2799
NB	-5.5	-15.1	-23.6	-44.2	-984	-2261	-3340	-2237
Que	17.7	-27.4	-53.5	-63.2	348	-436	-827	-327
Ont	45.1	54.8	94.1	194.0	727	690	997	808
Man	-1.8	-6.6	-17.2	-25.5	-203	-651	-1619	-846
Sask	-2.3	-2.7	-10.3	-15.3	-278	-287	-1019	-537
Alta	5.3	59.5	101.7	166.4	395	3206	4465	2768
BC	11.4	17.9	10.0	39.2	673	768	337	590
Reg. Sum	50.4	34.9	27.2	112.5	281	163	101	178
Outside Canada	-11.2	-18.9	-31.1	-61.2				
Canada	39.2	16.1	-3.8	51.4	217	79	-21	88

TABLE 6B.1: Total Federal Fiscal Balance By Region, Cash Flow Basis (millions of 1990 dollars)

	Nfld	PEI	NS	NB	Que	Ont	Man	Sask	Alta	BC	Terr	Sum	Outside	Canada
1961	-414	-133	-1128	-611	700	1163	-404	-626	20	74	-276	-1636	-1030	-2665
1962	-457	-160	-1177	-603	476	705	-404	-656	0	404	-282	-2154	-1031	-3185
1963	-424	-172	-1144	-596	658	1058	-367	-339	95	524	-272	-977	-1116	-2093
1964	-394	-171	-1112	-575	1242	2576	-185	-292	278	927	-301	1992	-1126	866
1965	-523	-230	-1212	-608	1194	3398	-216	-207	383	1118	-288	2807	-1172	1636
1966	-554	-232	-1362	-692	876	2892	-404	-193	516	1109	-301	1654	-1530	125
1967	-656	-231	-1540	-850	186	2659	-421	-223	632	1172	-330	396	-1610	-1214
1968	-633	-235	-1649	-837	-231	3072	-442	-279	665	1255	-303	382	-1315	-932
1969	-686	-255	-1581	-758	469	5017	-373	-408	1013	2084	-251	4270	-1291	2979
1970	-724	-284	-1362	-790	-335	4008	-477	-772	917	1584	-222	1544	-1493	51
1971	-854	-325	-1534	-956	-1220	4099	-564	-899	847	1668	-261	0	-1404	-1404
1972	-978	-330	-1702	-1061	-2018	4174	-581	-1021	931	1585	-374	-1375	-1325	-2699
1973	-1061	-331	-1926	-1131	-1383	4879	-576	-779	1990	2373	-273	1782	-1404	377
1974	-1360	-357	-2562	-1422	-3399	3227	-523	182	8930	1955	-228	4445	-2041	2403
1975	-1727	-466	-3193	-2012	-6727	-1419	-959	-178	8363	695	437	-8058	-2337	-10395
1976	-1458	-503	-3297	-1990	-5189	-1083	-937	63	7323	874	-544	-6741	-1878	-8619
1977	-1808	-543	-3788	-2278	-7720	-3628	-1434	-288	7613	-25	-595	-14495	-2246	-16740
1978	-2103	-595	-3873	-2469	-9456	-4705	-1755	-715	6755	-207	-622	-19744	-3153	-22897
1979	-1892	-534	-3818	-2384	-9206	-5901	-1935	-414	11397	100	-585	-15171	-3141	-18312
1980	-2026	-530	-4455	-3250	-11954	-10736	-2216	313	20402	-247	-665	-15365	-3433	-18798
1981	-1799	-511	-3995	-2883	-11859	-8987	-2041	415	23213	504	-667	-8611	-3563	-12174
1982	-2263	-601	-4042	-2881	-15585	-10197	-2396	-557	16914	-1241	-1560	-24409	-4517	-28926
1983	-2519	-596	-4142	-2558	-13263	-7326	-2404	-1167	8450	-1658	-1639	-28822	-4920	-33741
1984	-2595	-696	-4613	-2692	-12847	-8579	-2614	-1632	7145	-2590	-1857	-33571	-5580	-39151
1985	-2961	-711	-4204	-2865	-11828	-8120	-2578	-1711	5881	-2650	-1837	-33585	-6409	-39994
1986	-2697	-608	-3893	-2493	-7232	133	-2190	-2069	2067	-1275	-2054	-22312	-7477	-29790
1987	-2377	-572	-3314	-2332	-5551	2476	-2598	-3038	1430	-445	-1517	-17837	-8443	-26280
1988	-2320	-641	-3319	-2368	-5382	3758	-2777	-2694	1629	52	-1521	-15581	-8904	-24485
1989	-2353	-616	-3314	-2328	-5635	1779	-2515	-2306	1950	361	-1626	-16602	-9173	-25776
61-69	-4741	-1820	-11905	-6129	5570	22538	-3217	-3222	3602	8666	-2604	6736	-11219	-4483
70-79	-13964	-4267	-27053	-16493	-46652	3650	-9740	-4821	55065	10603	-4141	-57813	-20421	-78234
80-89	-23911	-6082	-39293	-26651	-101135	-45798	-24329	-14446	89080	-9187	-14943	-216695	-62421	-279116
TOTAL	-42617	-12169	-78251	-49274	-142218	-19610	-37285	-22490	147747	10082	-21688	-267773	-94060	-361833

TABLE 6B.2: Per Capita Federal Fiscal Balance By Region, Cash Flow Basis (1990 dollars)

	Nfld	PEI	NS	NB	Que	Ont	Man	Sask	Alta	BC	Terr	Sum	Outside	Canada
1961	-904	-1267	-1531	-1022	133	186	-438	-676	15	45	-7260	-90		-146
1962	-977	-1499	-1577	-996	89	111	-431	-706	0	243	-7050	-116		-171
1963	-891	-1589	-1524	-979	120	163	-387	-363	68	309	-6628	-52		-111
1964	-815	-1573	-1473	-940	222	388	-193	-310	194	531	-7170	103		45
1965	-1071	-2108	-1603	-989	210	501	-224	-218	264	622	-7034	143		83
1966	-1124	-2129	-1802	-1121	152	415	-419	-202	352	592	-6994	83		6
1967	-1315	-2121	-2026	-1372	32	373	-437	-233	424	603	-7506	19		-60
1968	-1252	-2137	-2150	-1339	-39	423	-455	-290	437	627	-6728	18		-45
1969	-1334	-2299	-2040	-1207	78	679	-381	-425	650	1011	-5349	203		142
1970	-1401	-2581	-1741	-1260	-56	531	-485	-820	575	744	-4441	72		2
1971	-1635	-2898	-1945	-1505	-202	532	-571	-971	520	764	-4925	0		-65
1972	-1844	-2923	-2140	-1658	-333	534	-586	-1117	562	707	-6556	-63		-124
1973	-1976	-2905	-2395	-1749	-227	617	-579	-861	1178	1031	-4548	81		17
1974	-2509	-3102	-3155	-2174	-555	401	-519	203	5186	823	-3800	199		107
1975	-3145	-3982	-3893	-3026	-1089	-174	-945	-196	4704	286	-6930	-355		-458
1976	-2613	-4264	-3978	-2940	-832	-131	-917	68	3984	354	-8493	-293		-375
1977	-3229	-4561	-4547	-3330	-1228	-434	-1397	-308	3980	-10	-9160	-623		-719
1978	-3741	-4914	-4622	-3588	-1501	-558	-1700	-757	3406	-81	-9427	-840		-974
1979	-3354	-4377	-4534	-3446	-1452	-694	-1882	-436	5551	39	-8868	-639		-771
1980	-3580	-4309	-5273	-4677	-1872	-1253	-2162	326	9529	-93	-9921	-639		-782
1981	-3167	-4158	-4717	-4142	-1842	-1042	-1989	428	10377	184	-9663	-354		-500
1982	-3999	-4923	-4756	-4133	-2412	-1172	-2320	-570	7306	-445	-21971	-993		-1177
1983	-4412	-4803	-4833	-3639	-2048	-833	-2298	-1180	3612	-589	-22761	-1163		-1361
1984	-4536	-5568	-5339	-3803	-1979	-964	-2478	-1630	3055	-909	-25445	-1344		-1567
1985	-5213	-5600	-4811	-4029	-1807	-890	-2407	-1693	2477	-916	-24177	-1324		-1576
1986	-4756	-4788	-4434	-3497	-1096	14	-2032	-2037	870	-435	-26673	-870		-1162
1987	-4178	-4437	-3753	-3262	-835	262	-2394	-2999	598	-149	-19701	-688		-1013
1988	-4063	-4966	-3742	-3294	-803	392	-2557	-2675	671	17	-19497	-594		-933
1989	-4106	-4737	-3715	-3216	-832	182	-2305	-2306	789	115	-20324	-624		-968
61-69	-1076	-1858	-1747	-1107	111	360	-374	-380	267	509	-6858	35		-28
70-79	-2545	-3651	-3295	-2468	-748	62	-958	-520	2965	466	-6715	-246		-336
80-89	-4201	-4829	-4537	-3769	-1553	-530	-2294	-1433	3929	-322	-20013	-859		-1104
AVERAGE	-2660	-3501	-3243	-2494	-759	-50	-1238	-792	2460	208	-11345	-370		-505

TABLE 6B.3: Index of Relative Per Capita Federal Revenue,
Cash Flow Basis (National Average =100)

	Nfld	PEI	NS	NB	Que*	Ont	Man	Sask	Alta	BC	Terr	Canada
1961	51	60	69	59	84	127	89	67	104	115	158	100
1962	54	55	68	59	87	124	90	74	103	116	148	100
1963	52	53	68	59	86	124	87	78	100	117	134	100
1964	52	51	68	62	87	124	91	73	96	117	139	100
1965	52	50	70	65	82	126	87	78	97	120	165	100
1966	55	56	72	65	80	125	89	82	102	117	160	100
1967	53	52	77	65	80	124	92	79	105	117	198	100
1968	54	54	77	64	77	126	93	76	105	116	190	100
1969	51	53	78	65	77	126	91	69	105	119	196	100
1970	53	55	82	68	78	126	91	64	106	113	194	100
1971	56	56	83	69	78	125	91	67	105	115	181	100
1972	55	60	84	69	77	125	91	70	106	113	189	100
1973	53	57	81	66	75	122	88	75	117	118	198	100
1974	48	52	72	63	68	107	82	102	226	104	200	100
1975	45	59	73	65	69	106	83	103	227	102	191	100
1976	50	60	75	65	71	107	83	100	207	107	170	100
1977	49	60	75	62	72	105	81	96	215	105	198	100
1978	49	61	75	62	74	105	81	93	202	107	196	100
1979	47	56	69	61	69	98	75	100	254	103	195	100
1980	40	47	60	54	61	86	66	108	338	96	176	100
1981	42	46	64	61	61	87	65	104	324	94	165	100
1982	46	54	71	59	57	93	71	101	297	96	186	100
1983	51	60	80	64	68	104	76	94	220	97	194	100
1984	52	63	82	65	72	104	76	95	213	92	199	100
1985	55	62	85	65	75	109	79	89	183	92	201	100
1986	61	78	88	70	82	119	86	81	119	96	171	100
1987	62	74	89	73	83	120	83	78	110	97	171	100
1988	63	77	88	73	82	122	81	75	109	96	169	100
1989	63	77	89	73	82	121	82	77	107	97	169	100
61-69	53	54	72	63	82	125	90	75	102	117	165	100
70-79	50	58	77	65	73	113	85	87	176	109	191	100
80-89	54	64	80	66	72	107	77	90	202	95	180	100
AVG	52	59	76	65	76	114	83	84	162	107	179	100

*   Numbers for Quebec cannot be directly compared to those for other regions because of
    opting out.

TABLE 6B.4: Index of Relative Per Capita Federal Expenditure,
Cash Flow Basis (National Average =100)

	Nfld	PEI	NS	NB	Que	Ont	Man	Sask	Alta	BC	Terr	Canada
1961	96	124	146	110	73	111	108	99	98	107	533	100
1962	101	130	146	107	77	110	107	106	97	96	507	100
1963	98	137	148	110	77	112	105	95	93	97	484	100
1964	98	138	150	115	80	110	106	93	91	96	528	100
1965	112	164	159	121	77	109	106	95	91	97	544	100
1966	113	163	164	123	76	110	113	95	89	93	510	100
1967	114	150	171	129	79	108	113	90	87	90	546	100
1968	108	147	171	123	80	109	113	89	87	90	483	100
1969	111	153	170	121	80	108	114	93	87	87	436	100
1970	109	158	153	119	82	109	112	98	86	87	373	100
1971	114	160	152	123	85	106	111	102	86	88	357	100
1972	115	155	153	122	86	104	109	106	85	88	402	100
1973	119	154	161	125	85	106	109	105	82	87	352	100
1974	122	142	164	127	88	102	101	102	93	87	318	100
1975	121	155	165	136	90	101	99	99	87	86	350	100
1976	113	165	171	135	87	102	101	90	89	90	375	100
1977	120	162	173	133	91	99	103	89	86	90	390	100
1978	128	165	170	135	95	97	105	93	81	88	380	100
1979	118	149	164	132	92	99	107	95	87	87	373	100
1980	107	128	159	141	91	100	101	87	102	86	353	100
1981	101	125	153	138	93	102	100	89	97	84	344	100
1982	115	140	150	128	93	98	103	93	96	86	579	100
1983	128	143	159	123	93	96	105	96	96	86	608	100
1984	124	151	161	120	91	96	103	101	102	86	624	100
1985	139	151	153	124	90	99	104	99	92	86	601	100
1986	144	159	160	127	89	98	112	107	81	88	667	100
1987	136	152	151	127	88	99	119	126	84	87	537	100
1988	135	165	151	129	88	100	121	119	83	84	530	100
1989	135	160	150	127	88	103	116	113	79	83	541	100
61-69	106	145	158	118	78	110	109	95	91	95	508	100
70-79	118	156	163	129	88	103	106	98	86	88	367	100
80-89	126	147	155	128	90	99	109	103	91	86	539	100
AVG	117	150	159	125	86	104	108	99	89	89	470	100

*   Numbers for Quebec cannot be directly compared to those for other regions because of
     opting out.

TABLE 6B.5: Index Of Relative Per Capita Revenue / Relative Per Capita Expenditure, Cash Flow Basis (National Average =100)

	Nfld	PEI	NS	NB	Que	Ont	Man	Sask	Alta	BC	Terr	Canada
1961	53	48	47	54	115	114	83	67	106	107	30	100
1962	53	43	47	55	113	112	84	69	106	120	29	100
1963	53	39	46	54	111	111	83	82	107	120	28	100
1964	53	37	45	54	109	113	86	78	106	123	26	100
1965	47	31	44	53	106	115	83	82	107	124	30	100
1966	49	34	44	53	106	114	79	86	115	126	31	100
1967	46	35	45	50	101	115	81	87	121	130	36	100
1968	50	37	45	52	97	116	82	85	121	129	39	100
1969	46	34	46	54	96	116	79	75	121	137	45	100
1970	48	35	54	57	95	116	81	65	123	130	52	100
1971	49	35	54	56	92	118	82	66	122	131	51	100
1972	48	39	55	57	89	119	84	66	124	129	47	100
1973	44	37	50	53	89	116	81	71	143	135	56	100
1974	40	37	44	49	78	105	81	100	244	120	63	100
1975	37	38	44	48	76	105	83	104	260	119	55	100
1976	44	36	44	48	82	105	83	110	232	119	45	100
1977	41	37	43	47	79	105	79	108	250	117	51	100
1978	38	37	44	46	78	108	77	101	249	122	52	100
1979	40	37	42	46	74	98	70	105	292	119	52	100
1980	37	37	38	38	67	86	65	123	331	112	50	100
1981	41	37	42	44	66	86	65	118	335	112	48	100
1982	40	39	47	46	61	95	69	109	308	112	32	100
1983	40	42	50	52	73	108	73	98	230	113	32	100
1984	42	42	51	54	79	109	74	93	208	107	32	100
1985	40	41	55	53	83	110	76	90	199	106	33	100
1986	42	49	55	55	91	121	77	76	146	109	26	100
1987	46	49	59	57	94	122	70	62	132	112	32	100
1988	46	47	58	57	93	122	67	63	131	114	32	100
1989	47	49	59	58	93	118	70	69	136	117	31	100
61-69	50	38	46	53	106	114	82	79	112	124	33	100
70-79	43	37	47	51	83	110	80	90	204	124	52	100
80-89	42	43	52	51	80	108	71	90	216	111	35	100
AVG	45	39	48	52	89	110	77	87	179	120	40	100

TABLE 6B.6: Index of Relative Per Capita Market Income
(National Average = 100)

	Nfld	PEI	NS	NB	Que	Ont	Man	Sask	Alta	BC	Terr	Canada
1961	53	55	74	63	90	121	93	69	100	114	109	100
1962	51	53	72	62	89	120	97	90	99	111	100	100
1963	52	53	72	62	89	120	93	97	98	111	98	100
1964	52	56	72	64	90	120	95	83	95	113	101	100
1965	53	57	71	64	90	119	93	88	96	113	99	100
1966	53	57	70	66	90	119	90	89	98	110	95	100
1967	53	55	71	65	91	119	95	78	97	110	98	100
1968	53	55	72	65	89	120	96	82	99	108	98	100
1969	53	55	72	65	89	121	92	77	98	109	105	100
1970	55	59	72	67	89	121	91	69	98	107	114	100
1971	55	55	72	68	90	120	92	77	96	108	104	100
1972	53	57	74	67	90	119	90	74	97	108	100	100
1973	54	62	73	67	89	117	93	87	99	109	97	100
1974	55	63	74	68	90	115	92	93	102	109	99	100
1975	56	59	73	68	91	113	94	101	105	108	99	100
1976	56	63	72	68	92	113	90	96	104	110	99	100
1977	57	61	72	67	93	113	90	86	104	112	107	100
1978	56	63	73	67	92	112	90	88	108	112	106	100
1979	58	63	73	66	92	111	89	87	111	112	107	100
1980	56	61	71	65	93	109	86	85	115	114	107	100
1981	55	62	70	64	91	109	91	94	118	114	108	100
1982	56	62	72	66	91	110	92	92	117	111	110	100
1983	56	63	75	68	91	112	91	87	111	107	109	100
1984	56	65	76	69	91	115	93	84	107	103	114	100
1985	58	62	80	70	92	113	91	84	110	102	126	100
1986	58	67	80	71	91	114	90	87	108	99	123	100
1987	59	64	80	71	92	116	89	82	102	98	120	100
1988	60	67	78	71	92	117	87	79	103	97	121	100
1989	59	66	77	70	91	117	86	79	100	98	117	100
61-69	53	55	72	64	90	120	94	84	98	111	100	100
70-79	55	61	73	67	91	115	91	86	102	109	103	100
80-89	57	64	76	68	91	113	90	85	109	104	116	100
AVG	55	60	74	67	91	116	92	85	103	108	107	100

TABLE 6C.1:
Total and Per Capita Federal Fiscal Balances, Benefits Basis, 1961-1989
Sensitivity Case: Interest on Public Debt Allocated on Personal Tax Basis

Region	Total Balances (billions of 1990 dollars)				Annual Per Capita Balance (1990 dollars)			
	1960s	1970s	1980s	Total	1960s	1970s	1980s	Avg.
Nfld	-5.4	-15.6	-26.4	-47.5	-1232	-2841	-4647	-2965
PEI	-1.9	-4.5	-6.5	-12.9	-1970	-3841	-5159	-3715
NS	-12.8	-28.4	-41.2	-82.4	-1875	-3460	-4756	-3415
NB	-6.8	-18.1	-29.8	-54.7	-1228	-2715	-4211	-2769
Que	4.5	-53.2	-106.1	-154.8	90	-853	-1628	-828
Ont	35.1	36.0	10.7	81.8	565	458	91	365
Man	-4.5	-12.0	-27.8	-44.3	-521	-1184	-2624	-1475
Sask	-4.6	-7.2	-19.8	-31.6	-540	-777	-1975	-1117
Alta	0.9	47.9	71.1	119.9	669	2574	3161	1998
BC	4.8	1.8	-25.7	-19.1	277	99	-894	-188
Terr	-2.7	-4.4	-15.1	-22.2	-7083	-7090	-20236	-11621
Reg.Sum	6.7	-57.8	-216.7	-267.8	35	-246	-859	-370
Outside								
Canada	-11.2	-20.4	-62.4	-94.1				
Canada	-4.5	-78.2	-279.1	-361.8	-28	-336	-1104	-505

TABLE 6C.2:
Total and Per Capita Federal Fiscal Balances, Benefits Basis, 1961-1989
Sensitivity Case: Balanced Budget (No Interest on Public Debt)

Region	Total Balances (billions of 1990 dollars)				Annual Per Capita Balance (1990 dollars)			
	1960s	1970s	1980s	Total	1960s	1970s	1980s	Avg.
Nfld	-5.5	-14.6	-23.2	-43.2	-1237	-2658	-4078	-2707
PEI	-1.9	-4.3	-5.7	-11.9	-1971	-3647	-4552	-3439
NS	-12.6	-26.1	-34.0	-72.6	-1843	-3180	-3927	-3023
NB	-6.7	-16.6	-24.9	-48.3	-1218	-2491	-3526	-2453
Que	4.6	-38.4	-57.8	-91.6	94	-617	-890	-491
Ont	38.4	68.5	116.1	223.3	623	853	1251	919
Man	-4.3	-9.1	-19.1	-32.5	-494	-901	-1796	-1084
Sask	-4.6	-4.7	-11.8	-21.1	-538	-509	-1170	-746
Alta	1.1	56.0	100.8	157.9	78	2982	4432	2581
BC	5.5	11.8	4.8	22.0	321	500	164	329
Terr	-2.7	-4.0	-14.0	-20.7	-7012	-6522	-18976	-10906
Reg.Sum	11.3	18.9	31.1	61.3	64	-83	122	91
Outside								
Canada	-11.3	-18.9	-31.1	-61.3				
Canada	0.0	0.0	0.0	0.0				

TABLE 6D.1: Total Federal Fiscal Balance By Region, Benefits Basis (millions of 1990 dollars)

	Nfld	PEI	NS	NB	Que	Ont.	Man	Sask	Alta	BC	Terr	Sum	Outside	Canada
1961	-529	-154	-1262	-729	327	2797	-554	-826	-236	-191	-277	-1635	-1030	-2665
1962	-579	-184	-1321	-732	101	2416	-554	-869	-270	125	-284	-2152	-1031	-3185
1963	-554	-197	-1290	-725	258	2828	-515	-557	-194	245	-275	-974	-1116	-2093
1964	-528	-197	-1257	-705	805	4411	-337	-512	-15	633	-300	1996	-1126	866
1965	-663	-257	-1356	-742	718	5296	-377	-434	92	819	-288	2807	-1172	1636
1966	-698	-257	-1490	-823	339	4862	-560	-423	214	790	-302	1652	-1530	125
1967	-810	-258	-1657	-980	-395	4718	-582	-456	317	829	-329	396	-1610	-1214
1968	-800	-265	-1783	-980	-819	5350	-625	-525	287	843	-304	380	-1315	-932
1969	-862	-287	-1720	-915	-145	7374	-569	-645	630	1663	-255	4271	-1291	2979
1970	-916	-313	-1495	-952	-1035	6497	-670	-1006	511	1146	-226	1541	-1493	51
1971	-1055	-355	-1662	-1131	-2165	6874	-757	-1135	426	1222	-263	0	-1404	-1404
1972	-1193	-364	-1845	-1253	-3056	7199	-786	-1276	474	1100	-375	-1375	-1325	-2699
1973	-1282	-367	-2060	-1330	-2556	8160	-803	-1052	1511	1834	-275	1781	-1404	377
1974	-1587	-394	-2700	-1632	-4705	6765	-766	-92	8414	1372	-231	4445	-2041	2403
1975	-1979	-498	-3360	-2248	-8208	2506	-1220	-470	7800	58	-441	-8060	-2337	-10395
1976	-1745	-549	-3493	-2269	-6917	3541	-1250	-281	6650	122	-550	-6741	-1878	-8619
1977	-2119	-595	-4019	-2589	-9494	1427	-1791	-677	6823	-858	-601	-14493	-2246	-16740
1978	-2467	-661	-4182	-2854	-11260	1241	-2189	-1205	5750	-1281	-632	-19741	-3153	-22897
1979	-2231	-597	-4087	-2740	-10675	-730	-2299	-871	10512	-867	-586	-15171	-3141	-18312
1980	-2387	-596	-4719	-3626	-13295	-5496	-2583	-197	19518	-1316	-667	-15363	-3433	-18798
1981	-2231	-591	-4323	-3343	-13404	-2747	-2451	-208	22117	-754	-677	-8613	-3563	-12174
1982	-2704	-680	-4353	-3346	-17077	-3883	-2786	-1190	15689	-2510	-1568	-24408	-4517	-28926
1983	-2953	-674	-4427	-3021	-14735	-998	-2810	-1808	7203	-2963	-1634	-28822	-4920	-33741
1984	-3094	-785	-4933	-3226	-14598	-1226	-3089	-2394	5721	-4097	-1850	-33584	-5580	-39151
1985	-3492	-809	-4516	-3435	-13861	-145	-3115	-2539	4269	-4115	-1826	-33584	-6409	-39994
1986	-3208	-699	-4187	-3040	-9312	7997	-2726	-2885	472	-2692	-2033	-22312	-7477	-29790
1987	-2868	-661	-3604	-2859	-7750	10457	-3165	-3827	-166	-1904	-1489	-17836	-8443	-26280
1988	-2832	-730	-3640	-2918	-8044	12633	-3390	-3515	-109	-1556	-1479	-15580	-8904	-24485
1989	-2908	-715	-3729	-2946	-8745	12126	-3262	-3212	-102	-1529	-1581	-16602	-9173	-25776
61-69	-6022	-2056	-13135	-7330	1189	40052	-4674	-5248	825	5756	-2614	6743	-11219	-4483
70-79	-16574	-4693	-28903	-18998	-60072	43482	-12532	-8065	48872	3849	-4180	-57814	-20421	-78234
80-89	-28676	-6940	-42431	-31760	-120822	28719	-29378	-21775	74612	-23436	-14804	-216691	-62421	-279116
TOTAL	-51272	-13689	-84470	-58088	-179704	112253	-46584	-35088	124309	-13831	-21598	-267763	-94060	-361833

TABLE 6D.2: Per Capita Federal Fiscal Balance By Region, Benefits Basis (1990 dollars)

	Nfld	PEI	NS	NB	Que	Ont.	Man	Sask	Alta	BC	Terr	Sum	Outside	Canada
1961	-1156	-1471	-1712	-1219	62	449	-600	-893	-177	-117	-7292	-90		-146
1962	-1236	-1719	-1771	-1211	19	380	-592	-934	-197	75	-7108	-116		-171
1963	-1163	-1820	-1717	-1190	47	436	-543	-597	-138	144	-6704	-51		-111
1964	-1093	-1809	-1666	-1154	144	665	-352	-543	-10	363	-7150	103		45
1965	-1358	-2359	-1794	-1206	126	780	-391	-457	63	456	-7019	143		83
1966	-1416	-2358	-1970	-1333	59	698	-581	-443	146	422	-7035	83		6
1967	-1622	-2370	-2180	-1581	-67	662	-605	-476	212	426	-7474	83		-60
1968	-1580	-2408	-2325	-1569	-138	737	-644	-547	188	421	-6756	19		-45
1969	-1677	-2584	-2219	-1456	-24	999	-581	-673	404	807	-5420	18		142
1970	-1772	-2843	-1912	-1518	-172	860	-682	-1069	320	538	-4516	203		2
1971	-2021	-3165	-2106	-1781	-359	892	-767	-1226	262	559	-4962	72		-65
1972	-2251	-3223	-2321	-1958	-505	922	-793	-1396	286	491	-6572	0		-124
1973	-2387	-3216	-2562	-2056	-420	1032	-806	-1162	894	797	-4589	81		17
1974	-2928	-3427	-3325	-2495	-768	840	-760	-102	4886	578	-3858	199		107
1975	-3605	-4259	-4097	-3380	-1328	307	-1204	-518	4387	24	-6999	-355		-458
1976	-3127	-4653	-4214	-3352	-1109	428	-1223	-305	3618	49	-8596	-293		-375
1977	-3784	-4998	-4825	-3785	-1511	171	-1744	-724	3567	-343	-9239	-623		-719
1978	-4389	-5466	-4991	-4148	-1787	147	-2121	-1277	2900	-504	-9582	-839		-974
1979	-3955	-4893	-4854	-3959	-1684	-86	-2237	-916	5120	-335	-8882	-639		-771
1980	-4217	-4843	-5584	-5218	-2082	-641	-2520	-206	9116	-494	-9954	-639		-782
1981	-3927	-4808	-5104	-4803	-2082	-319	-2389	-215	9887	-275	-9811	-354		-500
1982	-4778	-5576	-5121	-4801	-2643	-446	-2697	-1218	6777	-900	-22084	-993		-1177
1983	-5172	-5437	-5166	-4297	-2276	-113	-2687	-1828	3080	-1053	-22690	-1163		-1361
1984	-5409	-6281	-5709	-4556	-2249	-138	-2928	-2391	2446	-1439	-25341	-1344		-1567
1985	-6148	-6367	-5166	-4831	-2118	-16	-2909	-2511	1798	-1422	-24027	-1324		-1576
1986	-5657	-5505	-4769	-4264	-1412	861	-2529	-2840	199	-918	-26399	-870		-1162
1987	-5041	-5120	-4082	-3998	-1166	1107	-2917	-3778	-69	-638	-19342	-688		-1013
1988	-4960	-5657	-4104	-4059	-1201	1317	-3122	-3490	-45	-509	-18961	-594		-933
1989	-5075	-5502	-4180	-4068	-1292	1244	-2990	-3212	-41	-487	-19764	-624		-968
61-69	-1367	-2100	-1928	-1324	25	645	-543	-618	55	333	-6884	35		-28
70-79	-3022	-4014	-3521	-2843	-964	551	-1234	-870	2624	185	-6780	-246		-336
80-89	-5038	-5510	-4899	-4490	-1852	286	-2769	-2169	3315	-813	-19837	-859		-1104
AVERAGE	-3204	-3936	-3502	-2940	-963	489	-1549	-1240	2065	-113	-11315	-370		-505

TABLE 6D.3: Index of Relative Per Capita Federal Revenue, Benefits Basis (National Average = 100)

	Nfld	PEI	NS	NB	Que*	Ont	Man	Sask	Alta	BC	Terr	Canada
1961	51	60	70	60	85	125	90	68	104	115	159	100
1962	54	56	69	60	87	122	90	74	104	116	150	100
1963	53	54	69	60	87	123	88	79	100	117	135	100
1964	53	52	69	62	88	122	91	73	97	118	140	100
1965	53	51	71	65	83	124	88	78	98	121	166	100
1966	56	57	73	66	81	124	90	83	103	118	161	100
1967	54	53	78	66	80	122	93	80	106	118	199	100
1968	55	55	78	65	78	124	94	77	106	117	191	100
1969	52	54	79	66	78	125	92	70	106	120	197	100
1970	54	56	83	69	79	125	91	65	107	114	195	100
1971	57	57	84	70	79	123	92	68	106	116	182	100
1972	56	61	85	70	78	123	92	71	107	115	190	100
1973	54	58	82	67	76	121	89	76	118	119	199	100
1974	49	53	73	64	69	106	83	103	227	105	201	100
1975	46	60	74	66	70	104	84	104	228	103	192	100
1976	51	61	76	66	72	105	85	101	208	108	171	100
1977	50	62	76	64	73	102	83	97	216	107	199	100
1978	51	63	77	64	75	103	83	95	204	109	198	100
1979	48	57	70	62	69	96	76	101	255	105	197	100
1980	41	48	61	55	61	85	67	109	339	97	177	100
1981	43	47	65	62	62	86	66	105	325	95	166	100
1982	47	56	72	60	58	92	72	102	298	97	187	100
1983	53	61	82	66	68	102	78	96	222	98	196	100
1984	54	64	83	66	72	103	78	96	214	93	200	100
1985	57	63	86	67	75	108	80	90	184	93	202	100
1986	62	80	89	71	82	117	88	82	120	97	172	100
1987	63	75	90	74	83	119	85	79	112	98	172	100
1988	64	79	90	74	82	120	82	76	110	97	170	100
1989	64	79	90	74	82	120	83	79	108	98	170	100
61-69	53	55	73	63	83	124	91	76	103	118	167	100
70-79	52	59	78	66	74	111	86	88	178	110	192	100
80-89	55	65	81	67	72	105	78	91	203	96	181	100
AVG	53	60	77	66	76	113	85	85	163	108	181	100

* Numbers for Quebec cannot be directly compared to those of other provinces because of opting out

TABLE 6D.4: Index of Relative Per Capita Federal Expenditure, Benefits Basis (National Average = 100)

	Nfld	PEI	NS	NB	Que*	Ont	Man	Sask	Alta	BC	Terr	Canada
1961	110	135	157	121	78	96	117	111	109	116	536	100
1962	116	143	157	119	81	95	116	119	108	106	511	100
1963	113	150	159	122	82	96	114	109	105	106	490	100
1964	114	151	162	127	85	94	115	106	103	105	528	100
1965	128	178	170	133	82	93	115	108	102	106	544	100
1966	128	175	173	134	81	94	122	108	100	102	514	100
1967	129	163	179	140	84	93	122	103	97	100	546	100
1968	124	160	179	134	85	93	122	101	98	100	485	100
1969	127	166	179	132	86	94	124	104	98	96	440	100
1970	124	169	161	130	88	94	121	109	97	96	377	100
1971	129	170	159	134	92	91	119	112	97	96	359	100
1972	130	166	160	133	93	90	117	116	95	96	403	100
1973	133	165	168	136	92	90	118	116	92	96	355	100
1974	135	153	170	137	95	88	109	111	102	95	321	100
1975	134	163	171	146	97	87	107	108	96	93	353	100
1976	127	176	178	147	95	86	110	101	100	98	379	100
1977	134	173	181	146	99	83	113	100	97	99	393	100
1978	145	180	180	150	102	79	117	106	95	99	385	100
1979	133	162	173	145	98	84	117	107	98	97	374	100
1980	120	139	166	153	95	87	109	99	111	95	355	100
1981	117	138	161	152	98	86	109	102	107	94	348	100
1982	131	154	158	142	98	83	111	106	108	96	582	100
1983	145	157	167	137	98	80	114	110	108	97	608	100
1984	141	165	169	135	96	80	113	117	115	96	623	100
1985	157	166	161	140	96	82	115	115	105	97	599	100
1986	163	174	168	143	96	80	123	124	96	99	663	100
1987	154	166	159	143	94	81	131	143	98	97	531	100
1988	153	180	159	145	96	81	134	136	98	96	521	100
1989	155	175	160	144	97	82	131	131	96	96	531	100
61-69	121	158	168	129	83	94	119	108	102	104	510	100
70-79	132	168	170	140	95	87	115	109	97	97	370	100
80-89	144	162	163	143	96	82	119	118	104	96	536	100
AVG	133	163	167	138	92	88	117	112	101	99	471	100

* Numbers for Quebec cannot be directly compared to those of other provinces because of opting out

TABLE 6D.5: Index of Relative Per Capita Revenue / Relative Per Capita
Expenditure, Benefits Basis (National Average = 100)

	Nfld	PEI	NS	NB	Que*	Ont	Man	Sask	Alta	BC	Terr	Canada
1961	47	45	45	49	109	131	77	61	96	99	30	100
1962	47	40	44	50	108	129	78	63	96	110	29	100
1963	46	36	43	49	106	128	77	73	96	110	28	100
1964	46	35	43	49	103	131	79	69	94	112	27	100
1965	42	29	42	49	101	134	77	73	96	114	31	100
1966	44	32	42	49	100	131	74	77	103	116	31	100
1967	42	32	43	47	95	132	76	78	109	119	36	100
1968	44	35	43	49	92	133	77	76	107	117	39	100
1969	41	32	44	50	91	133	74	67	108	124	45	100
1970	43	33	52	53	90	132	76	60	110	119	52	100
1971	44	34	53	52	86	135	77	61	110	121	51	100
1972	44	37	53	53	84	137	79	62	112	119	47	100
1973	40	35	49	49	83	134	76	65	128	124	56	100
1974	37	35	43	46	73	120	76	92	222	111	63	100
1975	35	37	43	45	72	120	78	97	237	111	55	100
1976	40	35	43	45	76	122	77	100	209	110	45	100
1977	37	36	42	44	74	124	74	97	222	108	51	100
1978	35	35	43	43	73	130	71	89	215	110	51	100
1979	36	35	41	43	70	115	65	94	261	108	53	100
1980	34	34	37	36	64	98	61	110	305	103	50	100
1981	36	34	40	41	63	100	61	103	303	101	48	100
1982	36	36	46	42	59	111	65	96	277	101	32	100
1983	36	39	49	48	69	127	68	87	206	102	32	100
1984	38	39	49	49	75	129	69	82	187	96	32	100
1985	36	38	53	48	78	132	70	79	175	96	34	100
1986	38	46	53	50	86	146	72	66	126	99	26	100
1987	41	45	57	52	88	147	65	55	114	101	32	100
1988	42	44	56	51	85	149	62	56	112	101	33	100
1989	42	45	56	52	84	147	63	60	113	103	32	100
61-69	44	35	43	49	101	131	76	71	101	114	33	100
70-79	39	35	46	47	78	127	75	82	183	114	52	100
80-89	38	40	50	47	75	129	66	79	192	100	35	100
AVG	40	37	46	48	84	129	72	77	160	109	40	100

Commentaries

Kathleen Macmillan, Canadian International Trade Tribunal

The Mansell and Schlenker paper provides a careful and well-explained analysis of regional fiscal balances in Canada. This type of examination is a critical element in any consideration of the benefits of our economic union and, as such, this paper contributes in an important way to the current constitutional debate.

The authors' calculations of federal expenditures and revenues by province show large negative net fiscal balances for Ontario and Alberta for most the estimation period. It is similar to the Reid and Snoddon paper, also presented at this conference, except that, in addition to the tabulation of equalization payments and transfers to people, the Mansell and Schlenker estimates include federal spending on goods and services and resource rents captured by federal taxation. As a result, Alberta is found by Mansell and Schlenker to be the largest net contributor to Confederation over the period examined, whereas Ontario held this distinction in the Reid and Snoddon analysis.

The limitations of this type of static balance sheet analysis are acknowledged by the authors and discussed by conference participants. Fiscal balances studies do not indicate the impact of a host of government programs such as monetary, industrial, trade, or agricultural policies that do not require disbursements. Federal policies of this nature can have farther reaching regional economic impacts than fiscal measures, as the West could attest in recent years. Balance sheet analyses are also poor predictors of the future and tell us little about how effectively regions, and particularly smaller regions, could provide for themselves under another form of constitutional arrangement. Finally, accounting analyses reveal nothing about how labour or investment capital have reacted in response to fiscal expenditures.

In this final respect, I take issue with the authors' statement that fiscal imbalances contributed substantially to an outflow of economic activity and population from Alberta. This conclusion would have to be based on more than the calculations provided in this paper. As the paper itself recognized earlier, a number of studies have attempted to verify a relationship between fiscal variables and migration patterns and have been largely unsuccessful in quantifying any kind of relationship, let alone a substantial one.

Another of the paper's conclusions is that federal fiscal policy has had a destabilizing effect on Alberta's economy and that an independent Alberta would be less economically volatile than if the province remained part of Canada. Again, I find little basis for this finding in the paper's analysis and note that this conclusion is at odds with Reid and Snoddon's view that an independent Alberta would be more unstable economically. Although there is little disagreement that federal tax policies such as the National Energy Program reduced the *level* of provincial income, there is no evidence that they contributed to its variability. To conclude that it did, one would have to be certain that the provincial government would have done a better job of smoothing economic peaks and troughs than federal taxes and transfers have in the past. In any event, I wonder to what extent federal fiscal policy can really stabilize provincial economies, beyond the effect of the various automatic stabilizers, particularly as our growing debt makes expenditure policies a less attractive and effective policy tool.

The authors' basic message is a plea for more fairness in Canadian fiscal policy. The authors view fairness in terms of a better sharing of fiscal balances. Applying this view, they demonstrate that, until recently, Alberta has been unfairly treated in Confederation. However, much of Alberta's huge fiscal surplus is attributable to the intrusive and highly misguided National Energy Program (NEP), the type of tax policy that one seriously hopes would not be repeated in the future. My own view of fiscal fairness does not include resource rents in the equation, although I accept that, inconsistently, rents from hydroelectric development in Québec and other provinces were not taxed by federal governments as were energy revenues under the NEP. In defining fiscal fairness, I would also focus on the equality of fiscal goals, as our current equalization formula does, and not on equalizing fiscal flows.

In closing, I compliment the authors on their carefully detailed and explained analysis. Any consideration of alternative federal arrangements requires a thorough understanding of the workings of the current system. However, I would urge those interpreting these results to realize the limitations of analyses of this type, no matter how well they are conducted. First, other elements than fiscal balances enter into a consideration of regional fairness and the costs of benefits of Confederation. Second, these studies do not show how an economy or its factors of production have reacted to fiscal patterns in the past or how they are likely to react under different constitutional arrangements. What studies like this can do is dispel myths about fiscal capacity under a different form of economic union. But to dispel myths and not to contribute to them, they must be properly interpreted. Although, undoubtably, decisions about changes to our economic union will be made based on reasons that have very little to do with sound economic thinking, analyses such as those of Mansell and Schlenker are an important backdrop to these deliberations.

Paul A.R. Hobson, Acadia University

General Comments

This paper employs computations by province of net federal fiscal balances—the difference between federal revenues collected and federal expenditures (inclusive of transfers)—to make inferences about horizontal equity in the Canadian federation. In addition, an argument is made that the implied direction of federal fiscal policy by region has been destabilizing in the periphery, including Alberta.

Central to the computation of these net federal fiscal balances is the impact of the pricing policy under the National Energy Program (NEP). The results are dominated by the implicit transfer from Alberta to Ontario resulting from a domestic price for oil and gas set artificially below the world price. Alberta shows a consistent federal fiscal surplus—a net withdrawal from the provincial economy. However, this is simply with reference to an accounting entry. The real question is: Has Canada as a whole and Alberta in particular lost in an economic sense? To answer this would require a full-blown general equilibrium analysis. It can nonetheless be argued that the extent of redistribution that has occurred is not inconsistent with that prescribed in the literature on fiscal federalism on grounds of fiscal equity and fiscal efficiency.

It should be recalled that there are three key components of federal tax-expenditure programs: Programs aimed at equalization; programs aimed at regional development; programs aimed at individuals. Stabilization occurs automatically through equalization transfers and CAP transfers to governments as well as through transfers to individuals such as those through UI. Discretionary stabilization programs must come largely through regional development expenditures including federal government procurement. Fiscal equalization, EPF and CAP are major program areas and all involve substantial redistribution across provinces. To argue the broad view that there should be a federal fiscal deficit during a province's downturn is then to argue that the important equalizing role of the federal government should be unravelled. Rather, only the narrow view is appropriate. While there is a role for an increase in discretionary federal expenditures during an economic downturn, these may remain small relative to, say, equalization and interpersonal transfers and be reflected only in a change in the federal fiscal balance, not in its sign.

The Concept of Narrow-Based Fiscal Equity

Budgetary measures undertaken by provincial governments may give rise to horizontal inequity within the federation—otherwise identical individuals who happen to reside in different provinces are treated differently in the presence of the public sector. There are two sources of differences in, so-called, net fiscal benefits (NFBs)—the value of public services received less taxes paid by residents—across provinces. First, to the extent that provinces have access to different levels of per capita resource revenues with which to finance the public sector, individuals' comprehensive incomes will differ due to the resulting difference in NFBs. Second, to the extent that provincial budgets are ultimately redistributive, then, in the presence of regional disparities in personal income levels, again individuals' comprehensive incomes will differ due to the resulting differences in NFBs.

Moreover, in the presence of differences in NFBs across provinces, the federal personal income tax will itself be horizontally inequitable. Since NFBs are not included in the federal personal income tax base, otherwise identical residents of provinces with relatively high levels of NFBs will be favoured by a federal income tax structure that is uniformly applied across provinces.

"Broad-based" horizontal equity would require that equals be treated equally in the presence of the public sector regardless of province of residence. This would require the full equalization of NFBs. The concept of "narrow-based" horizontal equity holds that differences in NFBs arising from provincial budgetary actions be taken as given; in effect, residents are granted the property rights to NFBs created through the budgetary actions of their respective provincial governments. In this case, horizontal equity with regard to the federal personal income tax requires only partial equalization of NFBs; equalization of the tax benefit derived from the non-taxation of NFBs.

The Economic Council of Canada has advocated that the principle of broad-based horizontal equity should be applied in a federation other than in cases where property rights are constitutionally assigned. Thus, in the case of NFBs deriving from the use of resource rents to finance the provincial public sector, the narrow-based principle of horizontal equity should be applied. This would imply that only a portion of resource rents should be equalized, namely in proportion to the marginal federal tax rate.

In addition, it should be emphasized that the same applies to all resource rents, including those derived from hydroelectricity. Moreover, it is rents rather than royalties that properly constitute the base for equalization.

All this calls into question the discussion of regional equity in the paper. In the context of Figure 6.1, the argument is made that Albertans have been discriminated against in the application of federal policies. In particular, it is argued that the pricing policy under the NEP resulted in a redistribution from Alberta to Central Canada and that this cannot be justified given the principle of narrow-based horizontal equity. Yet, correctly applied, the narrow-based view of horizontal equity does require some redistribution, the extent of which need not be inconsistent with Figure 6.1. What is clear is that Figure 6.1 does not demonstrate that the principle of horizontal equity alone cannot be used to justify the measured discrimination against Alberta.

Certainly, a strong case can be made for equalization of a portion of the oil and gas rents which accrued to Alberta during the energy boom, and this was done indirectly through the NEP. At the same time, it should be noted that while there may be some justification for the redistribution which resulted from the NEP on the basis of fiscal equity, it was clearly detrimental with regard to the objective of nation building.

A Look at the Annual Data

The adjustment of the data to incorporate fully the pricing policy under the NEP dominates the data. It is worth noting, however, that Alberta's fiscal deficit was significantly diminished with the collapse of the energy market in the mid-1980s. Indeed, on a benefits basis (Table 6D.2) Alberta has shown a fiscal surplus since 1987. It cannot be argued that Alberta has been the milch-cow of Confederation; rather, Ontario appears to have resumed its historical role as milch-cow.

Summary

The real question at issue here is the extent to which redistribution under the NEP was justifiable. As indicated above, on grounds of nation building it probably was not. On grounds of horizontal equity there is, however, a strong case for equalizing a portion of resource rents. The narrow-based view of horizontal equity stated in the paper misses the important requirement that, although recognition of provincial property rights over resource rents obviates the need for full equalization, horizontal equity with regard to the federal personal income tax does require equalization of the tax benefit arising from the non-inclusion of resource rents used to finance the provincial public sector in the tax base.

There is also an efficiency argument in favour of such redistribution that would require the full equalization of resource rents in order to prevent fiscally-induced migration. However, the significance of fiscally induced migration is empirically contentious and so the discussion above has focused solely on equity criteria.

All this suggests a number of points with regard to reforming Canada's equalization program. First, it is resource rents that should be subject to equalization, not royalties. Moreover, it is only that portion of resource rents used to finance the provincial public sector which should be subject to equalization, and then only that portion, say 40%, which represents the tax benefit arising from non-inclusion in the federal base. This would apply to all resource rents, including hydroelectric rents and not just rents from oil and gas. Second, this should be undertaken in the context of a national average standard for equalization such as prevailed prior to 1982, rather than the present five-province standard.

It is worth concluding with some reflections on Musgrave's classic separation of government into an allocative branch, a distributive branch, and a stabilization branch. On grounds of both efficiency and equity, a strong case can be made for redistribution through intergovernmental transfers. The extent of such redistribution is greater on grounds of efficiency and broad-based horizontal equity than it is on grounds of narrow-based horizontal equity. In the presence of substantial disparities in resource endowments and personal incomes across provinces, this redistributive function will likely dominate the stabilization role of the federal government. In any event, there is no justification for the suggestion in the paper that countercyclical policies would require running a federal fiscal deficit during a down-turn in any province's economic cycle. Many federal programs that are stabilizing—such as CAP—are also redistributive across provinces. And discretionary expenditures—such as regional development—are minuscule besides the major intergovernmental and interpersonal redistributive programs. This is not to say that countercyclical federal fiscal policies do not have a role; simply, in light of the important redistributive role of the federal government, there is no basis for expecting a federal fiscal deficit during a province's down-turn.

Alberta and the Economics of Constitutional Change

7 Closing Commentary

by Roger S. Smith

The issues addressed at this conference are ones before all Canadians. The complexity of the issues has been apparent in the conference papers and in the discussions, and it is precisely this complexity which makes the exchange of views so essential. These papers make a contribution, but economists recognize the limitations of their discipline and the need to integrate their contribution to the constitutional debates with that of others. Nonetheless, the economic impact of constitutional arrangements will bear heavily on any future assessment of the strength of the Canadian nation, and deserves the attention of Canada's best economic minds.

The papers in this conference focussed on some (certainly not all) of the economic implications of different constitutional arrangements. The three scenarios were:

1. a more centralized Canada without Québec;

2   a more decentralized Canada with Québec; and

3   an independent Alberta (with some consideration of an independent West—including the Prairie provinces and British Columbia).

This choice was intended to provide breadth to the discussion. Nevertheless, conference discussion reflected that many participants found two of the scenarios to be of limited interest. Several thought that a Canada without

Québec would be less rather than more centralized. And most thought an
independent Alberta an unattractive alternative.

The major papers considered each of the three scenarios from five
perspectives:

1.   the provision of government goods and services (GGS);

2.   the distribution of transfer payments to provinces and to individuals;

3.   the division and structure of our tax system;

4.   the likely fiscal balances, calculated both on a cash-flow and a benefits basis.

5.   the fifth paper explored more generally the economic surplus created by
     Confederation, particularly the benefits to Albertans, and the effects of the
     alternative constitutional arrangements on this surplus.

Discussants, drawn from across Canada, did much to expand the
perspectives of the five papers.

What have we learned from the papers and the discussion?

There have been major benefits from past constitutional arrangements.

First, and perhaps importantly from the perspective of Albertans, is the fact
that the existing constitutional arrangements, at least from an economic
perspective, have provided substantial economic benefits to Alberta. In spite
of the large transfer of funds from Alberta to other parts of Canada over the
past three decades (see Mansell and Schlenker [M&S], and Reid and
Snoddon [R&S] in this volume), there have been large benefits to Alberta
from the existing federal system. Whether these benefits outweigh the costs
is where the debate is engaged, but Albertans (and others) cannot afford to
overlook the benefits. Given the potential importance of the benefits to the
constitutional discussions, it is unfortunate that the benefits are not
measured in these papers.

How large are the economic benefits derived from the increased market
power that enabled the FTA and other trade agreements? What is the value
to each Albertan and his or her children of having the option to move to
other provinces in the face of rising unemployment in an extremely volatile
economy? What are the savings from sharing the cost of expenditures on
defense, foreign relations, immigration administration and other services?
What would the costs be to Alberta of a collapsed economic union, be it due
to the separation of Québec or to greater fragmentation?

The paper by Chambers and Percy [C&P], as well as comments by Wendy Dobson and Richard Harris among others, focussed attention on the benefits of an economic union, but included no quantitative estimates. In contrast, the papers by M&S and R&S assessed in dollar terms some (and again it is important to recognize the partial nature of the estimates) of the costs to Alberta, and to Ontario and British Columbia, of the status quo, or of remaining within Canada without Québec. If meaningful cost-benefit comparisons on constitutional arrangements are to be made, more comprehensive measures of various cost and benefit streams may be helpful. At the same time, there is awareness that static dollar measures are of limited use in a dynamic world, and that much more than economics is involved. There is the danger that the "measured" will receive undue attention when the "unmeasured" may be of greater import. The conference discussion reflected this concern.

Some costs of the existing arrangement are large.

The papers by Mansell and Schlenker and Reid and Snoddon provided information on the size (if imperfectly measured) of some of the costs of Confederation. Given the careful and detailed past work by Mansell and Schlenker, the $2500 (1990 dollars) per capita annual cost to Albertans of supporting Confederation over the past three decades comes as no surprise. The $147 billion equals $59,000 for every person now in Alberta, or over $235,000 for a family of four. The political impact of these numbers cannot be ignored.

The fiscal balance estimates by M&S received peripheral comments from discussants of other papers as well as from Paul Hobson and Kathleen Macmillan. There was some concern about balance sheet exercises in general, but most seemed to agree with Ken Norrie that such exercises have an important role to play at a time when changes in constitutional arrangements are contemplated. Nevertheless, there was concern that too much weight might be placed on Mansell and Schlenker's numbers for a variety of reasons. First, demographics determine some of the transfers, and Alberta with a younger population quite rightly receives less of OAS and GIS payments on a per capita basis. This will change over time. Second, the large net costs of the past created by the National Energy Program (NEP) and high energy prices no longer exist. Alberta is currently close to being in fiscal balance (as measured by M&S), and this may well be the situation in the future. Professors Harris, Hobson, Hum, and Norrie all urged that the benefits of Confederation not be viewed in terms of a decade such as the period from 1975 to 1985 when net outflows from Alberta were high due to the NEP. Alberta's fiscal (im)balance on a cash-flow basis at the end of the 1980s was no more than 10% that at the beginning of the decade. On a "benefit" basis, Alberta was roughly in balance. Nevertheless, most agreed with Professor Mansell that an important part of new constitutional arrangements would be adequate future protection against measures such as the NEP. How to best achieve that "adequate protection," however, did not receive much attention at the conference. Professor Hum appeared to capture the feeling of many with his observation that "a constitution is for a long time" and this we must keep in mind.

In addition to the fiscal balance estimates, some other numbers developed for the conference were of interest. For example, Reid and Snoddon found that 1988 UI revenues would have had to rise by $541 per capita in the Atlantic provinces (and $111 in Québec) to finance expenditures on a balanced budget basis. That equals $2200 for a family of four in the Atlantic provinces.

The net transfer from Ontario for equalization, EPF, CAP, OAS, UI, CPP, and family allowances was about $1100 per capita in 1988. It was about $300 for Alberta. How many Albertans could have told you that the per capita net contribution of Ontario was nearly four times that of Alberta in 1988? The gain to the Atlantic provinces for the seven transfer programs considered by Reid and Snoddon was $2,000 per capita, or $8,000 for a family of four.

These numbers are big, and R&S note that the cost to provinces of taking over the areas where the above transfer programs now exist would be in the order of $40 billion to $50 billion. The costs of this "decentralization" to the have-not provinces would be enormous. R&S point out that it is a change that the Atlantic provinces simply could not afford to support in the absence of compensation.

The conference discussion recognized that the size of these transfers is important. However, both the authors and the discussion highlighted the partial nature of these calculations, and the resulting danger of coming to *any* conclusions based on them. For example, none of the calculations reflected the significant net transfers made through agricultural programs, transportation programs, trade protection, and regulation—all of which are important. Nor, as the authors acknowledged, and Ken Norrie emphasized, did any of the estimates consider the effects of shifts in factors of production, both labour and capital, which would result from significant changes in transfer programs.

Has Canada benefited from past transfer payment programs?

The transfers of resources across provinces have been large, but have they contributed to the overall development of Canada? Have they, by reducing differences between regions of the country, strengthened Canadian Confederation? Or has the result been that production in one part of the country has been hampered with little gain elsewhere? As Mansell and Schlenker ask, in referring to Courchene's (1978, 1981) earlier work, "is it *unlikely* that the net inflow regions have a higher average real per capita income than would otherwise be the case?" This is an important question, and one which the papers of this conference did not address. The importance of transfer payment programs in Canada makes it central to any constitutional discussion.

Charts 7.1 and 7.2 reflect at least part of the continuing problem faced by Canada. Chart 7.1 (from *The Economist*, December 22, 1990) shows the convergence of per capita personal income among the different regions of the United States since the end of the 1920s. Chart 7.2 shows the relative lack of convergence in Canada. Indices in the United States converge from a range of 50 to 135 to a range of 93 to 107. Those in Canada converge much less, and range from 71 to 114 in 1990. Even with the sizable transfers to develop human and physical capital, there has been little convergence in the productivity of individuals in the different regions of Canada. If Canada continues with its large transfer programs, will this only contribute to the maintenance of tensions in the country as neither the contributing regions nor the recipient regions experience real benefit over time? This question deserves continuing attention.

Is there a case for greater tax powers at the provincial level?

Bev Dahlby's paper brings the division of revenue sources into the constitutional discussions. As he notes, the limited discussion of taxing powers is rather remarkable. Dahlby's concept of minimizing the marginal cost of public funds (MCPF) is useful, but received as little attention at the conference as it has in the general constitutional discussions. Given the problems and uncertainties that accompany the use of transfers, the division of taxing powers undoubtedly results from many objectives other than minimizing the MCPF.

Dahlby reviews the principles for assigning tax power as set forth by Musgrave (1983), and the conclusions reached by Boadway (1991) and by Mintz and Wilson (1991) when these principles are appropriately modified for the Canadian federation. These authors conclude that the federal government should have primary control over personal and corporate

CHART 7.1:
Personal Income per Head as % of US Average

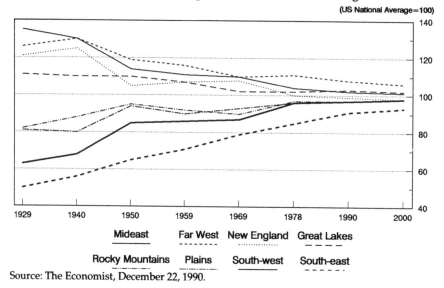

(US National Average=100)

Mideast   Far West   New England   Great Lakes

Rocky Mountains   Plains   South-west   South-east

Source: The Economist, December 22, 1990.

CHART 7.2:
Personal Income per Head as % of Canadian Average

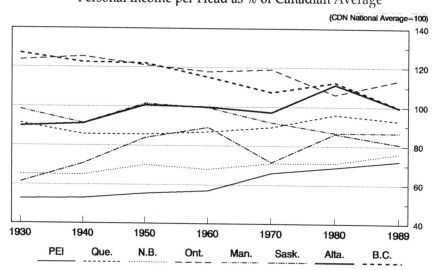

(CDN National Average=100)

PEI   Que.   N.B.   Ont.   Man.   Sask.   Alta.   B.C.

Source: Statistics Canada.

income taxes and that the provinces should control the indirect taxes. In
contrast, Dahlby would give the direct taxes to the provinces, leaving
indirect taxes to the federal government. The main argument for Dahlby's
approach appears to be that with provinces responsible for social programs,
there are real advantages to integrating the tax and social systems. He also
suggests that the "have" provinces should contribute directly to the "have
not" provinces, rather than channel equalization payments through the
federal government.

A further need, not discussed by Dahlby but consistent with Boadway's
division of taxing powers, is some means for gradually shifting the authority
over natural resource taxes to the federal government. Inefficiencies created
by fiscal residuals received little attention in the conference discussion. But,
be it based on equity arguments or inefficiencies created by large fiscal
residuals, the long run health of the federation may depend on federal
control over this revenue source. This is not a popular line of argument in
many provinces, but if the Canadian federation is to be healthy in the longer
run, it is not one which can be lightly dismissed.

Both Dahlby's paper and the conference discussion focussed on some of
the shortcomings of Musgrave's "accepted theory" of the division of taxing
powers. Wayne Thirsk suggested that the usual focus on taxes as being either
"source" or "residence" based was likely to be most helpful in determining
assignment of tax bases by level of government. Normally, those that are
residence based are least likely to be exported or affected by tax competition,
and are more appropriate for lower levels of government. Professor Winer
noted that "accepted theory" simply does not recognize federalism—it is
designed for a system where state or provincial level of government is not a
consideration. A number of participants also referred to the Swiss system
where lower levels of government have control over direct taxes—and the
apparent workability of such a system. Indeed, the frequency with which the
Swiss model arose during the day's discussion suggests that many
economists would sympathize with at least a careful look at radical
restructuring of taxing powers, such as that outlined by Professor Dahlby.

Professor McMillan, in discussing the Dahlby paper, noted the imbalance
between taxes raised and perceived benefits from expenditures on goods and
services by the different levels of government. He observed that the ratio of
expenditures to self-raised revenues was considerably greater than 1.0 for
provincial and local governments, and far below 1.0 for the federal
government. Although transfers from higher levels make possible a
significant part of the expenditures at the lower levels, it is perhaps not
surprising that citizens feel they get more for their tax dollar from lower
levels of government. That this may create a bias toward greater

decentralization of taxing authority should be kept in mind. Professor McMillan also makes the point that an increase in provincial own-tax revenues at the expense of federal revenues would likely have to be accompanied by provinces assuming responsibility for part of the federal debt. Otherwise Ottawa's flexibility would be reduced as debt service costs rise as a share of federal own source revenue. Ottawa would resist this, particularly if the debt is partly due to programs that have been transferred to the provincial sphere of responsibility.

Benefits from increased decentralization or fragmentation exist, but are they large enough?

The papers and discussion contributed to an understanding of some possible, if limited, benefits from an independent Alberta. Boothe notes that significant economies of scale exist for few functions, and, thus, at least on these grounds there is little basis for the centralization of powers. In addition, he notes the advantages in terms of responsiveness and accountability of moving the levying of taxes and delivery of services closer to the people. Thus, he argues, the criteria of responsiveness, accountability, and efficiency lend support for a relatively high degree of decentralization within the Canadian federal state. One Boothe assumption relating to responsiveness which many discussants appeared to question was that "people's preferences diverge as distance between them grows."

In the discussion of Boothe's paper, it became clear that the concept of "responsiveness" is closely related to "efficiency" since it is meaningless to provide efficiently services that no one wants. It is also clear that when more than one criterion exists it is essential to assign weights to each if alternative constitutional arrangements are to be ranked and choices made. In this regard the property tax revolts of the past fifteen years in the United States, and the more recent experience of the United Kingdom with the poll tax, may cause public finance economists to reassess their weighting of "accountability" and "responsiveness" relative to criteria such as "equity" and "efficiency" (see Smith [1990]). In any case, even with considerable attention to accountability and responsiveness, the efficiency and stabilization gains from a larger state lead Professor Boothe to rank a more decentralized Canada with Québec and an independent Western Canada as his first two choices.

Professor Winer, in his discussion of Boothe's paper, made a number of interesting points. He noted the possible advantages of "competitive federalism" where one level of government does not monopolize an expenditure area. As Professor Winer asked, "Do we really think we will be best served if we give monopolies to each level of government?" Professor Winer also emphasized the front and centre place that Scott and Breton's concept of "organizational costs" must have in discussions concerning the delivery of government services. Ideally, we may well find that each service has its own optimal service area if it is to be provided on the most efficient scale. However, coordination between a large number of overlapping jurisdictions may be exceptionally costly. The result of these costs is that a higher level of centralization is desirable than otherwise would be true. Finally, although not referring specifically to Boothe's paper, Professor Winer suggested that the Charter of Rights is likely to lead to a gradual diminution of provincial powers and increase in federal powers as individual provinces are prevented from infringing on individual rights in a number of areas.

Professor Courchene, in commenting on the Boothe paper, cast his net wide, noting that economic ties have become increasingly north-south, and that it will be the east-west social and cultural ties of the future rather than the east-west transportation links of the past that will bind Canada together. This suggests the need for substantial powers at the centre (although Courchene's comments did not spell out how he would divide up the spending responsibilities). Professor Courchene noted the added tensions to the Canadian Confederation created by the stronger north-south ties. He questioned the willingness of Ontario to continue supporting transfer payments to other parts of Canada when those payments no longer come back to purchase Ontario's manufactured goods or its financial services, but instead purchase goods and services from the United States and other countries. With the importance of the American market, particularly for Alberta, Professor Courchene acknowledged the difficulties for Alberta of a monetary system in which the Canadian dollar is not tied to the American dollar. This is likely to lead to growing pressures for some form of North American monetary union. Given the distinctness of the Alberta economy, Courchene felt that the additional protection provided to Alberta by the proposed Council of the Confederation would be an important change.

Mansell and Schlenker appear to share Boothe's view that Alberta may benefit significantly from increased decentralization of some government powers in Canada. However, they may be overly optimistic in terms of the increased economic stability they think would have existed in Alberta if the National Energy Program had not existed—a point made by discussant Kathleen Macmillan. Professor Thirsk also questioned the propensity of the provincial government to bank nonrenewable resource revenues in times of boom in order to support higher levels of spending in times of bust. The rates at which the Government of Alberta proved itself capable of reducing

tax rates and increasing expenditures from 1975 to 1985 in the face of rising
resource revenues does not support the optimism of Mansell and Schlenker.

Chambers and Percy clearly favour a confederation over an independent
Alberta. At least as far as their economic analysis goes, it would appear that
they are relatively agnostic as to whether the federation is one with or
without Québec. Both the costs and the benefits of an independent Québec
look to be relatively modest. Wendy Dobson, in discussing the Chambers
and Percy paper, was forceful in her views that we need to be careful
concerning assumptions made about the aftermath of the break-up of
Canada's economic union. This pertains to both arrangements under the FTA
and those between parts of Canada. In her view, we may underestimate the
costs of the disruption of the existing union. In particular, if the Canadian
economic union is broken, it is likely that any resulting entities would have
to renegotiate the trade agreement with the United States. Professor Dobson
noted the increased importance of economic and political clout in a world of
slow economic growth. In such a world both "managed trade" and "trade
conflicts" become more common, and the bargaining power of Canada as an
economic union will be stronger than that of a fragmented Canada. She also
points to the fact that strong linkages between Québec and Ontario mean
that Ontario will be damaged by the departure of Québec, and this in turn
will have an adverse impact on Alberta and the West.

Professor Harris, in his comments, supported the view of Chambers and
Percy on the importance of labour mobility; he cited the black market price
of the green card in the United States as an indication of the high value that
is placed on access to attractive labour markets. Thus, there is a large benefit
associated with the relatively free movement of Canadians among provinces.
And there are substantial gains to be reaped from the reduction of remaining
barriers to such movement.

The papers by Dahlby, and by Reid and Snoddon, make clear their wish
to draw no conclusions concerning the implications of their analysis for a
more or less centralized confederation. Reid and Snoddon emphasize the
"partial" nature of their analysis, due to the many programs excluded from
the analysis, as well as to the static partial equilibrium framework with the
rigid assumptions behind their results. Dahlby, although noting the
substantial shift in tax revenues that would flow to provincial governments if
they had exclusive use of the personal and corporate income taxes,
apparently considers his proposal to deserve much more analysis before
conclusions are reached.

Conclusion

The papers and accompanying discussion indicate some of the costs of a Canada with and without Québec. Like all Canadians, conference participants were left to decide what weights should be put on some of the unmeasureables, and how much the analysis of the past and present tells them about likely scenarios for the future.

The conference made clear that the transfers to some regions of the country have been enormous, and will continue to be so under existing arrangements. It is also clear that imbalances in natural resource revenues have been a major source of contention, in both "have" and "have not" provinces. Thus, a diminished role for certain transfer programs (UI is a clear example) and an increased role for the federal government in capturing resource rents may be central to the longer run stability of the Canadian federation. It not apparent that the current constitutional discussions are adequately addressing these two important issues.

In sum, the conference format and papers structured a discussion which did much to highlight issues that must be addressed in any constitutional reform. Much is left to be done if Albertans, and those from other provinces, are to understand adequately the benefits and costs of different constitutional arrangements. We must also gain a better understanding of net benefits from past transfer programs if we are to continue them with equanimity. And we must grasp the diversity of programs that are a net benefit to us, as well as those where we may be supporting other Canadians. It is appropriate that the conference ended without reaching conclusions on many of the issues that have been raised. Surely this reflects increased awareness of the knowledge base we must build. All would agree that the papers in this volume are an important contribution to this base.

References

Boadway, Robin. (1990). *Constitutional design in a federation: An economic perspective.* Paper prepared for the Business Council on National Issues Symposium on Canada's Post Meech Lake Constitutional Options, Toronto.

Courchene, Thomas J. (1978). *Avenues of adjustment: The transfer system and regional disparities.* In *Michael Walker (Ed.), Canadian confederation at the crossroads.* Vancouver: Fraser Institute.

Courchene, Thomas J. (1978, Autumn). A market perspective on regional disparities. *Canadian Public Policy 7.*

Mintz, J.M. & Wilson, T.A. (1991). *The allocation of tax authority in the Canadian federation.* Paper presented to the Economic Dimensions of Constitutional Change Conference, John Deutsch Institute for the Study of Economic Policy, Queen's University, Kingston, ON.

Musgrave, Richard A. (1983). Who should tax, where, and what? In *C.E. McLure, Jr. (Ed.), Tax assignment in federal countries.* Canberra: Australian National University Press, Center for Research on Federal Financial Relations.

Scott, A.D. & Breton, A. (1978). *The economic constitution of federal states.* Toronto: University of Toronto Press.

Smith, R.S. (1990, April/May). Why the Canadian property tax(payer) is not revolting. *Canadian Tax Journal 38.*